THE GREYING OF INDIA

THE GREYING OF INDIA

Population Ageing in the Context of Asia

Rajagopal Dhar Chakraborti

SAGE PUBLICATIONS
NEW DELHI ❖ THOUSAND OAKS ❖ LONDON

First published in 2004 by

Sage Publications India Pvt Ltd
B-42, Panchsheel Enclave
New Delhi 110 017

Sage Publications Inc	**Sage Publications Ltd**
2455 Teller Road	1 Oliver's Yard
Thousand Oaks	55 City Road
California 91320	London EC1Y 1SP

Published by Tejeshwar Singh for Sage Publications India Pvt Ltd, Phototypeset in 9.5/11.5 Leawood at C&M Digitals (P) Ltd., Chennai and printed at Chaman Enterprises, New Delhi.

Library of Congress Cataloging-in-Publication Data
Chakraborti, Rajagopal Dhar.
    The greying of India: population ageing in the context of Asia / by Rajagopal Dhar Chakraborti.
    p. cm.
    Includes bibliographical references and index.
    1. Aged—India—Social conditions—Statistics. 2. Aged—India—Economic conditions—Statistics. 3. Age distribution (Demography)—India. 4. India—Population policy. 5. India—Statistics, Vital. I. Title.

HQ1064.I4C425   305.26'0954'021—dc22   2004   2003018550

ISBN: 0–7619–9802–0 (US-Hb)   81–7829–279–3 (India-Hb)

Sage Production Team: Sunaina Dalaya, Rinki Gomes, Rajib Chatterjee and Santosh Rawat

Dedicated to my late father, Krishnagopal Dhar Chakraborti and my dear mother, Geeta Dhar Chakraborti, who aged gracefully together.

CONTENTS

List of Tables   9
List of Figures   17
List of Abbreviations   19
Foreword by Tim Dyson   21
Preface   25
Acknowledgements   31

1. Ageing in Asia: A Broad Overview   33
2. What Causes Population Ageing?   81
3. What is Ageing?   159
4. Ageing and Development   193
5. Status of the Aged   239
6. Graceful Ageing   303

Appendices   349
Glossary   431
Select Bibliography   445
Index   459
About the Author   469

CONTENTS

List of Topics

List of Figures

List of Abbreviations

Foreword by Tim Dyson

Preface

Acknowledgements

1. Ageing in Asia: A Broad Overview

2. What Causes Population Ageing?

3. What is Ageing?

4. Ageing and Development

5. Statistics of the Aged

6. Graceful Ageing

Appendices

Glossary

Bibliography

Index

About the Author

LIST OF TABLES

1.1	Estimates and Medium-fertility Variant Projections of the Elderly (60 plus) in Different World Regions, 1950–2050	35
1.2	Number of the Aged in the World (Region-wise)	36
1.3	Distribution of the Aged Population (Continent-wise)	38
1.4	The Aged in Asia, Absolute Numbers and Proportion of the Total Population of 60 plus and 80 plus, 1999 and 2050	39
1.5	Changing Intergenerational Balance in Selected Regions/Countries of the World, 1950–2050	42
1.6	The Aged Dependency Ratio from 1950–2050 in the Different Regions of the World	45
1.7	Potential Support Ratio (PSR) in Different Regions of the World, 1950–2050	46
1.8	Potential Support Ratio (PSR) in the Countries of Asia, 2000 and 2050	47
1.9	Parent Support Ratio (PaSR) in Various Regions of the World, 2000 and 2050	50
1.10	Parent Support Ratio (PaSR) in the Countries of Asia, 2000 and 2050	51
1.11(a)	Age Distribution of the Oldest among the Old for World Population (in thousands), 1950 and 1995	54
1.11(b)	Age Distribution of the Oldest among the Old for World Population (in thousands), projections for 2000 and 2050	55

1.12 Number of 80 plus and Centenarians and Life
       Expectancy at Age 60 for Males and Females in
       all Countries of Asia   56
1.13 Women as Percentage of the Aged Population in
       1999/2000 and the Sex Ratio (males per 100 females)   60
1.14 Women among the Aged: As Percentages of all
       Elderly (60 plus and 80 plus) and the Sex Ratio
       (males per 100 women)   61
1.15 Percentage of Elderly in the Labour Force, 1995   65
1.16 Workforce Participation of the Elderly in Asia   67
1.17 Illiteracy Rates among the elderly in Select Asian
       Countries for Select Years, 1980–2010   69
1.18 Marital Status of the Elderly in Different
       World Regions   72
1.19 Marital Status of the Elderly in Asia   72
1.20 Healthy Life Expectancy Level (Years) in
       Several Asian Countries   76

2.1   The Elderly in Different Regions of Asia and the MDRs,
       1950–2000   83
2.2   The Elderly in Different Regions of Asia and the MDRs,
       2000–2050   84
2.3   Speed of Population Ageing in Selected Countries   85
2.4   Factors Affecting Death and Birth Rates at Each
       Stage of Demographic Transition   88
2.5   List of the Countries that have Reached the
       Final Stage of Demographic Transition   90
2.6   Total Fertility Rate (TFR) and Life Expectancy (e_0^0)
       in Various Stages of Demographic Transition   90
2.7   Life Expectancy at Birth, Total Fertility Rate (TFR),
       Human Development Index (HDI), Per Capita
       Income, Demographic Transition Index (DTI) and
       the Current Stage of Demographic Transition
       in Different Countries in Asia, 1998   93
2.8   The Correlation Coefficients and the Regression
       Equations between Demographic Transition Index (DTI)
       and other Economic and Demographic Variables   97
2.9   Stages of Demographic Transition in Asian
       Countries, 1950–2050   100
2.10 Proportions of Aged, Life Expectancy at Birth
       in Different Regions of Asia, 1950–2050   103

2.11 The Correlation Coefficients and the Regression Equations between the Proportion of Aged and the Life Expectancy at Birth for Different Regions of Asia, the MDRs and the World   105

2.12 Proportions of Aged, Total Fertility Rate (TFR) in Different Regions of Asia, 1950–2050   106

2.13 Proportions of Aged, Total Fertility Rate (TFR) and Life Expectancy in the World and MDRs, 1950–2050   108

2.14 The Correlation Coefficients and the Regression Equations between Proportion Aged and the Total Fertility Rates (TFRs) for Different Regions of Asia, the MDRs and the World   109

2.15 Proportion of Aged, Life Expectancy and TFR in India, Thailand and Japan, 1950–2050   110

2.16 The Correlation Coefficients and the Regression Equations between the Proportion of Aged and the Total Fertility Rates (TFRs) for India, Japan and Thailand   112

2.17 The Correlation Coefficients and the Regression Equations between the Proportion of Aged and the Life Expectancy at Birth for India, Japan and Thailand   112

2.18(a) Life Expectancy of Males/Females at Age 60 in Various Countries of Asia   113

2.18(b) Life Expectancy of Males/Females at Age 60 in Various States of India   114

2.19 Life Expectancies for Both Sexes Combined, in Japan, Iceland and France, 1950–2000   116

2.20 Changes in the Proportion of the Aged Population in Japan, for Different Time Periods between 1950 and 1985   117

2.21 Proportions of Aged 65 plus to the Economically Dependent (15–64) in Japan under Alternative Variant Assumptions, 1950–80   119

2.22 Age-Child Ratio in Japan under Alternative Variant Assumptions, 1950–80   119

2.23 Life Expectancy and Age-specific Mortality Rates by Sex and Age in Japan for Select Years, 1930–2000   121

2.24(a) Male Life Expectancy and Percentages of
         Deaths by Cause from Ten Important Causes
         of Death in Japan, 1935–2000   122
2.24(b) Female Life Expectancy and Percentages of
         Deaths by Cause from Ten Important Causes
         of Death in Japan, 1935–2000   123
2.25   Fertility Indicators in Japan, 1925–2000   125
2.26   Factors Influencing Increase or Decrease in Supply
         of and Demand for Children during Demographic
         Transition   131
2.27   Indices of Ageing by Distance from the
         Metropolitan Centre, 1995   135
2.28   Proportion of Elderly in Urban and Rural
         Populations in Various Asian Countries   137
2.29   Patterns of Urban and Rural Fertility, Various
         Countries (mid-1970s)   138
2.30   Mortality Change in Major World Regions and
         Asia, 1950–55 and 1995–2000   139
2.31   UN Forecasted Mortality Change in Major
         World Regions and Asia, 2000–2050   140
2.32   Mortality Levels, 1950–2000, and their
         Determinants in Some Countries of Asia   144
2.33   Correlation Coefficient between Life
         Expectancy and Infant Mortality Rate with
         Various Socioeconomic Parameters in the
         Asian Countries   148
2.34   Effect of Fertility, Mortality and Migration on
         Momentum and Growth of the Aged Population   155

3.1   Proportion of Aged 65 or Over in Different
         Regions/Countries of the World, 1950–2050   161
3.2   Median Age in Different Regions/Countries of
         the World, 1950–2050   165
3.3   Percentage Aged 0–14 Years in Different
         Regions/Countries of the World, 1950–2050   166
3.4   Aged-Child Ratio in Different Regions/
         Countries of the World, 1950–2050   168
3.5   Aged Dependency Ratio in Different Regions/
         Countries of the World, 1950–2050   170
3.6   Youth and Total Dependency Ratios in Different
         Regions/Countries of the World, 1950–2050   172

3.7   Estimates and Projections of Life Expectancy
at Ages 60, 65 and 70, 1901–2001   176

3.8(a)   Calculation of the P-Index of Ageing in 1995 in
India based on UN Data   179

3.8(b)   Calculation of the P-Index of Ageing in 2025 in
India based on UN Data   179

3.8(c)   Calculation of the P-Index of Ageing in 2050 in
India based on UN Data   180

3.9(a)   Calculation of the P-Index of Ageing in 1995 in
Japan based on UN Data   180

3.9(b)   Calculation of the P-Index of Ageing in 2025 in
Japan based on UN Projections   181

3.9(c)   Calculation of the P-Index of Ageing in 2050 in
Japan based on UN Data   181

3.10   Ageing in India under H, I and Q Indices   182

3.11   Age Distribution of the Indian Population since 1950   186

3.12   Different Indices of Population Ageing   187

4.1   National Health Expenditure of GDP, 1960–1997,
in Developed Countries (in percentage)   206

4.2   Health Care Expenditures as Percentages of
GDP in Several Asian Countries   206

4.3   The Elderly in Voting Age Population in Some
Regions/Countries, 1995, 2025 and 2050   215

5.1   Share of the Aged to the Total Population
Obtained from NSS Surveys and Population
Censuses for Each Sex   243

5.2   Percentage of the Total and the Elderly Population
in India in the Rural Areas   243

5.3   Rural–Urban Differences in Fertility Indicators
of India   245

5.4   Expectation of Life at Birth (in years) by Sex and
Residence from 1970–75 to 1991–95 in India   246

5.5   Rural–Urban Differences in Old-age
Dependency Ratio (per 1000) in India   247

5.6   Old Age and Youth Dependency Ratios, by Urban
and Rural Sector in Some Asian Countries   248

5.7   Rural–Urban Sex Ratio (Male per 100 Females)
of Populations 60 Years of Age and Older for
Selected Asian Countries   250

5.8   Percentage Distribution of those Aged 60 and
above by Sex, since 1961   255

5.9   Rural–Urban Differences in Elderly Sex Ratio
(Number of Females per 1000 Males) in India   256

5.10   Sex Ratio (Number of Females per 1000 Males)
among Aged Persons in Selected Countries   257

5.11   Marital Status of the Aged in India   259

5.12   Literacy among the Aged and General Population
in India   260

5.13   Percentage Distribution of Literate Population
Aged 60 and above by the Level of Education,
India, 1981 and 1991   262

5.14   Proportion of Aged Persons by Number of
Surviving Children   263

5.15   Living Arrangements of the Elderly in India   264

5.16   Percentage of Co-residence of Elderly Aged 60
and over in Selected Asian Countries   265

5.17   Work Participation Rate for the Elderly and
General Population in India, 1991   269

5.18   Percentage Distribution of Main Workers
Aged 60 plus by Industrial Category, Sex
and Residence   270

5.19   Percentage Distribution of Elderly Workers by
Class of Worker Status   272

5.20   Percentage Distribution of Elderly Persons by
State of Economic Independence for Each Sex   273

5.21   Percentage Distribution of Economically
Dependent Aged Persons by Category of
Persons Supporting   274

5.22   Government-sponsored Schemes for Old Age
Income Security in India   277

5.23   Percentage Distribution of Aged Persons (Who
Were Ever Engaged in Wage/Salaried Jobs or
as Casual Labour) by Category of
Retirement Benefits   281

5.24   Coverage of Schemes Providing Cash Benefits
to the Aged, Disabled and/or Survivals, 1992   282

5.25   Percentage of Aged Persons with Financial
Assets/Property   284

5.26   Percentage of Aged Persons Reporting a
Chronic Disease by Sex   286

5.27 Prevalence Rate of Physical Disability among
the Aged by Type for Each Sex   288
5.28 Percentage of Aged Persons Participating in
Social Activities   294
5.29 Maximum and Minimum Values of Elderly
Status Indicators among the Indian States   296
5.30 Elderly Status Index (ESI) for the Major
Indian States   297

LIST OF FIGURES

1.1 Ageing Trends in the World, Asia, and in the More and Less Developed Regions of the World, 1950–2050   36

1.2 Elderly in the More Developed Regions (MDRs) and Less Developed Regions (LDRs) of the World, 1999   37

1.3 Elderly in the More Developed Regions (MDRs) and Less Developed Regions (LDRs) of the World, 1950   37

1.4 Distribution of the Aged Population, Continent-wise, 1999   38

1.5 Trends in the Dependency Ratio in the Whole World, More Developed Regions (MDRs), Less Developed Regions (LDRs), and Asia, 1950–2050   44

1.6 Potential Support Ratio (PSR) in Different Regions of the World, 1999 and 2050   49

1.7 Sex Distribution of the World Elderly, 1950   58

1.8 Sex Distribution of the World Elderly, 1995   59

1.9 Projected Sex Distribution of the World Elderly, 2050   59

2.1 Fertility and Mortality Rates during the Process of Demographic Transition   91

2.2 Scatter of Life Expectancy and Proportion of Aged in Asian Regions, MDRs and the World, 1950–2050   102

2.3 Scatter of TFR and Proportion of Aged in Asian Regions, the World and the MDRs, 1950–2050   107

2.4 Scatter of Life Expectancy and Percentage of Aged in India, Japan and Thailand, 1950–2050   111

2.5   Scatter of TFR and Proportion of Elderly in
        Japan, India and Thailand, 1950–2050   111

3.1(a) Half-age Pyramid in India, 1950   184
3.1(b) Half-age Pyramid in India,1980   185
3.1(c) Half-age Pyramid in India, 2000   185
3.2   Ageing Trends in India, 1950–2000 under
        Different Indices   188

LIST OF ABBREVIATIONS

ADL	Activities of Daily Living
AGE	Americans for Generational Equity
AIDS	Acquired Immunodeficiency Syndrome
ASEAN	Association of Southeast Asian Nations
BIMARU	Bihar, Madhya Pradesh, Rajasthan and Uttar Pradesh
CBR	Crude Birth Rate
DALE	Disability Adjusted Life Expectancy
CDR	Crude Death Rate
DF	Degree of freedom
DHS	Demographic and Health Survey
DTI	Demographic Transition Index
ESCAP	Economic and Social Commission for Asia and the Pacific
ESI	Elderly Status Index
FAO	Food and Agriculture Organization of the United Nations
FDI	Foreign Direct Investment
GATT	General Agreement on Tariffs and Trade
GDP	Gross Domestic Product
GNP	Gross National Product
HDI	Human Development Index
HIV	Human Immunodeficiency Virus
ICPD	International Conference on Population and Development
IDBA	International Database on Ageing (United States Bureau of the Census)
ILO	International Labour Organization
IMF	International Monetary Fund
IMR	Infant Mortality Rate
IUSSP	International Union for the Scientific Study of Population
KAP	Knowledge, Attitudes and Practices (Survey)

LDRs	Less Developed Regions
LtDRs	Least Developed Regions
MDRs	More Developed Regions
NCOP	National Council for Older Persons
NGO	Non-governmental Organisation
NIE	Newly Industrialising Economy
NOAPS	National Old Age Pension Scheme
NSSO	National Sample Survey Organisation
OASIS	Old Age Social and Income Security
OECD	Organisation for Economic Cooperation and Development
PPP	Purchasing Power Parity
PaSR	Parent Support Ratio
PSR	Potential Support Ratio
R&D	Research and Development
RPG	Rapid Population Growth
SAP	Structural Adjustment Programme
SRA	Statutory Retirement Age
TFR	Total Fertility Rate
UNAIDS	United Nations Programme on HIV/AIDS
UNDP	United Nations Development Programme
UNESCO	United Nations Educational, Scientific and Cultural Organization
UNFPA	United Nations Population Fund
UNHCR	United Nations High Commissioner for Refugees
UNIFEM	United Nations Development Fund for Women
WFS	World Fertility Survey
WHO	World Health Organization
WTO	World Trade Organization

FOREWORD

One of the benefits of the science of demography is that, in broad terms, and particularly in relation to the medium run, it enables us to make statements about the future with a reasonable degree of assurance.

The 20th century saw massive improvements in mortality in most of Asia. In 1900, the average life expectation for the continent as a whole was probably less than 30 years. According to the United Nations (UN) this figure had risen to about 41 years by 1950. And for the quinquennium 2000–2005, the UN puts the average life expectancy for males and females in Asia at 65.8 and 69.2 years respectively.

Eventually, all levels of human fertility have had to respond to this dramatic and sustained reduction in mortality. Populations in Asia have been subject to the same basic dictate that has earlier applied to populations in Europe and North America: a fall in birth rates so that they were roughly in balance with the much reduced death rates.

However, and not surprisingly, the timing, speed and nature of the ensuing Asian fertility declines have been somewhat different from those which occurred in other parts of the world; and, of course, with considerable variation of experience *within* Asia. For example, fertility rates fell relatively early in Japan, relatively late in much of northern India and Pakistan, relatively fast in Thailand, and, faster still in China. Most of the fall in the continent's fertility occurred in the second half of the 20th century.

Where Asian women had an average of almost six births each during the period 1950–55, the UN estimates that this figure fell to about 2.5 births per woman by 2000–2005.

Of course, fertility decline accounts for the basic process of population ageing. And, as this timely, stimulating and challenging book illustrates, it is inevitable that Asia is going to experience *very* considerable population ageing in the decades which lie immediately ahead. Indeed, in much of the continent, population ageing is going to occur at quite unprecedented rates. This ageing will almost certainly be accompanied by (and will help to produce) an increasing degree of population feminisation—because death rates for females tend to be significantly lower than those for males (especially at later ages). Furthermore, and largely because of the fall in fertility, Asian women are increasingly living lives which are rather more independent of men. In most countries the age of women at marriage is rising. For young women especially, a life dominated by the institution of marriage and considerable domestic and child care responsibilities, is becoming less attractive. Again, there is considerable variation within the continent, but undoubtedly this will be the general *direction* of change everywhere in the long run.

As this book shows, the challenges from population ageing that will arise from these developments are already fairly clear. These are challenges which many countries are going to have to tackle in circumstances where average levels of income per person are still low. Moreover, because of fertility decline (and increased human mobility) elderly people in Asia will probably have fewer adult children around to interact with and assist them than has generally been the case during recent decades.

However, while undeniably challenging, the prospect of population ageing will generally be welcomed. Population ageing is a *global* trend; lessons learnt in other parts of the world will often be transferable to Asia (and vice versa). Also, mortality decline and associated improvements in health will mean that people will be able to continue to work even at older ages. The concept of permanently 'retiring' from employment, say at age 60 or 65—which in any case is rather foreign to much of Asia—will almost certainly wane over the longer run. Properly managed, this can be a beneficial trend, partly because most people consider productive work to be a defining part of their lives, and partly because for society as a whole early retirement is a huge waste of precious human resources. Furthermore, mortality decline would mean a decline in the levels of widowhood in the future. In any given age group, married people will have a greater chance of their spouse still being alive for companionship and support. These are all good developments. The challenges will lie in developing and tailoring appropriate employment structures for the working elderly, developing satisfactory policies of income and family support for those who can no longer work, and grappling with the inevitable fact that health care expenditures for older people tend to rise sharply with increasing age.

Rajagopal Dhar Chakraborti is to be congratulated in raising very important issues regarding Asia's future. It is to be hoped that policy makers everywhere will turn to consider them sooner rather than later.

Tim Dyson
Professor, Development Studies Institute (DESTIN),
London School of Economics and Political Science,
London.

PREFACE

Reduction in fertility and mortality rates has been one of the major goals of civilisations. For thousands of years, human population did not grow because of high mortality. The Industrial Revolution on the other hand required more men than were available to run the wheels of progress and consequently, human effort did help contain death and death rates through continued experiments with research and development over generations. Today, civilised society has attained so much success that it has more people than the wheels of advancement need. Where private choice has clashed with public interest, governments have come forward with incentives and disincentives on family size. The result has been spontaneous. Fertility is on the decline the world over, despite differences in intensity.

However, instead of rejoicing over the now favourable demographic setup, mankind has once again been rocked by an 'age-quake'.[1] The proportions of people aged 60 years and above are rising and are expected to grow rapidly over the next 50 years. This 'demographic time bomb',[2] is nearing explosion in the economically advanced nations. Asia is not far behind either; the economically advanced countries of East Asia are almost at par with their counterparts elsewhere in the world. It is clearly visible in the South-east Asian countries that have successfully increased life expectancy and reduced fertility. This trend is now visible in South Asia too. Ironically, in those South Asian countries where the number of children is still very high, the elderly make up the second largest group among the geographic sub-regions of the world, as reported in World Population Prospects,[3] a United Nations publication.

While ageing research has been well developed and well documented in Europe and other developed countries, including Japan, it has yet to take shape in most other parts of Asia. To a great extent the lack of interest on ageing research in Asia owes its origin to the belief that the family support system is and will continue to be fool-proof insurance against all problems faced during old age. It is true that the family is an effective provider of old age support in India and most other Asian countries, and that in the absence of institutional support it will probably continue to serve an important role. At the same time, the family also has its limitations, which are becoming increasingly apparent, as social and economic development under-mines traditional values and as elderly populations grow in relation to the population expected to provide support to them.

It has been argued that the increasing proportions of the elderly would make their own conditions pitiable by drawing heavily on their family's humble resources, resulting in very low-quality life. They would consume larger shares of national income, burdening future generations of taxpayers. Saving and investment would decline. Simultaneously, national productivity would also decline as the median age of the workers grows.

The reduction in fertility rates means that fewer children are available per parent to take care of them during their old age. The cost of parent caring per child has risen and in the face of continuing financial crisis most children do not have adequate financial resources to take care of their elderly parents. Where resources are not scarce, psychological barriers which prevent children from caring for their parents have emerged. The opportunity of sharing costs often unites many unwilling heads.

Having survived several periods of ill health during the transition from high mortality, the elderly require special geriatric care. Most hospitals do not house such facilities and where they do exist, they are usually cost prohibitive. Even then, on average, 10 to 15 per cent of hospital beds in countries which offer such facilities are occupied by senior citizens. The health economics principle suggests that long confinement cases be treated at home for better resource utilisation. Previously, the unemployed women cared for the elderly at home. Now, with increasing female participation in the labour force, such caring avenues have narrowed greatly.

Housing shortages and the consequent reduction in housing space are robbing the elderly of their grossly eroded rights to privacy.

An increasing number of the elderly are found looking for work and they usually have to be satisfied with low wages and work insecurity combined with unhealthy working conditions. Widows form a large number of the elderly—Asian women married to men 10 to 15 years older than them and who, therefore, have to endure longer periods of widowhood. Their conditions are worsened by the fact that they are unable to fend for themselves. Abandonment of elderly widows, even from educated families, is on the rise.

The West has tried to find a solution to this crisis by making available institutional support outside the family system. Such attempts, however, are not viable in countries where funds are scarce and where living outside one's own family is a difficult proposition. Also, apart from their emotional value, the aged are of very little economic value to the family. With health care and long-term care costs rising at a rapid rate, negligence of the aged may take on serious proportions.

At a time when the western world is reshaping programmes for the elderly, in order to contain costs as well as to mitigate the intergenerational conflict, many Asian countries have barely begun to think about their elderly; and, given the pace of population ageing in Asia and the corresponding lack of adjustment mechanisms, a 'time bomb' or 'agequake' may not be very far.[4]

This book analyses the demographic and socio-economic characteristics such as size, age-sex composition, spatial distribution, and social and economic conditions of the ageing populations in India in the context of Asia. It identifies the factors responsible for ageing, and answers the following questions: Is fertility a more dominating factor than mortality? What role does migration play in changing the age composition of the population? The book also investigates the implications of future trends and patterns of the ageing population on socio-economic development programmes relating to health, savings, investment, consumption patterns, residence, workforce participation, migration, social security etc. It carefully scrutinises the role of the family in supporting the aged. This book identifies some of the major policy options that have been attempted to insure the elderly against all risks, including health hazards, and allow older adults to maintain as much economic independence and self-sufficiency as possible without disturbing the intergenerational balance. It envisages responsibility on the aged and their family members for their own improved living. The whole process of the elderly enjoying a better mode of living through life sustenance, self-esteem and freedom has been re-christened as 'graceful ageing'. The right to honourable death is also a part of graceful ageing. The suggested measures do not deviate much from the concept of 'active ageing' of the World Health Organization (WHO) and the International Plan of Actions on

Ageing. It seeks to provide a humane touch to the concept of ageing in the context of Asian peculiarities.

While we have given broad ageing scenarios for most Asian countries, given the diversity that exists within Asia, special emphasis has been laid on Japan, Thailand and China, in addition to India which is our primary area of study. Geographically, these countries are situated in different regions; economically also, they exist on different levels. Japan is the most developed nation in Asia with a GNI per capita of $35,990 in 2001, the fourth highest in the world. In comparison, Thailand's per capita income was $1,970 in the same year which placed it in the lower middle-income category. In 2001, India had a per capita income of $460 and was placed 161st in the world. China, though much better placed than India, is a new entrant in the lower middle-income country category by the definition of the World Bank.[5] As is well known, China has an economic system distinctly different from the countries mentioned here; all these countries are at different stages of transition, demographically and economically, and the same trend is maintained in population ageing too.

While working on this book, we observed that the question 'who are the aged' has not been settled adequately. Though people aged 60 or 65 are considered the most convenient yardstick there are several ways through which ageing can be measured, each with its own peculiarity. Often, the use of one measure in preference over others alters ageing indices significantly. In this book we introduce the various ways in which ageing can be measured, including their potential limitations with the hope that further research will bring us closer to a more scientifically acceptable measuring technique. We introduce the concept of Elderly Status Index based on some of the essential parameters of elderly life. This index helps us ascertain the relative position of the elderly, both across regions and over time, provided comparable data is available.

To facilitate demographic comparisons across regions, this book uses UN estimates and medium variant projections. Where UN data does not exist, the research uses data from other established agencies. This book draws heavily from the survey report, the *Aged in India*, prepared by the country's most prestigious statistical agency, the National Sample Survey Organisation (NSSO). A comparison of the NSS 42nd Round (July 1986–June 1987) data with the NSS 52nd Round (July 1995–June 1996) data gives a fairly good idea about the changes that the aged have experienced in India over the last decade.

This book is divided into six chapters. *Chapter one* introduces the Asian perspective of population ageing. *Chapter two* seeks to identify the factors responsible for population ageing in Asia. *Chapter three* discusses the various conceptual and measurement issues relating to population ageing. *Chapter four* explores the major consequences of population ageing. *Chapter five* reviews the status of the elderly and prepares an Elderly Status Index from the available data on the demographic characteristics of the elderly. *Chapter six* introduces the concept of graceful ageing.

The book also includes five appendices. The Statutory Retirement Age (which technically signals the onset of ageing in a country) of several countries has been given in *Appendix one*. *Appendix two* lists all the major policies and programmes for the elderly of the different governments in India. The International Plan of Actions on the Ageing, including the political resolutions of the recently held Madrid Congress are discussed in *Appendix three*. *Appendix four* lists the major chronic conditions affecting older people. *Appendix five* gives the ordinance on elderly people in Viet Nam. Technical terms used in the book are explained in the *Glossary*.

NOTES AND REFERENCES

1. Paul Wallace, *Agequake: Riding the Demographic Rollercoaster Shaking Business and Our World*, Nicolas Brearly Publishing, London, 1999.
2. M.S. Teitelbaum and J.M. Winter, *The Fear of Population Decline*, Academic Press, Orlando, 1985; also see J. McLoughlin, *The Demographic Revolution*, Faber and Faber, London, 1991.
3. United Nations, *World Population Prospects: The 1998 Revision*, ST/ESA/SER.A/180, Department of Economic and Social Affairs, Population Division, New York, 1999.
4. The metaphor of a 'time bomb' or 'age quake' used by some analysts to explain ageing trends may seem inappropriate. Bomb explosions or earthquakes occur with tremendous force, but such force is rapidly spent. A more appropriate metaphor for rapid ageing is that of a glacier, since a glacier moves at a slow pace but with enormous effects wherever it goes and with a long-term momentum that is unstoppable.
5. According to the World Bank's *World Development Indicators 2002*, a low-income country is one where the per capita income is $745 or less. A lower middle income country has a per capita income range from $746 to $2,975 and a upper middle income country from $2,976 to $9,205 and high income countries have GNP per capita above $9,205.

ACKNOWLEDGEMENTS

My interest in population ageing dates back to the early 1980s when some teachers at St Xavier's College, Calcutta, decided to promote a home for the aged. While the home is yet to be developed, the emotions I felt at the time were strong enough to sustain my interest in the aged to this date. I acknowledge with deep gratitude the Jesuit Fathers at St Xavier's College, Calcutta, and my dear friend, Dr Dipak Chatterjee for initiating my interest and motivation in the aged.

A research of this magnitude cannot be undertaken without the combined effort of several people. My teachers, colleagues, friends and other co-workers have provided me with valuable guidance and assistance at various stages of research. Although it is impossible for me to thank each of them individually, I take this opportunity to acknowledge my teacher, Professor Tim Dyson of the London School of Economics (LSE) for all his kind research advice during my Visiting Fellowship at the LSE last year. I am also grateful to Tim, as he is fondly called by demographers the world over, for agreeing to write the Foreword to this book. Professor Ashish K. Banerjee, also my teacher and the current Vice Chancellor of Calcutta University, helped me considerably during my research as well. I thank Ms Jane Falkingham, my classmate at the LSE, for her research inputs. A very special thanks also to Dr Emily Grundy of the London School of Hygiene and Tropical Medicine; Professor Eileen Crimmins of the University of South California; Professor Joseph Troisi, Deputy Director at the United Nations International Institute on Ageing at Malta; Professor Sen-dou Chang, of the University of Hawaii; Dr Yasuhiko Saito of Nihon University, Japan; Professor Eldon Wegner of the University of Hawaii, Manoa; Dr Jim Shon, a political analyst and a former legislator of Hawaii; and several other scholars in the field who have helped me at various stages of my research. I am indebted to Chinese demographers like Professor

Cangping Wu, Professor Li Jianmin, Professor Zhenwu Zhai, Dr Du Peng, Dr Chengrong Duan, Dr Tha Lin, Dr John J.D. Zhu, Dr Zhang Zaisheng and Dr Weimin Chen for their valuable insights.

I take this opportunity to also thank the authorities of Calcutta University and the Department of South & South-east Asian Studies, for providing me with valuable logistical support with which to carry out my research on ageing. I thank Professor Suranjan Das, the Pro-Vice Chancellor for Academic Affairs, Calcutta University, and Professor Asish K. Roy, for all their help.

My trips to the UK and USA would not have been possible without funding from The Wellcome Trust International and the East-West Center. Both the trips helped in laying the groundwork for this book. I also thank the authorities of the Asian Scholarship Foundation, Bangkok, for selecting me for the Asia Fellowship, which will give me further opportunities to work on ageing in many Asian countries. I am also indebted to the faculty and staff of all the research institutes and libraries that have assisted me with academic and logistic support.

A big thank you also to Dr Alexandre Sidorenko, Chief, UN Programme on Ageing, for permitting me to use the International Plan of Actions on Ageing in Appendix three; Dr Ellen Carnevale, Director of Communications, Population Reference Bureau, for allowing me to use some technical terms in the glossary; and Dr Shubha Soneja, HelpAge India, for her acquiescence to use one of their booklets on elderly programmes in India.

I take this opportunity to also acknowledge my family: my brothers, Probodhgopal (also my mentor), for his intellectual support, Subodhgopal, for his help in ensuring that I worked on the project uninterruptedly, and Bijoygopal who was always ready to help in the research and writing of the book; my brother-in-law, Udayan Bhattacharya, for his manifold assistance; my sisters, Jyotsana and Devaki, for seeing me through personal tragedy at the time of writing this book; and my parents, for the best possible upbringing and values.

Finally, I thank Debjani M. Dutta, Sage Publications, for all her professional help and support.

Rajagopal Dhar Chakraborti
Institute of Population and Development, Nankai University,
Tianjin, China,
January 2003.

CHAPTER ONE

AGEING IN ASIA: A BROAD OVERVIEW

Population ageing—the process by which older individuals come to form a proportionately larger share of the total population—is one of the most distinctive demographic events in the world today. Initially experienced in the more developed countries, the process is now rapidly approaching the developing world. Although not a global phenomena yet, various predictions indicate that population ageing is going to become a major global issue in the years to come. Virtually all countries will face population ageing, albeit with varying intensity and at different points in time. This chapter presents a broad overview of ageing, its geographic and temporal spread over different regions of the world and over different countries of Asia. It uses United Nations Medium Variant Projections[1] to provide a rough idea of the numbers of older persons that the various regions of Asia and other parts of the world would have in the future. Again, as the proportions of aged persons rise, that of other age groups in the population would fall. The projections indicate that the proportion of younger people upto the age group of 15–24 years would fall in most places. The intergenerational balance that is seen today may not be observed in the future. The changing balance between age groups would make the aged more of a burden on society, and as resources are diverted from the young to the old, the world as a whole may experience malevolent intergenerational conflicts and tensions.[2] With improvements in life expectancy (and these improvements will take place at a faster rate for females than for males) there is, and there will be, a progressive ageing of the older population and, interestingly, a majority of them would be females. Apart from these demographic traits, the socio-economic characteristics of these people are, and will be, very interesting to watch, both for academics and policy makers. How many of them have spouses who are living? How many of them work outside the home? What is the condition of their health? To what level have they been educated? All these questions which bother policy makers and academics alike are answered in this chapter.

SPREAD OF AGEING: OVER TIME AND REGIONS

Ageing is spreading rapidly with time and over regions. Some of the major characteristics that mark the global spread of ageing are:

◆ The number of elderly has tripled over the last 50 years and this number is expected to further triple in the next 50 years;
◆ the growth rate of the elderly is much faster than the growth rate of the total population almost all over the world;
◆ the proportion of the elderly in total populations will double within the next 50 years;
◆ though currently the more developed regions of the world have relatively high proportions of the elderly, the older population is concentrated in the less developed regions and is growing at a faster rate.

In 1950, the number of persons aged 60 years or older was 205 million. Their numbers surged to 606 million in 2000. By 2050, these numbers are projected to rise to two billion. In 1950, only three countries had more than one million aged people: China, India and the United States of America. In 2000, Japan and the Russian federation joined the list. By 2050, 33 countries are expected to be on the list. In terms of percentage, the aged constituted 8.2 per cent of the total population in 1950; this percentage rose to 10 per cent of the world's population in 2000 and is projected to rise to 21.1 per cent in 2050, by which time the world population of the aged will be larger than the population of children between the ages 0–14 years. The current growth of the older population, which is 1.9 per cent, is significantly higher than that of the total population, estimated to be at 1.2 per cent. As the baby boom generation enters into old age, the difference between the two can be expected to increase in the near future. The projections indicate that by 2025–30, the aged population will grow by 2.8 per cent compared to 0.8 per cent for the total population. There will, however, be a fall in the growth rate of the elderly in 2045–50.

As is evident from Table 1.1 and also Figure 1.1, the percentage of the aged is rising. The number of aged is growing at a much faster rate in the More Developed Regions (MDRs)[3] than anywhere else, but the pace of ageing in developing countries is more rapid. Interestingly, the trends in Asia perfectly match the trends in the Less Developed Regions (LDRs)[4] and the world as a whole. Surprisingly, ageing is neither a current problem in the Least Developed Regions (LtDRs),[5] nor is it going to be a problem for another 50 years. Even in 2050, those aged 60 and above will constitute less than 10 per cent of the population in these regions.

In terms of absolute numbers, the incidence of ageing gets a totally different look. As Table 1.2 shows, the aged are concentrated in the LDRs of the world. Not only that, most of the additions to the aged population in the world will also be in these regions. In 1999,

Table 1.1
Estimates and Medium-fertility Variant Projections of the Elderly (60 plus) in Different World Regions, 1950–2050

(the figures are percentages of total population)

Regions	1950	1975	2000	2025	2050
World	8.2	8.6	10.0	15.0	21.1
MDRs	11.7	15.4	19.4	28.2	33.5
LDRs	6.4	6.2	7.7	12.6	19.3
Least Developed Regions (LtDR)	5.4	5.0	4.9	5.9	9.5
Africa	5.3	5.0	5.1	6.3	10.2
Oceania	11.2	11.0	13.4	19.7	23.3
Europe	12.1	16.4	20.3	28.8	36.6
Latin America	5.9	6.5	8.0	14.0	22.5
North America	12.4	14.6	16.2	25.1	27.2
ASIA	6.8	6.6	8.8	14.7	22.6
Eastern Asia[6]	7.4	7.4	11.3	20.8	30.7
South-central Asia[7]	6.1	6.1	7.1	11.1	18.7
Western Asia[8]	7.1	6.5	7.1	10.4	15.6
South-eastern Asia[9]	6.0	5.7	7.1	12.7	22.0

Source: United Nations, 'World Population Ageing 1950–2050', Population Division, Department of Economic and Social Affairs, ST/ESA/SER.A/207, New York, 2002.

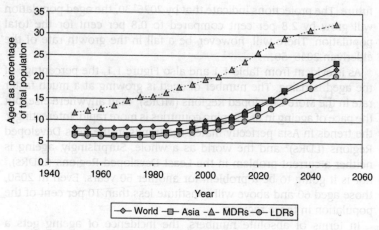

Figure 1.1 Ageing Trends in the World, Asia, and in the More and Less Developed Regions of the World, 1950–2050

Table 1.2
Number of the Aged in the World (Region-wise)

Country or Area	Aged, 2000 (number in thousands)	Aged, 2000 (percentage)	Aged, 2050 (number in thousands)	Aged, 2050 (percentage)
World	593,111	100.0	1,969,809	100.00
More Developed Regions	228,977	38.6	375,516	19.06
Less Developed Regions	364,133	61.4	1,594,293	80.94

Source: United Nations, 'Population Ageing', Population Division, Department of Economic and Social Affairs, New York, 1999.

the LDRs sheltered 61.4 per cent of the world's aged (see Figure 1.2). In 2050, they are projected to hold over 80 per cent of the world's aged. In contrast, in 1950, half of the world's elderly (46.6 per cent) were in the developed regions (see Figure 1.3).

Table 1.3 presents the distribution of the aged continent-wise. Asia holds the largest number of aged (53 per cent), followed by Europe (25 per cent). This pressure of increasing numbers of the

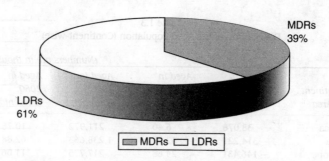

Figure 1.2 Elderly in the More Developed Regions (MDRs) and Less Developed Regions (LDRs) of the World, 1999

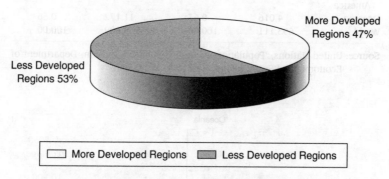

Figure 1.3 Elderly in the More Developed Regions (MDRs) and Less Developed Regions (LDRs) of the World, 1950

aged will further intensify in the next 50 years. In 2050, 81 per cent of the world's elderly will be in the LDRs of Asia, Africa and Latin America while only 19 per cent of them will reside in the developed regions of Europe and North America. Population ageing is therefore gradually emerging as the problem of the LDRs. To be more specific, if absolute numbers are any indication, not only was ageing an Asian problem in the last century, but it is going to continue to dominate Asia in the next century too. Figure 1.4 provides a pictorial representation of the distribution of the elderly for the year 1999.

Table 1.4 provides the absolute number as well as the proportion of the aged in most countries of Asia. As can be seen the largest number of the aged in Asia are in China, followed by India, Japan,

Table 1.3
Distribution of the Aged Population (Continent-wise)

(Numbers are in thousand)

Continent or Area	Aged in 2000 (Numbers)	Aged in 2000 (Percentage)	Aged in 2050 (Numbers)	Aged in 2050 (Percentage)
Africa	38,078	6.40	211,972	10.76
Asia	314,221	52.97	1,238,663	62.88
Europe	146,431	24.68	217,775	11.06
Latin America & Caribbean	40,037	6.75	180,622	9.17
Northern America	50,339	8.48	109,600	5.56
Oceania	4,016	0.67	11,172	0.56
World	593,111	100.00	1,969,809	100.00

Source: United Nations, 'Population Ageing', Population Division, Department of Economic and Social Affairs, New York, 1999.

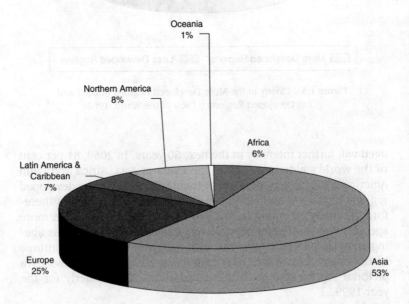

Figure 1.4 Distribution of the Aged Population, Continent-wise, 1999

Table 1.4
The Aged in Asia, Absolute Numbers and Proportion of the Total Population of 60 plus and 80 plus, 1999 and 2050

Area/ Country	60 Plus (number in thousands)		60 Plus (percentages of total population)		80 Plus (percentages of total elderly population)	
	1999	2050	1999	2050	1999	2050
Asia	314,221	1,238,663	9	24	9	18
Eastern Asia	162,560	506,694	11	30	10	23
China	126,161	439,583	10	30	9	23
Hong Kong	965	2,690	14	40	14	31
N. Korea	1,873	8,211	8	27	10	26
Japan	28,603	39,428	23	38	16	31
Macao	42	173	9	35	14	32
Mongolia	152	1,029	6	23	10	15
Republic of Korea	4,764	15,580	10	30	8	24
South-central Asia	102,141	486,724	7	20	8	14
Afghanistan	1,068	6,404	5	10	4	9
Bangladesh	6,418	42,835	5	20	7	9
Bhutan	128	697	6	12	8	13
India	75,190	323,855	8	21	8	15
Iran (Islamic Republic of)	4,177	26,638	6	23	9	13
Kazakhstan	1,824	4,392	11	24	10	18
Kyrgyzstan	417	1,527	9	21	9	16
Maldives	15	103	5	15	7	10
Nepal	1,297	7,338	6	15	7	9
Pakistan	7,490	54,250	5	16	8	15
Sri Lanka	1,768	6,928	9	27	10	20
Tajikistan	410	2,111	7	19	10	15
Turkmenistan	285	1,538	7	20	9	16
Uzbekistan	1,654	8,107	7	20	10	16
South-eastern Asia	36,510	177,513	7	23	8	16
Brunei Darussalam	16	126	5	24	9	23
Cambodia	527	2,967	5	14	7	11
East Timor	37	232	4	17	4	9
Indonesia	15,339	69,744	7	22	7	15
Laos	276	1,574	5	12	6	11

(continued)

Table 1.4
(Continued)

Area/ Country	60 Plus (number in thousands)		60 Plus (percentages of total population)		80 Plus (percentages of total elderly population)	
	1999	2050	1999	2050	1999	2050
Malaysia	1,413	7,940	6	21	9	18
Myanmar	3,322	15,942	7	25	7	16
Philippines	4,187	26,041	6	20	9	14
Singapore	362	1,259	10	31	13	36
Thailand	5,166	21,981	8	30	10	21
Viet Nam	5,866	29,707	7	23	10	17
Western Asia	**13,009**	**67,732**	**7**	**18**	**9**	**15**
Armenia	456	1,177	13	29	8	21
Azerbaijan	814	2,747	11	28	10	22
Bahrain	29	238	5	24	7	22
Cyprus	121	272	16	30	18	26
Gaza Strip	49	393	5	8	10	12
Georgia	908	1,459	18	28	11	23
Iraq	1,084	8,381	5	15	10	13
Israel	797	2,373	13	25	16	23
Jordan	293	2,531	5	15	9	14
Kuwait	65	867	3	25	8	19
Lebanon	267	1,155	8	22	8	17
Oman	102	937	4	11	7	12
Qatar	26	178	4	21	3	22
Saudi Arabia	952	8,142	5	15	7	14
Syrian Arab Republic	735	6,395	5	19	8	12
Turkey	5,537	24,148	8	24	8	17
UAE	112	877	5	24	6	23
Yemen	661	5,462	4	9	6	9

Source: Registrar General, India, New Delhi, Census Reports (Various Years); United Nations, *World Population Prospects: The 1998 Revision*, (Volumes I and II; Sales Nos. E.99.XIII.8 and E.99.XIII.9) Population Division, Department of Economic and Social Affairs New York, 2002; United Nations, *Demographic Yearbook 2000 series: R*, No. 31, Sales No. E/F.02.XIII.1, New York 2002 and *Demographic Yearbook: Historical Supplement 1948–1997 Series: R*, CD-Rom, No. 28/HS-CD Sales No. E/F 99.XIII.12, New York, 2002; United States Bureau of the Census, International Programs Center, International Data Base, web address: http://www.census.gov/ipc/www/idbnew.html

Indonesia, Pakistan, Bangladesh, Viet Nam, Turkey, Thailand, Philippines and Iran. The UN projections for 2050 indicate that the elderly would constitute 1,970 million of the world's population. Of these 1,239 million (63 per cent) would be in Asia. By 2050, ageing will be more pronounced in the developing countries.

The lowest numbers of the aged are currently seen in the Maldives, followed by Brunei, Qatar, Bahrain, East Timor, Macao and the Gaza Strip. This list will be altered significantly by 2050 with the first two countries retaining their position, followed by Macao, Qatar, East Timor, Bahrain and Gaza.

As a percentage of the total population, 11 countries of Asia have crossed the double-digit figure and are close to the developed nations. These are Japan, Hong Kong, South Korea, China, Singapore, Kazakhstan, Armenia, Azerbaijan, Cyprus, Georgia and Israel. In 2050, all Asian countries except the Gaza Strip and Yemen will have a double-digit figure. In Asia, as a whole, every 11th person is 'sixty plus'; by 2050, every fourth person will be an elderly.

CHANGING INTERGENERATIONAL BALANCE

The changing proportions of the aged have been accompanied, in most populations, by steady declines in the proportions of children. Over the last half-century, the proportion of children (0–14 years) dropped worldwide from 34.3 per cent in 1950 to 30 per cent in 2000. This percentage is projected to decline further to 21 per cent by 2050, when the proportion of the aged, for the first time in history, would match that of the younger generation below the age of 15. In the MDRs, the proportion of persons aged 60 and above are slightly higher than the proportion of children below 15 years of age. By the year 2050, the proportion of the aged would be more than double that of the children. As the baby boom generation grows old and the effect of fertility decline realised, the proportion of persons aged 15 to 59 (also called working population) will also slowly decline over the next half-century, though this trend may not be very discernible in the LDRs and most of Asia. However, in East Asia, the proportion of the working population is projected to fall by 10 points in the next half-century. In fact, in the first quarter of the next century, the pro-portion of this age group will rise in almost every country in Asia. The proportion of the working population will stabilise thereafter. Table 1.5 shows the changing balance between different age groups.

Table 1.5
Changing Intergenerational Balance in Selected Regions/Countries
of the World, 1950–2050

Regions/ Countries	Age Group	1950	1975	2000	2025	2050
World	0–14	34.3	36.7	30.0	24.3	21.0
	15–24	18.3	18.6	17.6	15.2	13.2
	15–59	57.6	54.7	60.0	60.7	58.0
	60+	8.2	8.6	10.0	15.0	21.1
MDRs	0–14	27.3	24.2	18.3	15.0	15.5
	15–24	17.0	16.8	13.6	10.9	10.8
	15–59	60.9	60.4	62.3	56.8	51.0
	60+	11.7	15.4	19.4	28.2	33.5
LDRs	0–14	37.6	41.1	32.8	26.0	21.8
	15–24	18.8	19.2	18.5	15.9	13.6
	15–59	56.0	52.7	59.5	61.4	59.0
	60+	6.4	6.2	7.7	12.6	19.3
ASIA	0–14	36.5	39.6	30.2	22.9	19.5
	15–24	18.9	19.0	17.9	14.8	12.6
	15–59	56.7	53.7	61.0	62.4	57.9
	60+	6.8	6.6	8.8	14.7	22.6
Eastern Asia	0–14	34.1	37.8	23.9	17.9	16.1
	15–24	18.5	18.8	15.4	12.2	11.0
	15–59	58.5	54.8	64.9	61.3	53.2
	60+	7.4	7.4	11.3	21.4	39.3
South-central Asia	0–14	38.6	40.7	35.2	25.7	20.8
	15–24	19.2	19.0	19.4	16.5	13.4
	15–59	55.3	53.2	57.8	63.1	60.6
	60+	6.1	6.1	7.1	11.1	18.7
South-eastern Asia	0–14	38.9	42.1	32.4	23.5	19.8
	15–24	19.4	19.7	19.8	15.1	13.0
	15–59	55.1	52.2	60.5	63.8	58.2
	60+	6.0	5.7	7.1	12.7	22.0
Western Asia	0–14	38.5	41.7	35.9	30.2	25.0
	15–24	20.0	19.4	19.7	17.4	14.2
	15–59	54.3	51.7	57.0	59.5	59.4
	60+	7.1	6.5	7.1	10.4	15.4
India	0–14	38.9	39.8	33.5	23.2	19.7
	15–24	19.4	18.8	18.8	15.7	13.1
	15–59	55.5	54.0	58.9	64.3	59.7
	60+	5.6	6.2	7.6	12.5	20.6

(continued)

Table 1.5
(Continued)

Regions/ Countries	Age Group	1950	1975	2000	2025	2050
China	0–14	33.5	39.5	24.8	18.4	16.3
	15–24	18.3	19.1	15.6	12.3	11.1
	15–59	59.0	53.6	65.0	62.1	53.8
	60+	7.5	6.9	10.1	19.5	29.9
Japan	0–14	35.4	24.3	14.7	12.1	12.5
	15–24	19.6	15.4	12.6	10.4	10.0
	15–59	56.9	64.0	62.1	52.8	45.2
	60+	7.7	11.7	23.2	35.1	42.3
Thailand	0–14	42.1	42.6	26.7	19.6	17.1
	15–24	20.4	20.2	18.9	13.0	11.6
	15–59	52.8	52.4	65.2	63.3	56.8
	60+	5.0	5.0	8.1	17.1	27.1

Source: United Nations, 'World Population Ageing 1950–2050', Population Division, Department of Economic and Social Affairs ST/ESA/SER.A/207, New York, 2002.

Age distribution changes have been very slow in the LDRs and Asia. Substantial changes are, however, expected to occur in the next 50 years. The proportion of older persons will more than double everywhere; in East Asia, it will rise by a factor of 3.5. The proportion of children will fall by about one-third in the LDRs and Asia. Interestingly, in most countries and regions as Table 1.5 shows, there would be a significant decline in the proportion of people in the college and university going age-group in the first half of this century. With the decline in the proportion of children (0–14 years) and (15–24 years), schools and colleges and universities will face many empty class rooms. Education planners the world over will need to take serious note of this.

DEPENDENCY BURDENS OF THE AGED

As most of the aged do not work, depending instead on their families, religious or communal institutions or the state, it is often stated that the aged are a burden on society. Since the earnings of all the institutions stated here originate directly or indirectly from the incomes of the working population, the ratios of the non-working age and working-age populations provide crude indicators of old age dependency. The ratio is calculated on the basis of the number of persons aged 65 and above per person in the age group of 15–64.[10] However, the ratio ought to be used very cautiously as not all working-age persons actually provide direct or indirect support[11] to their elders and also because older persons in many societies are the ones who support their adult children.[12]

The dependency ratio is on the rise all over the world. Table 1.6 provides the dependency ratio (for 65 and above) for different regions of the world from 1950–55 to medium variant projected levels of 2045–50. Figure 1.5 shows the dependency ratios in Asia, the MDRs, LDRs and for the world as a whole. Though dependency ratios are rising in Asia, they are still lower than the MDRs, Europe, North America and Oceania. However, this gap would decline in the future.

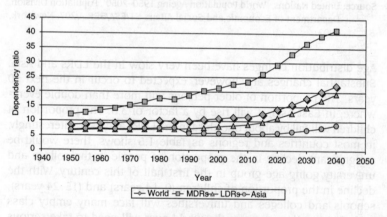

Figure 1.5 Trends in the Dependency Ratio in the Whole World, More Developed Regions (MDRs), Less Developed Regions (LDRs), and Asia, 1950–2050

The potential support ratio (PSR) is an alternative way of looking into the numerical relationship between the economically productive and the so-called aged dependants. It shows the number of persons 15–64 years per older persons aged 65 years or above. Mathematically, it is the inverse of the dependency ratio. The PSR is declining rapidly

Table 1.6
The Aged Dependency Ratio from 1950–2050 in the Different Regions of the World

Year	World	MDRs	LDRs	Africa	Asia	Europe	Latin America	North America	Oceania
1950-55	8.6	12.2	6.7	5.8	6.9	12.5	6.6	12.7	11.7
1955-60	8.9	12.8	6.9	5.6	7.2	13.0	6.9	14.2	12.3
1960-65	9.2	13.6	7.1	5.6	7.4	13.7	7.3	15.1	12.4
1965-70	9.3	14.3	7.0	5.8	7.2	14.7	7.7	15.5	12.2
1970-75	9.6	15.4	7.0	6.0	7.3	16.3	7.9	15.6	12.0
1975-80	9.8	16.5	7.1	5.9	7.4	17.6	8.0	15.9	12.2
1980-85	10.1	17.7	7.2	6.0	7.6	18.9	8.0	16.6	12.7
1985-90	9.8	17.4	7.2	5.9	7.7	17.8	8.0	17.5	13.2
1990-95	10.0	18.7	7.4	5.9	8.0	19.1	8.0	18.6	14.3
1995-2000	10.5	20.3	7.7	5.9	8.5	20.8	8.3	19.0	15.3
2000-2005	10.9	21.3	8.2	5.9	9.1	21.7	8.6	18.9	15.2
2005-10	11.3	22.6	8.5	5.8	9.6	23.3	9.0	18.8	15.4
2010-15	11.5	23.4	8.9	5.7	10.1	23.6	9.7	19.6	16.2
2015-20	12.5	26.1	9.7	5.8	11.1	25.7	10.8	22.2	18.4
2020-25	14.1	29.3	11.2	6.0	13.0	28.8	12.3	25.8	20.4
2025-30	15.8	33.0	12.8	6.5	14.9	32.7	14.3	30.2	22.7
2030-35	17.9	36.6	14.8	7.1	17.3	36.6	16.6	34.0	24.7
2035-40	20.2	39.2	17.2	7.8	20.4	39.9	19.0	35.4	26.4
2040-45	22.2	41.2	19.4	8.8	23.2	42.8	21.5	35.6	27.9
2045-50	23.8	42.7	21.1	10.0	25.1	45.2	24.1	35.5	28.8

Source: United Nations, *World Population Prospects: The 1998 Revision. Volume II: Sex and Age*, New York, 1999; and, United Nations *Demographic Year Book 2000 Series: R*, No.31, New York, 2002 and also *Demographic Yearbook: Historical Supplement 1948–1997 Series: R*, New York, 2002; United States Bureau of the Census, International Programs Center, International Data Base.

Notes: MDRs = More Developed Regions; LDRs = Less Developed Regions.

in most parts of the world. For the world as a whole, the PSR has fallen from 12 in 1950–55 to 10 in 1995–2000 and is expected to fall further to 4 in 2050. Between 1950–2050, the PSR will decline from 8 working age persons per older person to 2 in the MDRs. The ratio will fall by a larger fraction in the LDRs from 15 to 5. PSRs also have important implications for social security schemes. Table 1.7 provides the PSR for the different regions of the world, while the support ratios in different countries of Asia are drawn in Table 1.8. Figure 1.6 shows how the PSR will fall in different continents 50 years from now.

The PSR in most Asian countries is still very high. Only in seven countries (Japan, Hong Kong, Kazakhstan, Israel, Georgia, Cyprus and Armenia), is the PSR less than a double digit figure. In some countries, the support ratio is extraordinarily high. The support ratio is 36 in Qatar, 33 in Kuwait, 24 in East Timor, 23 in Bahrain, 21 in Yemen and Oman, and 20 in Saudi Arabia and Brunei. In India, the PSR is 13. But in the next half-century, the PSR will be a single digit figure in most of Asia, except in Yemen, the Gaza Strip and Afghanistan. Interestingly, once this happens there would hardly be

Table 1.7
Potential Support Ratio (PSR) in Different Regions of the World, 1950–2050

Regions	1950	1975	2000	2025	2050
World	11.6	10.1	9.1	6.3	4.1
MDRs	8.2	6.1	4.7	3.0	2.2
LDRs	14.9	14.0	12.2	7.8	4.6
Africa	16.9	16.8	16.6	14.3	9.5
Asia	14.4	13.4	10.9	6.7	3.8
Europe	8.0	5.7	4.6	3.0	1.9
Latin America	15.2	12.6	11.6	7.0	3.7
North America	7.9	6.3	5.4	3.4	2.8
Oceania	8.6	8.3	6.6	4.4	3.5
Eastern Asia	13.8	12.2	8.8	4.7	2.5
South-central Asia	15.5	14.6	13.2	9.1	5.0
Western Asia	13.0	12.5	12.5	9.1	5.6
South-eastern Asia	15.1	15.3	13.5	8.2	4.0

Source: United Nations, *World Population Ageing 1950–2050*, Population Division, Department of Economic and Social Affairs, ST/ESA/SER.A/207, New York, 2002.

Table 1.8

Potential Support Ratio (PSR) in the Countries of Asia, 2000 and 2050

Area/Country	Potential Support Ratio, 2000	Potential Support Ratio, 2050	Area/Country	Potential Support Ratio, 2000	Potential Support Ratio, 2050
Asia	**11**	**4**	Indonesia	14	4
Eastern Asia	**9**	**3**	Laos	16	9
China	10	3	Malaysia	15	4
China, Hong Kong SAR (a)	7	2	Myanmar	14	3
Democratic People's Republic of Korea	13	3	Philippines	17	5
Japan	4	2	Singapore	10	2
Macao	10	2	Thailand	12	3
Mongolia	15	4	Viet Nam	12	4
Republic of Korea	11	2	**Western Asia**	**13**	**5**
South-central Asia	**13**	**5**	Armenia	8	3
Afghanistan	19	10	Azerbaijan	10	3
Bangladesh	19	5	Bahrain	23	4
Bhutan	13	8	Cyprus	6	3
India	13	4	Gaza Strip	14	12
Iran (Islamic Republic of)	13	4	Georgia	5	3

(continued)

Table 1.8
(Continued)

Area/Country	Potential Support Ratio, 2000	Potential Support Ratio, 2050	Area/Country	Potential Support Ratio, 2000	Potential Support Ratio, 2050
Kazakhstan	9	4	Iraq	18	6
Kyrgyzstan	10	4	Israel	6	3
Maldives	15	7	Jordan	19	6
Nepal	15	7	Kuwait	33	4
Pakistan	17	6	Lebanon	11	4
Sri Lanka	10	3			
Tajikistan	12	5	Oman	21	9
Turkmenistan	14	5	Qatar	36	4
Uzbekistan	13	5	Saudi Arabia	20	6
South-eastern	**14**	**4**	Syrian Arab Republic	18	5
Asia					
Brunei Darussalam	20	4	Turkey	12	3
Cambodia	18	8	United Arab Emirates	30	4
East Timor	24	7	Yemen	21	12

Source: United Nations, *World Population Prospects: The 1998 Revision, Vol. II: Sex and Age*, New York, 1999 and *Demographic Year Book 2000 Series: R*, No.31, Sales No. E/F.02.XIII.1, New York, 2002 and also *Demographic Yearbook: Historical Supplement 1948–1997 Series: R*, CD-Rom, No.28/HS-CD, Sales No.E/F 99. XIII.12, New York, 2002; United States Bureau of the Census, International Programs Center, International Data Base, web address: http://www.census.gov/ipc/www/idbnew.html

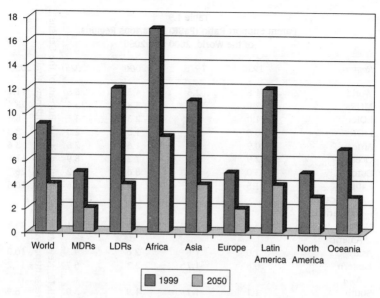

Figure 1.6 Potential Support Ratio (PSR) in Different
Regions of the World, 1999 and 2050

any difference between the PSR of developed regions and the rest of
the world.

Parent Support Ratio (PaSR)

People are living longer today and are thus more likely to experience
multiple chronic diseases, as a result of which increasing number of
adults are expected to maintain very old and frail relatives. An indicator of this trend is found in the Parent Support Ratio (PaSR), which
shows the number of persons aged 85 or above in relation to those
between 50 and 64 years of age. In 1950, at the global level, there
were less than two persons over 85 years per 100 persons within
the age group 50–64 years; this figure doubled in the 50 years that
followed but is projected to triple within the next 50 years. The rich-
poor divide is very prominent hereto. In the MDRs the PaSR is currently
9 and is projected to rise to 28.4 by 2050. France has the highest
PaSR at 13 and Japan is expected to have the highest PaSR in 2050
at 56. In the LDRs, the PaSR is currently 2.3 and is expected to rise

Table 1.9
Parent Support Ratio (PaSR) in Various Regions
of the World, 2000 and 2050

Regions	1950	1975	2000	2025	2050
World	1.8	2.6	4.3	5.5	11.1
MDRs	2.9	4.4	8.8	13.5	28.4
LDRs	1.0	1.4	2.3	3.5	8.3
LtDRs	0.8	0.9	1.5	2.0	3.0
Africa	0.9	1.2	1.6	2.5	3.6
Oceania	2.9	3.6	7.2	8.9	17.8
Europe	3.0	4.3	8.6	12.2	26.7
Latin America and the Caribbean	1.5	2.2	3.5	4.6	10.6
North America	3.4	5.6	9.9	11.1	24.8
Asia	1.0	1.5	2.6	4.3	10.0
Eastern Asia	0.8	1.7	3.3	5.7	17.2
South-central Asia	1.1	1.1	1.9	3.0	5.9
Western Asia	1.6	2.5	2.9	3.8	7.2
South-eastern Asia	1.2	1.3	2.0	2.8	7.7

Source: United Nations, *World Population Ageing 1950–2050*, Population Division, Department of Economic and Social Affairs, ST/ESA/SER.A/207, New York, 2002.

to 8.3 by 2050. In the LtDRs, the PaSR is less than 2 and is not expected to exceed 3 in the next 50 years. This projection of the PaSR too indicates that the impact of population ageing will be very limited in the LtDRs. As note 5 at the end of the chapter lists, 9 Asian countries out of the world's 49 nations fall into this category. Table 1.9 gives the PaSR for different regions of the world, including Asia and its regions.

The PaSR for individual countries in Asia are given in Table 1.10. The PaSR is not disquieting in Asia yet, except in the developed regions of the East and erstwhile parts of Soviet Russia. But in 2050, this figure would be a cause for concern in Japan, Hong Kong, Macao, Korea and Singapore.

Table 1.10
Parent Support Ratio (PaSR) in the Countries of Asia, 2000 and 2050

Area/ Country	PaSR 2000	PaSR 2050	Area/ Country	PaSR 2000	PaSR 2050
Asia	**2.6**	**10.0**	Indonesia	1.6	6.6
Eastern Asia	**3.3**	**17.2**	Laos	2.0	3.1
China	2.5	14.5	Malaysia	2.2	9.4
China, Hong Kong SAR (a)	5.8	35.7	Myanmar	2.4	7.4
Democratic People's Republic of Korea	1.9	8.9	Philippines	1.7	5.8
Japan	8.1	56.0			
China, Macao SAR	4.9	30.9	Singapore	4.4	35.0
Mongolia	2.5	7.2	Thailand	1.7	13.1
Republic of Korea	2.3	26.6	Viet Nam	4.0	8.9
			Western Asia	**2.9**	**7.2**
South-central Asia	**1.9**	**5.9**	Armenia	3.7	16.0
Afghanistan	0.5	1.2	Azerbaijan	5.9	15.7
Bangladesh	1.5	3.2	Bahrain	1.1	14.8
Bhutan	1.8	3.8	Cyprus	7.4	21.4
India	1.9	6.7	Gaza Strip (Occupied Palestinian Territory)	4.3	4.2
Iran (Islamic Republic of)	1.3	5.3	Georgia	6.5	21.4
Kazakhstan	4.2	11.1	Iraq	1.5	5.2
Kyrgyzstan	4.6	9.1	Israel	8.2	17.5
Maldives	1.4	3.8	Jordan	2.6	5.3
Nepal	1.3	2.7	Kuwait	0.6	11.9
Pakistan	1.8	4.0	Lebanon	3.4	9.2
Sri Lanka	2.1	13.7			
Tajikistan	5.4	7.7	Oman	1.2	3.9
Turkmenistan	3.8	7.6	Qatar	0.3	11.3
Uzbekistan			Saudi Arabia	1.2	4.6
South-eastern Asia	**2.0**	**7.7**	Syrian Arab Republic	1.8	5.2

(continued)

Table 1.10
(Continued)

Area/ Country	PaSR 2000	PaSR 2050	Area/ Country	PaSR 2000	PaSR 2050
Brunei Darussalam	2.1	14.1	Turkey	2.9	9.2
Cambodia	1.1	2.7	United Arab Emirates	1.2	21.1
East Timor	0.5	2.4	Yemen	1.3	1.3

Source: United Nations, *World Population Prospects: The 1998 Revision, Vol. II: Sex and Age*, New York, 1999 and *Demographic Yearbook 2000 Series: R*, No.31, Sales No. E/F.02.XIII.1, New York, 2002 and *Demographic Yearbook: Historical Supplement 1948–1997 Series: R*, CD-Rom, No.28/HS-CD Sales No.E/F 99, XIII.12, New York, 2002; United States Bureau of the Census, International Programs Center, International Data Base, web address: http://www.census.gov/ipc/www/idbnew.html

DEMOGRAPHIC PROFILE OF THE OLDER POPULATION

For most nations, regardless of their geographic location or developmental stage, there are two notable aspects of the global ageing process:

1. Progressive demographic ageing of the older population itself;
2. feminisation of ageing.

The rapid growth of the oldest groups among the older population is of special importance to public policy. Although numerically people aged 80 plus do not constitute a significant force yet, this age group is the fastest growing among all the other age groups and projections indicate that it will maintain this lead for the next 50 years. Increase in age is usually accompanied by considerable change in individual needs. As age advances, health declines. Normal Activities of Daily Living (ADL)[13] such as bathing, dressing and eating as well as the Instrumental Activities of Daily Living (IADL)[14] such as shopping, telephoning, cooking and money management, cannot be carried out without support. This suggests an escalation in the demand for long-term care.[15]

An increase in the share of the female section of the older population is another notable demographic profile among the aged. Since mortality rates are usually higher among men than among women, even at older ages, the percentage of women tends to increase with advancing age. In most countries, older women greatly outnumber older men. As women normally marry men senior to them, a greater number of older women are more likely to be widowed. This trend is more pronounced in Asian countries where the age gap between spouses is much higher than in other developed regions. Apart from widowhood, women also have less access to skill formation, education, health care and other sources of private and public support.[16] Indeed, the concerns of the 'oldest old' should be viewed primarily as the concerns of older women.

Ageing of the Aged

Population ageing is characterised not only by an increasing proportion of old people and their growing numbers, but also by ageing within the elderly population and ageing of the labour force. If the age 60 years and above introduces social and economic complications, the ageing of the older population aggravates the problem further. It is estimated that rapid ageing will produce an extremely aged population in the decades ahead. Currently, the 'oldest old' (80 years or older) constitute 11 per cent of the population aged 60 years or older. In Asia today, every 11th aged person is 80 years old or above. Every fifth among them would be over 80 in the next 50 years. In 18 countries of Asia, 'oldest old' among old constitutes a double-digit figure now. Most Asian countries except five (Bangladesh, Afghanistan, Yemen, East Timor and Nepal) would attain the double-digit figure by 2050. Incidentally, these five countries would have 9 per cent of their elderly as 'eighty plus'.

The oldest old are the fastest-growing segment of the elderly population. By 2050, those in the age bracket 80 and above would constitute 19 per cent of the elderly population. Not only that, there would be a considerable shift from 'young elderly' to 'old elderly'. In 1950, people in the age group of 60–64 constituted 36.3 per cent of the elderly population. Their proportion fell to 31.5 per cent in 1995 and is projected to fall further to 25.9 per cent by 2050. People in the age group 80 and above constituted 6.7 per cent of the total population in 1950. This percentage rose significantly to 11.5 per cent in 1995 and is projected to rise further to 18.9 per cent by 2050. Tables 1.11(a) and 1.11(b) provide the five-year age distribution among the aged for four selective years. From the tables one can see that the age pyramid of the global population is changing in a big way in favour of the oldest among the old.

The number of centenarians (aged 100 years or older) is projected to increase from 115,000 in 1995 to 2.2 million people in 2050. In Asia their numbers are expected to rise from 36,000 to 1.09 million during the same period. China, which had 9,000 centenarians in 1995, is expected to house half a million of them by 2025. Interestingly, the

Table 1.11(a)
Age Distribution of the Oldest among the Old for World Population
(in thousands), 1950 and 1995

Age	1950 Estimates of Aged			1995 Estimates of Aged		
	Male	Female	Total	Male	Female	Total
60–64	34,930	39,380	74,310	82,881	87,815	170,696
	(38.3)	(34.6)	(36.3)	(34.3)	(29.3)	(31.5)
65–69	25,160	31,259	56,419	66,303	75,926	142,229
	(27.6)	(27.5)	(27.5)	(27.4)	(25.3)	(26.2)
70–74	16,627	21,578	38,205	45,073	58,263	103,335
	(18.2)	(19.0)	(18.6)	(18.6)	(19.4)	(19.1)
75–79	9,194	13,004	22,198	26,066	37,505	63,572
	(10.1)	(11.4)	(10.8)	(10.8)	(12.5)	(11.7)
80–84	5,234	8,499	13,733	14,179	24,313	38,492
	{5.7}	{7.5}	{6.7}	{8.9}	{13.5}	{11.5}
85–89				5,520	11,690	17,210
90–94				1,424	3,861	5,286
95–99				215	753	968
100 plus				25	89	115
Total	91,145	113,720	204,865	241,686	300,215	541,903
	(100.00)	(100.00)	(100.00)	(100.00)	(100.00)	(100.00)

Source: United Nations, *World Population Prospects: The 1998 Revision*, (Volumes I and II; Sales Nos. E.99.XIII.8 and E.99.XIII.9) and the *Demographic Yearbook 2000 Series:R*, No.31, Sales No. E/F.02.XIII.1, New York, 2002 and *Demographic Yearbook: Historical Supplement 1948–1997 Series: R*, CD-ROM, Sales No. E/E99.XIII.12, New York, 2002; national statistics; United States Bureau of the Census, International Programs Center, International Data Base.

Notes: In 1950, age distribution beyond 80 has not been estimated. The figures corresponding to 80–84 age group therefore refers to 80 plus. { } Indicate percentage in the 80 plus category; figures in brackets ( ) indicate percentage.

Table 1.11(b)
Age Distribution of the Oldest among the Old for World Population
(in thousands), projections for 2000 and 2050

Age	2000 Projections			2050 Projections		
	Male	Female	Total	Male	Female	Total
60–64	90,241	96,434	186,674	254,152	256,991	511,143
	(33.3)	(28.8)	(30.8)	(28.0)	(24.2)	(25.9)
65–69	71,536	80,213	151,749	213,005	225,149	438,154
	(26.4)	(24.0)	(25.1)	(23.5)	(21.2)	(22.2)
70–74	53,021	65,813	118,834	168,134	189,519	357,653
	(19.6)	(19.7)	(19.6)	(18.5)	(17.8)	(18.2)
75–79	32,112	46,370	78,481	130,932	161,531	292,463
	(11.9)	(13.9)	(13.0)	(14.4)	(15.2)	(14.8)
80–84	15,471	25,828	41,299	83,612	118,316	201,928
	{8.8}	{13.6}	{11.5}	{15.6}	{21.6}	{18.9}
85–89	6,496	13,641	20,138	40,078	69,263	109,341
90–94	1,754	4,855	6,609	13,349	30,717	44,066
95–99	287	1,053	1,340	2,871	10,001	12,872
100 plus	31	124	155	340	1,849	2,189
Total	270,949	334,331	605,279	906,473	1,063,336	1,969,809

Source: United Nations, *World Population Prospects: The 1998 Revision, Vol. II: Sex and Age*, New York, 1999.
Notes: {} Indicate percentage in the 80 plus category; figures in ( ) brackets indicate percentage.

number of female centenarians would be nine times more than their male counterparts. Japan, which has 7,000 people aged 100 plus is expected to experience an increase in this number to over a quarter of a million; 85 per cent of these people would be females. In India, living beyond the age of 100 is considered to be a divine blessing. Only 3,000 such people are currently blessed in this way. However, the manner in which the Indian society will react when their '100 plus' people reach 111,000 by 2050 remains to be seen.

The world is experiencing a dramatic increase in longevity. Life expectancy at birth (for both sexes combined) has risen from 46.5 years in 1950–55 to 65.4 years in 1995–2000. Of those surviving upto the age of 60, the men are expected to live for another 17 years and women another 20 years. However, there are still large differences in the mortality levels of different regions/countries. Table 1.12 presents the Asian pattern of ageing among the aged. Interestingly, life expectancy at the age of 60 in Asian countries does not show much variation.

Table 1.12
Number of 80 plus and Centenarians and Life Expectancy at Age 60 for
Males and Females in all Countries of Asia

Area/Country	80 Plus, Male/Female 1950 (in thousands)	Centenarians, Male/Female 1995 (in thousands)	Centenarians, Male/Female 2050 (in thousands)	Life Expectancy Male/Female at age 60, 1995–2000
Asia	1732/2612	10/26	173/916	16/19
Eastern Asia	625/1385	3/13	91/691	17/20
China	471/1087	1/8	47/425	16/19
China, Hong Kong SAR (a)	2/4	0/0	2/8	20/24
Democratic People's Republic of Korea	8/14	0/0	1/10	16/20
Japan	126/250	1/6	40/232	21/25
Macao	0/1	0/0	0/0	19/23
Mongolia	1/1	0/0	0/0	
Republic of Korea	17/28	0/0	1/17	16/20
South-central Asia	763/744	6/8	58/133	16/18
Afghanistan	4/4	0/0	0/0	14/14
Bangladesh	50/50	0/0	1/1	15/16
Bhutan	0/0	0/0	0/0	17/18
India	457/466	1/2	34/77	16/17
Iran (Islamic Republic of)	46/44	4/5	11/20	18/19
Kazakhstan	21/31	0/0	0/4	15/20
Kyrgyzstan	7/10	0/0	0/1	16/20
Maldives	0/0	0/0	0/0	16/17
Nepal	14/16	0/0	0/0	15/16
Pakistan	109/78	0/0	8/16	17/18
Sri Lanka	31/17	0/0	1/7	18/20
Tajikistan	3/3	0/0	0/2	17/21
Turkmenistan	3/4	0/0	0/1	15/19
Uzbekistan	17/19	1/1	2/5	17/20
South-eastern Asia	261/353	1/2	13/54	16/18
Brunei Darussalam	0/0	0/0	0/0	18/21
Cambodia	0/0	0/0	0/0	14/16
East Timor	0/0	0/0	0/0	13/15

(continued)

Table 1.12
(Continued)

Area/Country	80 Plus, Male/Female 1950 (in thousands)	Centenarians, Male/Female 1995 (in thousands)	Centenarians, Male/Female 2050 (in thousands)	Life Expectancy Male/Female at age 60, 1995–2000
Indonesia	128/147	0/0	1/12	16/17
Laos	2/3	0/0	0/0	15/16
Malaysia	0/0	0/0	1/5	17/19
Myanmar	17/28	0/0	3/5	15/16
Philippines	26/51	0/0	1/7	16/18
Singapore	2/3	0/0	2/8	19/22
Thailand	26/37	0/0	3/5	18/21
Viet Nam	0/1	0/1	2/13	16/20
Western Asia	**84/131**	**1/3**	**11/38**	**17/20**
Armenia	6/10	0/0	0/1	16/20
Azerbaijan	9/14	0/1	1/5	17/21
Bahrain	0/0	0/0	0/0	17/20
Cyprus	1/2	0/0	0/1	20/23
Gaza Strip	0/0	0/0	0/0	17/19
Georgia	0/0	0/0	0/2	17/21
Iraq	4/5	0/0	3/5	17/19
Israel	2/2	0/0	2/5	20/23
Jordan	3/2	0/0	0/1	17/19
Kuwait	0/0	0/0	0/1	18/22
Lebanon	6/7	0/0	0/0	17/18
Oman	0/1	0/0	0/0	17/19
Qatar	0/0	0/0	0/0	17/19
Saudi Arabia	3/3	0/0	1/3	17/19
Syrian Arab Republic	7/6	0/0	0/1	16/18
Turkey	18/38	0/1	2/11	17/19
United Arab Emirates	0/0	0/0	2/1	18/20
Yemen	0/0	0/0	0/0	15/16

Source: Registrar General, India, New Delhi, Census Reports (Various Years); United Nations, *World Population Prospects: The 1998 Revision*, (Volumes I and II; Sales Nos. E.99.XIII.8 and E.99.XIII.9) and the *Demographic Yearbook 2000 Series:R*, Sales No.E/F.02.XIII.1, New York, 2002 and *Demographic Yearbook: Historical Supplement 1948–1997 Series:R*, No.28/HS-CD Sales No.E/F99.XIII.12, New York, 2002; United States Bureau of the Census, International Programs Center, International Data Base; ILO, *Estimates and Projections of the Economically Active Population, 1950–2010*, 4th ed., International Labour Office, Geneva, 1996; United States Social Security Administration, *Social Security Programs Around the World –1997*, Washington, D.C.

Japan tops the list in Asia with regard to both male and female life expectancy at the age of 60. The life expectancy for males and females is 21 and 25 respectively. The male life expectancy at age 60 is 13 in East Timor; this is Asia's lowest. For females, it is 14 in Afghanistan. Most countries are close to the Asian average at 16 and 19.

Feminisation of the Elderly

Some major demographic trends that are observed vis-à-vis the women among the aged are:

1. Women constitute a significant majority of the older population; the female share increases with age.
2. The sex ratios, with increase in age, will rise in favour of women in the next half-century.
3. The elderly sex ratios are not as favourable to women in the developing countries as they are in the developed regions.

The majority of older persons are women. Today around 55 per cent of those aged 60 plus are women. This percentage has remained almost the same since 1950 and is not expected to change in the next 50 years. A perusal of Figures 1.7, 1.8 and 1.9 clearly establishes this fact.

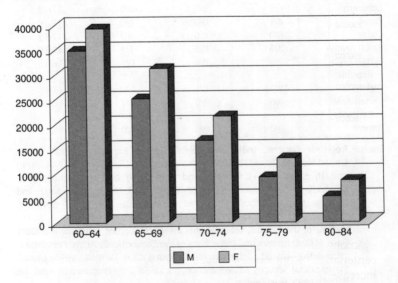

Figure 1.7   Sex Distribution of the World Elderly, 1950

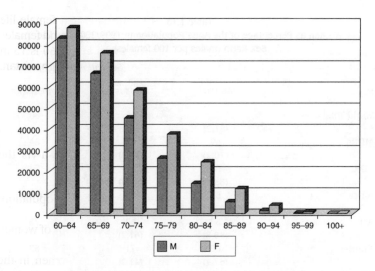

Figure 1.8 Sex Distribution of the World Elderly, 1995

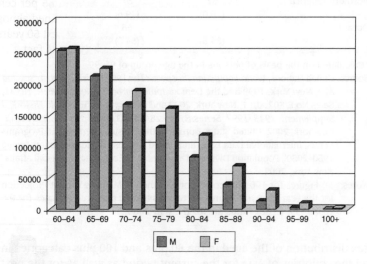

Figure 1.9 Projected Sex Distribution of the World Elderly, 2050

Among the 80 plus, 65 per cent are women. In 1995, 77 per cent of the centenarians were women and by 2050, this number is expected to increase to 84 per cent. Table 1.13 shows the distribution of aged women over different regions of the world. Table 1.14 provides the

Table 1.13
Women as Percentage of the Aged Population in 1999/2000 and the
Sex Ratio (males per 100 females)

(Sex ratios are in brackets)

Region	60 Plus	80 Plus	Centenarian
World Total	55	65	80
	(81.2)	(53.1)	
MDRs	59	69	84
	(70.2)	(44.2)	
LDRs	53	61	73
	(88.4)	(64.9)	
Africa	55	59	69*
	(83.1)	(69.0)	
Asia	53	62	75
	(88.8)	(61.2)	
Europe	60	71	83
	(67.4)	(41.0)	
Latin America & the	55	61	73
Caribbean	(81.7)	(65.1)	
Northern America	57	67	84
	(76.0)	(49.6)	
Oceania	54	65	77*
	(84.5)	(54.5)	

*Calculated on the basis of persons in the age group of 95–99.

Source: United Nations, *World Population Prospects: The 1998 Revision, Vol. II: Sex and Age*, New York, 1999 and the *Demographic Yearbook 2000 Series:R*, No.31, Sales No.E/F.02.XIII.1, New York, 2002 and *Demographic Yearbook: Historical Supplement 1948–1997 Series:R*, No.28/HS-CD Sales No.E/F 99.XIII.12, New York, 2002; United States Bureau of the Census, International Programs Center, International Data Base; and United Nations, 'World Population Ageing 1950–2050', Population Division, Department of Economic and Social Affairs, New York, 2002.

Notes: (a) Figures for 100 plus correspond to the UN Medium Variant Projection for the year 2000; (b) figures for 60 plus and 80 plus are estimates for the year 1999; (c) sex ratios are for the year 2000.

sex distribution of the aged in the 80 plus and 100 plus categories in all the countries of Asia for the current period as well as for the next 50 years for which projections are available. The women outweigh the men in almost all the countries in Asia. The reason for this 'women surplus' is that the women generally live longer than men; the residual effect of the Second World War, which killed a large number of men, also plays an important role here. The percentage of

Table 1.14
Women among the Aged: As Percentages of all Elderly (60 plus and
80 plus) and the Sex Ratio (males per 100 women)

(Sex ratios are in brackets)

Area/Country	Women in 60 Plus, 1999 (percentage)	Women in 80 Plus 1999 (percentage)	Area/Country	Women in 60 Plus, 1999 (percentage)	Women in 80 Plus 1999 (percentage)
Asia	53 (88.8)	62 (61.2)	Thailand	55 (82.9)	63 (64.9)
Eastern Asia	**53** (**87.9**)	**66** (**51.6**)	**Singapore**	**53** (**86.9**)	**62** (**62.3**)
China	52 (91.4)	65 (54.1)	Cambodia	64 (56.1)	59 (68.5)
Hong Kong	51 (93.9)	63 (60.5)	East Timor	50 (96.7)	54 (68.0)
North Korea	61 (81.0)	74 (50.1)	Indonesia	54 (84.5)	58 (69.4)
Japan	56 (77.0)	67 (46.8)	Lao People's Democratic Republic	53 (88.0)	58 (78.9)
Macao	56 (79.0)	67 (48.9)	Malaysia	53 (89.7)	56 (76.4)
Mongolia	55 (81.6)	64 (53.7)	Myanmar	53 (86.9)	54 (75.6)
Republic of Korea	59 (72.0)	74 (41.1)	Philippines	53 (83.0)	58 (61.5)
South-central Asia	**52** (**92.2**)	**55** (**81.4**)	**Western Asia**	**54** (**86.3**)	**61** (**62.5**)
Afghanistan	51 (98.2)	54 (90.8)	Armenia	58 (74.2)	69 (47.7)
Bangladesh	49 (100.4)	54 (98.2)	Azerbaijan	59 (71.0)	75 (32.4)
Bhutan	53 (89.0)	57 (75.2)	Bahrain	46 (117.1)	49 (101.1)
India	52 (91.8)	55 (81.8)	Cyprus	55 (81.4)	58 (69.9)
Iran (Islamic Republic of)	49 (93.7)	53 (83.7)	Gaza Strip	56	46
Kazakhstan	62 (59.8)	78 (27.1)	Georgia	60 (66.3)	74 (35.4)
Kyrgyzstan	60 (66.6)	75 (33.8)	Iraq	53 (90.6)	56 (82.1)

(continued)

Table 1.14
(Continued)

(Sex ratios are in brackets)

Area/Country	Women in 60 Plus, 1999 (percentage)	Women in 80 Plus 1999 (percentage)	Area/Country	Women in 60 Plus, 1999 (percentage)	Women in 80 Plus 1999 (percentage)
Maldives	47 (111.8)	52 (84.4)	Israel	57 (75.3)	60 (61.0)
Nepal	49 (96.7)	52 (82.7)	Jordan	51 (103.2)	51 (91.6)
Pakistan	50 (100.3)	48 (112.5)	Kuwait	44 (202.6)	58 (62.8)
Sri Lanka	52 (104.3)	52 (90.7)	Lebanon	54 (84.9)	59 (70.9)
Tajikistan	56 (78.1)	68 (46.0)	Oman	49 (107.0)	57 (79.3)
Turkmenistan	58 (71.7)	71 (39.4)	Qatar	26 (245.4)	49 (151.9)
Uzbekistan	58 (74.2)	71 (40.4)	Saudi Arabia	47 (115.4)	56 (81.7)
South-eastern Asia	55 (84.6)	61 (69.9)	Syrian Arab Republic	53 (90.4)	56 (82.1)
Brunei Darussalam	50 (102.4)	53 (91.3)	Turkey	53	60
Viet Nam	59	72	United Arab Emirates	29	52
			Yemen	56	58

Source: United Nations, *World Population Prospects: The 1998 Revision, Volume II: Sex and Age*, New York, 1999 and *Demographic Yearbook 2000 Series:R*, No.31, Sales No.E/F.02.XIII.1, New York, 2002, and also *Demographic Yearbook: Historical Supplement 1948–1997 Series:R*, No.28/HS-CD Sales No.E/F 99.XIII.12, New York, 2002; United States Bureau of the Census, International Programs Center, International Data Base, web address: http://www.census.gov/ipc/www/idbnew.html

women in the older age groups is higher in the MDRs than in the LDRs. This is again due to the differences in the life expectancy between the sexes in the MDRs.

The position of women among the aged in different regions of the world and different countries of Asia are represented in Table 1.13 and Table 1.14. A perusal of these tables shows that the highest number of elderly women of all categories (60 plus, 80 plus and 100 plus) are seen in Europe, although the other regions of the world are not far behind.

In all the Asian countries, except Bangladesh, Iran, Maldives, Nepal, Oman, Bahrain, Saudi Arabia, Kuwait, UAE and Qatar, women constitute the majority (over 50 per cent) of the 60 plus population. Even in these countries, barring Qatar and UAE, the population of elderly women ranges from 44–49 per cent. In Qatar, they constitute 26 per cent of the population while in the UAE they form 29 per cent. In North Korea, Cambodia, Kazakhstan, Kyrgyzstan and Georgia, the proportion of women vis-à-vis the total population is at 60 per cent and above. In South Korea and Azerbaijan, this percentage is close to 60 (59 per cent). In the 80 plus category, women are a majority everywhere except in Pakistan, Gaza Strip, Qatar and Bahrain. The largest number of old elderly women are seen in Kazakhstan (78 per cent), followed by Kyrgyzstan and Azerbaijan (both 75 per cent), Georgia and North Korea (both 74 per cent).

SOCIO-ECONOMIC CHARACTERISTICS OF THE ELDERLY

The well-being of the elderly depends largely on certain socio-economic conditions such as: labour force participation, literacy, marital status and health. In most developed economies, where social security coverage is universal, the labour force participation rates are low. Even people in these countries leave their jobs before retirement.[17] Some are required to leave a job simply because of shortage of employment opportunities;[18] yet others leave the labour market, because their skills and knowledge become redundant.[19] However, the picture is different in developing countries. Given little or no social security, the aged cannot afford to leave the job market, even if their skills become obsolete. This, however, is possible only in the informal agricultural sectors, where job arrangements are generally informal. There is therefore a large concentration of older workers in agriculture and the allied informal sectors.[20]

Education is an important determinant of the status of an individual. It is not less important in the lives of the elderly either. There is a very high correlation between educational levels and the health and economic status of the older generations. Older people with higher educational backgrounds are generally more open, tolerant and liberal. As educational levels of the elderly improve, intergenerational cultural tensions become weaker and society grows in more healthy ways. Higher levels of literacy among the aged are likely to substantially alter their interests, needs and abilities to their own advantage, and improve the quality of their lives.

Marital status is another important determinant of the well-being of the elderly. Apart from being an index of isolation, the data on the marital status of the elderly signals many important features of their health. Married people have consistently lower rates of mortality than single, widowed and divorced people of the same age and sex; these longevity benefits are greater for men than for women.[21] A similar differential has been found for morbidity. Married people suffer fewer accidents and assaults,[22] have fewer acute and chronic conditions, fewer activity limitations, a lower probability of becoming disabled and less psychiatric morbidity.[23] With such a favourable health climate, medical expenses of the married are lower than those who are unmarried.[24] Some studies, however, have found that single women are healthier than married women.[25]

Labour Force Participation of the Elderly

The participation of older persons in the labour markets in the LDRs is far greater because of the limited coverage of retirement schemes and meagre incomes there. The labour force participation rates for older workers tend to be lower in countries with high per capita incomes, and older men have higher participation rates than older women. As Table 1.15 exhibits, 42 per cent of elderly males in the world today work outside the home to earn a living. At the same time 16 per cent of females also need to work outside the home to earn a living. As we move to the developed regions, the percentages of economically active elderly population decline. In the MDRs, 23 per cent of elderly males work outside their home for a living, as compared to 52 per cent in the LDRs and 76 per cent in the LtDRs. In the MDRs, 10 per cent of older women are economically active, compared to 20 per cent in the LDRs and 44 per cent in the LtDRs.

In Europe only 7 per cent of elderly women are in the labour force, as compared to 34 per cent in Africa. With regard to elderly males, two-thirds of them are in the workforce in Africa against only 17 per cent in Europe. Looking to individual countries, Guinea-Bissau, a

Table 1.15
Percentage of Elderly in the Labour Force, 1995

Regions	Male	Female
World	42	16
MDRs	23	10
LDRs	52	20
LtDRs[26]	76	44
Africa	67	34
Asia	51	19
Europe	17	7
Latin America	48	12
Northern America	24	13
Oceania	22	8

Source: United Nations, *World Population Prospects: The 1998 Revision, Volume II: Sex and Age*, New York, 1999 and *Demographic Yearbook 2000 Series:R*, No.31, Sales No.E/F.02.XIII.1, New York, 2002 and *Demographic Yearbook: Historical Supplement 1948–1997 Series:R*, No.28/HS-CD Sales No.E/F 99.XIII.12, New York, 2002; United States Bureau of the Census, International Programs Center, International Data Base.

country in western Africa has been recorded to have the largest percentage of elderly males (91 per cent) in the workforce; Hungary has the lowest percentage of 2 per cent. In Asia, Myanmar tops the list with 74 per cent of elderly males in the workforce. Among the females, Mozambique, a country in Africa, has the distinction of topping the world elderly workforce participation with 77 per cent. In many countries, the labour force participation of the elderly females is reported to be zero. These include Brunei Darussalam, Bahrain, Qatar, UAE and Belize.

Most Asian countries exhibit low levels of participation of the elderly in the workforce. The elderly have fewer job opportunities as they are attributed with low physical and mental alertness. They are also considered unfit for jobs and occupations requiring modern skills. They cannot accept many jobs either, especially those which require mobility and where wages are low. The transport system is generally unfriendly towards the elderly too; a great majority of them acquire some degree of disability during their life and are therefore unable to use the public transport system.

In countries where agriculture is still a dominant occupation, participation of the elderly in the workforce is still very high. In Bangladesh,

Bhutan, Myanmar and East Timor, over 70 per cent of the elderly form a part of the workforce. In India, Iran, Indonesia, Laos, Philippines, Afghanistan etc., participation rates are just over 60 per cent. In most industrialised nations, the elderly participation rates are low. In the erstwhile Soviet Union, these rates are abysmally low—Kazakhstan (15 per cent), Kyrgyzstan (16 per cent), Armenia (27 per cent), Azerbaijan (30 per cent), and Georgia (31 per cent).

The participation of elderly women in labour markets is much lower when compared to their male counterparts. Rice cultivating agriculture is the only occupation in which elderly women have found acceptance. In countries where rice cultivation has given way to a more machine oriented occupation system, the chances of women finding productive work has been greatly reduced. In Bahrain, Qatar, Brunei, Gaza Strip and Yemen, elderly women are not gainfully employed outside their home. In many other countries (in the erstwhile USSR, western Asia, Sri Lanka) the participation of women in the labour force is much below a double-digit figure. This is what is seen in the economically developed countries. Women's participation in labour markets, on the other hand, is highest in East Timor at 47 per cent. Table 1.16 shows the workforce participation of the elderly in all the countries of Asia for which data is available.

Literacy Status of the Aged

Most countries in the MDRs have attained universal literacy. Illiteracy is so non-existent in these countries that statistical information on its spread among the aged is hard to find. Although illiteracy among older persons has consistently declined in the most less developed countries, it still remains generally high. Combining the data for 105 less developed countries, a UN Report[27] estimates that 75 per cent of the elderly were illiterate in 1980; in 2000 this percentage dropped to 56 per cent. Projections show that in 2010, only 43 per cent of the elderly would be illiterate in the less developed countries. The incidence of illiteracy is higher among elderly females than males. In 1980, the illiteracy rate among elderly females was 85 per cent compared to 63 per cent for elderly males. This gender gap in illiteracy increased further in 2000 when the aggregate rate was 69 per cent among older women compared to 41 per cent among older men. Projections indicate that over the next decade, the aggregate rate will decrease to 55 per cent for older women and to 30 per cent for older men. This data

Table 1.16
Workforce Participation of the Elderly in Asia

Area/ Country	Elderly Labour Force (Males/Females) (percentage of elderly)	Area/ Country	Elderly Labour Force (Males/Females) (percentage of elderly)
Asia	51/19	Singapore	27/7
Eastern Asia	**43/16**	**Thailand**	**50/27**
China	42/14	Viet Nam	53/32
Hong Kong	.	Cambodia	51/38
N. Korea	47/20	East Timor	73/47
Japan	49/21	Indonesia	62/32
Macao	.	Laos	64/35
Mongolia	51/32	Malaysia	47/21
Republic of Korea	46/25	Myanmar	74/45
South-central Asia	**60/19**	**Philippines**	**67/35**
Afghanistan	69/27	Western Asia	46/18
Bangladesh	72/42	Armenia	27/8
Bhutan	74/31	Azerbaijan	30/10
India	61/19	Bahrain	46/0
Iran (Islamic Republic of)	64/13	Cyprus	40/13
Kazakhstan	15/16	Gaza Strip	31/0
Kyrgyzstan	16/6	Georgia	34/17
Maldives	50/33	Iraq	49/5
Nepal	72/38	Israel	30/10
Pakistan	61/18	Jordan	47/6
Sri Lanka	38/8	Kuwait	44/5
Tajikistan	20/7	Lebanon	44/4
Turkmenistan	24/7	Oman	41/5
Uzbekistan	19/6	Qatar	58/0
South-eastern Asia	**59/32**	**Saudi Arabia**	**53/3**
Brunei	50/0	Syrian Arab	
		Republic	48/10
		Turkey	50/30
		UAE	53/0
		Yemen	59/12

Source: United Nations, *World Population Prospects: The 1998 Revision, Volume II: Sex and Age*, New York 1999 and *Demographic Yearbook 2000 Series:R*, No.31, Sales No E/F.02.XIII.1, New York, 2002 and *Demographic Yearbook: Historical Supplement 1948–1997 Series:R*, No.28 HS-CD Sales NO.E/F 99.XIII.12, New York, 2002; United States Bureau of the Census, International Programs Center, International Data Base, web address: http://www.census.gov/ipc/www/idbnew.html.

clearly establishes that not many attempts have been made to ensure literacy among women till the 1950s in most parts of the developing world. However, each successive generation has realised the importance of education, much more than the preceding ones. This is evident from the UN estimates[28] which show that illiteracy rates among the 60–64 age group were 71 per cent compared to 78 per cent for the 70 plus age group in 1980; this changed to 49 and 62 per cent respectively in 2000. In 2010, the rates are projected to drop to 36 per cent for persons in the age group 60–64 and 49 per cent for persons aged 70 or above. Huge differences in illiteracy levels exist among different countries of the world. In some African countries like Burkina Faso, Gambia, Mali and Niger adult illiteracy is almost universal. Again, some developing countries like Argentina, Uruguay and Tajikistan have attained almost universal literacy among their aged populations. Within Asia, countries like Sri Lanka, Korea and Israel have attained commendable achievements in elderly literacy. At the same time, elderly literacy rates are still very low in Afghanistan, Bangladesh, Nepal, Pakistan and India. It also appears that some countries are more successful than others in reducing adult illiteracy. Countries in East Asia and South-central East Asia have reduced their adult illiteracy levels faster than the countries of South Asia. Even within South-central Asia, Sri Lanka and the Maldives have experienced considerable success in eradicating illiteracy from the elderly population. Table 1.17 provides elderly illiteracy rates for select Asian countries.

Marital Status of the Elderly

Tables 1.18 and 1.19 provide data on the marital status of the aged. While living with a spouse has proved beneficial for the elderly, a large number of them are single. Older men are more likely to be married than older women. While 79 per cent of the older men are currently married in the world, the corresponding figure for older women is 43 per cent. In Asia, the corresponding figures are 78 and 44 per cent respectively. Interestingly, there is not much global difference in the marital status of older persons. Most older persons living without a spouse are widowed. Aged women are the victims of early widowhood and low levels of economic support. Women are more likely to outlive their spouses because they have lower death rates than men at any age and, on average, are younger than their husbands.

Table 1.17

Illiteracy Rates among the Elderly in Select Asian Countries for Select Years, 1980–2010

(in percentage)

Country	Age Groups	1980 Male	1980 Female	1980 Total	2000 Male	2000 Female	2000 Total	2010 Male	2010 Female	2010 Total
Afghanistan	60–64	90.0	99.6	94.9	81.3	98.5	89.8	70.4	96.3	83.2
	65–69	93.3	99.8	96.7	84.8	99.0	92.0	79.2	97.7	88.4
	70 plus	95.1	99.9	97.7	86.4	99.2	93.1	81.3	98.5	90.1
Bangladesh	60–64	70.1	94.8	82.2	63.8	88.5	75.5	59.2	83.7	71.0
	65–69.	71.5	96.1	83.9	65.8	90.6	77.6	62.0	86.5	73.8
	70 plus	75.3	96.6	85.6	67.4	92.1	80.3	65.8	88.5	76.3
China	60–64	61.9	94.4	78.3	25.3	61.6	42.9	11.4	34.3	22.7
	65–69	70.6	96.3	84.1	34.3	76.7	55.5	16.2	45.4	30.9
	70 plus	78.0	97.8	89.8	42.8	85.6	67.0	25.3	61.6	45.7
India	60–64	65.8	91.2	78.2	51.0	81.5	66.6	42.3	73.1	57.9
	65–69	69.4	92.9	81.0	55.2	84.5	70.3	46.6	77.7	62.9
	70 plus	72.1	94.2	83.0	59.2	87.2	74.1	51.0	81.5	67.6
Israel	60–64	10.7	25.5	18.5	5.2	13.8	9.8	5.1	7.2	2.8
	65–69	12.5	29.0	21.3	6.9	18.0	13.0	6.8	9.6	3.5
	70 plus	14.2	31.8	23.5	7.8	19.5	14.7	10.3	13.8	5.2
Indonesia	60–64	54.5	86.0	70.8	39.8	53.4	24.6	14.4	32.7	24.0
	65–69	62.3	90.2	77.0	48.8	63.7	31.3	18.8	42.6	31.7
	70 plus	69.6	93.3	82.8	57.4	72.7	38.6	24.6	53.4	40.9

(continued)

Table 1.17
(Continued)

(in percentage)

Country	Age Groups	1980			2000			2010		
		Male	Female	Total	Male	Female	Total	Male	Female	Total
Malaysia	60–64	52.2	86.8	69.9	24.0	53.9	39.0	13.0	30.0	21.6
	65–69	60.4	91.1	75.7	30.1	64.8	48.2	17.6	41.3	29.7
	70 plus	66.9	93.9	80.7	37.1	73.8	57.3	24.0	53.9	40.5
Maldives	60–64	19.8	24.2	22.0	10.2	11.5	10.7	6.9	7.3	7.1
	65–69	23.0	28.2	25.6	11.9	13.6	12.8	8.2	9.1	8.6
	70 plus	26.4	32.7	29.6	14.3	16.8	15.5	10.2	11.5	10.8
Nepal	60–64	86.1	99.2	86.1	71.3	97.1	83.8	77.9	94.2	60.4
	65–69	88.2	99.6	86.2	76.7	97.5	86.8	81.7	95.9	66.5
	70 plus	90.4	99.8	90.4	79.6	98.0	89.0	84.5	97.1	71.3
Myanmar	60–64	20.3	58.7	40.5	16.2	40.2	28.8	13.6	29.4	21.8
	65–69	21.2	63.8	41.1	17.5	45.3	29.0	14.8	34.6	25.6
	70 plus	22.6	68.6	48.8	18.3	48.9	32.7	16.2	40.2	29.4
Pakistan	60–64	81.4	97.0	88.6	66.8	91.6	79.1	58.9	87.8	73.0
	65–69	84.6	97.7	90.7	71.7	93.1	82.5	62.7	89.9	76.5
	70 plus	87.4	98.3	92.4	75.1	95.1	85.3	66.8	91.6	79.8
Philippines	60–64	28.5	6.6	32.7	11.7	13.4	12.5	7.3	7.9	7.6
	65–69	31.1	41.0	36.3	14.1	17.3	15.8	9.3	10.3	9.8
	70 plus	34.8	46.6	41.1	17.9	22.7	20.6	11.7	13.4	12.6

(continued)

Table 1.17
(Continued)

(in percentage)

Country	Age Groups	1980			2000			2010		
		Male	Female	Total	Male	Female	Total	Male	Female	Total
Sri Lanka	60–64	16.2	45.9	29.9	9.3	24.4	17.1	7.2	15.4	11.6
	65–69	18.9	51.4	34.4	11.2	30.5	21.4	8.1	20.0	14.6
	70 plus	21.1	56.2	37.7	12.7	35.2	24.4	9.3	24.4	17.7
Korea (S)	60–64	13.4	39.7	27.4	3.3	11.5	7.6	0.9	2.6	1.8
	65–69	18.4	48.2	34.7	9.8	16.7	11.6	2.1	7.2	4.8
	70 plus	23.8	56.7	44.1	13.4	23.4	17.7	3.3	11.5	8.5
Tajikistan	60–64	7.6	21.3	16.2	1.1	3.9	2.5	0.3	0.9	0.6
	65–69	11.4	30.5	22.6	2.1	6.0	4.2	0.6	2.3	1.4
	70 plus	16.6	41.5	31.0	3.4	9.4	7.0	1.1	3.9	2.7
Thailand	60–64	25.0	62.4	44.6	5.4	10.5	8.3	4.6	9.1	6.9
	65–69	29.9	73.9	53.1	8.3	16.3	9.3	5.4	10.5	8.2
	70 plus	35.8	83.9	63.9	9.3	18.8	12.4	8.3	16.3	13.0

Source: United Nations, *World Population Ageing 1950–2050*, Population Division, Department of Economic and Social Affairs, ST/ESA/ SER.A/207, New York, 2002.

Table 1.18
Marital Status of the Elderly in Different World Regions

Area	Elderly Currently Married Male/Female 1995 (percentage of total)	Area	Elderly Currently Married Male/Female 1995 (percentage of total)
World Total	79/43	Less Developed Regions	78/43
More Developed Regions	80/43	Least Developed Regions	85/39

Source: United Nations, *World Population Prospects: The 1998 Revision, Vol. II: Sex and Age*, New York, 1999 and *Demographic Yearbook 2000 Series:R*, No.31, Sales No.E/F.02.XIII.1, New York, 2002 and *Demographic Yearbook: Historical Supplement 1948–1997 Series:R*, No.28/HS-CD Sales No.E/F 99.XIII.12, New York, 2002; United States Bureau of the Census, International Programs Center, International Data Base, web address: http://www.census.gov/ipc/www/idbnew.html.

Table 1.19
Marital Status of the Elderly in Asia

Area/Country	Elderly Currently Married Male/Female (percentage of total)	Area/Country	Elderly Currently Married Male/Female (percentage of total)
Asia	78/44	South-eastern Asia	82/41
Eastern Asia	**76/48**	Brunei	83/50 [A]
China	73/48 [A]	Thailand	80/47 A
Hong Kong	82/50 [A]	Singapore	83/45 A
North Korea	.	Viet Nam	84/45 B
Japan	86/51 [A]	Cambodia	.
Macao	.	East Timor	.
Mongolia	.	Indonesia	84/36 [A]
Republic of Korea	87/37 [A]	Laos	.
South-central Asia	**81/38**	Malaysia	84/44 [A]
Afghanistan	83/37 [C]	Myanmar	71/39 [B]
Bangladesh	95/43 [A]	Philippines	81/49 [A]

(continued)

Table 1.19
(Continued)

Area/Country	Elderly Currently Married Male/Female (percentage of total)	Area/Country	Elderly Currently Married Male/Female (percentage of total)
Bhutan	.	**Western Asia**	**86/50**
India	78/35 [B]	Armenia	87/44 [B]
Iran (Islamic Republic of)	89/66 [A]	Azerbaijan	.
Kazakhstan	83/34 [B]	Bahrain	87/42 [A]
Kyrgyzstan	85/35 [B]	Cyprus	84/55 [A]
Maldives	66/35 [B]	Gaza Strip	.
Nepal	79/49 [A]	Georgia	85/39 [B]
Pakistan	86/50 [B]	Iraq	89/50 [B]
Sri Lanka	82/53 [A]	Israel	84/49 [B]
Tajikistan	84/38 [B]	Jordan	92/46 [A]
Turkmenistan	78/36 [B]	Kuwait	92/41 [A]
Uzbekistan	83/38 [B]	Lebanon	.
		Oman	82/33 [A]
		Qatar	89/36 [B]
		Saudi Arabia	.
		Syrian Arab Republic	89/50 [B]
		Turkey	86/53 [A]
		UAE	82/29 [C]
		Yemen	.

Source: United Nations, *World Population Prospects: The 1998 Revision, Volume II: Sex and Age*, New York, 1999 and *Demographic Yearbook 2002 Series:R*, No.31, Sales No.E/F.02.XIII.1, New York, 2002 and *Demographic Yearbook: Historical Supplement 1948–1997 Series:R*, CD-ROM, No.28/HS-CD Sales No.E/F 99.XIII.12, New York, 2002; United States Bureau of the Census, International Programs Center, International Data Base, web address: http://www.census.gov/ipc/www/idbnew.html.

Notes: A = reference year 1990 and after;
B = reference year 1980–89;
C = 1970–79
Currently married includes where possible those in consensual unions.

In an overwhelming majority of countries in Asia, 80 per cent of elderly men are lucky to have spouses who are still living. In Bangladesh, Kuwait and Jordan the proportion of such men has crossed 90 per cent. Astonishingly, in the Maldives only 66 per cent of elderly males have spouses who are still living. Elderly women are not all that lucky. In Hong Kong, Japan, Iran, Iraq, Turkey, Cyprus, Brunei, Pakistan, Sri Lanka, and Syria, more than half of the elderly women have spouse who are still living. In Yemen, there are only 29 per cent of such women.

Health Status of the Aged

The health status of the elderly can be represented through several variables. The most convenient form is the healthy life expectancy. It summarises the expected number of years to be lived in what might be termed the equivalent of 'full health'. The WHO has christened this concept Disability Adjusted Life Expectancy (DALE) to provide a clearer picture of the issues involved.

To estimate DALE, the years of ill health are weighed according to severity and subtracted from the expected overall life expectancy to give the equivalent number of years of healthy life. There are significant regional variations in DALE estimations. This is natural as health standards vary in different regions. While Japanese males lead a healthy life expectancy of 17.6 years from the age of 60, the aged in most countries of South-central and Western Asia do not enjoy a healthy life for more than 10 years after the age of 60. China and Viet Nam have improved dramatically vis-à-vis their health profiles and healthy life expectancy, while Thailand has not shown any significant improvement over the past decade. Myanmar has not done very well either, with a healthy life expectancy of just 49.1 years, substantially behind its South-east Asian neighbours. The healthy life expectancy in India is also very low at 52 years. In Sri Lanka, healthy life expectancy is almost at par with many developed countries. This shows that even countries with the same levels of income can have very different healthy life expectancies.

As in the case of general life expectancy, women also live longer, more healthy lives than men. Studies have consistently shown that as countries get richer, the decline in male mortality tends to be less than that of female mortality. The same patterns hold when healthy life expectancies are measured. In the early 1900s, the gap between female and male life expectancy was two to three years in the richer countries around the world. By 1999, the women were living, on average, seven to eight years longer than the men in the same countries. A variety of reasons can explain why women live more healthy lives. First, women are generally more health conscious. Second, men smoke more and exercise much less. Third, men in richer countries tend to have poorer diets than the women. Fourth, in poorer countries men suffer more disabling injuries than women. Fifth, men contract more diseases than women. However, South Asian countries are notable exceptions. In Afghanistan, Bangladesh, Nepal, Maldives and Bhutan, the healthy life expectancy of women is shorter than those of the men. In Western Asia, males and females have similar levels of healthy life expectancy, which is unusual. Also, the status of women in these societies is often not good; less care is given to female children, and they run a higher risk of reproductive deaths than in other countries. Table 1.20 shows the healthy life expectancy of men and women in several countries of Asia.

The WHO rankings in Table 1.20 show that the years lost to disability are substantially higher in poorer countries because it is here that the debilitating effects of several tropical diseases such as malaria, cholera and dengue strike children and young adults equally. In addition, blindness, paralysis and accidents impinge on the health of the people of any age group. People in the healthiest regions lose about 9 per cent of their lives to a disability as compared to 14 per cent in the worst-off countries. The Japanese enjoy the longest healthy life expectancy of 74.5 years among 191 countries; this is in sharp contrast to Sierra Leone, which has a healthy life expectancy of less than 26 years and is the lowest ranking country in this respect. A major factor that makes Japan number one in the rankings is the low rate of heart disease in the country, a direct result of their traditional low fat diet. The effect of tobacco has also been mild (until recently) with low lung cancer rates. Yet, how much longer the Japanese can maintain this lead is questionable. The national diet is changing, with high fat foods such as red meat becoming common. Smoking is also becoming popular.

In terms of DALE, the rest of the top 10 nations are Australia (73.2 years); France (73.1 years); Sweden (73.0 years); Spain (72.8 years); Italy (72.7 years); Greece (72.5 years); Switzerland (72.5 years); Monaco (72.4 years); and Andorra (72.3 years). DALE is estimated to equal or exceed 70 years in 24 countries and 60 years in over half the countries for which data is available. At the other extreme are the 32 countries where DALE is estimated to be less than 40 years. Many of these are countries with major epidemics of HIV/AIDS, among others. The United States is ranked at number 24 under this system. As is shown in Table 1.20, most of developing regions of Asia are ranked

Table: 1.20

Healthy Life Expectancy Level (Years) in Several Asian Countries

Country	Total At Birth	Male At Birth	Male At 60	Female At Birth	Female At 60	DALE RANK
Afghanistan	33.8	35.1	7.1	32.5	5.8	168
Armenia	59.0	56.9	9.7	61.1	12.0	41
Azerbaijan	55.4	53.3	12.2	57.5	14.6	65
Bahamas	58.1	57.2	12.4	59.1	12.6	110
Bangladesh	49.3	50.6	8.8	47.9	8.0	140
Bhutan	49.2	50.1	9.3	48.2	8.8	138
Brunei Darussalam	64.9	63.8	13.3	65.9	15.1	59
Cambodia	47.1	45.6	9.0	48.7	10.1	148
China	62.1	60.9	11.8	63.3	14.3	82
Cyprus	66.3	66.4	14.5	66.2	14.1	25
Democratic People's Republic of Korea	55.4	54.9	11.1	56.0	12.1	51
India	52.0	52.2	9.9	51.7	10.9	135
Indonesia	57.4	56.5	11.6	58.4	12.5	104
Iran (Islamic Republic of)	58.8	59.0	11.3	58.6	11.4	97
Malaysia	61.6	59.7	10.6	63.4	12.7	90
Maldives	52.4	54.2	10.1	50.6	8.6	131
Mongolia	52.4	50.3	10.8	54.5	12.7	132
Myanmar	49.1	47.7	9.2	50.5	10.1	139
Nepal	45.8	47.5	10.2	44.2	9.6	142
Oman	59.7	59.2	10.3	60.3	12.0	72
Pakistan	48.1	50.2	9.8	46.1	8.7	125
Philippines	59.0	57.0	11.5	60.9	13.6	114
Qatar	60.6	59.3	9.2	61.8	11.6	66
Republic of Korea	66.0	63.2	12.3	68.8	16.0	88
Saudi Arabia	59.5	58.3	10.5	60.7	12.1	58
Singapore	67.8	66.8	14.5	68.9	16.2	30
Sri Lanka	61.1	58.6	12.5	63.6	14.6	76
Syrian Arab Republic	58.5	58.2	10.7	58.7	11.3	115

(continued)

Table: 1.20
(Continued)

Country	Total At Birth	Male At Birth	Male At 60	Female At Birth	Female At 60	DALE RANK
Iraq	52.6	52.6	9.3	52.5	9.5	129
Israel	69.9	69.3	16.2	70.6	17.1	23
Japan	73.8	71.2	17.6	76.3	21.4	1
Jordan	58.5	58.2	10.3	58.8	11.3	102
Kazakhstan	54.3	50.5	10.9	58.1	14.6	123
Kuwait	64.7	64.6	12.4	64.8	13.0	68
Kyrgyzstan	52.6	49.6	8.5	55.6	11.8	124
Lao People's Democratic Republic	44.7	43.7	9.6	45.7	10.6	147
Lebanon	60.7	60.3	11.3	61.1	12.2	96
Tajikistan	50.8	49.6	9.0	52.0	10.3	121
Thailand	59.7	57.7	13.2	61.8	14.4	100
Turkey	58.7	56.8	11.2	60.5	13.4	73
Turkmenistan	52.1	51.2	8.8	53.0	9.5	129
United Arab Emirates	63.1	62.3	11.5	63.9	13.3	50
Uzbekistan	54.3	52.7	9.9	55.8	11.6	101
Viet Nam	58.9	58.2	11.4	59.7	12.3	117
Yemen	49.1	48.9	8.5	49.3	8.8	141

Source: WHO, *The World Health Report 2001*, Annex Table 4, Geneva, 2002.

above 100 by the DALE measure, the notable exceptions being Sri
Lanka at 76 and China at 82. India ranks 135, Thailand 100,
Bangladesh 140, Pakistan 135, and Afghanistan 168.

NOTES AND REFERENCES

1. Under this projection, it is assumed that the fertility rate of all countries that
   had a total fertility above replacement level in 1990–95 would reach replacement level at some point before 2050 and remain at that level until 2050. For
   countries with total fertility at or below the replacement level in 1990–95, the
   assumption is that fertility levels would remain below replacement level during the whole of the projection period.
2. See Chapter four. Also W.A. Jackson, *Political Economy of Population Ageing*,
   Edward Elgar Publishing, Cheltenham, 1998.
3. More Developed Regions (MDRs) comprise all the regions of Europe and
   Northern America, Australia/New Zealand and Japan.
4. Less Developed Regions (LDRs) comprise all the regions of Africa, Asia (excluding Japan), Latin America and the Caribbean, and the regions of Melanesia,
   Micronesia and Polynesia.
5. As of 12th April 2001, 49 countries have been recognised by the United
   Nations General Assembly as LtDRs. The list includes the nine Asian countries: Afghanistan, Bangladesh, Bhutan, Cambodia, Laos, Maldives, Myanmar,
   Nepal, and Yemen.
6. China, China Hong Kong, China Macao, North Korea, Japan, Mongolia and
   South Korea.
7. Afghanistan, Bangladesh, Bhutan, India, Iran, Kazakhstan, Kyrgyzstan,
   Maldives, Nepal, Pakistan, Sri Lanka, Tajikistan, Turkmenistan, Uzbekistan.
8. Armenia, Azerbaijan, Bahrain, Cyprus, Georgia, Iraq, Israel, Jordan, Kuwait,
   Lebanon, occupied Palestinian Territory, Oman, Qatar, Saudi Arabia, Syrian
   Arab Republic, Turkey, UAE, Yemen.
9. Brunei Darussalam, Cambodia, East Timor, Indonesia, Lao, Malaysia,
   Myanmar, Philippines, Singapore, Thailand, Viet Nam.
10. In fact there are three dependency ratios. These are:
    Total dependency ratio = Proportion of total (aged and the children) dependants
                            to the total population aged 15–64.
    Aged dependency ratio = Proportion of aged dependants to the total population
                            aged 15–64.
    Child dependency ratio = Proportion of children dependants to the total pop-
                            ulation aged 15–64.
11. C.M. Taeuber, 'Sixty-five Plus in America', Current Population Reports, Special
    Studies, P23–178, U.S. Department of Commerce, Economics, and Statistics
    Administration, Bureau of the Census, Washington, D.C., 1992.
12. D.L. Morgan, T.L. Schuster and E.W. Butler, 'Role Reversals in the Exchange of
    Social Support', *Journal of Gerontology*, 46(5), 1991.

13. S. Katz, A.B. Ford, A.W. Moskowitz, B.A. Jackson and M.W. Jaffe, 'Studies of Illness in the Aged. The Index of ADL: A Standardized Measure of Biological and Psychosocial Function', *Journal of American Medical Association (JAMA)*, 185: 914–19, 1963.

14. M.P. Lawton and E.M. Brody, 'Assessment of Older People: Self-maintaining and Instrumental Activities of Daily Living', *Gerontologist*, 9: 179–86, 1969.

15. E. Crimmins, 'Trends in Mortality, Morbidity, and Disability: What Should We Expect for the Future of our Ageing Populations', in *International Population Conference, Beijing, 1997, Vol. 1*, International Union for the Scientific Study of Population (IUSSP), Liege, Belgium, 1997.

16. United Nations, *Ageing in a Gendered World: Women's Issues and Identities*, International Research and Training Institute for the Advancement of Women (INSTRAW), Sales No. E.99.III.C.I, 1999.

17. Jonathan Gruber and David A. Wise (eds), *Social Security and Retirement Around the World*, University of Chicago Press, Chicago, Illinois, 1999.

18. E. Drury, 'Age Discrimination Against Older Workers in the European Union', in *Studies on the Four Pillars, Geneva Papers on Risk and Insurance: Issues and Practice*, No. 73, 1994.

19. P.E. Taylor and A. Walker, 'Intergenerational Relations in the Labour Market: The Attitudes of Employers and Older Workers', in A. Walker (ed.), *The New Generational Contract, Intergenerational Relations, Old Age and Welfare*, University College London Press, London, 1996.

20. International Labour Office, *World Labour Report 2000: Income Security and Social Protection in a Changing World*, Geneva, 2000.

21. L.A. Lillard and C.W.A. Panis, 'Marital Status and Mortality: The Role of Health', *Demography*, 33: 313–27, 1996.

22. Y.B. Cheung, 'Accidents, Assaults, and Marital Status', *Social Science Medicine*, 47(9): 1325–29, 1998.

23. S. Wyke and G. Ford, 'Competing Explanations for Associations Between Marital Status and Health', *Social Science Medicine*, 34: 523–32, 1995.

24. I.M.A. Joung, J.B.W. Van der Meer and J.P. Mackenbach, 'Marital Status and Health Care Utilization', *International Journal of Epidemiology*, 24: 569–75, 1995.

25. N. Goldman, S. Korenman and R. Weinstein, 'Marital Status and Health Among the Elderly', *Social Science Medicine*, 40: 1717–30, 1995.

26. LtDRs as defined by the United Nations General Assembly in 1994, include 48 countries of which 33 are in Africa, nine are in Asia, one in Latin America and 5 in Oceania.

27. United Nations, 'World Population Ageing 1950–2050', Department of Economic and Social Affairs Population Division, ST/ESA/SER.A/207, New York, 2002.

28. *ibid.*

CHAPTER TWO

WHAT CAUSES POPULATION AGEING?

Having been introduced to the demographic aspect of ageing in chapter one, this chapter delves into the process that causes population ageing. 'Viewed as a whole the problem of ageing is no problem at all. It is only the pessimistic way of looking at a great triumph of civilization…' said the famous demographer, Frank W. Notestein[1] in 1954. Population ageing is one of humanity's greatest triumphs.

Civilised society has always wanted to reduce human mortality rates and once it successfully accomplished this the population began to grow from the low level of stationary population, helping in industrialisation and economic growth. This was followed by the belief that population growth precedes economic development. However, the problem of Rapid Population Growth (RPG) soon began to upset human prosperity and civilised society needed some intervention in the area of human fertility. The technological breakthroughs in the regulation of human reproductivity, economic development, spread of education and judicial mix of incentive and disincentive policies did bring about some change. However, the pace of change has varied. In some places it has been rapid; in others, it has taken time. There still remain many areas where this transition has not even begun yet. However, it is from these massive changes in fertility that there has risen a growing concern for the aged.

This chapter seeks to identify the factors responsible for the current state of ageing in Asia. Why is ageing faster in some countries but slower in others? The analysis starts off from an elementary level discussion of demographic transition and the different stages through which the different countries of Asia have passed over time. It discusses, in detail, the factors contributing to fertility and mortality transitions in Asia, for when both fertility and mortality are contributing factors in the process of ageing, it is worth asking which factor dominates over the other. Since migrations also influence the age profile of a population in any given place, this chapter looks into the various complex issues relating to the flow of people that alters age distribution. Finally, the chapter also discusses population momentum and ageing.

VARYING SPEEDS OF AGEING

Towards the end of the last century, the speed of ageing was much higher in the MDRs than in the other regions of Asia. Within Asia, ageing was highly pronounced in the eastern part and was almost similar to the speed observed in the MDRs. South-eastern Asia came in at a distant second while South-central Asia a poor third. During this period, there was no ageing in Western Asia. Table 2.1 shows the spread of ageing in different regions of Asia and the MDRs from 1950 to 2000.

This whole pattern is expected to undergo a sea change in the first half of this century. Asia will outdo the MDRs of the world by over 100 per cent. Within Asia too, the rankings in terms of the speed of ageing will be altered in a big way. The speed of ageing will be highest in South-eastern Asia (214 per cent), followed by South-central Asia (186 per cent), Eastern Asia (170 per cent) and Western Asia (154 per cent). During the same period, Africa will be at 140 per cent, Europe at 82.6 per cent, Latin America and the Caribbean at 182 per cent, Northern America at 70 per cent and Oceania at 80.6 per cent. See Table 2.2 for speed of ageing in different regions of Asia and the MDRs between 2000–2050.

Ageing in the MDRs started much earlier than in the LDRs. However, for a meaningful comparison of the speed of ageing in the developed countries, one needs to move beyond 1950. Table 2.3 provides data on the speed of ageing (65 plus) for select countries for a much longer time period.

The speed of ageing in the select Asian countries shown in Table 2.3 appears to be remarkable. It would take Asia, Japan, Thailand and

Table 2.1

The Elderly in Different Regions of Asia and the MDRs, 1950–2000

(percentage of total population)

Regions	1950	1955	1960	1965	1970	1975	1980	1985	1990	1995	2000	Percentage Change in 50 years
Asia	6.7	6.7	6.5	6.4	6.5	6.6	6.8	7.2	7.6	8.2	8.8	31.3
MDRs	11.7	12.1	12.6	13.4	14.5	15.4	15.5	16.4	17.7	18.4	19.5	66.6
Eastern Asia	7.4	7.5	7.3	7.2	7.2	7.4	7.9	8.6	9.3	10.3	11.2	51.4
South-central Asia	6.1	6.0	5.9	5.8	5.9	6.0	6.1	6.2	6.4	6.7	7.0	14.8
South-eastern Asia	5.9	5.6	5.4	5.3	5.3	5.3	5.6	5.8	6.3	6.7	7.2	22.0
Western Asia	7.1	6.8	6.7	6.5	6.7	6.5	6.1	6.0	6.4	6.8	7.1	0.0

Source: United Nations, *World Population Prospects: The 1998 Revision, Vol. I: Comprehensive Tables*, Department of Economic and Social Affairs, Population Division, New York, 1999.

Table 2.2

The Elderly in Different Regions of Asia and the MDRs, 2000–2050

(percentage of total population)

Regions	2000	2005	2010	2015	2020	2025	2030	2040	2050	Percentage Change in 50 years
Asia	8.8	9.3	10.2	11.6	13.1	14.9	17.1	20.5	23.5	167.0
MDRs	19.5	20.2	21.9	23.7	25.8	27.7	29.2	31.1	32.5	66.6
Eastern Asia	11.2	12.1	13.6	16.0	17.8	20.5	24.0	27.9	30.2	169.6
South-central Asia	7.0	7.4	7.9	8.9	10.1	11.5	13.0	16.1	20.0	185.7
South-eastern Asia	7.2	7.7	8.3	9.5	11.2	13.0	15.1	19.2	22.6	213.8
Western Asia	7.1	7.2	7.7	8.6	9.7	11.0	12.2	15.1	18.0	153.5

Source: United Nations, *World Population Prospects: The 1998 Revision, Vol. I: Comprehensive Tables*, Department of Economic and Social Affairs, New York, 1999.

Table 2.3
Speed of Population Ageing in Selected Countries

Country	*Years Attaining the Specified Percentage of the Aged Among the Total Population*			*Years Required for Proportion of Aged to Double from 7 per cent*
	7 per cent	*10 per cent*	*14 per cent*	
Japan	1970	1985	1994	24
France	1864	1943	1979	115
Germany	1932	1942	1972	40
Sweden	1887	1948	1972	85
Switzerland	1931	1960	1982	51
United Kingdom	1929	1946	1976	47
USA	1942	1972	2013	71
Asia	2010	2025	2035	25
Thailand	2005	2020	2030	25
India	2020	2030	2045	25

Source: Before 1950: United Nations, *The Ageing of Population and its Economic and Social Implications*, Population Studies, No. 26, New York, 1956. After 1950: United Nations, *World Population Prospects, The 1998 Revision, Vol. II: The Sex and Age Distribution of World Population*, Department of Economic and Social Affairs, Population Division, New York, 1999.

India only 24 to 25 years for their aged to double their numbers from 7 to 14 per cent. This is distinctly much shorter than the time required in any of the other selected developed countries. When the speed of ageing is rapid, its social and economic impacts are obviously much larger than otherwise would have been in the situation where the change takes place rather slowly.[2] The process of greying in Asia, therefore, has very different implications, from the point of view of both family and government than is the case in the developed world.

Why is the speed of population ageing so rapid in Asia? This is primarily due to the rapid demographic transition that has been projected for Asia in the years to come. In Japan, the speed of ageing is already very high because of rapid fertility decline in the post-war years. It is remarkable that the Crude Birth Rate (CBR), which was 34.3 per 1,000 in 1947, had been halved to 17.2 in 1957; thereafter the fertility level has never moved beyond 20 per 1,000. The CBR is now even less than 10 per 1,000. This fertility transition is the major factor behind the rapid ageing experienced in Japan. In other countries too, demographic transition plays a major role in the ageing process. To appreciate the implications of demographic transition on ageing, given here is a brief discussion on the theory of demographic transition. This theory, though it may sound somewhat old-fashioned, is still relevant to most Asian countries.

THEORY OF DEMOGRAPHIC TRANSITION

The theory of demographic transition arose, in part, as a reaction to the crude biological explanations of fertility decline in Europe following World War I. It rationalised fertility decline in terms of social and economic factors. The factory system and urbanisation reduced the role of the family in industrial production. It was also responsible for reducing the economic value of children. Meanwhile, the costs of raising children rose. The new system of education that came up as a result of industrialisation also postponed their entry into the workforce. Finally, the lessening of infant mortality reduced the number of births needed to achieve a given family size. The discovery of new medicines and improvements in health indicators began to reduce mortality rates, everywhere, starting with the European countries.

The shift from high to low levels of fertility and mortality has been explained through the different stages in the demographic transition theory. Formally, the theory is a historical generalisation and not truly a scientific theory offering predictive and testable hypotheses. The first person to talk about demographic transition was Thompson.[3] He tried to explain the transition process in terms of three geographic population regions. These regions have the following characteristics with regard to mortality and fertility conditions:

♦ *Group A*: Population of some parts of Western Europe where birth and death rates have declined very rapidly.
♦ *Group B*: Population of Southern and Eastern Europe where birth and death rates are in transition moving towards decline.

♦ *Group C:* Population of Africa, Asia and Latin America where birth and death rates are uncontrolled and have given rise to population explosion or stationary population through Malthusian checks, viz., diseases, hunger, etc.

Laundry[4] suggested three stages in demographic transition—primitive, intermediary and contemporary. The credit for the development of the modern concept of the transition theory goes to Notestein.[5] His theory was widely accepted as the explanation for fertility and mortality decline until the 1970s. More recently, careful research on fertility and mortality experiences in various countries have forced a reappraisal and refinement of the demographic transition theory. Many new variables and attributes such as language, religion, nuclear family and the social acceptability of deliberate fertility control are now recognised as important determinants of the theory. These researches have strengthened the logical foundation of the theory and made it more acceptable in various demographic explanations.

The modern-day transition theory is explained in four stages. In Stage I, which prevails in pre-industrial societies (i.e., the world before the 17th century), both birth and death rates are high. One offsets the other and there is little or no population growth. As countries begin to modernise, however, death rates fall and countries enter Stage II, where death rates are low while birth rates continue to remain high. This is the stage of RPG. Most of the developing countries of Asia, Africa and Latin America are at this stage. However, countries cannot remain in this stage for long.

With further modernisation, fertility is subject to deliberate control. Birth rates decline and countries enter Stage III of demographic transition. Finally, when both birth and death rates fall to a very low level and balance each other, we have Stage IV or the final stage of demographic transition. At this point, population size stabilises. Countries rarely ever have zero growth rates. If they attain a population growth rate which is below 0.4, they can be considered to have attained a stable population. Among the earliest nations to reach the final stage of demographic transition were Germany, Hungary and Sweden, who achieved stability during the 1970s. The factors which determine birth and death rates at each stage are summarised in Table 2.4.

To sum up with Demeny: 'In traditional societies, fertility and mortality are high. In modern societies, fertility and mortality are low. In between there is demographic transition.'[6]

Table 2.4
Factors Affecting Death and Birth Rates at Each Stage of Demographic Transition

Stage I	Stage II	Stage III	Stage IV
Pre-industrialisation: Stable Population Growth	Rapid Population Growth (RPG)	Continued and Decreasing Population Growth	Stable Low Population Growth
High Death Rates	Falling Death Rates	Death Rates Low	Death Rates Low
Widespread giant killer diseases such as malaria, cholera and plague.	Improved medical care e.g., vaccinations, hospitals, doctors, new drugs and scientific inventions.	Stage II conditions are further reinforced.	Further consolidation from Stage III.
Recurrences of famine, uncertain food supplies and poor diet.	Improved sanitation and water supply.		
Poor hygiene, no piped clean water or sewage disposal.	Improvements in food production in terms of quality and quantity.		
	Improved transport to move food and doctors.		
	A decrease in child mortality.		
High Birth Rates	High Birth Rates	Falling Birth Rates	Low Birth Rates
No or little family planning. Parents have many children because few survive.	Stage I conditions remain intact.	Family planning utilised, contraceptives, abortions, sterilisation and other government incentives.	Stage III conditions are further reinforced.

(continued)

Table 2.4
(Continued)

Stage I	Stage II	Stage III	Stage IV
Pre-industrialisation: Stable Population Growth	*Rapid Population Growth (RPG)*	*Continued and Decreasing Population Growth*	*Stable Low Population Growth*
Many children are needed to work the land.		A lower infant mortality rate means less pressure to have children.	
Children are a sign of virility.			
Some religious beliefs and cultural traditions encourage large families.		Increased mechanisation and industrialisation means less need for labour.	
		Increased desire for material possessions and less desire for large families.	
		Emancipation of women.	

Today, all countries are either in Stage II or Stage III of demographic transition. The *World Population Report*, 1998, prepared by the United Nations,[7] shows that 49 countries in the world have moved to the Stage IV of demographic transition by virtue of their annual growth rate being lower than 0.4 per cent. Table 2.5 lists these countries.

TRANSITION STAGES IN TERMS OF TFR AND LIFE EXPECTANCY

The boundary of each stage of demographic transition can be set in terms of the Total Fertility Rate (TFR) and Life Expectancy (e_0^0)[8] from

Table 2.5
List of the Countries that have Reached the Final Stage of
Demographic Transition

Continents	Countries
Asia	Japan (0.2), Kazakhstan (−0.3), Armenia (−0.3) and Georgia (−1.1)
Europe	Belarus (−0.3), Bulgaria (−0.7), Czech Republic (−0.2), Hungary (−0.4), Poland (0.1), Moldavia (0.0), Romania (−0.4), Russian Federation (−0.2), Slovakia (0.1), Ukraine (−0.4), Denmark (0.3), Estonia (−1.2), Faeroe Islands (−0.9), Finland (0.3), Latvia (−1.5). Lithuania (−0.3), Sweden (0.2), UK (0.2), Albania (−0.4), Croatia (−0.1), Gibraltar (−0.7), Greece (0.3), Holy See (0.3), Italy (0.0), San Marino (0.0), Slovenia (0.0), Spain (0.0), Yugoslavia (0.1), Belgium (0.1), France (0.4), Germany (0.1) and Netherlands (0.4).
America	Dominica (−) 0.1, Cuba (0.4), Grenada (0.3), Montserrat (−0.3), St. Kitts and Nevis (−0.8), United States Virgin Islands (−0.9), Greenland (0.1), Suriname (0.4), St. Pierre and Miquelon (0.3).
Oceania	Niue (−1.9), Pitcairn (0.0), Tokelau (0.0) and Tonga (0.3).

Source: United Nations, *World Population, 1998*, United Nations Publications, ST/ESA/SER.A/176, New York, 1999.
Note: The figures in brackets indicate the annual population growth rates.

Table 2.6
Total Fertility Rate (TFR) and Life Expectancy (e_0^0) in Various Stages of
Demographic Transition

Stage in Demographic Transition	Life Expectancy at Birth (e_0^0)	Total Fertility Rate (TFR)	Representation in Figure 2.1 (rectangle)
Stage I	Less than 45 years	Greater than 6.0	M_1F_1
Stage II	Between 45 and 55 years	Between 4.5 and 6.0	M_2F_2
Stage III	Between 55 and 65 years	Between 3.0 and 4.5	M_3F_3
Stage IV	Above 65 years	Less than 3	M_4F_4

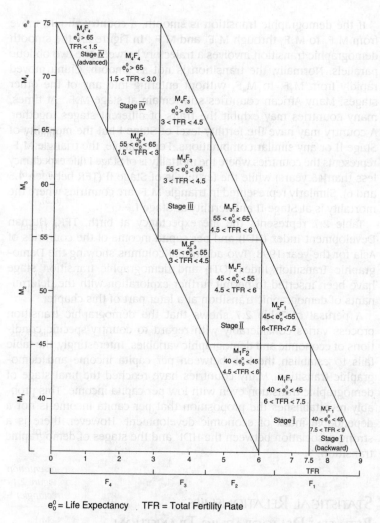

e_0^0 = Life Expectancy   TFR = Total Fertility Rate

Figure 2.1   Fertility and Mortality Rates during the
Process of Demographic Transition

the historical experiences. Table 2.6 lays down the probable domains of TFR and Life Expectancy (e_0^0) in each stage. Such an attempt makes it convenient to locate the stage(s) of demographic transition of a country over its known demographic history.

If the demographic transition is smooth, a country should move from M_1F_1 to M_4F_4 through M_2F_2 and M_3F_3. In Figure 2.1 the smooth demographic transition involves a trajectory between the two oblique parallels. Normally, the transition is not as smooth. China moved rapidly from M_1F_1 to M_4F_4 without entering into any of the other stages. Many African countries still remain at stage M_1F_1. At times, many countries may exhibit the traits of different stages together. A country may have the fertility level of Stage I but the mortality of Stage II or any similar combinations. For example, the triangle M_1F_2 represents the countries where the mortality is of Stage I (life expectancy less than 45 years) while the fertility is of Stage II (TFR between 4.5 and 6). Similarly represented in triangle M_2F_1 are countries where the mortality is at Stage II and fertility at Stage I.

Table 2.7 represents the life expectancy at birth, TFR, Human Development Index (HDI) and per capita income of the countries of Asia for the year 1998. Two additional columns showing the Demographic Transition Index (DTI) and demographic transition stage have been inserted to permit further exploration with the determinants of demographic transition at a later part of this chapter.

A perusal of Table 2.7 shows that the demographic transition process varies considerably with regard to country-specific conditions of economic and demographic variables. Interestingly, the table fails to establish the link between per capita income and demographic transition. Many countries have reached the final stage of demographic transition even with low per capita income. This probably re-establishes the proposition that per capita income is not a dependable index of economic development. However, there is a strong association between the HDI[9] and the stages of demographic transition.

STATISTICAL RELATIONSHIPS BETWEEN DEMOGRAPHIC TRANSITION INDEX (DTI) AND OTHER ECONOMIC AND DEMOGRAPHIC INDICATORS

To recognise the variables which determine demographic transition, this section fits the data for all the Asian countries, as given in Table 2.7, for the determination of the correlation coefficient and the regression

Table 2.7

Life Expectancy at Birth, Total Fertility Rate (TFR), Human Development Index (HDI), Per Capita Income, Demographic Transition Index (DTI) and the Current Stage of Demographic Transition in Different Countries in Asia, 1998

Country/Area	Life Expectancy at Birth	Total Fertility Rate (per women)	Human Development Index	Per Capita Income (US $)	Demographic Transition Index	Demographic Transition Stage
ASIA	**66**	**2.6**			**0.755**	**4th**
Eastern Asia	**71**	**1.8**			**0.899**	**4th**
China	70	1.8	0.650	750.00	0.884	4th
Hong Kong	78	1.3	0.909	23,670	1.0	4th
North Korea	72	2.0	0.766	**Lower Middle Income**	0.895	4th
Japan	80	1.4	0.940	32,380	1.0	4th
Macao	78	1.4		**High Income**	1.0	4th
Mongolia	66	2.6	0.669	400	0.755	4th
South Korea	72	1.6	0.894	7,970	0.931	4th
South-central Asia	**62**	**3.4**		**430#**	**0.625**	**3rd**
Afghanistan	45	6.9		**Low Income**	0.064	1st
Bangladesh	58	3.1	0.371	350	0.595	3rd
Bhutan	61	5.5	0.347	**Low Income**	0.419	M_3F_2
India	63	3.1	0.451	430	0.666	3rd

(continued)

Table 2.7
(Continued)

Country/Area	Life Expectancy at Birth	Total Fertility Rate (per women)	Human Development Index	Per Capita Income (US $)	Demographic Transition Index	Demographic Transition Stage
Iran	69	2.8	0.758	1,770	0.779	4th
Kazakhstan	68	2.3	0.695	1,310	0.810	4th
Kyrgyzstan	68	3.2	0.633	350	0.729	M_4F_3
Maldives	65	5.4	0.683	1,230	0.486	M_3F_2
Nepal	57	4.4	0.351	210	0.462	3rd
Pakistan	64	5.0	0.453	480	0.508	M_3F_2
Sri Lanka	73	2.1	0.716	810	0.900	4th
Tajikistan	67	4.1	0.575	350	0.483	M_4F_3
Turkmenistan	65	3.6	0.660	630*	0.649	3rd
Uzbekistan	68	3.4	0.659	870	0.710	M_4F_3
South-eastern	**66**	**2.7**			**0.745**	**4th**
Asia						
Brunei	76	2.8	0.859	High Income	0.880	4th
Cambodia	53	4.6	0.422	280	0.387	2nd
East Timor	48	5.3			0.252	2nd
Indonesia	65	2.6	0.679	680	0.740	4th
Laos	53	5.8	0.465	330	0.278	2nd
Malaysia	72	3.2	0.834	3,600	0.786	M_4F_3
Myanmar	60	2.4	0.481	Low Income	0.687	3rd

(continued)

Table 2.7
(Continued)

Country/Area	Life Expectancy at Birth	Total Fertility Rate (per women)	Human Development Index	Per Capita Income (US $)	Demographic Transition Index	Demographic Transition Stage
Philippines	68	3.6	0.677	1,050	0.692	M_4F_3
Singapore	77	1.4	0.896	30,600	1.00	4th
Thailand	69	1.7	0.838	2,200	0.879	4th
Viet Nam	67	2.6	0.560	330	0.769	4th
Western Asia	**68**	**3.8**			**0.674**	**M_4F_3**
Armenia	70	1.7	0.674	480	0.894	4th
Azerbaijan	70	2.0	0.623	490	0.866	4th
Bahrain	73	2.9	0.872	7,660	0.827	4th
Cyprus	78	2.0	0.979	**High Income**	0.981	4th
Gaza Strip	71	7.3			0.399	4th
Georgia	73	1.9	0.633	**Lower Middle Income**	0.918	4th
Iraq	62	5.3	0.538	930	0.452	M_3F_2
Israel	78	2.7	0.981	15,940	0.917	4th
Jordan	70	4.9	0.729	1,520	0.603	M_4F_2
Kuwait	76	2.9	0.848	22,110*	0.870	4th
Lebanon	70	2.7	0.796	3,560	0.803	4th
Oman	71	5.8	0.771	**Upper Middle Income**	0.535	M_4F_2

(continued)

Table 2.7
(Continued)

Country/Area	Life Expectancy at Birth	Total Fertility Rate (per women)	Human Development Index	Per Capita Income (US $)	Demographic Transition Index	Demographic Transition Stage
Qatar	72	3.7	0.840	**High Income**	0.740	M_4F_3
Saudi Arabia	71	5.8	0.778	6,790*	0.535	M_4F_2
Syria	69	4.3	0.749	1,020	0.504	M_4F_3
Turkey	69	2.5	0.782	3,160	0.806	4th
UAE	75	3.4	0.855	18,220	0.810	M_4F_3
Yemen	58	7.6	0.356	300	0.186	M_3F_1

Source: i. United Nations, *World Population, 1998*, United Nations Publications, ST/ESA/SER.A/176, New York, 1999 for demographic data; ii. World Bank, *World Development Report 1999/2000*, Oxford University Press, New York, 2000, for data on per capita income.

Notes: * Data relates to 1997; # relates to only South Asia; Low Income: $760 or less; Lower Middle Income: $761 to $3,030; Upper Middle Income: $3,031 to $9,360; High Income: $9,361 or more.

Table 2.8
The Correlation Coefficients and the Regression Equations between
Demographic Transition Index (DTI) and other Economic and
Demographic Variables

Interrelationship between	Correlation Coefficient	Regression Equation	Degree of Association
Human Development Index and Demographic Transition Index	R = 0.6148 p <= 5.3e–06 (t = 5.229, DF = 45)	Y = 0.6338 * x + 0.2881	Fairly positive
Per capita Income and Demographic Transition Index	R = 0.03125 p <= 0.8482 (t = 0.1927, DF = 38)	y = 2.479e–05 * x + 0.6948	No or very little correlation
Life Expectancy at Birth and Demographic Transition Index	R = 0.7888 p <= 0 (t = 9.43, DF = 54)	Y = 0.01622 * x + – 0.3923	Strong positive
Total Fertility Rate and Demographic Transition Index	R = –0.7091 p <= 0 (t = –7.391, DF = 54)	Y = –0.1039 * x + 1.032	Strong inverse

equation between the Demographic Transition Index (DTI) and the other economic and demographic indicators. The correlation coefficients and the regression equations are summed up in Table 2.8

The high positive correlation between the DTI and life expectancy, and the high negative correlation between the DTI and TFR, clearly establish the strength of the DTI, suggested here as a composite index of fertility and mortality transition. The following section defines the DTI, suggests its estimation procedures and finally estimates the DTI for all Asian countries for a selected five-year time period from 1950 to 2050.

DEMOGRAPHIC TRANSITION INDEX

The Demographic Transition Index (DTI) of a country 'i' may be defined as the weighted average of relative TFR and life expectancy of that country with respect to the highest and lowest rates in the region. Here we have assigned equal weightages to both mortality and fertility indictors, in the absence of any theoretical foundation suggesting an alternative. Mathematically speaking,

$$DTI = 0.5 \ [(TFR_{max} - TFR_i)/ \ (TFR_{max} - TFR_{min})]$$
$$+$$
$$0.5 \ [1 - (e^0_{0 \ max} - e^0_{0i})/ \ (e^0_{0 \ max} - e^0_{0 \ min})]$$

where TFR_{max} = highest TFR; TFR_{min} = lowest TFR; $e^0_{0 \ max}$ = highest life expectancy at birth; $e^0_{0 \ min}$ = lowest life expectancy at birth; e^0_{0i} = life expectancy at birth of the country.

In Asia, the highest TFR is that of Yemen i.e., 7.6; the lowest TFR is the replacement fertility level i.e., 2.1.[10] The highest life expectancy is 80 (found in Japan) and the lowest is 45 (in Afghanistan). Therefore,

$$DTI = 0.5 \ [(7.6 - TFR)/5.5] + 0.5 \ [1-(80 - e^0_0)/35]$$

When a country completes its demographic transition, the DTI becomes 1 or very close to it. The more distant the DTI is from 1; the further the country is from the completion of a demographic stage. A perusal of the last two columns of Table 2.6 indicates that a country is most likely to move to Stage IV when its DTI is above 0.750. Stage III starts as early as 0.450. This is misleading.

The use of the DTI has distinct advantages over the arbitrary stage marking. Nepal is currently in Stage III of demographic transition, but its DTI is only 0.462. The country needs to go a long way to complete its demographic transition but that is not clear from the stage of demographic transition it is at. Again, it is true that some countries and geographical areas have completed the transition process or are very close to its completion. These are the countries of East Asia and South-east Asia. Here too, East Timor, Cambodia and Laos Republic are yet to reach the final stage of demographic transition.

In South-central Asia, only Sri Lanka appears to be closer to the completion of its demographic transition. The DTI in Sri Lanka is 0.900. Among the counties of South-central Asia, Iran and Kazakhstan have a DTI of over 0.750. The DTI of India is only 0.666. In Western Asia, despite the initial delays, the process of demographic transition has already set in; ten countries have a DTI of above 0.8. Except in Yemen, Gaza Strip and Iraq, the demographic transition is very close to completion in most of Western Asia. There has been a tremendous reduction in mortality though fertility is still very high. To a great extent, the latter is deliberate.

DEMOGRAPHIC TRANSITION IN ASIA, 1950–2050

Based on the United Nations' estimates and projections, this section seeks to locate the transition process of Asian countries for six discrete five-year groupings between 1950–2050. Table 2.9 sums up the findings.

The MDRs and Europe reached their final stage of demographic transition in 1950–55 when most of Asia was in the first stage of the transition process. Interestingly, most of Asia reaches the final stage of transition in the beginning of the new century. However, there exist significant regional variations in the transition process. Mortality transition always precedes fertility transition. In Western Asia, fertility transition takes a much longer time to mature than elsewhere. To some extent, this picture is true for most of the Islamic world in Asia too. In most countries of Eastern and South-eastern Asia, fertility transition seems to be more rapid than elsewhere. Unlike most of Europe, very few countries of Asia experience a smooth transition from Stage I to Stage IV, through Stages II and III. This entire pattern has its bearing on population ageing.

DEMOGRAPHIC TRANSITION AND AGEING

It is the stage and rapidity of demographic transition that determines the population-ageing process. Ageing is determined by both fertility and mortality reductions. Early and quick initiation of demographic transition leads to rapid ageing of the population. These transitions, are in general, universal and seemingly irreversible, although the process has not yet been completed for many developing countries.

Changes in fertility and mortality can cause population ageing, either jointly or independently from each other. Studies show that fertility transition from the traditional high levels to modern low levels is the primary cause of population ageing. This is essentially because of the fact that lower fertility reduces the relative size of the younger population. If fertility declines to a low level and remains there for long, ageing of the population increases very rapidly. A large number of people have

Table 2.9
Stages of Demographic Transition in Asian Countries, 1950–2050

Country/Area	1950–55	1970–75	1980–85	2000–2005	2020–25	2040–50
MDRs	4th	4th	4th	4th	4th	4th
LDRs	1st	2nd	3rd	4th	4th	4th
Europe	4th	4th	4th	4th	4th	4th
N. America	M_4F_3	4th	4th	4th	4th	4th
ASIA	M_1F_2	2nd	3rd	4th	4th	4th
Eastern Asia	M_1F_2	3rd	4th	4th	4th	4th
China	1st	M_3F_2	4th	4th	4th	4th
Hong Kong	3rd	4th	4th	4th	4th	4th
North Korea	2nd	M_3F_2	M_4F_3	4th	4th	4th
Japan	M_3F_4	4th	4th	4th	4th	4th
Macau	2nd	M_4F_3	4th	4th	4th	4th
Mongolia	1st	M_2F_1	M_3F_2	4th	4th	4th
South Korea	2nd	3rd	4th	4th	4th	4th
South-central Asia	1st	2nd	2nd	3rd	4th	4th
Afghanistan	1st	1st	1st	2nd	M_3F_4	4th
Bangladesh	1st	1st	M_2F_1	3rd	M_3F_4	4th
Bhutan	1st	1st	2nd	3rd	M_3F_4	4th
India	1st	2nd	3rd	4th	4th	4th
Iran	M_2F_1	M_2F_1	M_3F_2	M_4F_3	4th	4th
Kazakhstan	3rd	3rd	4th	4th	4th	4th
Kyrgyzstan	2nd	M_3F_2	4th	4th	4th	4th
Maldives	1st	M_2F_1	M_3F_1	M_4F_2	4th	4th
Nepal	1st	1st	M_2F_1	3rd	M_3F_4	4th
Pakistan	1st	M_2F_1	2nd	3rd	4th	4th
Sri Lanka	M_3F_2	M_4F_3	M_4F_3	M_4F_3	4th	4th
Tajikistan	M_2F_1	M_3F_1	M_4F_2	M_4F_3	4th	4th
Turkmenistan	M_2F_1	M_3F_1	M_3F_2	3rd	4th	4th
Uzbekistan	M_2F_1	M_3F_1	M_4F_2	M_4F_3	4th	4th
South-eastern Asia	M_1F_2	2nd	3rd	4th	4th	4th
Brunei	M_3F_1	M_4F_1	M_4F_3	4th	4th	4th
Cambodia	1st	1st	M_1F_2	M_3F_4	M_3F_4	4th
East Timor	1st	1st	M_1F_2	M_2F_3	M_3F_4	4th
Indonesia	M_1F_2	2nd	M_2F_3	4th	4th	4th
Laos	1st	1st	2nd	3rd	4th	4th
Malaysia	M_2F_1	M_3F_2	M_4F_3	4th	4th	4th
Myanmar	1st	2nd	3rd	4th	4th	4th
Philippines	M_2F_1	M_3F_2	3rd	4th	4th	4th
Singapore	M_3F_1	M_4F_2	4th	4th	4th	4th
Thailand	M_3F_1	M_3F_2	3rd	4th	4th	4th
Viet Nam	M_1F_2	2nd	3rd	4th	4th	4th
Western Asia	M_2F_1	M_3F_2	M_3F_2	4th	4th	4th

(continued)

Table 2.9
(Continued)

Country/Area	1950–55	1970–75	1980–85	2000–2005	2020–25	2040–50
Armenia	3rd	4th	4th	4th	4th	4th
Azerbaijan	M_3F_2	M_4F_3	M_4F_3	4th	4th	4th
Bahrain	M_2F_1	M_3F_1	M_4F_2	4th	4th	4th
Cyprus	M_4F_3	4th	4th	4th	4th	4th
Gaza Strip	3rd	3rd	4th	4th	4th	4th
Georgia	3rd	4th	4th	4th	4th	4th
Iraq	1st	M_3F_1	M_3F_1	M_4F_3	4th	4th
Israel	M_4F_3	M_4F_3	M_4F_3	4th	4th	4th
Jordan	1st	M_3F_1	M_3F_1	M_4F_2	M_4F_3	4th
Kuwait	M_3F_1	M_4F_1	M_4F_1	M_4F_3	4th	4th
Lebanon	M_3F_2	M_4F_2	M_4F_3	4th	4th	4th
Oman	1st	M_2F_1	M_3F_1	M_4F_3	4th	4th
Qatar	M_2F_1	M_3F_1	M_4F_1	M_4F_3	4th	4th
Saudi Arabia	1st	M_2F_1	M_3F_1	M_4F_3	4th	4th
Syria	M_2F_1	M_3F_1	M_3F_1	M_4F_3	4th	4th
Turkey	M_2F_1	M_3F_2	3rd	4th	4th	4th
UAE	M_2F_1	M_3F_1	M_4F_2	M_4F_3	4th	4th
Yemen	1st	1st	M_2F_1	M_3F_2	M_4F_3	4th

Source: Calculated from United Nations, *World Population Prospects: The 1998 Revision*, Department of Economic and Social Affairs, Population Division, New York, 1999.

been born during the past high fertility stages when compared with those born during the current low fertility periods. When the low fertility transition continues for long, the large cohorts of the population born during the high fertility period will grow older and enter the elderly age bracket, while the younger cohorts remain relatively smaller. When the smaller cohorts of the population who are born after the onset of low fertility begin to enter the elderly age brackets, the ageing of the population may be stabilised. There may also be a temporary decline in the proportion of ageing but they can never revert to the proportion of the aged that existed before the onset of fertility transition.[11]

The decline in mortality rate also plays an important role in population ageing. Mortality first declines among infants and children. This inflates the number of children in the population. In other words, it causes population rejuvenation. In the later stages, mortality decline takes place among all age groups. During this phase, mortality transition contributes to population ageing. In countries where mortality rates at young ages are already low, a further decline in mortality tends to largely affect adults and the elderly, thereby contributing to population ageing. When mortality transition of the latter forms is accompanied by a general downward and stable fertility transition, population ageing becomes more pronounced.

This theoretical hypothesis between population ageing, mortality and fertility indicators may now be tested for Asian countries. As discussed, life expectancy at birth is an indicator of mortality in the country while the TFR indicates the fertility pattern in the country. Table 2.10 provides the relevant time series data for different regions of Asia, the MDRs and the world.

A perusal of Figure 2.2 shows that, when the life expectancy at birth is below 50, the proportion of the aged does not increase very much, and, in fact, even decreases slightly in response to the improvement of life expectancy. Beyond that level, however, the proportion of aged starts to rise rather quickly as life expectancy increases. It may also be seen from the graph that the MDRs indicate significant deviations from the Asian or the global pattern. The regional differences are essentially due to the presence of fertility and migration.

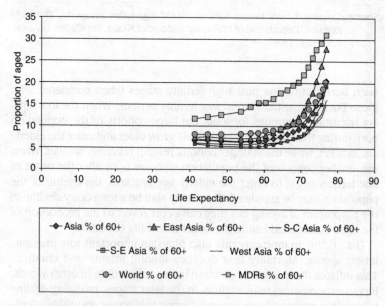

Figure 2.2 Scatter of Life Expectancy and Proportion of Aged in Asian Regions, MDRs and the World, 1950–2050

Table 2.10
Proportions of Aged, Life Expectancy at Birth in Different Regions of Asia, 1950–2050

Year	Asia e_o^o	Asia Percentage of 60 plus	East Asia e_o^o	East Asia Percentage of 60 plus	South-central Asia e_o^o	South-central Asia Percentage of 60 plus	South-east Asia e_o^o	South-east Asia Percentage of 60 plus	West Asia e_o^o	West Asia Percentage of 60 plus
1950–55	41.3	6.7	42.9	7.4	39.3	6.1	40.5	5.9	45.2	7.1
1955–60	44.8	6.7	46.7	7.5	42.8	6.0	43.6	5.6	48.8	6.8
1960–65	48.4	6.5	51.4	7.3	45.5	5.9	46.4	5.4	52.2	6.7
1965–70	53.7	6.4	60.5	7.2	48.1	5.8	49.3	5.3	54.9	6.5
1970–75	56.3	6.5	64.2	7.2	50.2	5.9	51.9	5.3	57.9	6.7
1975–80	58.5	6.6	66.4	7.4	52.7	6.0	54.7	5.3	60.5	6.5
1980–85	60.4	6.8	67.7	7.9	54.9	6.1	58.0	5.6	62.9	6.1
1985–90	62.5	7.2	68.2	8.6	57.7	6.2	61.4	5.8	65.3	6.0
1990–95	64.5	7.6	69.6	9.3	60.2	6.4	63.7	6.3	66.2	6.4
1995–2000	66.3	8.2	71.0	10.3	62.3	6.7	65.7	6.7	68.0	6.8
2000–2005	67.9	8.8	72.3	11.2	64.0	7.0	67.5	7.2	70.3	7.1
2005–10	69.4	9.3	73.4	12.1	65.8	7.4	69.2	7.7	71.6	7.2
2010–15	70.8	10.2	74.4	13.6	67.4	7.9	70.8	8.3	72.8	7.7
2015–20	72.0	11.6	75.3	16.0	68.9	8.9	72.1	9.5	73.9	8.6
2020–25	73.2	13.1	76.2	17.8	70.4	10.1	73.3	11.2	74.9	9.7
2025–30	74.2	14.9	77.0	20.5	71.7	11.5	74.4	13.0	75.8	11.0
2030–40	75.6	17.1	78.0	24.0	73.3	13.0	75.7	15.1	77.0	12.2
2040–50	76.9	20.5	79.1	27.9	75.0	16.1	77.1	19.2	78.3	15.1

Source: Calculated from United Nations, *World Population Prospects: The 1998 Revision*, Department of Economic and Social Affairs, Population Division, New York.

Notes: 1. The data on proportion of aged belongs to the beginning of each five-year period.

2. Life expectancy is combined for both sexes.

The data on the proportions of the aged and life expectancy generates the following regression equations and correlation coefficients in various regions. To facilitate comparisons, we also estimate the regression equations and correlation coefficients for the world and the MDRs (see Table 2.11).

The bivariate distribution of the proportion of aged and life expectancy as shown in Figure 2.2 reflects a non-linear relationship. Even then, linear regression and correlation coefficients have been used, mainly to identify the nature of association between the two. The association is positive everywhere. The unexplained variations, however, are high, as expected.

In Table 2.12, we provide data on the percentage of aged and the TFR in different regions of Asia for the 100-year period. As expected, the relationship is negative. Figure 2.3 puts the data on a scatter diagram along with that of the MDRs and world average. The objective is to facilitate comparisons with Asia and the MDRs in particular, and the world as a whole. The relationship between the proportion of aged and the TFR is more diverse among the Asian regions; this is not so in the case of life expectancy.

Table 2.13 provides data on the proportions of aged, the TFR and life expectancy in the MDRs and the rest of the world for the period 1950–2050.

Let us now derive the regression equations and correlation coefficients between the proportion of aged and TFR in the same way as has been done with life expectancy. Here too, the bivariate distribution does not generate a linear relationship, but linear regressions have been derived for the same reason. See Table 2.14.

It is true that a decrease in the TFR raises the proportion of aged, but the relationship between the TFR and the proportion of aged does not appear to be as strong as the life expectancy. For all the regions of Asia, the correlation is close to zero. For the broader geographic regions of Asia, the MDRs and the world as a whole the associations, however, are not all that weak. From this exercise, one could be tempted to conclude that mortality factors play a more important role than fertility in population ageing. However, to establish a definite conclusion we need to deconstruct the change in the proportion of aged into fertility, mortality and initial age distribution components. However, before we engage in that exercise, let us use the country data on the relationship between the proportion of aged, life expectancy at birth and TFR for Japan, India and Thailand to determine the relative nature of the correlation between fertility and mortality elements on ageing. Table 2.15 provides the time series country data for India, Japan and Thailand on proportions of aged, life expectancy and TFRs.

Table 2.11
The Correlation Coefficients and the Regression Equations between
the Proportion of Aged and the Life Expectancy at Birth for
Different Regions of Asia, the MDRs and the World

Regions	Correlation Coefficient	Regression Equation	Degree of Association
Asia	R = 0.7829 p <= 0.0001341 (t = 5.188, DF = 17)	y = 0.2024 * x + −2.911	Fairly positive
East Asia	R = 0.7379 p <= 0.0002961 (t = 4.638, DF = 18)	y = 0.2276 * x + −2.658	Fairly positive
South-central Asia	R = 0.8621 p <= 5.4e − 06 (t = 7.218, DF = 18)	Y = 0.151 * x + −0.932	Fairly positive
South-eastern Asia	R = 0.795 p <= 5.79e − 05 (t = 5.56, DF = 18)	Y = 0.163 * x + −1.669	Fairly positive
West Asia	R = 0.843 p <= 1.12e − 05 (t = 6.648, DF = 18)	y = 0.1284 * x + −0.3442	Fairly positive
World	R = 0.8472 p <= 1.72e − 05 (t = 6.575, DF = 17)	y = 0.2068 * x + −2.245	Fairly positive
MDRs	R = 0.7586 p <= 0.0002607 (t = 4.8, DF = 17)	y = 0.3192 * x + −4.274	Fairly positive

Figures 2.4 and 2.5 represent the scatter of points between life expectancy and the percentage of elderly, and also between the TFR and the percentage of elderly.

The correlation coefficients and the regression equations for the TFR and the proportion of aged are summed up in Table 2.16.

The correlation coefficients and the regression equations for life expectancy at birth and the proportions of aged are summed up in Table 2.17.

For India, both TFR and life expectancy are very strongly associated with the proportion of aged. For other countries, this relationship is not as strong as it is in India. But all over, life expectancy

Table 2.12
Proportions of Aged, Total Fertility Rate (TFR) in Different Regions of Asia, 1950–2050

Year	Asia TFR	Asia Percentage of 60 plus	East Asia TFR	East Asia Percentage of 60 plus	South-central Asia TFR	South-central Asia Percentage of 60 plus	South-east Asia TFR	South-east Asia Percentage of 60 plus	West Asia TFR	West Asia Percentage of 60 plus
1950–55	5.91	6.7	5.71	7.4	6.08	6.1	6.03	5.9	6.38	7.1
1955–60	5.63	6.7	5.12	7.5	6.06	6.0	6.07	5.6	6.25	6.8
1960–65	5.62	6.5	5.19	7.3	6.01	5.9	5.90	5.4	6.18	6.7
1965–70	5.69	6.4	5.46	7.2	5.91	5.8	5.81	5.3	5.91	6.5
1970–75	5.09	6.5	4.49	7.2	5.72	5.9	5.31	5.3	5.57	6.7
1975–80	4.22	6.6	3.13	7.4	5.24	6.0	4.81	5.3	5.19	6.5
1980–85	3.70	6.8	2.47	7.9	4.92	6.1	4.18	5.6	4.96	6.1
1985–90	3.39	7.2	2.36	8.6	4.44	6.2	3.58	5.8	4.73	6.0
1990–95	2.85	7.6	1.88	9.3	3.79	6.4	3.05	6.3	4.05	6.4
1995–2000	2.60	8.2	1.77	10.3	3.36	6.7	2.69	6.7	3.77	7.1
2000–2005	2.43	8.8	1.81	11.2	2.97	7.0	2.40	7.2	3.49	7.2
2005–10	2.28	9.3	1.86	12.1	2.59	7.4	2.23	7.7	3.26	7.7
2010–15	2.18	10.2	1.88	13.6	2.34	7.9	2.16	8.3	3.08	7.7
2015–20	2.14	11.6	1.88	16.0	2.25	8.9	2.11	9.5	2.87	8.6
2020–25	2.10	13.1	1.89	17.8	2.17	10.1	2.10	11.2	2.65	9.7
2025–30	2.07	14.9	1.89	20.5	2.13	11.5	2.09	13.0	2.43	11.0
2030–40	2.04	17.1	1.89	24.0	2.11	13.0	2.08	15.1	2.21	12.2
2040–50	2.03	20.5	1.89	27.9	2.10	16.1	2.08	19.2	2.09	15.1

Source: Calculated from United Nations, *World Population Prospects: The 1998 Revision*, Department of Economic and Social Affairs, Population Division, New York.

Note: The data on proportions of aged belongs to the beginning of each five-year period.

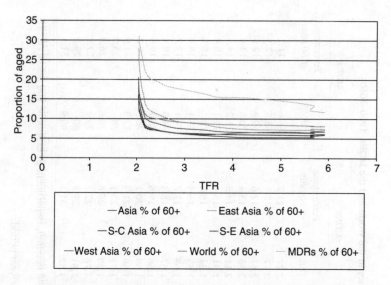

Figure 2.3 Scatter of TFR and Proportion of Aged in Asian Regions, the World and the MDRs, 1950–2050

has a stronger influence on ageing than total fertility, though the effect of fertility on ageing cannot be ignored either. That mortality is a more important element in population ageing than fertility variables has been discovered from French and Italian data. Caselli and Vallin concluded that even if Italian fertility remained at a very low level of 1.4 children per woman through the year 2040, more than half the increase in the proportion of the population aged 60 or above would be due to change in mortality, and less than half to the earlier fertility trends.[12]

FERTILITY AND MORTALITY ELEMENTS IN POPULATION AGEING IN INDIA

The regression analysis shown in the earlier tables proves that decline in mortality and improvement in life expectancy play major roles in determining ageing. At the same time the role of fertility in the ageing of the Indian population cannot be understated either. In

Table 2.13

Proportions of Aged, Total Fertility Rate (TFR) and Life Expectancy in the World and the MDRs, 1950–2050

Year	World			MDRs		MDRs	
	TFR	e^o_0	Percentage of 60 plus	TFR	Percentage of 60 plus	e^o_0	Percentage of 60 plus
1950–55	4.99	46.5	8.1	2.77	11.7	66.6	11.7
1955–60	4.92	49.6	8.1	2.77	12.1	68.5	12.1
1960–65	4.95	52.4	8.1	2.67	12.6	69.8	12.6
1965–70	4.91	56.0	8.2	2.36	13.4	70.5	13.4
1970–75	4.48	58.0	8.4	2.11	14.5	71.2	14.5
1975–80	3.92	59.7	8.5	1.91	15.4	72.1	15.4
1980–85	3.58	61.3	8.6	1.84	15.5	73	15.5
1985–90	3.34	63.1	8.8	1.83	16.4	74.1	16.4
1990–95	2.93	64.1	9.2	1.68	17.7	74.1	17.7
1995–2000	2.71	65.4	9.6	1.57	18.4	74.9	18.4
2000–2005	2.57	66.5	10	1.56	19.5	75.7	19.5
2005–10	2.44	67.8	10.3	1.59	20.2	76.5	20.2
2010–15	2.35	69.2	11.1	1.65	21.9	77.3	21.9
2015–20	2.29	70.6	12.3	1.71	23.7	78	23.7
2020–25	2.23	71.9	13.6	1.75	25.8	78.6	25.8
2025–30	2.17	73.1	15.1	1.78	27.7	79.2	27.7
2030–40	2.08	74.5	16.8	1.81	29.2	80	29.2
2040–50	2.03	76.0	19.5	1.82	31.1	80.9	31.1

Source: Calculated from United Nations, *World Population Prospects: The 1998 Revision*, Department of Economic and Social Affairs, Population Division, New York.

Note: The data on proportion of aged belongs to the beginning of each five-year period.

Table 2.14
The Correlation Coefficients and the Regression Equations between Proportion Aged and the Total Fertility Rates (TFRs) for Different Regions of Asia, the MDRs and the World

Regions	Correlation Coefficient	Regression Equation	Degree of Association
Asia	R = −0.6874 p <= 0.001955 (t = −3.786, DF = 16)	Y = −1.905 * x + 16.26	Negative but not very strong
East Asia	R = −0.3036 p <= 0.2067 (t = −1.314, DF = 17)	Y = −1.286 * x + 15.3	Negative and low
South-central Asia	R = −0.2668 p <= 0.2697 (t = −1.141, DF = 17)	y = −0.4964 * x + 9.36	Negative and low
South-eastern Asia	R = −0.3161 p <= 0.1877 (t = −1.374, DF = 17)	Y = −0.7621 * x + 10.4	Negative and low
West Asia	R = −0.1402 p <= 0.5672 (t = −0.5837, DF = 17)	y = −0.2433 * x + 8.551	Negative and low
World	R = −0.7416 p <= 0.0006049 (t = −4.422, DF = 16)	y = −2.209 * x + 18.02	Negative but fairly strong
MDRs	R = −0.6226 p <= 0.006332 (t = −3.182, DF = 16)	y = −9.284 * x + 37.41	Negative but not very strong

fact, if there were a decline in the mortality rate unaccompanied by a fall in fertility, the typical age pattern would have tilted towards the younger age group. It is the fertility decline that affects the number of births and reduces the size of the younger people in the population. Tables 2.18(a) and 2.18(b) provide data on the life expectancy of males and females (at age 60) in various countries of Asia and within different states of India respectively.

The Indian experience of mortality decline broadly conforms to the Asian pattern. The SRS data indicates that the elderly in the states of Kerala and Punjab live much longer than those in the other Indian states. They also live much longer than the elderly in many regions

Table 2.15

Proportion of Aged, Life Expectancy and TFR in India, Thailand and Japan, 1950–2050

Year	India e_o^o	India TFR	India Percentage of 60 plus	Japan e_o^o	Japan TFR	Japan Percentage of 60 plus	Thailand e_o^o	Thailand TFR	Thailand Percentage of 60 plus
1950–55	38.7	5.97	5.6	63.9	2.75	7.7	47.0	6.59	4.8
1955–60	42.6	5.92	5.6	66.8	2.08	8.1	50.6	6.39	4.5
1960–65	45.5	5.81	5.7	69.0	2.02	8.9	53.9	6.39	4.5
1965–70	48.0	5.69	5.8	71.1	2.00	9.6	56.7	6.11	4.7
1970–75	50.3	5.43	6.0	73.3	2.07	10.7	59.6	4.99	4.8
1975–80	52.9	4.83	6.2	75.5	1.81	11.7	61.2	4.25	4.7
1980–85	54.9	4.47	6.5	76.9	1.76	12.9	64.9	2.96	5.4
1985–90	57.6	4.07	6.6	78.3	1.66	14.8	67.2	2.57	5.9
1990–95	60.3	3.56	6.9	79.5	1.49	17.4	68.8	1.94	6.7
1995–2000	62.6	3.13	7.2	80.0	1.43	20.5	68.8	1.74	7.6
2000–2005	64.2	2.72	7.6	80.3	1.47	23.1	69.4	1.74	8.7
2005–10	65.8	2.31	8.1	80.7	1.54	25.8	71.0	1.78	9.6
2010–15	67.3	2.10	8.8	81.1	1.61	29.3	72.8	1.85	10.8
2015–20	68.8	2.10	9.8	81.5	1.68	31.2	74.2	1.90	12.7
2020–25	70.4	2.10	11.1	81.9	1.73	32.1	75.3	1.90	15.2
2025–30	71.6	2.10	12.6	82.3	1.75	32.9	75.8	1.90	18.1
2030–40	73.1	2.10	14.2	82.8	1.75	34.2	76.2	1.90	21.4
2040–50	74.6	2.10	17.4	83.6	1.75	37.4	76.7	1.90	26.8

Source: Calculated from United Nations, *World Population Prospects: The 1998 Revision*, Department of Economic and Social Affairs, Population Division, New York.

Notes: 1. The data on proportion aged belongs to the beginning of each five-year period. 2. Life expectancy is combined for both sexes.

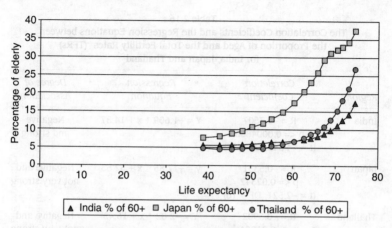

Figure 2.4 Scatter of Life Expectancy and Percentage of
Aged in India, Japan and Thailand, 1950–2050

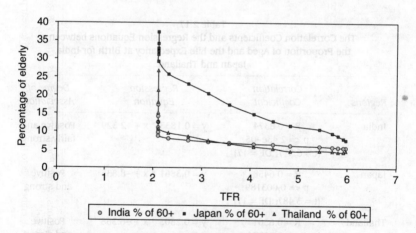

Figure 2.5 Scatter of TFR and Proportion of Elderly in Japan,
India and Thailand, 1950–2050

of Asia. However, a perusal of the Indian data indicates significant errors in the reported ages of the living population and those deceased. The state of Bihar, with its poor living conditions, has an elderly life expectancy similar to that of the MDRs of Asia.

The influence of fertility on the ageing of the Indian population can be recognised from the following calculation. In 1950, the aged (60 plus)

Table 2.16
The Correlation Coefficients and the Regression Equations between the Proportion of Aged and the Total Fertility Rates (TFRs) for India, Japan and Thailand

Regions	Correlation Coefficient	Regression Equation	Degree of Association
India	R = −0.7507 p <= 0.0004865 (t = −4.546, DF = 16)	Y = −1.609 * x + 14.37	Negative and strong
Japan	R = −0.5331 p <= 0.02342 (t = −2.521, DF = 16)	y = −17.85 * x + 52.53	Negative and not very strong
Thailand	R = −0.5902 p <= 0.01054 (t = −2.925, DF = 16)	Y = −2.02 * x + 16.43	Negative and not very strong

Table 2.17
The Correlation Coefficients and the Regression Equations between the Proportion of Aged and the Life Expectancy at Birth for India, Japan and Thailand

Regions	Correlation Coefficient	Regression Equation	Degree of Association
India	R = 0.8374 p <= 2.43e−05 (t = 6.317, DF = 17)	y = 0.1833 * x + −2.329	Positive and fairly strong
Japan	R = 0.6458 p <= 0.003189 (t = 3.487, DF = 17)	y = 0.3861 * x + −8.835	Positive and strong
Thailand	R = 0.6501 p <= 0.00294 (t = 3.528, DF = 17)	y = 0.2503 * x + −6.368	Positive and strong

constituted 5.6 per cent of the total population. This means that in a country of 357.6 million, 20.02 million were aged. In 2000, 7.6 per cent of a population of 1.01 billion turned 60 plus. The number of elderly therefore swelled to 77.03 million. In terms of percentage, this works out to be a 285 per cent increase in the number of elderly over the past five decades. If the proportion of the aged were kept

Table 2.18(a)
Life Expectancy of Males/Females at Age 60 in Various Countries of Asia

Area/Country	e_{60}^0 (M/F), 1995–2000	Area/Country/States of India	e_{60}^0 (M/F), 1995–2000	Area/Country/States of India	e_{60}^0 (M/F), 1995–2000
Asia	16/19	Western Asia	17/20	South-eastern Asia	16/18
Eastern Asia	17/20	Armenia	16/20	Brunei Darussalam	18/21
China	16/19	Azerbaijan	17/21	Cambodia	14/16
China, Hong Kong SAR (a)	20/24	Bahrain	17/20	East Timor	13/15
Democratic People's Republic of Korea	16/20	Cyprus	20/23	Indonesia	16/17
Japan	21/25	Gaza Strip	17/19	Laos	15/16
Macao	19/23	Georgia	17/21	Malaysia	17/19
Mongolia	16/20	Iraq	17/19	Myanmar	15/16
Republic of Korea	16/18	Israel	20/23	Philippines	16/18
South-central Asia	16/18	Jordan	17/19	Singapore	19/22
Afghanistan	14/14	Kuwait	18/22	Thailand	18/21
Bangladesh	15/16	Lebanon	17/18	Viet Nam	16/20
Bhutan	17/18	Oman	17/19		
India	16/17	Qatar	17/19		
Iran (Islamic Republic of)	18/19	Saudi Arabia	17/19		
Kazakhstan	15/20	Syrian Arab Republic	16/18		
Kyrgyzstan	16/20	Turkey	17/19		
Maldives	16/17	United Arab Emirates	18/20		
Nepal	15/16	Yemen	15/16		
Pakistan	17/18				
Sri Lanka	18/20				
Tajikistan	17/21				
Turkmenistan	15/19				
Uzbekistan	17/20				

Table 2.18(b)
Life Expectancy of Males/Females at Age 60 in Various States of India

Country/States of India	e^o_{60} (M/F), 1991–95	States of India	e^o_{60} (M/F), 1991–95	States of India	e^o_{60} (M/F), 1991–95
India	15.3/17.1	Himachal Pradesh	18.6/16.2	Punjab	20.7/20.8
Andhra Pradesh	14.4/15.1	Karnataka	15.0/17.1	Rajasthan	14.7/16.0
Assam	13.9/15.5	Kerala	18.1/20.6	Tamil Nadu	15.0/15.7
Bihar	16.5/16.7	Maharashtra	16.1/18.1	Uttar Pradesh	14.9/15.7
Gujarat	14.6/15.6	Madhya Pradesh	14.5/15.3	West Bengal	15.0/16.4
Haryana	17.5/18.7	Orissa	16.0/15.4		

Source: Sample Registration System (SRS) based *Abridged Life Tables, 1991–95*, Registrar General, India, New Delhi; Census of India, 1991, *Ageing Population of India: An Analysis of the 1991 Census Data*, Registrar General of India, New Delhi, 1999; United Nations, *World Population Prospects: The 1998 Revision*, Volumes I and II, Sales Nos. E.99.XIII.8 and E.99.XIII.9, New York, 1999; United Nations, *Demographic Yearbook: Historical Supplement 1948–1997 Series:R*, CD-ROM, No.28/HS-CD Sales No.E/F99.XIII.12, United Nations, New York, 2002.

Notes: e^o_{60} = life expectancy at 60 years; M/F = Male/Female Indian states are shown in bold Italics. The data for the Indian states is for the years 1991–95.

constant at 5.6 per cent in 2000, the number of elderly would have been 56.76 million. This works out to be a 184 per cent increase. In effect, 56.8 million out of the 77.03 million elderly (that is 73.7 per cent) grew from the population growth. The remaining 26.7 per cent has been due to the ageing of the population. The importance of population growth in the ageing of the population only highlights the role of fertility.

As Table 2.15 (given earlier) indicates, the TFR has dropped significantly from 5.97 children per woman in 1950–55 to the current level of 3.5 children per woman. It is also projected that this number will reach the replacement level of 2.1 children by 2010–15.[13] The Indian data indicates vast variation in the TFR among the various administrative regions. The TFR is highest in Arunachal Pradesh at 5.3, followed by Uttar Pradesh at 5.1. Projections indicate that even in 2021, the states of Arunachal Pradesh, Bihar, Jammu & Kashmir, Madhya Pradesh, Meghalaya, Nagaland, Rajasthan, Sikkim, Tripura and Uttar

Pradesh will have a TFR of above 3.0. However, the states of Kerala, Tamil Nadu and Goa have already attained the replacement level of fertility. Urban India, too, is very close to reaching that level. Further improvements in economic growth with consequent increase in employment and economic opportunities, rising aspirations about the quality of life and effective implementation of reproductive and child health programmes are expected to consolidate improvements in fertility. These changes will accelerate the ageing of the Indian population.

FERTILITY VS MORTALITY FACTORS IN POPULATION AGEING

Japanese life expectancies in recent years have surpassed those of Iceland and France (see Table 2.19). France and Iceland have recorded one of the highest male and female life expectancies in the world. This has encouraged many to consider that improved mortality is solely responsible for such rapid ageing in Japan. However, apart from mortality, there are several other factors working on ageing; the task is to decompose the various factors contributing towards ageing. However, the question of how to remove the influence of these several factors from population ageing remains.

Based on Kitagawa's methodology of decomposition,[14] we now seek to decompose the difference between the percentages of the population aged 65 and above for Japan for two different years. The annual data on the proportion of those aged 65 plus are clubbed into five-year, 10-year, 20-year, 30-year and 35-year time periods to facilitate short run and long run decomposition of data on the aged. Such a grouping also helps smooth annual ups and downs in fertility and mortality movement. Table 2.20 shows the result of the decomposition for various time periods.

A perusal of the table allows us to draw the following observations:

1. The effect of initial age distribution was most dominant in all the time periods except during the longer period of 30 and 35 years. This is the effect of previous age distribution or the cohort effect. However, it is obvious that baseline age distribution has a considerable effect on the proportion of the elderly. The effect of initial age distribution was most dominant in all the time periods, except during the longer period of 30 and 35 years. This is also known as the cohort effect.

Table 2.19
Life Expectancies for Both Sexes Combined, in Japan, Iceland and France, 1950–2000

Country	1950–55	1955–60	1960–65	1965–70	1970–75	1975–80	1980–85	1985–90	1990–95	1995–2000
Japan	63.9	66.8	69.0	71.1	73.3	75.5	76.9	78.3	79.5	80.0
France	66.5	69.6	71.0	71.5	72.4	73.7	74.7	76.0	77.1	78.1
Iceland	72.0	73.0	73.4	73.4	74.3	76.3	76.8	77.8	78.3	79.0

Source: United Nations, *World Population Prospects: The 1998 Revision*, Volumes I and II, Department of Economic and Social Affairs, Population Division, New York, 1999.

Table 2.20
Changes in the Proportion of the Aged Population in Japan,
for Different Time Periods between 1950 and 1985

Period	Population Aged 65 plus at the Beginning of the Time Period	Population Aged 65 plus at the End of the Time Period	Absolute Change	Effects of Fertility	Effects of Mortality	Effect of the Initial Age Distribution
1950–55	4.94	5.35	0.41	0.07	0.01	0.32
1955–60	5.32	5.69	0.37	0.01	0.01	0.35
1960–65	5.73	6.28	0.56	−0.04	0.07	0.53
1965–70	6.29	7.01	0.72	−0.12	0.02	0.83
1970–75	7.06	7.87	0.81	−0.01	0.04	0.78
1975–80	7.92	9.08	1.16	−0.02	0.08	1.09
1980–85	9.10	10.25	1.15	−0.05	0.09	1.11
1950–60	4.94	5.70	0.76	0.32	0.05	0.39
1955–65	5.32	6.24	0.93	0.06	0.11	0.76
1960–70	5.73	7.03	1.30	−0.06	0.28	1.09
1965–75	6.29	7.86	1.57	−0.26	0.28	1.54
1970–80	7.06	8.99	1.93	0.11	0.37	1.45
1975–85	7.92	10.22	2.30	0.01	0.42	1.88
1950–70	4.94	6.96	2.03	0.91	0.40	0.70
1955–75	5.32	7.82	2.51	0.17	0.75	1.59
1960–80	5.73	9.04	3.32	−0.05	1.24	2.13
1965–85	6.29	10.19	3.90	−0.36	1.40	2.87
1950–80	4.94	9.01	4.07	1.74	1.32	1.00
1955–85	5.32	10.18	4.86	0.52	2.04	2.30
1950–85	4.94	10.19	5.25	2.38	1.93	0.94

Source: Japan Ageing Research Center (JARC), Aging in Japan 2000, JARC, Tokyo, 1998.

2. Only during 1950–55, 1950–60, 1950–70, 1950–80 and 1950–85 was the effect of fertility higher than that of mortality. All these have 1950 as the beginning of the time period.
3. For all the other time periods where 1950 was not the base, the effect of mortality was much stronger than the effect of fertility in population ageing.

Mortality factors seem to play a dominating role in determining population ageing in Japan. Given here is one more decomposition exercise to ascertain the relative effects of fertility and mortality on population ageing. Ogawa[15] suggested a methodology to quantify the relative effects of the two. Since population ageing was very pronounced during 1950–80, the exercise is conducted for this time period. The computational method employed projects the age structure of the population of 1950, one year at a time upto the year 1980 on the basis of a set of observed age-specific fertility rates and survival ratios. Within this framework, four possible alternative projections emerge:

Variant 1: Age-specific mortality constant while fertility rates are changing.
Variant 2: Age-specific fertility constant while mortality rates are changing.
Variant 3: Both age-specific fertility and mortality rates are constant.
Variant 4: Both age-specific fertility and mortality rates are changing.

Since fertility and mortality factors generally contribute to population ageing, statistically, their relationship can be stated as: the total change in an index of the population of the aged = fertility component + mortality component + residual element.

Total change in the index of the aged population between 1950–80 = The index in 1980 under variant 4 – The index in 1980 under variant 3.

Fertility component = The index in 1980 under variant 1 – The index in 1980 under variant 3.

Mortality component = The index in 1980 under variant 2 – The index in 1980 under variant 3.

Based on these variants, the estimates of the proportion of the population aged 65 plus to the economically aged population are given in Table 2.21 for different years, starting from 1950. These measures which have been introduced as the aged dependency ratio in chapter one, are sometimes also referred to as the Index of Aged Population.

Substituting the values of each component, we get the following results. Total change = 13.14 – 8.91 = 4.23; fertility component = 10.47 – 8.91 = 1.56; mortality component = 11.19 – 8.91 = 2.28; the residual component (the migration etc.) = 4.23 – (1.56 + 2.28) = 0.39; This shows that mortality factors make a significant contribution in population ageing, more than fertility elements. Improved mortality, therefore, played a major role in the population ageing in Japan. This reconfirms our correlation results.

Table 2.21
Proportions of Aged 65 plus to the Economically Dependent (15–64)
in Japan under Alternative Variant Assumptions, 1950–80

Assumptions	1950	1960	1970	1980
Variant 1	8.27	8.47	8.97	10.47
Variant 2	8.27	8.81	9.65	11.19
Variant 3	8.27	8.47	8.70	8.91
Variant 4	8.27	8.81	8.95	13.14

Source: N. Ogawa, 'Ageing of the Population', in *Population of Japan*, Economic and Social Commission for Asia and the Pacific (ESCAP), United Nations, 1984.

Table 2.22
Age-Child Ratio in Japan under Alternative Variant Assumptions, 1950–80

Assumptions	1950	1960	1970	1980
Variant 1	13.96	18.08	26.73	30.67
Variant 2	13.96	14.77	16.52	19.69
Variant 3	13.96	14.35	15.44	16.24
Variant 4	13.96	18.69	28.64	37.32

Source: N. Ogawa, 'Ageing of the Population', in *Population of Japan*, Economic and Social Commission for Asia and the Pacific (ESCAP), United Nations, 1984.

The full impact of fertility change on population ageing, however, cannot be understood in the estimates of the proportion of aged and the aged dependency ratios. To ascertain this we need to undertake another decomposition exercise on the aged–child ratio, based on Ogawa's technique. Ogawa's technique has been described earlier, only the computations and the results are given here.

Since the total change in the index of ageing = fertility component + mortality component + residual element; *total change* in the index of ageing between 1950–80 = The index in 1980 under variant 4 – The index in 1980 under variant 3; *Fertility component* = The index in 1980 under variant 1 – The index in 1980 under variant 3. *Mortality component* = The index in 1980 under variant 2 – The index in 1980 under variant 3.

Substituting the values of each component, we get the following results. *Total change* = 37.32 − 16.24 = 21.08; *Fertility component* =

$30.67 - 16.24 = 14.43$; *Mortality component* $= 19.69 - 16.24 = 3.45$; The residual component (the migration etc.) $= 21.08 - 14.43 - 3.45 = 3.20$. This shows that fertility factors are 4.2 times more dominant than mortality factors. In terms of the aged–child ratio, one cannot deny the importance of fertility in the ageing of populations, at least in the context of Japanese populations.

For China, the decomposition exercises indicate that between 1950 and 1990, fertility factors played a more important role than mortality factors in ageing.[16] Fertility decline caused the proportion of the elderly to increase by 2.7 per cent, while mortality decline caused it to increase by 0.8 per cent. Between 1990 and 2030, on the assumption of low fertility (TFR drops to 1.6), fertility factors would still dominate more than mortality elements. However, if fertility remains at the replacement level and does not drop further (i.e., TFR = 1.8), mortality may be the more dominating factor.[17] Two reasons can be cited in defence of fertility overtaking mortality in the ageing of populations:

1. Mortality decline helps all age groups and therefore when there is a general decline in mortality, the proportion of age groups in the total population does not alter. Fertility decline, however, reduces the proportion of the youth in the total population.
2. In most countries nearing demographic transition, further mortality decline means a marginal decline in the very old age category of the population when their proportion in the total population is already very low.

DETERMINANTS OF IMPROVED MORTALITY IN JAPAN

Life expectancy in Japan improved during the post-war years essentially because of rapid declines in infant and child mortality. The primary causes of mortality in childhood are infectious and parasitic diseases. However, the use of antibiotics and other measures can take care of this problem. On the other hand, old age diseases are of an attritional and degenerative nature. Modern technology is not capable of bringing about massive improvements in this area yet. Thus, the factors which contribute to the improvements in life expectancy are also responsible for rejuvenating the population.

Life expectancy in Japan has been lengthened by reducing mortality in each age group. Table 2.23 sums up the changes in age specific mortality rates for five broad age groups, from the period 1930, for both males and females. It is possible to notice the contribution

Table 2.23
Life Expectancy and Age-specific Mortality Rates by Sex and Age in Japan for Select Years, 1930–2000

Male	1930	1950	1960	1970	1980	1990	2000
Life Expectancy	44.82	59.57	65.32	69.31	73.35	75.92	77.72
Age Specific Mortality Rate							
All Ages	18.6	11.5	8.3	7.7	6.8	7.4	8.6
0–14	53.9	24.3	10.7	5.3	2.7	1.8	1.2
15–39	39.2	24.5	11.2	8.0	5.1	4.1	3.9
40–64	116.7	83.1	64.2	51.5	37.5	32.0	28.3
65–74	158.3	130.3	113.0	98.4	68.9	52.8	47.0
75 plus	2105.9	2021.6	2283.5	1810.3	1647.6	1509.2	483.2
Female							
Life Expectancy	46.54	62.97	70.19	74.66	78.76	81.90	84.60
Age Specific Mortality Rate							
All Ages	17.7	10.4	7.0	6.2	5.6	6.0	6.8
0–14	50.8	22.4	8.7	3.9	2.0	1.3	1.0
15–39	45.5	22.2	7.9	4.4	2.7	2.0	1.8
40–64	80.9	60.3	40.2	29.7	19.4	14.6	12.7
65–74	112.0	92.0	73.7	58.5	38.2	26.3	20.0
75 plus	1874.3	1627.4	1810.0	1744.7	1403.5	1186.7	311.4

Source: Calculated by the author from Ministry of Health, Labour and Welfare, *The 18th Life Tables*, and *Abridged Life Tables for 2000*, and *Vital Statistics of Japan*, Statistics and Information Department, Minister's Secretariat, Ministry of Health, Labour and Welfare, Japan. The demographic data may also be seen on the official website of National Institute of Population and Social Security Research, http://www.ipss.go.jp/English/S_D_I/Indip.html#t_5.

Note: Life expectancy data for 1930 relates to average for 1926–30, that for 1950 is average of 1950–52.

of each age group to the lengthening of life expectancies because of the decrease in mortality within that group.

Table 2.23 indicates that between 1955–60, mortality reductions in the early age group (0–14) contributed overwhelmingly to the lengthening of life expectancies in Japan, for both males and females. However, with time, the role of reduced early age and youth mortality in the lengthening of life expectancies decreases and that of higher ages increases. For example, reduced mortality in the age group 75 plus contributed negatively in the lengthening of life expectancies during 1950–60, but its contribution in 1980 was extremely high.

Over the years the causes of death in Japan have changed. Those diseases, which were once responsible for high mortality during the years immediately after the Second World War, were much less important in the later part of the last century. Table 2.24(a) and Table 2.24(b)

Table 2.24(a)
Male Life Expectancy and Percentages of Deaths by Cause from Ten Important Causes of Death in Japan, 1935–2000

	1935	1950	1960	1970	1980	1990	1995	2000
Life expectancy	46.92	59.57	65.32	69.31	73.35	75.92	76.38	77.72
Cause of Death								
All causes of death	100.0	100.0	100.0	100.0	100.0	100.0	100.0	100.0
Malignant neoplasmas	4.2	7.0	13.5	17.3	23.9	29.4	31.8	34.1
Heart disease	3.3	5.6	9.2	11.9	16.4	18.4	13.9	13.7
Cerebrovascular disease	10.4	11.2	20.9	25.0	20.9	13.0	13.9	12.0
Pneumonia	9.4	6.0	5.3	3.9	4.8	8.7	8.5	8.9
Accidents	3.4	5.1	7.9	8.5	5.4	5.0	5.6	4.8
Suicide	1.4	2.1	3.0	2.3	3.3	2.8	2.8	4.1
Liver diseases	0.8	1.0	2.1	2.8	3.4	3.0	2.3	2.1
Diabetes melitus	0.2	0.2	0.4	1.0	1.0	1.0	1.4	1.2
Hypertensive disease	...	1.0	1.9	2.2	1.7	0.8	0.6	0.4
Tuberculosis	11.1	13.9	5.2	2.8	1.2	0.6	0.5	0.4

Table 2.24(b)
Female Life Expectancy and Percentages of Deaths by Cause from
Ten Important Causes of Death in Japan, 1935–2000

	1935	1950	1960	1970	1980	1990	1995	2000
Life expectancy	49.63	62.97	70.19	74.66	78.76	81.90	82.85	84.60
Cause of Death								
All causes of death	100.0	100.0	100.0	100.0	100.0	100.0	100.0	100.0
Malignant neoplasmas	4.4	7.3	13.0	16.3	20.6	23.1	24.6	26.7
Heart disease	3.6	6.2	10.2	13.4	17.9	22.2	16.5	17.1
Cerebrovascular disease	9.2	12.2	21.6	26.0	24.3	17.1	18.3	15.9
Pneumonia	8.7	6.0	5.3	4.0	4.3	7.9	8.8	9.2
Accidents	1.5	2.1	2.8	3.3	2.4	2.6	4.1	3.3
Suicide	1.0	1.5	2.6	2.1	2.3	2.1	1.7	2.0
Liver diseases	0.6	0.9	1.6	1.9	1.7	1.7	1.3	1.1
Diabetes melitus	0.2	0.2	0.5	1.2	1.3	1.3	1.7	1.3
Hypertensive disease	...	1.2	2.4	3.0	2.8	1.6	1.2	0.9
Tuberculosis	11.6	12.9	3.7	1.5	0.5	0.2	0.2	0.2

Source: Calculated by the author from Ministry of Health, Labour and Welfare, *The 18th Life Tables*, and *Abridged Life Tables for 2000* and *Vital Statistics of Japan*, Statistics and Information Department, Minister's Secretariat, Ministry of Health, Labour and Welfare. The demographic data is also available on the official website of the National Institute of Population and Social Security Research, http://www.ipss.go.jp/English/S_D_I/Indip.html#t_5.

Note: Life expectancy data for 1935 relates to average for 1935–36

provide life expectancy and percentage cases of death for both males and females between 1935 and 2000. These tables also facilitate our understanding of the role played by improvements in mortality reductions by each cause of death towards lengthening of life expectancy. Between 1950 and 1970, declines in death from infectious and parasitic diseases were the most important cause behind the improvements in life expectancy. However, later on, the declines in mortality from non-infectious or degenerative types of diseases have become much more important.

In the years following the Second World War, improvements in deaths from tuberculosis, gastro-enteritis and pneumonia contributed enormously towards higher life expectancy. Their role was marginalised in later years when improvements in heart disease, cerebrovascular disease, hypertensive disease and diabetes contributed to the improved life expectancy for both males and females in a big way .

FERTILITY DECLINE AND ITS DETERMINANTS IN JAPAN

Our foregoing discussion shows that reduced fertility has played an important role in determining population ageing in Japan.

In this section, we will investigate the factors responsible for this massive fertility decline in Japan. Table 2.15 (given earlier) gives us estimates and projections on the TFR of Japan from 1950–2050 based on United Nations' medium variant estimations and projections. Table 2.25 provides us with a much wider fertility picture of Japan.

Whatever estimates we decide to use, there is no denying the fact that the TFR in Japan has gone down heavily. In addition, fertility has reached a level lower than the replacement level, i.e., the level of fertility at which a couple has only enough children to replace themselves, or about two children per couple. Speaking more technically, a Net Reproduction Rate (NRR) of 1 means that each generation of mothers has exactly enough daughters to replace itself in the population. In Table 2.25, we have underlined the year 1974 as it is from this year that the TFR in Japan has been lower than the replacement level. The lowest TFR recorded was in 1998 at 1.38. If the current TFR continues, the Japanese population should become extinct before the next millennium. However, Japan possesses several characteristics of a fertility-friendly country:

♦ Relatively weak feminist movement, compared to other developed nations;
♦ labour force participation by married Japanese women; even though this is on the rise it is much lower than other developed countries;
♦ stable marriage and relatively low divorce rates;
♦ a ban on oral contraceptives for medical reasons.

Table 2.25
Fertility Indicators in Japan, 1925–2000

Year	Births ('000)	Crude Birth Rate	Total Fertility Rate	Net Reproduction Rate	Year	Births ('000)	Crude Birth Rate	Total Fertility Rate	Net Reproduction Rate
1925	2,086	34.9	5.11	1.56	1964	1,717	17.7	2.05	0.96
1930	2,085	32.4	4.71	1.52	1965	1,824	18.6	2.14	1.01
1937	2,181	30.9	4.36	1.49	1970	1,934	18.8	2.13	1.00
1940	2,116	29.4	4.11	1.44	1971	2,001	19.2	2.16	1.02
1947	2,679	34.3	4.54	1.72	1972	2,039	19.3	2.14	1.01
1948	2,682	33.5	4.40	1.76	1973	2,092	19.4	2.14	1.01
1949	2,697	33.0	4.32	1.75	1974	2,030	18.6	2.05	0.97
1950	2,338	28.1	3.65	1.51	1975	1,901	17.1	1.91	0.91
1951	2,138	25.3	3.26	1.39	1976	1,833	16.3	1.85	0.88
1952	2,005	23.4	2.98	1.29	1977	1,755	15.5	1.80	0.86
1953	1,868	21.5	2.69	1.18	1978	1,709	14.9	1.79	0.86
1954	1,770	20.0	2.48	1.09	1979	1,643	14.2	1.77	0.84
1955	1,731	19.4	2.37	1.06	1980	1,577	13.6	1.75	0.84
1956	1,665	18.4	2.22	0.99	1981	1,529	13.0	1.74	0.83
1957	1,567	17.2	2.04	0.92	1982	1,515	12.8	1.77	0.85
1958	1,653	18.0	2.11	0.96	1983	1,509	12.7	1.80	0.86
1959	1,626	17.5	2.04	0.94	1984	1,490	12.5	1.81	0.87
1960	1,606	17.2	2.00	0.92	1985	1,432	11.9	1.76	0.85
1961	1,589	16.9	1.96	0.91	1986	1,383	11.4	1.72	0.83
1962	1,619	17.0	1.98	0.92	1987	1,347	11.1	1.69	0.81
1963	1,660	17.3	2.00	0.94	1988	1,314	10.8	1.66	0.80

(continued)

Table 2.25
(Continued)

Year	Births ('000)	Crude Birth Rate	Total Fertility Rate	Net Reproduction Rate	Year	Births ('000)	Crude Birth Rate	Total Fertility Rate	Net Reproduction Rate
1989	1,247	10.2	1.57	0.76	1995	1,187	9.6	1.42	0.69
1990	1,228	10.0	1.54	0.74	1996	1,207	9.7	1.43	0.69
1991	1,223	9.9	1.54	0.74	1997	1,192	9.5	1.39	0.67
1992	1,209	9.8	1.50	0.72	1998	1,203	9.6	1.38	0.67
1993	1,185	9.8	1.46	0.70	1999	1,177	9.4	1.34	0.65
1994	1,238	10.0	1.50	0.72	2000	1,170	9.5	1.36	0.65

Source: (i) Statistics and Information Department, *Vital Statistics of Japan*, Minister's Secretariat, Ministry of Health, Labour and Welfare; (ii) National Institute of Population and Social Security Research, *Latest Demographic Statistics*.

Notes: For 1947–72 excluding the Okinawa prefecture. The demographic data may also be seen on the official website of Naional Institute of Population and Social Security Research, http://www.ipss.go.jp/English/S_D_I/Indip.html#t_5.

Japanese society, however, is constrained by many factors that have created an environment of low fertility:

♦ Increasing competition at all levels;
♦ unpopularity of marriage;
♦ mass consumption society;
♦ women against fertility.

Let us elaborate on each of these to appreciate fully, their role in reducing fertility levels in Japan.

Increasing Competition at all Levels

Since the days of the Meiji Restoration in 1868 when Japan looked forward to continuous economic development, scarcity of resources has dominated the Japanese planning process. Japan has no oil reserves and produces very little iron ore. Most of the food requirements of the country are met through imports. Despite these constraints the Japanese are unstoppable in their efforts to develop. Among other factors, the deeply rooted doctrine of Confucianism has played an important role here. The role of Confucianism in Japanese society is similar to that of Protestantism in Europe during the Industrial Revolution. The development–motivating elements that Max Weber found in Protestantism can also be seen in Confucianism.[18] This doctrine, too, emphasises the ethical value of hard work, asceticism, frugality and regularity in the daily conduct of life. When Japan began to feel the scarcity of resources, people understood that only the fittest could survive. The result was the emergence of fierce competition at every level of life. Rigorous entrance examinations for high ranking universities and for large and prestigious corporations become common. Severe and ruthless examinations become an intrinsic part of Japanese life. Under such circumstances, marriage become unpopular, and children, financially and psychologically expensive.

Unpopularity of Marriage

Marriage has become highly unpopular in Japan. The age of individuals at first marriage is among the highest in the world. According to

Vital Statistics, 1998, the mean age at first marriage was 28.6 years for males and 26.7 years for females during that year. For females, the mean age was 23 years in 1950 and 25.2 years in 1980. A higher age at marriage shortens the reproductive span of married couples. According to the 1995 census, only 12.2 per cent of females and 6.2 per cent of males in the age group 20–24 were married. Even in the age group 24–29, considered to be the most reproductive age group, only 48.6 per cent of females and 31.5 per cent of males were married. Fecundability starts declining from age 30 and by 35, it becomes three-fourths of the full capacity of the 24–29 level. Late entry into marital life, therefore, acts as a biological depressant to fertility. But why is marriage so unpopular?

1. Housing is extremely costly. No male is expected to marry unless he has his own accommodation.
2. Weeding ceremonies are elaborate and expensive. Girls are also required to bring with them dowry and other expensive items after marriage.
3. The economic necessity to get married has been weakened with more women taking up employment.
4. The new system of the lover's hotel where Japanese couples are able to enjoy sex without getting married is on the rise.
5. In the young age group of 18–35, the males outnumber the females and this demographic advantage allows them to be choosy about their choice of a marital partner. Japanese women want their men to have the 3 Hs: Higher wealth/income, Higher height and Higher qualification.
6. The traditional matchmaking system, popularly known as *miai kekkon,* has become very weak with the growth of urbanisation and the accompanying increase in anonymity and individualistic attitude, lack of community ties etc.

Mass Consumption Society

Eighty per cent of Japanese are from the middle class. Income differentials among families are also very low. Durable consumption goods are status symbols in society. A family comprising more than two children is considered to be a hindrance; one that would be unable to attain a status centred around the holding and use of expensive consumer durable goods.

Women against Fertility

Although Confucianism introduced the competitive spirit in Japanese society and helped people seek attainment of the highest possible levels of efficiency, the doctrine envisaged no special status for females. With the rapid spread of education and the acceptance of jobs outside the home, women could no longer accept themselves simply as childbearing machines. The women's protest came silently in the form of the anti-machismo movement. The current unprecedented decline of fertility simply reflects the disenchantment of women with the current state and mode of family, marriage and reproduction, which are male-dominated and often patriarchal.

DETERMINANTS OF FERTILITY DECLINE

There are six major theories on fertility decline. These are:

1. There is the classical demographic transition theory of Thompson and Notestein described earlier. This theory attributes fertility decline to changes in social life that accompany, and are presumed to be caused by, industrialisation and urbanisation. These changes initially produce a decline in mortality, which sets the stage for fertility decline by increasing the survival of children and hence the size of families. Urbanisation and industrialisation also create a way of life in which rearing more than a few children is expensive enough to discourage most parents from having large families. This theory, however, is not consistent with the fertility experiences of Asia and Latin America where fertility transition has taken place even within the traditional agrarian set-up.
2. Lesthaeghe[19] tried to incorporate economic modernisation within the demographic transition theory. According to him rising affluence and secularisation brings with it economic modernisation which causes a shift in values towards individualism and self-fulfilment. This theory fits very well with the data from Europe, but not with data from the developing countries where fertility is declining despite little apparent change in traditional values.
3. Caldwell's theory of wealth flows attributes fertility decline to the emotional nucleation of the family.[20] This change may come through either economic or cultural forces. At the centre of the

theory is the idea that nucleation makes children, not parents, the net economic beneficiaries of family life. Caldwell calls this process a reversal of 'wealth flows'. This theory finds ready application in sub-Saharan Africa where extended families are strong and lineage elders are likely to benefit from high fertility. However, this theory fails to explain fertility transition in many parts of East Asia, which occurred even within the extended family system. The theory cannot be applied to Western Europe either, where family nucleation existed for centuries before fertility decline.[21]

4. The neo-classical microeconomic theory of fertility as developed by Leibenstein,[22] Becker,[23] and Schultz,[24] emphasises three proximate determinants of couples' fertility choices: (a) relative costs of children versus other goods; (b) couples' income; and (c) their preference for children versus competing forms of consumption. This theory provides a quantifiable framework for investigating fertility change, but fails to study the effects of institutional and environmental conditions on the determinants of fertility.

5. Easterlin elaborates the microeconomic fertility model by adding to it a sociological variable, the supply of children.[25] There are three proximate determinants in the Easterlin model: (a) the supply of children (i.e., the number of children that parents would bear in the absence of fertility regulation); (b) demand for children (i.e., the number of surviving children they would like to have); and (c) the costs of fertility regulation where the costs are psychic, social and monetary costs. This framework is useful for quantitative determination of fertility decline. Table 2.26 summarises the factors that help increase or decrease the supply of, and demand for, children in the four stages of transition.

6. The ideational theory of Cleland and Wilson[26] attributes the timing of fertility transition to the diffusion of information and new social norms about birth control. The diffusion of ideas and the processes through which diffusion occurs—social interaction and influence—are increasingly being recognised as important for the timing of fertility decline.

From this review of the important theories on fertility decline, the factors which play important roles in fertility transition can be summarised as follows:

1. Fertility transitions occur when a variety of institutional, cultural and environmental conditions, together, motivate a substantial portion of people to adopt fertility control measures.

Table 2.26
Factors Influencing Increase or Decrease in Supply of and Demand
for Children during Demographic Transition

Stage of Transition	Factors Influencing Increase in Supply of Children	Factors Influencing Decrease in Supply of Children	Factors Influencing Increase in Demand for Children	Factors Influencing Decrease in Demand for Children
I	Early marriage; high marriage rate	Poor health of women (sterility); prevalence of breast feeding; post-partum abstinence	Economic contribution of children; parents' desire for male children; high infant mortality	
II	Improved health of women			Decrease in infant mortality; school attendance of children
III	Decline in breast feeding; decline in practice of post-partum abstinence	Higher marriage age		Accelerated decrease of infant mortality; increased school attendance of children; access to family planning
IV	Use of milk substitutes as baby food	Later marriage; lower marriage rate		Low infant mortality; change in status of women; favourable attitude to family planning

2. Within a given geographic/cultural region, the first country to undergo fertility transition is likely to experience cultural, social structural and environmental changes. This country may act as an example for the rest in the region. In such a case, the follower countries might not go through such structural changes.

3. The speed with which lower fertility concepts travel from one place to another depends on the educational level of the people, the development of communication infrastructure, social networking of people, the extent to which the common language is used, and the nature of the local and national leadership.

4. Mortality decline is usually a necessary condition for fertility decline but that may not be a sufficient condition for that decline.

5. The actual level of fertility in a region depends on the availability and acceptability of control mechanisms.

POPULATION AGEING AND MIGRATION

The earlier discussion establishes that population ageing in Japan has been caused by a decline in both fertility and mortality. However, in a study at the sub-national level in Japan, this relationship is found to be insignificant. The correlation coefficient between the degree of ageing and TFR among 47 prefectures of Japan has been found to be only 0.46 in 1990. For the same year, the correlation coefficient between the degree of ageing and female life expectancy has been found to be (-0.22). On the contrary, it was recognised that the correlation between the degree of ageing and net migration rate for 1985–90 was higher (0.64) than that for fertility and mortality indicators. Thus, migration is an important determinant of ageing in sub-national populations such as prefectures and municipalities.

One cannot deny the importance of migration in population ageing. The volume of such migration depends on the levels of urbanisation already achieved, economic conditions in urban and rural areas, accessible transportation and communication, and social factors such as education, housing and social services. The ageing effect of such migration depends on the causes of such migration and the conditions under which such migration takes place. If the country is predominantly agricultural and the level of urbanisation low, net migration from the rural to urban areas would also be low. As the economy develops, either through the improved productivity of agriculture or industrial development, then net migration to the urban areas or the level of urbanisation rises quickly. When the level of urbanisation reaches a high level, the rural-to-urban migration begins to taper off, primarily because of the shrinking size of the rural population from which such migration originates.

The major theory that operates behind the rural to urban flow of people is the demographic push and pull. In the early stage of demographic transition, when improvements in fertility lag behind those in mortality, population expands. Such improvements in mortality and also in fertility generally come through industrialisation. The beginning of industrialisation also indicates the beginning of the disparity between rural and urban areas. People begin to leave rural areas to alleviate the pressure on the land. This is push-oriented migration. On the other hand, when economic development takes off and the need for additional labour force becomes more intense in urban areas, there is a shift of population towards the urban centres. This is called pull-oriented migration.[27] This idealised model, which hardly describes the real experience of developing countries, has been the subject of continuous modification and refinement. However, the critical point here is that, in this scenario, migration is generally perceived to be positive for development and, presumably, beneficial for the ageing rural populations.

This simple model ignores the fact that it is usually the youngest and the most skilful who tend to leave their villages for the towns. This, in turn, offers scope for a second interpretation on migration and development. Migration not only exacerbates the ageing effects of fertility decline by removing the youthful and most energetic cohorts, but it also reduces rural productivity by removing those with the most productive skills. The conditions of the rural elderly become worse with the weakening of their support systems within the family and also because of fewer number of opportunities for economically productive activities. In this scenario, migration is detrimental to development and is likely to lead to the erosion of rural production and deterioration in the welfare of the elderly village populations. The exodus of the youthful cohorts ultimately reduces the capacity of the village to reproduce itself. This creates the danger of depopulation as the remaining elderly populations die.

There is an element of truth in both viewpoints depending upon the development potential of the area concerned and upon the stage of a hypothesised development sequence. This sequence is related to the phases of the demographic transition as reflected in the patterns of fertility and mortality decline. However, although all societies are experiencing a transition towards ageing populations, this transition is not uniform with respect to pattern and impact. At the same time, ageing transition depends on the pattern of rural-to-urban migration. In countries where rural-to-urban migration is familial in nature, the age composition of the migrant population may not differ very much from that of the rural population. The urban population will grow because of the new flow of people but this will not effect the age composition of the population there. On the other hand, if the migration were age and sex selective, the immediate results would be one of rejuvenation of the population, as the migrants tend to be younger than the resident population. When the migrants stay in the urban centres for long, they grow old and contribute to the growing elderly in due course. This prospect of the ageing of the urban population is reinforced if urban growth and migration slows down at some point. Those migrants who came to the urban areas during the peak of industrialisation remain as an unusually large cohort of population and cause a sudden ageing of the population structure in urban areas at a later date.

However, the impact on rural-to-urban migration on ageing has been poorly developed in demographic literature. The methodological difficulties relating to the definition of rural and urban areas and the paucity of suitable data are the major factors hindering any careful study on the impact of migration on ageing. While each country makes a distinction between rural and urban areas, the distinction between rural and urban populations, however, is not clear. In every census and large-scale survey, respondents are allocated to a rural or urban area of residence, depending upon rules of enumeration, giving the impression that it is within this area that they will live and work. In reality, there are continuous short-term movements of human circulation between rural and urban areas, not reflected in the long-term, rural-to-urban migration; these are migrations that are paralleled by flow of goods and money in the form of remittances. People living in the urban sector very often return to their villages at short-term intervals and regularly send remittances in cash or kind back to their families in the rural sector. The short-term circulation of people is generally not captured in the majority of the censuses or large-scale surveys. Hence, simply comparing the population structure of a rural area, as derived from such data sources, may give a very misleading impression of the rural-urban population movements.

This problem is more acute in those countries where the population is enumerated on the basis of where it 'usually lives' and significant numbers are recorded in the places of registration rather than where the people normally live. This problem is particularly felt in China, Indonesia, the Philippines and Thailand. A more refined definition of migration adopted in the National Migration Survey of Thailand, for example, raised the proportion of the migrant population of Bangkok from 8 per cent to 22 per cent when the survey results were compared with those of the 1990 census of population.[28] It is known that the populations of Bangkok change by about 10 per cent, between the wet and dry season.

In all the South-east and East Asian countries for which data exists, the elderly populations of the rural areas are more in number than those of urban areas (see Table 2.27). The differences between the proportions of populations 60 years of age and above in urban and rural sectors are very high in Japan and the Republic of Korea, the two most developed countries in the region. The Republic of Korea is perhaps an extreme case, with almost one in five of the rural population classified as elderly, compared with only about one in every 14 in the urban population.

Table 2.27
Indices of Ageing by Distance from the Metropolitan Centre, 1995

	Percent in Elderly	Aged Dependency	Elderly Child Ratio
Tokyo	11.5	15.6	78.6
30–40 Km	10.2	13.7	66.3
40–50 Km	11.6	16.0	73.3
50–60 km	12.7	18.0	74.8
60–70 Km	15.5	22.8	93.9
Osaka	12.6	17.5	82.0
30–40 Km	12.7	17.9	77.5
40–50 Km	14.7	21.0	94.7
Nagoya	12.3	17.3	75.1
20–30 Km	10.9	15.1	62.5
30–40 Km	13.5	19.3	79.6
40–50 Km	15.7	23.4	934

Source: Japan Bureau of Statistics, 1995 Population Census of Japan.

In Japan, the *shi* areas, or the areas consisting of *shi* municipalities are regarded as urban areas, while the *gun* areas or those of *machi* or *cho* and *mura* or *son* municipalities are regarded as rural areas. In

1995, the percentage of total population in the elderly ages of 65 and above were recorded at 19 per cent for *gun* areas against the 13.7 per cent for *shi* areas. In addition, DIDs, or Densely Inhabited Districts known as urban areas for statistical purposes, indicated that 12.5 per cent of the total population in these areas were in the elderly ages, whereas the non-DIDs, or the areas not included in DIDs, recorded them at 18.3 per cent in 1995. Interestingly, the percentage of the total population in the elderly ages of 65 and above in 1990 were recorded at 21.8 per cent for municipalities with less than 5,000 inhabitants; this number decreased gradually with the increase in the population size of the municipality. Population ageing also increases beyond a 30-km radii from the centre of the major cities of Tokyo, Osaka and Nagoya (see Table 2.27).

In the Asian countries under consideration, fertility, while declining overall, is generally higher in the rural sectors as compared to the urban sectors (see Table 2.28). If only fertility declined, other things remaining unchanged, population ageing ought to have been more in the urban areas than in the rural. However, other factors are not equal, and migration from rural to urban areas is clearly critical in transferring youthful cohorts from the villages to the cities to generate the observed patterns. *Urban areas are made youthful by accretion and rural areas age as residual populations move through the process of migration.*

See Table 2.29 for patterns of urban and rural fertility in various countries of Asia for the mid-1970s.

It is also interesting to observe that in China and Viet Nam, where there is little observed difference between urban and rural patterns of ageing, the censuses there severely underestimate the volume of population mobility. The census enumeration through the system of household registration tends to omit vast numbers of the 'floating' population, who work in the larger towns outside their households. As most of these 'floaters' are young adults, the impact of migration upon the age structure of the rural populations of these countries is underestimated. However, the volume of remittances sent by these floating people to the villages may be an important factor in the continued viability of rural economies and in the support of the increasingly elderly populations.

Along with the exodus of the young adult cohorts from the rural population, there is also a return movement of retirees who have spent several years away, either overseas or in the urban sector to the rural areas. Together they reinforce the population ageing of rural

Table 2.28
Proportion of Elderly in Urban and Rural Populations in
Various Asian Countries

Countries	Proportion of Urban Population to Total Population (percentage)	Proportion of Elderly (60 years and above) to Total Urban Population (percentage)	Proportion of Elderly (60 years and above) to Total Rural Population (percentage)
Japan (1995)	78.1	19.5	25.4
India (1991)	25.7	6.3	7.6
Republic of Korea (1995)	78.5	6.9	17.9
Brunei Darussalam (1991)	66.6	3.5	5.3
China (1990)	26.2	8.1	8.7
Indonesia (1995)	35.9	5.6	7.4
Malaysia (1991)	50.6	5.3	6.7
Philippines (1990)	48.6	5.0	5.5
Thailand (1990)	18.7	6.3	7.7
Cambodia (1996)	14.4	5.0	5.4
Laos PDR (1995)	17.1		5.7
Viet Nam (1992)	19.5	7.4	7.7

Source: United Nations *Demographic Yearbook, 1998, Demographic Yearbook 1996,* New York, Department of Economic and Social Affairs, ST/ESA/STAT/SER. R/27, Table 8; Incomplete data for Laos PDR from 'A demographic perspective on women in development in Cambodia, Laos People's Democratic Republic, Myanmar and Viet Nam', *Asian Population Studies Series No. 148,* Economic and Social Commission for Asia and the Pacific, ST/ESCAP/1869, Table 39 New York.

areas. The 'return migrants' contribute to the replenishment of older age cohorts and by returning aggravate the potential old age support problems in the villages vis-à-vis local sources of labour. However, the 'return migrants', although older, often also bring back to their village communities, wealth and knowledge in the form of acquired skills and other resources, such as pensions. This in turn helps create a climate for potential investment in small businesses or land development.

A detailed discussion on the inter-linkage between population ageing and migration, in the context of Asian countries, however, takes place in chapter five where the social and economic status of the aged is looked into in greater depth.

Table 2.29
Patterns of Urban and Rural Fertility, Various Countries (mid-1970s)

	Total Fertility Rate: Rural	Total Fertility Rate: Other Urban	Total Fertility Rate: Major Urban
Indonesia	4.9	4.3	4.6
Malaysia	5.0	4.5	3.5
Philippines	6.0	4.0	3.5
Republic of Korea	5.0	4.2	3.3
Thailand	5.0	3.6	2.5

Source: United Nations, *Fertility Behaviour in the Context of Development*, Department of International Economic and Social Affairs, Population Studies No. 100, ST/ESA/SER.A/100, p.193, New York, 1987.

Note: The three categories, Rural, Urban and Major Urban, come from definitions adopted in the World Fertility Survey. Urban areas were identified through individual national definitions, while Major Urban centres included cities which exceeded the one million population, all national capitals regardless of population, and the largest city in any country where no city exceeding one million inhabitants existed.

DETERMINANTS OF MORTALITY DECLINE

During the period 1950–55, Asian nations exhibited life expectancies at birth that were around 10 years below those of Latin America and the Caribbean,[29] while the mortality situation closely resembled that of Africa.[30] However, by 1995–2000, Asia was no longer the same on mortality indicators. The Crude Death Rate (CDR) was lower than that of Europe.[31] The life expectancy in Eastern Asia was almost close to that of Europe.[32] Not only that, one Asian nation, Japan, attained the highest healthy life expectancy in the world. During the last half-century, Asia's success with regard to the improvement in life expectancy and decrease in the Infant Mortality Rate (IMR) was by far the best among all the major geographic regions of the world. This is evident from Table 2.30. Not only that, it is also expected that in future too, most health improvements will be in Asia. Although Africa as a continent will do better, the developing regions of Asia will exhibit immense improvement, both on life expectancy and infant mortality. A comparative picture has been drawn in Table 2.31, based on the United Nations Medium Variant Projections.

Historically, life expectancy in populous Asian countries like China, Japan and India, for whom data is available, was very low compared

Table 2.30
Mortality Change in Major World Regions and Asia, 1950–55 and 1995–2000

Regions/Countries	Expectation of Life at Birth			Infant Mortality Rate (per thousand)		
	1950–55	1995–2000	Growth per Annum	1950–55	1995–2000	Decline per Annum
Asia	**41.3**	**64.5**	**0.5**	**180**	**63**	**2.6**
Eastern Asia	42.9	71.0	0.6	181	38	3.2
South-central Asia	39.3	62.3	0.5	186	73	2.5
South-eastern Asia	40.5	65.7	0.6	154	46	2.4
Western Asia	45.2	68.0	0.5	189	51	3.1
Africa	**37.8**	**51.4**	**0.3**	**179**	**87**	**2.0**
Europe	**66.2**	**73.3**	**0.2**	**72**	**12**	**1.3**
Latin America and Caribbean	**51.4**	**69.2**	**0.2**	**126**	**36**	**2.0**
North America	69.0	76.9	0.2	29	7	0.5
Afghanistan	31.6	43.5	0.26	227	160	1.49
Bangladesh	36.6	55.6	0.42	180	91	1.97
Cambodia	39.4	51.6	0.27	165	116	1.09
China	40.8	68.4	0.6	195	46	3.3
India	38.7	60.3	0.5	190	78	2.5
Japan	63.9	79.5	0.4	51	4	1.0
Laos People's Democratic Republic	37.8	50.7	0.3	180	115	1.44
Nepal	36.3	54.6	0.34	210	96	2.53

Source: United Nations, *World Population Prospects: The 1998 Revision, Volume I: Comprehensive Tables*, Department of Economic and Social Affairs, Population Division, New York, 1999.

Table 2.31
UN Forecasted Mortality Change in Major World Regions and Asia, 2000–2050

Regions/Countries	Expectation of Life at Birth			Infant Mortality Rate (per thousand)		
	2000–2005	2045–50	Improvement in Years	1995–2000	2040–50	Improvement
Asia	67.4	77.1	9.7	57	19	38
Eastern Asia	72.3	79.7	7.4	38	13	25
South-central Asia	63.3	74.9	11.6	73	25	48
South-eastern Asia	67.0	77.3	10.3	46	12	34
Western Asia	70.0	78.5	8.5	51	12	39
Africa	51.3	69.5	18.2	87	40	47
Europe	73.7	80.8	7.1	12	6	6
Latin America and Caribbean	70.4	77.8	7.4	36	11	25
North America	77.7	82.7	5.0	7	5	2
Oceania	74.4	80.6	6.2	24	8	16
MDRs	75.6	82.1	6.5	9	5	4
LDRs	64.1	75.0	10.9	63	20	43
Afghanistan	43.2	62.4	19.2	151	68	83
Bangladesh	60.7	75.0	14.3	79	15	64
Cambodia	56.2	72.2	16.0	103	22	81
China	71.2	79.0	7.8	41	14	27
India	64.2	75.4	11.2	72	27	45

(continued)

Table 2.31
(Continued)

Regions/Countries	Expectation of Life at Birth			Infant Mortality Rate (per thousand)		
	2000–2005	2045–50	Improvement in Years	1995–2000	2040–50	Improvement
Japan	81.5	88.0	6.5	4	4	0
Laos People's Democratic Republic	54.5	72.2	17.7	93	24	69
Nepal	59.8	74.9	15.1	83	15	68

Source: United Nations, *World Population Prospects: The 1998 Revision, Volume I: Comprehensive Tables,* Department of Economic and Social Affairs, Population Division, New York, 1999; United Nations, 'World Population Ageing 1950–2050', Population Division, Department of Economic and Social Affairs, ST/ESA/SER.A/207, New York, 2002.

to Europe and North America. One reason for this was the great population densities of these countries, which facilitated the rise and spread of epidemic diseases. The epidemics that occurred in Europe were known to have travelled from Asia. The other reason was the low level of income of the people.

The first prominent measure of 'good health for all' was the attainment of a life expectancy of 50 years. While most developed countries in the West had reached this level before the beginning of the 20th century, Japan was the first Asian country to reach this level in 1945. Korea reached it 10 years later; India in 1970 and Bangladesh in 1983.[33]

In most of Asia, mortality has been falling throughout this century as a result of infectious and parasitic diseases, tuberculosis and other respiratory diseases, together with diarrhoea and dysentery. Earlier tuberculosis was a major killer; malaria, cholera, smallpox, beriberi were no less merciful. However, these diseases have now been defeated by the rising standards of living almost all over the world.

These early successes were achieved not so much by improvements in health services, but more by the ability of modern transport to alleviate famine by getting food to the affected areas, and by sanitary engineering and strong administration. For example, in the late 19th century, the plague was conquered in Taiwan through deep burial, house burning and rat-catching. Similar systematic methods were used against malaria and other diseases, but the level of success differed between diseases and regions. In the years immediately after the Second World War, huge gains in life expectancy were achieved, apparently in most countries in Asia. The development of antibiotics and powerful pesticides and a new determination that health and social welfare should be placed higher on the political agenda by most of colonial administrations and the colonised people played a major role.

Between 1946 and 1953 Sri Lanka's life expectancy jumped 12 years, and between 1956 and 1971 that of the state of Kerala in India also increased by 12 years. Caldwell[34] concludes that this was possible because these societies were fairly well educated and egalitarian with considerable empowerment of women. The health system was sensitive to the needs of the poor, uneducated or inarticulate and respectful towards women. Knodel and Jones[35] also found women's education and empowerment to be significant determinants of decline in mortality in Asian regions. The outlook towards death is another important element. Only an educated and cultured society can regard death as the worst possible outcome of any life, qualitatively different from all other possibilities in life. It is education which make individuals feel that they have to work hard to minimise mortality risks that not only affect them, but also the people close to them.[36] Such realisation makes mortality decline a self-sustaining process. Caldwell[37] also identified an alternative route to low mortality, the socialist one, that met with notable success in the USSR in the 1920s and 1930s, and greater success in China, Cuba and Viet Nam during the last 50 years.

DETERMINANTS OF MORTALITY

Mortality depends on the various social and economic acheivements of society. Income has long been considered an important parameter. But subsequent research not only identified several other variables but also refined the concept of income; Social scientists these days are very sceptical about using per capita income, instead, they have found Purchasing Power Parity (PPP) and the HDI to be more useful. To establish the quantitative linkage between mortality and various other social and economic parameters, Table 2.32 combines data on mortality along with other major social and economic variables which is purported to influence mortality. Table 2.33 sums up the correlation coefficient between life expectancy/infant mortality rate with various socioeconomic and demographic variables.

Purchasing Power Parity

A perusal of mortality data in relation to the data on material standard of living, shown by the PPP reveals some very interesting facts. Every country with a life expectancy below 66 years in the period 1995–2000 had a per capita purchasing power of less than $ 3,500 (in 1997 US dollars), while every country with a life expectancy of above 75 years had a per capita purchasing power of over $16,000. Nevertheless, the statistical correlation between them was found to be only 0.110038. Again, one must skip Sri Lanka in this model. This country had a life expectancy of 57 years in the period 1950–55, much higher than what was anticipated considering its per capita income. Again, its life expectancy reached 73.1 years by the period

...regard death as the worst possible thing of one's life, relatively
...part of them all, other losses of life... is one... make
Individuals feel that they... fear... and to limit mortality to
...es that not only affect them, but also the people...
Such realisation comes from... to save self... success
Curiously, also... attempts to... lower mortality. The
society, one that not with notable success in the USSR in the 1970s
and 1980s and... later success in China... and Viet Nam during
the last 50 years.

Table: 2.32

Mortality Levels, 1950–2000, and their Determinants in Some Countries of Asia

Country/Area	Total Fertility Rate (per women) 1995–2000	Expectation of Life at Birth (years) 1995–2000	Expectation of Life at Birth (years) 1950–55	Female Excess over Male Life Expectancy 1995–2000	Infant Mortality Rate (per thousand) 1995–2000	Infant Mortality Rate (per thousand) 1950–55	Socioeconomic Measures (late 1990s) — Purchasing Power Parity Per Capita (US$)	Socioeconomic Measures (late 1990s) — Human Development Index	Socioeconomic Measures (late 1990s) — Percentage of GDP Spent on Health 1990–95	Female Education: Percentage of Age Group in — Primary School	Female Education: Percentage of Age Group in — Secondary School
Afghanistan	6.90	45.5	31.6	1.0	151	227	–	0.37	–	–	–
Armenia	1.70	70.5	64.8	6.4	26	50	2,280	0.67	–	93	90
Azerbaijan	1.99	69.9	61.3	8.6	36	68	1,520	0.62	–	87	88
Bangladesh	3.11	58.1	36.6	0.1	79	180	1,050	0.37	1.2	105	12
Bhutan	5.50	60.7	35.2	2.5	63	191	–	0.35	–	–	–
Brunei Darussalam	2.80	75.5	60.4	4.7	10	68	–	0.89	–	–	–
Cambodia	4.60	53.4	39.4	3.5	103	165	–	0.42	0.7	46	–
China	1.80	69.8	40.8	4.1	41	195	3,570	0.65	2.1	116	51
Democratic People's Republic of Korea	2.05	72.2	47.5	6.2	22	115	–	0.77	–	–	–
East Timor	4.35	47.5	30.0	1.7	135	264	–	–	–	–	–

(continued)

Table: 2.32
(Continued)

Country/Area	Total Fertility Rate (per women) 1995–2000	Expectation of Life at Birth (years) 1950–55	Expectation of Life at Birth (years) 1995–2000	Female Excess over Male Life Expectancy 1995–2000	Infant Mortality Rate (per thousand) 1950–55	Infant Mortality Rate (per thousand) 1995–2000	Socioeconomic Measures (late 1990s): Purchasing Power Parity Per Capita (US$)	Socioeconomic Measures (late 1990s): Human Development Index	Socioeconomic Measures (late 1990s): Percentage of GDP Spent on Health 1990–95	Female Education: Percentage of Age Group in: Primary School	Female Education: Percentage of Age Group in: Secondary School
Hong Kong, China	1.32	61.0	78.5	5.6	79	6	24,540	0.91	–	–	–
India	3.13	38.7	62.6	0.6	190	72	1,650	0.45	0.7	91	–
Indonesia	2.58	37.5	65.1	3.7	160	48	3,450	0.68	0.7	112	39
Islamic Republic of Iran	2.80	46.1	69.2	1.5	190	35	5,530	0.76	–	–	–
Japan	1.43	63.9	80.0	6.1	51	4	23,400	0.94	5.8	102	97
Kazakhstan	2.30	56.5	67.6	9.7	85	35	3,290	0.70	2.2	86	91
Kyrgyzstan	3.21	55.4	67.6	8.6	95	40	2,040	0.63	3.7	–	–
Laos People's Democratic Republic	5.75	37.8	53.2	2.5	180	93	1,290	0.47	1.3	92	19
Macau	1.40	54.0	77.7	5.0	100	10	–	–	–	–	–

(continued)

Table: 2.32
(Continued)

Country/Area	Total Fertility Rate (per women)		Expectation of Life at Birth (years)		Female Excess over Male Life Expectancy 1995–2000	Infant Mortality Rate (per thousand)		Socioeconomic Measures (late 1990s)			Female Education: Percentage of Age Group in:	
	1995–2000	1950–55	1995–2000	1950–55	1995–2000	1950–55	1995–2000	Purchasing Power Parity Per Capita (US$)	Human Development Index	Percentage of GDP Spent on Health 1990–95	Primary School	Secondary School
Malaysia	3.18		72.0	48.5	4.4	99	11	10,920	0.83	1.4	93	61
Maldives	5.40		64.5	38.9	-2.4	185	50	3,230	0.68	–	–	–
Mongolia	2.60		65.8	42.3	2.9	148	51	–	0.67	4.8	–	87
Myanmar	2.40		60.1	36.9	3.3	206	79	–	0.48	–	–	–
Nepal	4.45		57.3	36.3	-0.5	210	83	1,090	0.35	1.2	87	23
Pakistan	5.03		64.0	38.9	2.2	190	74	1,590	0.45	0.8	49	–
Philippines	3.62		68.3	47.5	3.7	100	35	3,670	0.68	1.3	–	–
Republic of Korea	1.65		72.4	47.5	7.5	115	10	13,500	0.89	1.8	102	92
Singapore	1.68		77.1	60.4	4.4	66	5	29,000	0.90	2.8	–	–
Sri Lanka	2.10		73.1	56.6	4.5	91	18	2,460	0.72	1.4	105	78
Tajikistan	4.15		67.2	55.7	6.0	110	57	930	0.58	6.4	–	–
Thailand	1.74		68.8	47.0	6.2	132	29	6,590	0.84	1.4	97	37
Turkey	2.50		69.0	43.6	5.2	233	45	6,430	0.78	2.7	98	48

(continued)

Table: 2.32
(Continued)

Country/Area	Total Fertility Rate (per women)		Expectation of Life at Birth (years)		Female Excess over Male Life Expectancy	Infant Mortality Rate (per thousand)		Socioeconomic Measures (late 1990s)			Female Education: Percentage of Age Group in:	
	1995–2000	1950–55	1995–2000	1950–55	1995–2000	1995–2000	1950–55	Purchasing Power Parity Per Capita (US$)	Human Development Index	Percentage of GDP Spent on Health 1990–95	Primary School	Secondary School
Turkmenistan	3.60		65.4	53.0	7.0	55	115	1,410	0.66	2.8	–	–
Uzbekistan	3.45		67.5	56.4	6.4	44	98	2,450	0.66	3.5	79	92
Viet Nam	2.60		67.4	40.4	4.7	38	180	1,670	0.56	7.1	–	–

Source: United Nations, *World Population Prospects: The 1998 Revision, Volume I: Comprehensive Tables*, Department of Economic and Social Affairs, Population Division, New York, 1999; ESCAP, *1999 ESCAP Population Sheet*, Economic and Social Commission for Asia and the Pacific (ESCAP) Bangkok; World Bank, *World Development Report 1997*, New York, Oxford University Press 1997; and World Bank, *World Development Report 1998/99*, New York, Oxford University Press 1999.

Table 2.33
Correlation Coefficient between Life Expectancy and Infant Mortality Rate
with Various Socioeconomic Parameters in the Asian Countries

Correlation between	Coefficient
Total Fertility Rate (TFR) and Life Expectancy for Asian Countries, 1995–2000 data of Table 2.31	−0.789005
Total Fertility Rate (TFR) and Time Series Data for all of Asia, 1950–55 and 1995–2000	−0.921090
Life Expectancy and Infant Mortality Rate (IMR) for Asian Countries, 1995–2000 data of Table 2.31	−0.974843
Life Expectancy and Excess Female Life Expectancy for Asian Countries, 1995–2000 data of Table 2.31	0.532814
Life Expectancy and Purchasing Power Parity (PPP), for Asian Countries, 1995–2000 data of Table 2.31	0.110038
Life Expectancy and Human Development Index (HDI) for Asian Countries, 1995–2000 data of Table 2.31	0.874658
Life Expectancy and Proportion of GDP Spent on Health for Asian Countries, 1995–2000 data of Table 2.31	0.392665
Life Expectancy and Primary Female Education for Asian Countries, 1995–2000 data of Table 2.31	0.436397
Life Expectancy and Secondary Female Education for Asian Countries, 1995–2000 data of Table 2.31	0.747032
Infant Mortality Rate (IMR) and Primary Female Education for Asian Countries, 1995–2000 data of Table 2.31	−0.510917
Infant Mortality Rate (IMR) and Secondary Female Education for Asian Countries, 1995–2000 data of Table 2.31	−0.435368

1995–2000, only four years behind Singapore at a time when Sri Lanka's per capita income (as measured by the PPP) at US$ 2,460 was not even 10 per cent of that of Singapore at US$ 29,000.

Human Development Index

The correlation with the Human Development Index (HDI) ranking is as high as 0.874658. This definitely stands as a better determinant than the PPP. This ought to be since the HDI includes female education, which as our earlier discussion narrates, has a very strong influence on mortality. Strictly speaking the correlation is not valid in that the HDI has life expectancy as a component.

Proportion of Girls in Primary School

The correlation with the proportion of girls in primary school is 0.436397. However, this is not a good guide any longer as nearly all girls in most countries are in primary school. The outstanding exception is Pakistan where life expectancy is above 60 years despite only 49 per cent of girls being in primary school. The only other country where female education at the primary level is less than 50 per cent is Cambodia, but the life expectancy here is also low at 53.4.

Proportion of Girls in Secondary School

Life expectancy does rise fairly consistently with the proportion of girls in secondary school. The correlation is significantly strong at 0.747032. Infant mortality rates are also significantly correlated with female education. With the enrolment of girls in primary education the correlation coefficient is (–)0.510917. With the enrolment of girls in secondary schools the correlation is (–)0.435368. As more females join schools, the chances of survival of their children improve.

Proportion of GDP Spent on Health

The proportion of GDP spent on health seems to have a very weak effect on life expectancy. The correlation between the two is only 0.392665. India, Indonesia and Cambodia have all spent 0.7 per cent of their GDP on health but their life expectancies differ significantly. Sri Lanka spends 1.4 per cent of its GDP on health while an almost similar proportion is spent in Bangladesh, Laos, Nepal, Thailand, Malaysia and the Philippines. But Sri Lanka has attained a much higher life expectancy than any of these countries. The communist countries, both past and present, spend a significant part of their GDP on health too, though they are nowhere near that of Sri Lanka and far away from Japan which spends 5.8 per cent of its GDP on health.

Excess of Female Life Expectancy over Male Life expectancy

The correlation between general life expectancy at birth and female excess in life expectancy over males is found to be strong at 0.532814. This is quite natural, as an improvement in female life expectancy improves the general life expectancy and vice versa. Female life expectancy currently exceeds that of males by over five years in the Democratic People's Republic of Korea, Hong Kong, China, Japan, Turkey, and all of the ex-Soviet North and Central Asia (with China likely to reach this situation soon). In all these countries, except those in North and Central Asia, life expectancy is over 70 years, and the substantial decline in female mortality is a key factor in the improvement of general health. In some of these Central Asian countries like Uzbekistan, Kazakhstan, Kyrgyzstan, Turkmenistan and Tajikistan, the gap between *female and male life* expectancy is very high and the general life expectancy is lower than 70 years. One probable cause is alcohol or 'binge drinking' among the males,[38] which is responsible for high male mortality and the accompanying low life expectancy at birth. In contrast, the relatively small difference in life expectancy explains high mortality in East Timor. However, South Asia is a unique set-up outside this model. Here the general life expectancy has improved without much improvement in the male-female life expectancy gap. The low level of female autonomy in South Asian societies almost certainly leads not only to high female mortality but also to high child mortality. Maldives and Nepal still exhibit shorter female than male life expectancies, while in Afghanistan, Bangladesh, India, Bhutan, the Islamic Republic of Iran and Pakistan, female excess longevity is not more than 2.5 years. In most of South Asia, more females than males die in childhood though not in infancy because in infancy there is no discrimination in breast feeding between boys and girls. The early reproductive years also take a heavy toll on women's lives because of lack of nutrition and other expert care necessary during childbearing. Even then, female life expectancy has exceeded that of males only because of significant low female mortality in old age.

Infant Mortality

Infant mortality also contributes to the general standard of mortality in society. As infant mortality rises life expectancy falls. For Asian countries, the correlation coefficient between infant mortality rates (IMRs) and life expectancy was found to be (–) 0.974843. This relationship is fairly strong in countries where infant mortality is above or close to 100 and life expectancy is below or close to 50 years. In all countries where life expectancy has exceeded 70 years, infant mortality has been present in the early 20s or even earlier.

Decline in Fertility

The decline in fertility has also contributed to the decline in mortality. During the transition to low fertility, women experience motherhood at much less frequent intervals, deaths during pregnancies decline and infant mortality falls. The fall in infant mortality strengthens the likelihood of further fertility decline. For Asia as a whole, between 1950–55 and 1995–2000, the correlation coefficient between the time series data on TFR and life expectancy was as high as (–) 0.921090. The cross-section data on Asian countries, however, does not exhibit such a strong relationship. Among the Asian countries, Afghanistan, Bhutan, the Laos People's Democratic Republic, Maldives, Cambodia and Pakistan have TFRs of 5 or more children per woman. While life expectancy is generally low in these countries, Maldives and Pakistan have a high life expectancy at around 64 years.

HIV and AIDS

Since 1981, when the first cases of Acquired Immunodeficiency Syndrome (AIDS) were diagnosed, the world has been facing the deadliest epidemic in contemporary history. Human mortality from this disease has attained orders of a magnitude comparable only to those associated with visitations from other pestilence. Between 1347–51, over 20 million people died from the Black Death; another 20 million people died in 1917–19 because of the influenza epidemic.[39] The UNAIDS estimated that at the end of 1997, 29.4 million adults and 1.1 million children had been infected with the virus and that a further 11.7 million people had already lost their lives to AIDS.[40]

The UN sponsored 'World Population Prospect: The 1998 Revision'[41] shows the devastating toll that AIDS took on mortality. In the 29 African countries in which the impact of AIDS was studied, life expectancy at birth was projected to decline to 47 years in 1995–2000, whereas it would have been expected to reach 54 years in the absence of AIDS. This would mean a loss of full seven years. The mortality impact is more serious for those nine African countries with an adult HIV prevalence of 10 per cent or more: Botswana (22.09 per cent), Zimbabwe (21.52 per cent), Zambia (16.62 per cent), Namibia (16.12 per cent), Malawi (12.51 per cent), Mozambique (11.92 per cent), South Africa (11.80 per cent), Rwanda (11.16 per cent) and Kenya (10.43 per cent). In all these countries, the average life expectancy at birth was estimated to be 10 years or less in 1995–2000, much less than it would have been in the absence of AIDS. By 2010–15, the average life expectancy at birth in these countries is projected to be 17 years less than in the absence of AIDS.

The spread of HIV has thus compromised the first stage of the epidemiological transition in developing countries, which is defined as the passage from high to low mortality as infectious diseases are brought under control and are no longer the major cause of death.[42] With the emergence of HIV/AIDS, the epidemiological transition receives a setback in the affected African countries. Furthermore, the interaction of HIV with other infectious agents exacerbates the detrimental impact on longevity. For example, an HIV-positive person is seven times more likely to develop tuberculosis than a person not infected by HIV.[43] AIDS is yet to appear as an epidemic in Asian countries. A UN study indicates that only 1.98 per cent of the adult population in Cambodia, 1.81 per cent in Thailand and 0.65 per cent in India are HIV-positive.[44] If this proportion does not exceed 5 per cent, longevity will be reduced by 2.3 years by 2010–15. If the proportion somehow jumps to 5 per cent or 10 per cent, longevity will fall by 6.7 years by 2010–15.

Over Urbanisation

Since the 1980s cities are no longer seen as 'islands of privilege';[45] rapid population growth and the accompanied negative externalities on city environments have made living conditions highly unfavourable. The problem has been further aggravated with the Structural Adjustment Programmes (SAPs) and related reform measures, which make lesser amount of public money available for the city's maintenance. The large cities are now increasingly becoming 'centres of poverty and social collapse.'[46] Numerous health studies document the rates of morbidity and child mortality to be higher in several pockets of urban areas than in the neighbouring areas.[47] Studies by Brockerhoff and Brennan show that IMRs are higher in giant cities (population above 1.5 million) than in the medium-sized cities of Latin America and the Caribbean by 36 per cent and in North Africa and Asia by 19 per cent.[48] In Latin America and the Caribbean, the young children in the big cities are less likely than those in small cities to have received extensive health care directly or through their mothers and much less likely to be enrolled in school; they are more likely to have stunted growth, reflecting malnutrition.[49] The conditions in the big cities of Asia are not that bad today, but with growing population pressures, rising pollution, curtailment of public resources and accompanied unemployment, inequality and crimes, the health status of the people is bound to fall. Excessive urbanisation is set to be a major determinant of future mortality and morbidity unless appropriate corrective measures are adopted, which is not an easy task for the developing regions of Asia.

POPULATION MOMENTUM AND AGEING

An important and often misunderstood characteristic of human populations is the tendency of a highly fertile population that has been increasing rapidly in size to continue to do so for decades after the onset of even a substantial decline in fertility. This results from the youthful age structure of such a population. These populations contain large numbers of children still to attain adulthood and who in time will marry and procreate. Thus even a dramatic decline in fertility, which affects only the numbers at age zero, cannot prevent the continuing growth of the number of adults of childbearing age for at least two or three decades.

Eventually, of course, as these large groups pass through the childbearing years to reach middle and older ages, the smaller numbers of children resulting from fertility decline lead to a moderation in the rate of population growth. But the delays are lengthy, allowing a very substantial additional population growth even after fertility has declined. This phenomenon gives rise to the term *population momentum*,[50] which is of great significance to developing countries with rapid population growth and limited natural resources.

The world's population is about 6 billion today and over 7 billion people are expected to inhabit the earth by 2050 as today's children start families of their own. Demographers estimate that about 60 per cent of the world's population growth between now and 2050 will be due to population momentum. Population momentum is the primary force underlying this growth. Less developed countries have enormous potential for population growth at older ages as the large cohorts currently in the younger age groups reach adulthood later. In Asia, the population momentum would increase the population by more than 40 per cent, even if fertility fell immediately to the replacement level. Since fertility is still above the replacement level (NRR = 1.12 in 1995–2000), the proportionate increase in the population will ultimately be much greater.

Conceptually and empirically, momentum and ageing expresses the same change, though on different scales. Fundamentally, they are the manifestations of the underlying process of demographic trans-formation. Kim and Schoen[51] have shown that population momentum (defined technically as the ratio of the size of an ultimate stationary population to that of an initial population, when the initial population undergoes an immediate shift in fertility to replacement level), is linearly related to ageing.

Rowland[52] makes a cohort analysis to explain the transformation of the age structure and the associated changes in the numbers and circumstances of the aged. He interprets population ageing as a process of cohort flow. The numbers and proportion of the aged increase as larger cohorts reach later life. Cohort flow further changes the composition of the older population, as cohorts with different marital histories, educational levels, employment histories and ethnic characteristics move into later ages. The analysis, which has been called gerontological transition, also explains that population momentum is a major cause behind the swelling of the number of tomorrow's aged in Asian countries.

The projections on gerontological transition by Rowland[53] demonstrate the possible effects of fertility, mortality and migration transition on momentum and the number and proportions of the aged. The exercise indicates that in countries where mortality is declining, a delay in the beginning of the fertility transition and slow progress towards replacement level fertility contribute to vastly increased numbers in older ages. It also shows that if mortality declines quickly while fertility remains above the replacement level, an enormous increase in population momentum can occur and eventually flow on to the older ages. Net migration too has such a spectacular effect on population momentum in that the greater the inflow, the greater the total aged population. We reproduce, in Table 2.34, Rowland's projections

Table 2.34
**Effect of Fertility, Mortality and Migration on Momentum and
Growth of the Aged Population**

Assumptions	Peak Momentum		Aged 65 plus at the End of Transition	
	Millions	Percentages	Millions	Percentages
Western Slow Fertility Decline	6.7	61	4.6	20.1
Rapid Fertility Decline	4.2	58	3.0	20.1
Rapid Fertility Decline, Delayed	11.2	70	6.4	20.1
Slow Fertility Decline, Delayed	17.9	72	9.9	20.1
Western Slow Mortality Decline	6.7	61	4.6	20.1
Rapid Mortality Decline	27.2	93	11.6	20.1
Very Rapid Mortality Decline	27.2	104	14.0	20.1
Western Zero Net Migration	6.7	61	4.6	20.1
Low Net Migration (50,000 annually)	15.3	58	11.9	19.6
Medium Net Migration (100,000 annually)	23.9	57	19.3	19.5
High Net Migration (200,000 annually)	41.1	57	33.9	19.4

Source: Rowland, 1994.

on the aged and momentum, based on different assumptions on
fertility, mortality and migration.

NOTES AND REFERENCES

1. Quoted in 'Health and Ageing: A Discussion Paper', World Health
   Organization, Department of Health Promotion, Non-Communicable
   Disease Prevention and Surveillance, Geneva, 2002.
2. Japan Ageing Research Center (JARC), *Aging in Japan*, JARC, Tokyo, 2000.
3. Warren S. Thompson, *Population, Problems*, McGraw Hill, 1935.
4. Adolph Laundry, *La Revolution Demographique*, Receuil Sirey, Paris, 1934.

5. T.W. Schultz (ed.), *Food for The World*, University of Chicago Press, 1945.
6. Paul Demeny, 'On the End of the Population Explosion', *Population and Development Review*, 5(1): 141–62, 1979.
7. United Nations, *World Population, 1998*, United Nations Publications, (ST/ESA/SER.A/176), New York, 1999.
8. United Nations, *World Population at the Turn of the Century*, Population Studies No.111, DIECSA, ST/ESA/SER.A/111, New York, 1989.
9. Human Development Index is a composite index based on three indicators: longevity, as measured by life expectancy at birth; educational attainment, as measured by a combination of adult literacy (two-thirds weight) and the combined gross primary, secondary and tertiary enrolment ratio (one-third weight); and standard of living, as measured by GDP per capita (PPP US $).
10. Toshio Kuroda, 'Population Ageing in Asia and its Economic and Social Implications', in The Fourth Asian and Pacific Population Conference, 19–27 August 1992, Bali, Indonesia (Selected Papers), Economic and Social Commission for Asia and the Pacific (ESCAP), Asian Population Studies Series No. 124, United Nations, New York, 1993.
11. Milos Macura, 'Problems of Youth in an Ageing Population: Competition and Complementarity', in *Economic and Social Implications of Population Ageing*, United Nations, ST/ESA/SER.R/85, pp. 344–67, New York, 1988.
12. Graziella Caselli and Jacques Vallin, 'Mortality and Population and Ageing', *European Journal of Population*, 6(1): 1–25, 1990.
13. This is the United Nations Medium Variant Projections. The Office of the Registrar General suggests that the replacement level of fertility will be attained by about 2021.
14. Evelyn M. Kitagawa, 'Components of a Difference between Two Rates', *Journal of American Statistical Association*, 30: 1168–74, 1955.
15. N. Ogawa, 'Ageing of the Population', in *Population of Japan: United Nations*, Economic and Social Commission for Asia and the Pacific (ESCAP), Population Division, United Nations, New York, 1984: 249–68. (Country Monograph Series No. 11.)
16. Du Peng, 'Fertility Decline and Population Aging in China', *Chinese Journal of Population Sciences*, 7(4): 299–306, Alberton Press, 1995.
17. ibid.
18. Max Weber, *The Protestant Ethic and the Spirit of Capitalism*, translated by Talcott Parsons, New York, Charles Scribner's Sons, [1904]1930.
19. R. Lesthaeghe, 'A Century of Demographic and Cultural Change in Western Europe: An Exploration of Underlying Dimensions', *Population And Development Review*, 9(3): 411–35, 1983.
20. J.C. Caldwell, *Theory of Fertility Decline*, Academic Press, London, 1982.
21. J. Hajnal, 'European Marriage Patterns in Perspective', in David V. Glass (ed.), *Population in History: Essays in Historical Demography*, pp.101–43, Edward Arnold, London, 1965.
22. H.M. Leibenstein, *Economic Backwardness and Economic Growth*, John Wiley and Sons, New York, 1957.

23. G.S. Becker, 'An Economic Analysis of Fertility', in *Demographic and Economic Change in Developed Countries: A Conference of the Universities*, National Bureau Committee for Economic Research, Princeton University Press, Princeton, 1960.

24. T.W. Schultz, 'The High Value of Human Time: Population Equilibrium', *Journal of Political Economy*, 81(2): S2–S10, 1973.

25. R.A. Easterlin, and E.N. Crimmins, *The Fertility Revolution: A Demand-Supply Analysis*, University of Chicago Press, Chicago, 1985.

26. J. Cleland, and C. Wilson, 'Demand Theories of the Fertility Transition: An Iconoclastic View', *Population Studies*, 41(1): 5–30, 1987.

27. United Nations, *The Determinants and Consequences of Population Trends: New Summary of Findings on Interaction of Demographic, Economic and Social Factors*, Vol. I, Sales No. E.71.XIII.5, 1973.

28. A. Chamratrithirong, K. Archavanitkul, K. Richter, P. Guest, V. Thongthai, W. Boonchalaksi, N. Piriyathamwong and P. Vong-Ek, National Migration Survey of Thailand, Institute for Population and Social Research, Mahidol University, 1995.

29. Asia's life expectancy was 41.3 years compared to 51.4 years in Latin America.

30. The IMR in Asia was 179 in contrast to 180 in Africa. The Crude Death Rate (CDR) in Asia was 23.9 per thousand population against Africa's 26.6.

31. Asia's CDR was 8.3 in relation to Europe's 11.3.

32. Life expectancy in Eastern Asia was 69.6 years compared to Europe's 72.6 years.

33. John C. Caldwell, 'Pushing Back the Frontiers of Death', Academy of the Social Sciences in Australia, Cunningham Lecture for 1999.

34. J.C. Caldwell, 'Routes to Low Mortality in Poor Countries' *Population and Development Review*, 12(2): 171–220, 1986.

35. J. Knodel and G.W. Jones, 'Post-Cairo Population Policy: Does Promoting Girls' Schooling Miss the Mark?' *Population and Development Review*, 22(4): 683–702, 1996.

36. J. Simons, 'Cultural Dimensions of the Mother's Contribution to Child Survival', in J.C. Caldwell and G. Santow (eds), *Selected Readings in the Cultural, Social and Behavioural Determinants of Health*, pp. 132–45, Australian National University, Canberra, 1989.

37. See note 34.

38. J.C. Caldwell, 'Good Health for Many: The ESCAP Region, 1950–2000', *Asia-Pacific Population Journal*, 14(4): 21–38, 1999.

39. J.C. Caldwell, 'The Impact of the African AIDS Epidemic', *Health Transition Review*, 7(2): 169–88, 1997.

40. UNAIDS, Report on the Global HIV/AIDS Pandemic, Geneva, 1998.

41. United Nations, *World Population Prospects: The 1998 Revision, Vol. III: Analytical Report*, New York, 2000.

42. John Rogers and Marie C Nelson, 'The Epidemiological Transition Revisited or What Happens if We Look Beneath the Surface?', *Health Transition Review*, 7: 241–46, 1997.

43. J.R. Glynn, D.K. Warndorff, P.E.M. Fine, G.K. Msiska, M.M. Munthali and J.M. Ponnighaus, 'The Impact of HIV on Morbidity and Mortality from Tuberculosis in Sub-Saharan Africa: A Study in Rural Malawi and Review of the Literature', *Health Transition Review*, 7(2): 75–87, 1997.

44. ibid.

45. Paul Harrison, *Inside the Third World*, Penguin, Harmondsworth, 1982.

46. Paul Kennedy, *Preparing for the Twenty-First Century*, Random House, New York, 1993.

47. Carolyn Stephens, 'Healthy Cities or Unhealthy Islands? The Health and Social Implications of Urban inequality', *Environment and Urbnization*, 8(2): 9–30, 1996.

48. M. Brockerhoff and Ellen Brennan, 'The Poverty of Cities in Developing Regions', *Population and Development Review*, 24(1): 75–114, March, 1998.

49. ibid.

50. N. Keyfitz, 'On the Momentum of Population Growth', *Demography*, 8: 71–80, 1971.

51. Kim, Young J. and Robert Schoen, Population Momentum Expresses Population Ageing, Hopkins Population Center Papers on Population, WP–97–02, Johns Hopkins Population Center, Baltimore, Maryland, 1997.

52. D.T. Rowland, *Ageing in Australia: Population Trends and Social Issues*, Longman Cheshire, Melbourne, 1991.

53. D.T. Rowland, 'Population Policies and Ageing in Asia: A Cohort Perspective', in *The Ageing of Asian Populations*, Proceedings of the United Nations Round Table on the Ageing of Asian Populations, Bangkok, 4–6 May 1992, Department for Economic and Social Information and Policy Analysis, Sales no. ST/ESA/SER.R/125, United Nations, New York, 1994.

CHAPTER THREE

WHAT IS AGEING?

The definition of ageing varies from society to society and has been modified considerably over time. Ancient Chinese scholars divided human life into seven phases; during the 6th century BC, Pythogoras compared human life to the different seasons. In both cases, old age seems to have started after the age of 60.[1] According to traditional Indian culture, the lifespan of a human being is 100 years. Manu, the ancient law giver, in his *Dharmasastra* divided this span of life into four *'ashramas'* or life stages:

♦ *Brahmacharya*: the stage of learning skills and unquestioned devotion towards one's teachers.
♦ *Grihasthashrama*: the stage of performing the duties of a householder, which include raising and maintaining a family.
♦ *Vanaprastha*: the stage of gradual withdrawal from the world, without reducing one's responsibilities.
♦ *Sanyasa*: the stage of total renunciation of all attachments and submission.

The ageing process starts somewhere in the third and fourth stages. Concepcion interprets this theory to say that ageing in Hindu society starts at the ages of 36 or 40 years.[2] Nayar, however, considers ageing to start only after 50 years of age.[3] All these stages, however, are parts of an individual life cycle that finally leads to ageing.

Population ageing, however, is different from individual ageing. Individual ageing is a continuous process; a person ages inexorably from the time of birth to the moment of death,[4] whatever the form of the life cycle or stages. Populations, however, can become older or younger depending on the age structure composition of the people. The age of a population can be determined in several ways. Although proportions of those aged 60 years and above are generally used as an index of ageing, there are several other ways in which ageing can be measured. Each measure has its own merits and demerits. Sometimes, these alternative measures can give better results than the traditional indices. This chapter introduces the important traditional measures of ageing, including dependency measures, followed by several alternative measures. We begin with Ryder's alternative suggestion and then move to the P-index of ageing, which attributes higher values to the older among the old in order to emphasise the fact that if ageing were a problem, the older elderly face much larger difficulties. In this chapter we also evaluate the slope of the age pyramid as another unconventional measure of ageing. Finally, we also introduce an ageing index that takes into account the causal factors of ageing.

TRADITIONAL MEASURES OF AGEING

Among the various measures of population ageing, the proportions of persons aged 60 or 65 years and above, mean age,[5] median age, proportion of children under 15 years of age and aged-child ratio are frequently used factors to represent the various facets of ageing. The list is neither based on merit nor on popularity.

Proportions of Aged 60 or 65 Years and Above

This is the most commonly used measure of ageing. Most ageing data is presented through this measure. The major reason for its popularity is its simplicity and easy comprehensibility. This statistic measures ageing through the proportion of people aged 60 (or, 65) and above in the total population. Table 3.1 reproduces data on proportions of aged 65 and above for some countries and regions of Asia and the rest of the world. This measure, P_{65}, may be expressed as:

$$P_{65} = \int_{65}^{w} n(a)da \Big/ \int_{0}^{w} n(a)da \qquad (1)$$

Table 3.1
Proportion of Aged 65 or Over in Different Regions/Countries of the World, 1950–2050

Regions/Countries	1950	1960	1970	1980	1990	1995	2000	2025	2050
World	5.2	5.3	5.5	5.9	6.2	6.6	6.9	10.4	16.4
MDRs	7.9	8.6	9.9	11.6	12.5	13.6	14.4	20.9	25.9
LDR	3.9	3.9	3.8	4.1	4.4	4.7	5.1	8.5	15.0
Asia	4.1	4.2	4.0	4.4	4.9	5.4	5.9	10.1	17.3
Eastern Asia	4.5	4.9	4.5	5.1	6.1	6.8	7.7	14.2	23.2
South-central Asia	3.7	3.6	3.6	3.9	4.1	4.3	4.6	7.6	14.2
South-east Asia	3.7	3.3	3.3	3.6	4.0	4.3	4.7	8.5	16.7
Western Asia	4.4	4.1	4.3	4.3	3.9	4.4	4.8	7.3	13.1
China	4.5	4.8	4.3	4.7	5.6	6.1	6.8	13.2	22.6
Japan	4.9	5.7	7.1	9.0	12.0	14.6	17.1	26.7	31.8
Thailand	3.0	2.7	3.0	3.5	4.3	5.0	5.8	12.3	23.0
India	3.3	3.4	3.7	4.1	4.3	4.6	5.0	8.4	15.1

Source: United Nations, *World Population Prospects: The 1998 Revision, Vol. I: Comprehensive Tables*, United Nations Population Division, Department of Economic and Social Affairs, New York, 1999.

For ease of interpretation, this proportion is generally multiplied by 100 to get a percentage figure.

A population is said to be ageing when the proportion of people aged 65 plus is rising. This index may also be used to identify countries according to the stages of ageing. For example, populations with less than 4 per cent of people aged 65 and above may be classified as young, those with 4 to 6.9 per cent of people aged 65 and above as youthful, those with 7 to 9.9 per cent aged 65 and above as mature, and those with 10 per cent or more in the 65 plus and older category as old.[6] The United Nations suggests that a 7 per cent number is enough to make the population aged. By this measure, most of Asia, except Japan and a few countries of Eastern Asia have youthful ageing. But in the next 25 years, matured or old ageing would set into all the regions of Asia.

There is nothing special about the ages 65 or 60. They are merely arbitrarily defined entry points to old age that have certain socio-economic implications for those above this age. However, as the index of demographic ageing, they are purely conventional. Since 65 years has been used in developed countries as the entry point for ageing, we felt justified in choosing the Asian cut-off point at 60 years. There is no denying that people in the MDRs live longer than their counterparts in the poorer regions of the world. The average life expectancy at birth in the MDRs was 74.1 years in 1990–95 compared to 61.9 years in the poorer regions. In Asia, the figure was 64.5 years; in South-central Asia it was even lower at 60.2 years. The median age for the MDRs was 35.9 years in 1995; in Asia it was only 24.7 years. Among many others, the United Nations International Conference on Ageing Populations in the Context of Urbanization, 1988, also recommended the age of 60 as the age marking the onset of ageing.[7] Appendix one puts together the statutory retirement ages of 31 Asian countries for which data could be secured. Only two among them, Japan and Cyprus, maintain 65 as the retirement ages for both males and females. Males in Israel retire at the age of 65 while females at the age of 60. In Lebanon, the retirement age has been fixed at 64 years for both sexes. The retirement age in Kazakhstan is 61 years for males; females retire five years earlier. In all other countries, the retirement age is 60 years or less. At the same time, it is important to recognise the fact that chronological age is not always the best indicator of the changes that accompany ageing. Variations in the health status of individual older people of the same age can be dramatic. Decision-makers thus need to take both these factors into account when designing policies for their 'older' populations.

Mean Age

The mean age, M, of a population can be defined in terms of the number of persons in each age group, $n(a)$. For the continuous case, we have

$$M = \int_0^w an(a)da \Big/ \int_0^w n(a)da \qquad (2)$$

where a is age and w is the upper age limit. The discrete counterpart simply replaces integration by summation:

$$M = \frac{\sum_0^w a_i f_i}{N} \qquad (3)$$

where a_i is the different age group, f_i is the number of people in the respective age group and N is the total population. This measure, though theoretically useful, has not much use in ageing studies.

Median Age

The median age, Md, can be defined as the exact age that divides the age distribution into two equal halves. For the discrete case, where a limited number of age groups is used, it is necessary to identify the group containing the median first. The median may then be calculated as,

$$Md = l_1 + \left(\frac{N/2 - F}{f_m}\right) C \qquad (4)$$

where l_1 is the lower class boundary of the median class, N is the total population, f_m is the number of people in the median class, and F is the cumulative frequency below l_1. For the continuous case, the proportion at Md and below is,

$$PMd = \int_0^{Md} n(a)da \Big/ \int_0^w n(a)da = 2/1 \qquad (5)$$

A typical ageing population has its median age at 30 years or more. When the median age varies between 20 and 29 years, a country is in the intermediate stage of the ageing process, while a median age below 20 years indicates that the country's population is young.[8] By this token, none of the Asian regions are young today. Most of them, except Eastern Asia (including China) are in the intermediary stage. However, all regions except Western Asia would be ageing. Table 3.2 portrays the median age of the different regions of Asia and the rest of the world for a few years starting from 1950.

Proportion of Children under 15 Years of Age

This measure is simply the proportion of children under 15 years of age to the total population. This measure is called P_{15} and is used in the following formula:

$$P_{15} = \int_0^{15} n(a)da \Big/ \int_0^w n(a)da \qquad (6)$$

Often, 100 is multiplied to represent the measure in percentage terms. Any population with a value below 30 is typically regarded as old. In the next 25 years, all the regions of Asia would be under 30. Japan reached this level in the 1970s and China in the 1990s. India is projected to reach this target by 2010. Table 3.3 provides the percentage aged 0–14 years in different regions of the world, starting from 1950.

Table 3.2

Median Age in Different Regions/Countries of the World, 1950–2050

Regions/Countries	1950	1960	1970	1980	1990	1995	2000	2025	2050
World	23.5	22.8	21.6	22.6	24.3	25.4	26.6	32.7	37.8
MDRs	28.6	29.6	30.6	31.9	34.4	35.9	37.5	42.6	45.6
LDRs	21.3	20.1	19.0	20.0	22.0	23.2	24.4	30.9	36.7
Asia	21.9	20.9	19.7	21.0	23.2	24.7	26.3	33.8	39.3
South-central Asia	20.6	20.1	19.2	19.8	20.8	21.7	22.7	30.5	37.2
Western Asia	20.4	20.2	18.9	19.2	20.5	21.5	22.5	27.9	35.0
South-east Asia	20.2	19.5	18.2	19.2	21.4	22.8	24.3	32.8	38.3
Eastern Asia	23.5	22.7	20.6	23.0	26.2	28.3	30.7	39.6	44.1
China	23.9	21.8	19.7	22.1	25.3	27.6	30.0	38.9	43.7
Thailand	18.4	17.9	16.8	19.4	23.3	25.7	28.0	38.4	42.9
Japan	22.3	25.5	29.0	32.6	37.4	39.7	41.2	48.4	49.0
India	20.4	20.4	19.9	20.6	21.9	22.7	23.8	31.9	38.2

Source: Estimated from United Nations, *World Population Prospects: The 1998 Revision, Vol. I: Comprehensive Tables*, United Nations Population Division, Department of Economic and Social Affairs, New York, 1999.

Note: Definitions of the regions are given in chapter two.

Table 3.3

Percentage Aged 0–14 Years in Different Regions/Countries of the World, 1950–2050

Regions/Countries	1950	1960	1970	1980	1990	1995	2000	2025	2050
World	34.3	36.9	37.4	35.2	32.4	31.2	29.7	23.4	19.7
MDRs	27.3	28.1	26.0	22.4	20.6	19.6	18.2	15.7	15.3
LDRs	37.8	40.7	41.8	39.3	35.6	34.3	32.5	24.9	20.3
Asia	36.6	39.4	40.3	37.7	33.2	31.8	29.9	22.1	18.9
Eastern Asia	34.1	38.0	38.2	34.3	26.7	25.4	23.9	17.9	16.1
South-central Asia	38.7	40.4	41.7	40.0	38.4	37.0	34.8	24.5	20.1
South-east Asia	39.2	41.4	43.4	40.9	36.4	34.0	31.4	23.0	19.6
Western Asia	38.5	41.1	42.2	40.8	38.7	36.7	35.0	27.9	21.3
China	33.6	38.9	39.7	35.5	27.7	26.5	24.9	18.3	16.3
Japan	35.5	30.2	24.0	23.6	18.4	16.0	14.8	13.5	13.8
Thailand	42.5	44.7	46.2	40.0	32.0	28.0	25.3	18.9	16.8
India	38.9	39.8	40.4	38.5	36.4	35.4	33.3	23.0	19.6

Source: Estimated from United Nations, *World Population Prospects: The 1998 Revision, Vol. I: Comprehensive Tables*, United Nations Population Division, Department of Social and Economic Affairs, New York, 1999.

Aged-Child Ratio (or, Ageing Index)

This is the ratio of the number of elderly persons to the number of children. It takes into account the size and changes at both ends of the age distribution. This measure, R, may be expressed as:

$$R = \int_{65}^{w} n(a)da \bigg/ \int_{0}^{15} n(a)da \qquad (7)$$

This ratio is commonly multiplied by 100 and is also known as the *Ageing Index*. A value of over 30 may indicate an ageing population. Under this measure, the MDRs are ageing nations. However, in the next 25 years, all the regions of Asia, except Western Asia, would be aged and in another 50 years, ageing would have spread all across Asia. Table 3.4 provides the ratio of people aged 65 plus and children aged 0–14 in different regions of the world, starting from 1950.

DEPENDENCY MEASURES OF AGEING

These measures are not used for measuring the ageing of populations per se, but have been used as an approximation of the social and economic dependency created by the ageing of populations. Dependency terminologies are quite common these days and are used by professional demographers and politicians alike. This section introduces some of these popular expressions with demographic overtones.

Old Age Dependency Ratio

Generally, this is the ratio of those aged 65 years and above to those aged between 15 and 64 years of age. The latter age group are assumed to be economically active.

$$D_{65} = \int_{65}^{w} n(a)da \bigg/ \int_{15}^{64} n(a)da \qquad (8)$$

Table 3.4
Aged-Child Ratio in Different Regions/Countries of the World, 1950–2050

Regions/Countries	1950	1960	1970	1980	1990	1995	2000	2025	2050
World	15.2	14.4	14.7	16.8	19.1	21.2	23.2	44.4	83.2
MDRs	28.9	30.6	38.1	51.8	60.7	69.4	79.1	133.1	169.3
LDRs	10.3	9.6	9.1	10.4	12.4	13.7	15.7	34.1	73.9
Asia	11.2	10.4	9.9	11.7	14.8	17.0	19.7	45.7	91.5
Eastern Asia	13.2	12.9	11.8	14.9	17.8	26.8	32.2	79.3	144.0
South-central Asia	9.6	8.9	8.6	9.8	10.7	11.6	13.2	31.0	70.6
South-east Asia	9.4	8.0	7.6	8.8	11.0	12.6	15.0	37.0	85.2
Western Asia	11.4	10.0	10.2	10.5	10.1	12.0	13.7	26.2	61.5
China	13.4	12.3	10.8	13.2	20.2	23.0	27.3	72.1	138.7
Japan	13.8	18.9	29.6	38.1	65.2	91.3	115.5	197.8	230.4
Thailand	7.0	6.0	6.0	8.7	13.4	17.9	22.9	65.0	136.9
India	8.5	8.5	9.2	10.6	11.8	13.0	15.0	36.5	77.0

Source: Calculated from United Nations, *World Population Prospects: The 1998 Revision, Vol. I: Comprehensive Tables*, United Nations Population Division, Department of Economic and Social Affairs, New York, 1999.

Table 3.5 gives the aged dependency ratios for the same regions/ countries as in the earlier tables. Table 1.6 in chapter one provides data on the aged dependency ratios for more regions of the world for a much longer period of time. In 1950, in the world as a whole, around 12 persons supported one aged person. Projections indicate that there would be less than four persons supporting an aged person by 2050. In Japan already, less than four non-elderly persons exist for every elderly person.

Potential Support Ratio (PSR)

This is the number of persons aged 15 to 64 years per every person aged 65 years or older. Mathematically, the ratio can be expressed by the following formula:

$$PSR = \frac{\int_{15}^{64} n(a)da}{\int_{65}^{w} n(a)da} \qquad (9)$$

As can be seen, the PSR is an inverse of the old age dependency ratio. Tables 1.7 and 1.8 in chapter one supply the estimates of the PSR for many regions of the world as well as of Asia.

Parent Support Ratio (PaSR)

This is the number of persons aged 85 years and above per 100 persons in the age bracket 50 to 64 years. Mathematically, the PaSR may be expressed as:

$$PaSR = \frac{\int_{85}^{w} n(a)da}{\int_{50}^{64} n(a)da} \qquad (10)$$

Tables 1.9 and 1.10 in chapter one give the PaSRs for different regions of the world and various countries of Asia respectively.

Table 3.5

Aged Dependency Ratio in Different Regions/Countries of the World, 1950–2050

Regions/Countries	1950	1960	1970	1980	1990	1995	2000	2025	2050
World	7.9	8.4	8.8	9.1	9.2	9.6	10.2	13.6	20.4
MDRs	10.9	12.0	13.4	14.9	15.7	16.9	17.6	24.8	30.6
LDRs	6.3	6.6	6.5	6.8	6.8	7.2	7.6	11.3	18.8
Asia	6.5	6.9	6.7	7.1	7.3	7.9	8.4	13.0	21.3
Eastern Asia	6.8	7.9	7.3	7.8	8.3	9.1	10.1	17.7	27.7
South-central Asia	6.0	6.0	6.2	6.5	6.7	6.8	7.1	10.1	17.8
South-east Asia	6.1	5.6	5.8	6.1	6.3	6.5	6.9	12.7	20.8
Western Asia	7.2	7.0	7.4	7.3	6.4	7.2	7.4	10.1	16.6
China	7.3	8.5	7.6	8.0	8.4	9.1	10.0	19.4	37.2
Japan	7.6	8.2	9.3	11.8	14.7	17.4	20.1	30.9	36.9
Thailand	5.2	4.9	5.6	5.8	6.3	6.9	7.8	15.2	27.6
India	5.4	5.6	6.2	6.6	6.8	7.1	7.5	10.9	18.8

Source: Estimated from the United Nations, *World Population Prospects: The 1998 Revision Vol. I: Comprehensive Tables*, United Nations, New York, 1999.

Youth Dependency Ratio

This is the number of persons aged 0 to 14 years per 100 persons in the age group 15 to 64 years. Mathematically, this ratio may be expressed as:

$$D_{15} = \frac{\int_0^{14} n(a)da}{\int_{15}^{64} n(a)da} \qquad (11)$$

Total Dependency Ratio

This is the number of persons under age 15 plus persons aged 65 or older per one hundred persons aged 15 to 64. It is the sum of the youth dependency ratio and the old-age dependency ratio.

$$D_T = D_{65} + D_{15} = \frac{\int_{65}^{w} n(a)da}{\int_{15}^{64} n(a)da} + \frac{\int_0^{14} n(a)da}{\int_{15}^{64} n(a)da} \qquad (12)$$

Table 3.6 provides figures for youth and total dependency for select regions and countries for specific years between 1950 and 2050. Many interesting annotations can be drawn from the table:

1. Youth dependency is on the decline the world over and is anticipated to fall even further. In the developing world and in all the Asian regions and countries, except Japan, youth dependency rose in the third quarter of the last century. In the MDRs and Japan, the decline has been smooth. Conversely, old age dependency has been rising, except during the period when youth dependency had risen.
2. Total dependency has mostly been above 50, that is, at least half of the country's population has been continually dependant.
3. Youth dependency has been a major dependency in the developing world and Asia, and will remain so in most of Asia in the future too. However, in China and Thailand aged dependency will be the dominating dependency in 2050. For the developed world and Japan, youth dependency is already a secondary dependency. In the next half-century, youth dependency will constitute one-third

Table 3.6
Youth and Total Dependency Ratios in Different Regions/Countries of the World, 1950–2050

Regions/Countries	1950 Total	1950 Youth	1975 Total	1975 Youth	2000 Total	2000 Youth	2025 Total	2025 Youth	2050 Total	2050 Youth
World	65.2	56.7	73.7	63.8	58.4	47.5	53.2	37.3	57.7	33.1
MDRs	54.4	42.2	53.8	37.2	48.3	27.1	57.0	23.6	73.4	26.9
LDRs	71.0	64.3	81.8	74.7	61.1	52.9	52.5	39.7	55.7	33.9
Asia	68.3	61.4	78.0	70.5	56.5	47.3	49.0	34.1	56.8	30.6
Eastern Asia	62.9	55.6	74.1	65.9	46.2	34.9	47.8	26.4	66.0	26.7
South-central Asia	73.4	66.9	80.1	73.3	65.9	58.3	49.5	38.4	51.4	31.4
South-east Asia	74.4	67.8	84.0	77.5	58.9	51.5	46.7	34.5	56.1	31.0
Western Asia	75.2	67.5	85.3	77.3	68.5	60.5	59.0	48.0	57.1	39.3
China	61.3	54.1	78.2	70.4	46.4	36.4	46.2	26.8	63.9	26.7
Japan	67.8	59.5	47.5	35.8	46.8	21.6	69.6	20.5	95.8	24.5
Thailand	83.1	77.1	84.4	78.6	46.8	39.1	44.8	28.4	61.9	27.7
India	73.2	67.4	77.4	70.6	62.5	54.4	46.1	33.9	52.6	30.0

Source: Estimated from the United Nations, *World Population Prospects: The 1998 Revision, Vol. I: Comprehensive Tables*, United Nations, New York, 1999.

of old age dependency. Projections indicate that 95.8 per cent of Japanese populations will be dependent by 2050. If things do not change, 4.2 per cent of the country's population will have the responsibility of maintaining the rest of the population. Never before has any population of the world had to bear such a gigantic burden.

PROBLEMS OF DEPENDENCY MEASURES

Dependency measures, although useful in analysing the burden of ageing, suffer some inherent limitations:

1. Entry into the job market is not legally possible in most countries before the age of 18. So, the choice of age group 15–64 can only serve as proxy for the 18–64 age group; it cannot explain the actual burden. Nonetheless, it may be mentioned that individual year-wise data is not available for many countries.
2. Many people who fall within the 14–64 or 18–64 age group are not economically independent, while scores of 65 plus persons are economically solvent.
3. The dependency measure, calculated this way, does not take into account the age structure within the age segments used. As a consequence, a hypothetical population, with all its 65 plus population in the age group 65–69 and 15–64, will have the same dependency burden as any other population with a concentration for higher age sub-groups within broader age groups. Obviously, the dependency situation is not same for both populations.

ALTERNATIVE DEPENDENCY MEASURE

Attempts have been made to measure old age dependency in terms of the number of years lived by an average person according to the life table cohort in the age group.[9] Under the new index; old age dependency can be measured as,

$$D_{65} = \frac{\sum_{65}^{w} P(x, x + 4).AL(x, x + 4)}{\sum_{15}^{64} P(x, x + 4).AL(x, x + 4)} \qquad (13)$$

Where AL $(x, x + 4)$ is the average person years lived by the life table cohort in the age group $(x, x + 4)$. Young age dependency has also been defined in similar terms,

$$D_{15} = \frac{\sum\limits_{0}^{14} P(x,x + 4).AL(x,x + 4)}{\sum\limits_{15}^{64} P(x,x + 4).AL(x,x + 4)} \qquad (14)$$

The ratio of old age and young age burden is the Index of Ageing.

A COMPARATIVE EVALUATION OF THE AGEING INDICES

The major disadvantage of these measures is that they all produce different rank orders of population ageing when one compares different populations. Rosset[10] dismisses median and mean age as imperfect measures of demographic ageing. It was argued that France ranked first when the proportion of old was used to measure its population ageing, but stood 11th in terms of the median age. This is, however, a priori reasoning and does not render a persuasive argument against the use of the median age.

There are, however, considerable difficulties to be faced in examining the ageing trend of a population over the years. According to Table 3.5, India's population has been ageing consistently since 1950, according to the index of the proportion of people 65 years and older. However, changes in the median age (Table 3.1) have shown that the population became younger between 1960 and 1970. Going by the index of the proportion of those 65 years and older, the world is ageing continuously. When the ratio of those 65 years of age and older to those less than 15 years of age is used, the world population is shown to have become slightly younger between 1950 and 1960. Despite the trend of ageing improving from 1960, the pre-1950s trend could not be reached even in 1970.

One of the major difficulties of using the proportion of those 65 years and older as an index of population ageing is that it represents only two broad groups: (a) 65 years and above; and, (b) below 65 years. It ignores the age variations within each category. To be more specific, this measure ignores the extent of 'oldness'. The other significant problem with this measure is the arbitrariness involved in creating the 'old' category. This fixing of age at entry into 'old' ignores the sociological, biological, physiological or psychological dimensions of the problem. In the sociological perspective, ageing as having reached a certain number of years has very little significance. In fact, most sociological interest lies in understanding the changes in the relationship between the elderly and social institutions. The cut-off point between the aged and the non-aged is essentially unimportant. It is also not easy to look for a universal cut-off point; it should vary according to region, culture, society, economy and even gender.

Some people have tried to see old age as the beginning of retirement from the labour market. Here too, a cut-off point seems impossible. In chapter one, we have provided the Statutory Retirement Ages (SRAs) of many countries of the world. There is no single age that can be accepted. Moreover, SRAs are mainly applicable in the organised sector. For various other occupations, people are allowed to work beyond the SRA. In many countries, teachers are allowed to work for longer periods of their lives. Many employees are provided an extension beyond the retirement age. At the same time, there are a large number of people who work in the unorganised sectors where there are no formal retirement ages. Very few women participate in the labour market and therefore retirement as the beginning of old age may not be applicable to these women in the developing world.

The single year cut-off point loses its relevance in the context of increased longevity over the years. The world life expectancy at birth for both sexes combined was 46.5 years in 1950. It has been increasing since. Life expectancy shot up to 64.1 years in 1990. In the MDRs, where studies on population ageing first took place, life expectancy increased from 66.6 years in 1950 to 74.1 years in 1990. If 65 years was the cut-off point in 1950, it ought to be a higher cut-off point now.

Ryder's Alternative Measure

Ryder[11] proposed an alternative measure of population ageing by designating the entry into old age in terms of the number of years remaining until death. According to him, old age may be considered as the last 10 years of a life. These years may vary according to policy needs. Under this criterion, the population of aged is the proportion of people above the age corresponding to a life expectancy of 10 years. This is an attractive concept since the entry into old age becomes a floating concept, rather than fixed at the conventional 65 years. If this criterion (with 10 years of remaining life) were used in the United States, the entry at old age would have increased from 68.6 to 73.3 years between 1900 and 1970.[12]

For India, Malaker and Guha Roy[13] have estimated/projected life expectancy for 1901–2001 at ages 60, 65 and 70. We reproduce here, in Table 3.7, the data from their estimates to comment on the applicability of Ryder's measure in India.

If Ryder's concepts were used for measuring the aged, 60 years would have been the entry point for old age in 1931–41, 65 years in 1951–61 and 70 years in 1971–81. The concept is interesting but its use in practice gives rise to several problems. First, it presupposes the existence of a very good and reliable life table. Second, since the life table varies between regions and even between gender, we ought to calculate a series of ageing indices to understand the full impact of improved longevity on population ageing. Third, how to decide on the 'remaining years of life' is not known. The use of 10 years

Table 3.7
Estimates and Projections of Life Expectancy at Ages
60, 65 and 70, 1901–2001

Year	Life Expectancy at 60		Life Expectancy at 65		Life Expectancy at 70	
	Male	Female	Male	Female	Male	Female
1901–11	9.0	9.3	7.3	7.6	5.8	6.0
1911–21	9.0	9.5	7.3	7.7	5.8	6.2
1921–31	9.3	9.9	7.5	8.0	6.0	6.4
1931–41	10.0	10.6	8.0	8.6	6.3	6.8
1941–51	10.9	11.4	8.8	9.2	6.8	7.3
1951–61	12.3	12.8	9.8	10.3	7.6	8.0
1961–71	14.0	14.3	11.1	11.5	8.6	8.9
1971–81	16.2	16.1	12.8	13.0	9.7	9.9
1981–91	17.3	18.0	13.7	14.5	10.4	11.0
1991–2001	18.3	20.0	14.6	15.9	11.0	12.1

Source: Malaker and Guha Roy (1986).

underestimates the proportion of aged. For example, the use of this concept would mean that only 1.97 per cent people in India constituted the aged in 1970.[14] To make the concept more realistic in developing societies, the remaining years of life ought to be much higher. Fourth, for calculating the ageing index, Ryder's method uses the proportion of the aged in the total population method and therefore carries with it all the problems associated with that method.

P-INDEX OF AGEING

Any ageing index, which is based on a cut-off point, is essentially a head-count ratio.[15] Denoting the total population in a country as $n(p)$ and number of people aged 65 and over as $q(p)$, we have the *head count ratio* of the aged population as:

$$H(p) = \frac{q(p)}{n(p)} \qquad (13)$$

The head-count ratio came under criticism from Sen.[16] His paper marked the beginning of the literature looking for better measures of poverty. It is true that all the people with incomes below the cut-off poverty line are poverty-stricken. But the degree of deprivation and suffering is much higher for those people whose income is lower than those whose income is marginally distant from the cut-off line. A true poverty line must not only find the people living below this line, but the intensity of their deprivation as well. This can be done by providing greater weightage to those whose income gap from the poverty line is higher.

If old age is a problem, the people whose age increases from the cut-off ages must face larger difficulties. The typical head-count index cannot settle this problem. A new ageing index based on Sen's P-Index of Poverty may be very useful. The P-Index of Ageing has been suggested to introduce more refinements in ageing estimation.

Similar to Sen's 'income gap' of poverty, there can be an *age gap index*:

$$I(p) = \sum_{i}^{q(p)} \frac{(p_i - 65)}{q(p).65} \qquad (14)$$

The expression $(p_i - 65)/65$ can be thought as a measure of the extent to which the person 'i' is old. The age gap index is an average of the extent of oldness of the old. A true ageing index can neither ignore the proportion aged $H(p)$ or the extent of oldness, $I(p)$. The multiplication of $H(p)$ and $I(p)$ leads to Basus' Q-Index of Ageing:[17]

$$Q(p) = H(p).I(p) \tag{15}$$

When the age distribution of the aged is known, a further refinement within the H and I combination becomes possible. It may be called the P-Index of Ageing in line with Sen's P-Index of Poverty:[18]

$$P(p) = \sum_i^{q(p)} \frac{(p_i - 65)^2}{n(p).(65)^2} \tag{16}$$

Tables 3.8 (a), (b) and (c) show the estimation procedures for P-Indices of Ageing in India for the years 1995, 2025 and 2050. Similar exercises are done for Japan for 1995, 2025 and 2050 in Tables 3.9 (a), (b) and (c). Note that the United Nations data is available for the five-year age group. We assume here that all the members in each group fall in the middle of this age group. The 100 plus age group has been treated as another group, of 100–104 years. This is definitely a very crude technique of measuring the P-Index of Ageing and may cause some error in the estimate. However, for the first assumption, there is hardly any alternative. For the second assumption, the age of the 100 plus people could have been averaged from the 1991 census data, but that was avoided for three reasons: (a) 100 plus people constituted only 0.00032 per cent of the aged population in 1995; (b) census data on those aged 100 plus is very likely to be overestimated; and (c) no census data could be used for the projected period of 2025 and 2050.

Table 3.10 represents the H-Index, I-Gap, Q-Index and P-Index of ageing for both India and Japan for 1995, 2025 and 2050. The P and Q indices register a sharper increase in ageing in India from 1995 than the conventional head-count ratio. This is quite natural as the indices consider not only the proportion of aged, but also the oldness of the old. As life expectancy rises, the I-Gap also rises. The I-Gap is higher in Japan than in India for obvious reasons. Interestingly, according to both the P- and Q-Index, ageing in India would be more

Table 3.8(a)
Calculation of the P-Index of Ageing in 1995 in
India based on UN Data

Age Group	Number ('000)	$(p_i - 65)$	$(p_i - 65)^2$	$\sum_i^{q(p)}(p_i - 65)$	$\sum_i^{q(p)}(p_i - 65)^2$
65–69	18,195	2	4	36,390	72,780
70–74	12,375	7	49	86,625	606,375
75–79	7,396	12	144	88,752	1,06,5024
80–84	3,459	17	289	58,803	999,651
85–89	1,191	22	484	26,202	576,444
90–94	265	27	729	7,155	193,185
95–99	34	32	1,024	1,088	34,816
100 Plus	3	37	1,369	111	4,107
Total 65 Plus	42,918	91	4,029	305,126	3,552,382
	$q(p)$				
All Ages	933,665				
	$n(p)$				

Source: United Nations, *World Population Prospects: The 1998 Revision, Vol. I: Comprehensive Tables*, United Nations, New York, 1999.

Table 3.8(b)
Calculation of the P-Index of Ageing in 2025 in
India based on UN Data

Age Group	Number ('000)	$(p_i - 65)$	$(p_i - 65)^2$	$\sum_i^{q(p)}(p_i - 65)$	$\sum_i^{q(p)}(p_i - 65)^2$
65–69	44,157	2	4	88,314	176,628
70–74	31,171	7	49	218,197	1,527,379
75–79	19,494	12	144	233,928	2,807,136
80–84	10,672	17	289	181,424	3,084,208
85–89	4,718	22	484	103,796	2,283,512
90–94	1,434	27	729	38,718	1,045,386
95–99	259	32	1,024	8,288	265,216
100 Plus	29	37	1,369	1,073	39,701
Total:	111,934	91	4,029	873,738	11,229,166
	$q(p)$				
All Ages	1,215,672				
	$n(p)$				

Source: Same as Table 3.8(a).

Table 3.8(c)
Calculation of the P-Index of Ageing in 2050 in
India based on UN Data

Age Group	Number ('000)	$(p_i - 65)$	$(p_i - 65)^2$	$\sum_i^{q(p)} (p_i - 65)$	$\sum_i^{q(p)} (p_i - 65)^2$
65–69	79,371	2	4	158,742	317,484
70–74	60,082	7	49	420,574	2,944,018
75–79	44,815	12	144	537,780	6,453,360
80–84	27,949	17	289	475,133	8,077,261
85–89	13,518	22	484	297,396	6,542,712
90–94	4,518	27	729	121,986	3,293,622
95–99	903	32	1,024	28,896	924,672
100 Plus	111	37	1,369	4,107	151,959
Total 65 Plus	231,267	91	4,029	2,044,614	28,705,025
	$q(p)$				
All Ages	1,528,853				
	$n(p)$				

Source: Same as Table 3.8(a).

Table 3.9(a)
Calculation of the P-Index of Ageing in 1995 in
Japan based on UN Data

Age Group	Number ('000)	$(p_i - 65)$	$(p_i - 65)^2$	$\sum_i^{q(p)} (p_i - 65)$	$\sum_i^{q(p)} (p_i - 65)^2$
65–69	6,398	2	4	12,796	25,592
70–74	4,696	7	49	32,872	230,104
75–79	3,290	12	144	39,480	473,760
80–84	2,301	17	289	39,117	664,989
85–89	1,137	22	484	25,014	550,308
90–94	368	27	729	9,936	268,272
95–99	69	32	1,024	2,208	48,576
100 Plus	6	37	1,369	222	8,214
Total 65 Plus	18,265	91	4,029	161,645	2,269,815
	$q(p)$				
All Ages	125,472				

Source: Same as Table 3.8(a).

Table 3.9(b)
Calculation of the P-Index of Ageing in 2025 in
Japan based on UN Projections

Age Group	Number ('000)	$(p_i - 65)$	$(p_i - 65)^2$	$\sum_i^{q(p)} (p_i - 65)$	$\sum_i^{q(p)} (p_i - 65)^2$
65–69	6,912	2	4	13,824	27,648
70–74	7,382	7	49	51,674	361,718
75–79	7,665	12	144	91,980	1,103,760
80–84	5,159	17	289	87,703	1,490,951
85–89	3,137	22	484	69,014	1,518,308
90–94	1,571	27	729	42,417	1,145,259
95–99	482	32	1,024	15,424	493,568
100 Plus	75	37	1,369	2,775	102,675
Total	32,383	91	4,029	374,811	6,243,887
	$q(p)$				
All Ages	121,150				
	$n(p)$				

Source: Same as Table 3.8(a).

Table 3.9(c)
Calculation of the P-Index of Ageing in 2050 in
Japan based on UN Data

Age Group	Number ('000)	$(p_i - 65)$	$(p_i - 65)^2$	$\sum_i^{q(p)} (p_i - 65)$	$\sum_i^{q(p)} (p_i - 65)^2$
65–69	6,695	2	4	13,390	26,780
70–74	7,157	7	49	50,099	350,693
75–79	7,381	12	144	88,572	1,062,864
80–84	5,375	17	289	91,375	1,553,375
85–89	3,550	22	484	78,100	1,718,200
90–94	1,969	27	729	53,163	1,435,401
95–99	924	32	1,024	29,568	946,176
100 Plus	272	37	1,369	10,064	372,368
Total 65 Plus	33,323	91	4,029	414,331	7,465,857
	$q(p)$				
All Ages	104,921				
	$n(p)$				

Source: Same as Table 3.8(a).

Table 3.10
Ageing in India under H, I and Q Indices

	H-Index of Ageing	I-Gap of Ageing	Q-Index of Ageing	P-Index of Ageing
India 1995	0.0459	0.1093771	0.0050204	0.0009
India 2025	0.09208	0.1200897	0.0110579	0.00218
	(200.6)		(220.3)	(242.2)
India 2050	0.15126	0.1360142	0.0205735	0.00444
	(329.5)		(409.8)	(493.7)
Japan 1995	0.145570	0.1361540	0.0198199	0.0042817
Japan 2025	0.2672967	0.1780663	0.0475966	0.0121985
	(183.6)		(240.1)	(284.9)
Japan 2050	0.3176009	0.1912890	0.0607536	0.0168419
	(218.2)		(306.5)	(393.3)

Source: Same as Table 3.8(a).

intense than in Japan in the future. Calculations indicating this can be seen here.

The P and Q indices as explained here have several advantages as compared to the conventional methods of assessing the ageing index:

1. They take into account variations in age distribution within the aged population which the conventional index fails to take note of.
2. To understand the intensity of ageing in a population, several proportions of the aged are needed in a conventional analysis. Kuroda and Hauser[19] have suggested that calculations be made separately for the 'young old' and 'old old' categories. P and Q are composite indices that take note of proportion of aged and 'oldest of the old'. The former index also takes in to account the age distribution of the old.
3. A person is more likely to suffer from mental/physical isolation as his/her age moves away from the cut–off age. A person's physical ability also declines with age.

Despite the advantages, however, the use of the P- or Q-Index may cause several conceptual and estimation problems:

1. The age gap in the P or Q indices is not as relevant as the poverty gap is in the poverty analysis. The poverty gap is an index of the deprivation of the people from the poverty line cut-off. The age

gap concept, though useful, fails to establish what it is. It is not an indicator of deprivation, nor is it an index of isolation. A person may have an age much higher than the cut-off age; he/she may still be in a family set-up surrounded by children/grandchildren. An aged woman may be a widow, but the presence of other members in the family may keep her from being isolated. Whether a person is really isolated or not can be understood from this age gap.

2. With age a person's physical strength diminishes. Medical experts believe that this process starts at the age of 30. If so then the age gap model should have its cut-off point at 30.

3. The age gap concept is also not valid on the grounds of retirement. It is true that retirement has a cut-off age, but retirement benefits, where they do exist, do not diminish with age.

4. The concept of age gap seems to be relevant only in a model which plans for the health care of the aged.

5. The P or Q indices are not free from the arbitrariness involved in the selection of a cut-off age. Not only that, they are also very dependent on the selection of this age. If the cut-off age is low, the index is high. With improvement in longevity what is the necessity of a single cut-off age? 'The cut off age itself should be on a sliding scale, being moved upwards as the expected longevity of a population rises'.[20]

6. While the P or Q indices take note of the age distribution of the aged, they ignore the age distribution of all other sections of the population.

7. To understand the status of the aged, it is very important that we develop a composite index similar to the HDI giving due weightage to isolation, retirement benefit, health care and such other elements useful in an elderly life. In chapter five, we have tried to develop an Elderly Status Index (ESI) based on the NSS 52nd Round Survey on the aged in India.[21]

SLOPE OF POPULATION
PYRAMID AS AN AGEING INDEX

Demographers have used the population pyramid to graphically illustrate the age-sex structure of a population. The shape of the population pyramid changes over the years according to the changes in fertility and mortality trends of the population. A so-called young population has a broader base reflecting a large proportion of its youth when ages and the proportions of the population for the corresponding ages are graphed on the ordinate and on the abscissa, respectively.

As the population ages, the population pyramid with a broad base becomes irregular in shape as the proportion of the population with the higher age groups rises. The slope of the population pyramid can be used as a single summary index for measuring population ageing.[22] As the slope becomes steeper, the population is said to be ageing. Another possible index for measuring population ageing, therefore, is the slope of the least square trend line as it is applied to the population pyramid or the b-coefficient of the regression line. Ordinarily, the population pyramid is constructed sex-age specific so that one side of the pyramid reflects the age composition of the male population and the other side that of the female population. For measuring the population ageing of the total population we can also combine both sexes together. In such a case, the pyramids would have the appearance of a half-pyramid. Figures 3.1 (a), (b) and (c) show the half-pyramid for age distribution in India for the years 1950, 1980 and 2000. The least square lines drawn on the pyramids become steeper as we move from 1950 to 2000.

The slope of the half-pyramid, b, from 1950 to 2000 is estimated in Table 3.11.

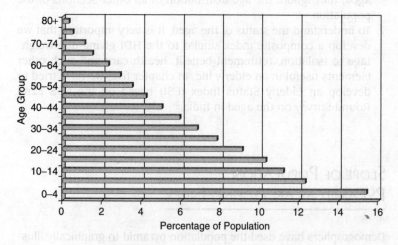

Figure 3.1(a): Half-age Pyramid in India, 1950

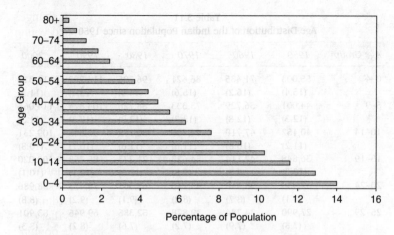

Figure 3.1(b): Half-age Pyramid in India, 1980

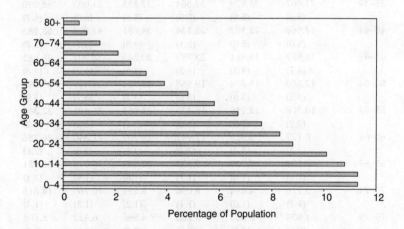

Figure 3.1(c): Half-age Pyramid in India, 2000

Based on the age distribution we estimate the regression coefficient, *b*, for all the years mentioned in the table. Table 3.12 presents ageing trends in India based on different indices.

The b-coefficient has been represented in the second row of Table 3.12. It would have been very useful if we had had a single-year age distribution; that was however not available. We have instead used the five-year age category with 17 such age groups represented by the

Table 3.11
Age Distribution of the Indian Population since 1950

Age Group	1950	1960	1970	1980	1990	2000
0–4	55,003	71,485	86,621	96,705	114,202	114,311
	(15.4)	(16.2)	(15.6)	(14.0)	(13.4)	(11.3)
5–9	44,001	56,729	73,333	88,726	104,874	114,065
	(12.3)	(12.8)	(13.2)	(12.9)	(12.3)	(11.3)
10–14	40,152	47,710	64,409	80,119	90,845	109,231
	(11.2)	(10.8)	(11.6)	(11.6)	(10.7)	(10.8)
15–19	36,848	42,114	54,623	71,273	85,758	102,020
	(10.3)	(9.5)	(9.8)	(10.3)	(10.1)	(10.1)
20–24	32,430	38,448	45,740	62,367	78,473	88,986
	(9.1)	(8.7)	(8.2)	(9.1)	(9.2)	(8.8)
25–29	27,990	34,784	39,878	52,385	69,946	83,901
	(7.8)	(7.9)	(7.2)	(7.6)	(8.2)	(8.3)
30–34	24,208	30,280	36,157	43,612	61,037	76,552
	(6.8)	(6.8)	(6.5)	(6.3)	(7.2)	(7.6)
35–39	21,007	25,929	32,564	37,855	51,003	68,020
	(5.9)	(5.9)	(5.9)	(5.5)	(6.0)	(6.7)
40–44	17,969	22,192	28,134	34,081	42,057	58,983
	(5.0)	(5.0)	(5.1)	(4.9)	(4.9)	(5.8)
45–49	14,987	18,981	23,799	30,345	35,907	48,683
	(4.2)	(4.3)	(4.3)	(4.4)	(4.2)	(4.8)
50–54	12,560	15,874	19,958	25,721	31,479	39,293
	(3.5)	(3.6)	(3.6)	(3.7)	(3.7)	(3.9)
55–59	10,308	12,715	16,474	21,061	26,891	32,365
	(2.9)	(2.9)	(3.0)	(3.1)	(3.2)	(3.2)
60–64	8,127	9,924	12,947	16,709	21,340	26,786
	(2.3)	(2.2)	(2.3)	(2.4)	(2.5)	(2.6)
65–69	5,339	7,200	9,323	12,547	15,778	20,921
	(1.5)	(1.6)	(1.7)	(1.8)	(1.9)	(2.1)
70–74	3,776	4,644	6,096	8,394	10,760	14,515
	(1.1)	(1.0)	(1.1)	(1.2)	(1.3)	(1.4)
75–79	1,934	2,203	3,288	4,596	6,422	8,708
	(0.5)	(0.5)	(0.6)	(0.7)	(0.8)	(0.9)
80 Plus	922	1,135	1,570	2,359	4,071	6,320
	(0.3)	(0.3)	(0.3)	(0.3)	(0.5)	(0.6)
Total	357,561	442,344	554,911	688,856	850,785	1,013,662
	(100.00)	(100.00)	(100.00)	(100.00)	(100.00)	(100.00)

Source: United Nations, *World Population Prospects: The 1998 Revision, Vol. I: Comprehensive Tables*, United Nations, New York, 1999.

Notes: The total may not tally because of rounding off. The figures in brackets indicate percentage.

middle age. The last open age group was treated like an 80–84 year age group. However, because of very little population in that age group, our estimation remains unaffected by this assumption.

As Table 3.12 shows, the Indian population has aged consistently except during the period between 1950 and 1960. In 1960, the Indian population had actually become much younger than in 1950. This trend, however, quickly reversed to the previous trend of ageing in 1970 and this upward trend of ageing continued subsequently. This particular pattern however was found only in the b-coefficient index. The aged-child ratio and the proportion of those aged 65 and above have increased consistently since 1950. The median age however declined between 1960 and 1970.

Table 3.12
Different Indices of Population Ageing

Measures	1950	1960	1970	1980	1990	2000
b-coefficient	−5.466	−5.339	−5.380	−5.673	−6.016	−6.646
Median	20.4	20.4	19.9	20.6	21.9	23.8
Percentage of 65 plus	3.3	3.4	3.7	4.1	4.3	5.0
Aged Child Ratio	8.5	8.5	9.2	10.6	11.8	15.0
Aged Dependency Ratio	5.4	5.6	6.2	6.6	6.8	7.5
Adjusted b-Coefficient	1.00	0.98	0.98	1.04	1.10	1.22
Adjusted Median	1.0	1.0	0.98	1.01	1.07	1.17
Adjusted percentage of 65 plus	1.0	1.03	1.12	1.24	1.30	1.51
Adjusted Aged Child Ratio	1.0	1.0	1.08	1.25	1.39	1.76
Adjusted Aged Dependency Ratio	1.0	1.04	1.15	1.22	1.26	1.39

Source: United Nations, *World Population Prospects: The 1998 Revision, Vol. I: Comprehensive Tables*, United Nations, New York, 1999.
Note: The indices have been standardised by their 1950 index values.

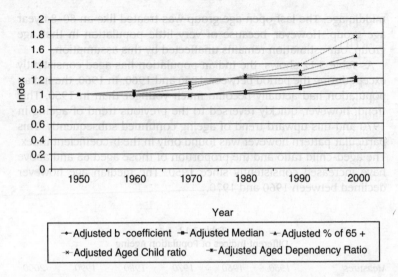

Figure 3.2: Ageing Trends in India, 1950–2000 under Different Indices

To draw ageing trends in India since 1950, utilising all these indices, we standardise them according to their 1950 index value.[23] The standardised indices have also been represented in Table 3.12. When placed in a graph (Figure 3.2), the trends exhibited by the b-coefficient hold remarkable similarity with the trends given by the median ages.

The degree of ageing appears to be most pronounced with the aged-child ratio. This index is most sensitive to the proportion of the young, i.e., those in the age group 0–14. Interestingly, the population in the age group 15–24, which formed almost 20 per cent of the total population since 1950 has been ignored in all the indices except the b-coefficient. The people who were in the age group 15–24 in 1950 are all aged in 2000. The traditional indices fail to take a note of the indirect contribution of all other groups on ageing. The new index directly takes into account the distribution of all age categories. This index is an approximate representation of the shape of the age structure of a population. The coefficient of determination (R^2) is also very high (0.9596 in 1950 and 0.991 in 2000) indicating that the fit of the regression line is very good. The *slope of population pyramid*, thus allows us to analyse ageing through the age distribution of the total population, which no other indices do.

Ageing as a Function of Fertility and Mortality

As discussed in chapter two, population ageing is mainly caused by changes in fertility and mortality. A measure of population ageing should, therefore, include fertility and mortality variables. Population ageing is also influenced by migration. In countries where migration is common, the ageing measure should include that as well.

The rate of change in the proportion of aged persons (65 plus) at time t, can be expressed as:

$$\frac{dp_{65}(t)}{dt} = \frac{N_{65}(t)\{[d(t) - d_{65}(t)] + [a_{65}(t) - b(t)]\}}{N(t)} \tag{17}$$

where P_{65} is the proportion of the population aged 65 and above; d is the death rate of the population; N_{65} is the size of the population aged 65 plus; N is the size of total population; d_{65} is the corresponding death rate of the population aged 65 and over; b is the birth rate of the population; and a_{65} is the rate of new members added to the population aged 65 and above. The change in the proportion aged at time t is expressed as the proportion at that time weighed by the sum of difference between the death rate of the population and the death rate of the population aged 65 plus at time t and differences between the birth rate of population and the rate of ageing into population aged 65 and over at time t. Here, the term $[d(t) - d_{65}(t)]$ indicates population loss, while the term $[a_{65}(t) - b(t)]$ shows population gain in the subgroup. Equivalent terms can be added for in- and out-migration when they are common:

$$\frac{dp_{65}(t)}{dt} = \frac{N_{65}(t)\{[d(t) - d_{65}(t)] + [a_{65}(t) - b(t)] + [0(t) - o_{65}(t)] + [i_{65}(t) - i(t)]\}}{N(t)} \tag{18}$$

where i and o indicate the rate of in-migration and the rate of out-migration, respectively, for the total or a sub-population.

Similarly, the rate of change in the proportion of children can be expressed through:

$$\frac{dp_{15}(t)}{dt} = \frac{N_{15}(t)\{[d(t) - a_{15}(t) - d_{15}(t)] + [b_{15}(t) - b(t)]\}}{N(t)} \tag{19}$$

where all terms have the same meaning as explained earlier. The term a_{15} refers to those members of the age group who are aging out of the group. The term b_{15} refers to the new births added to the age group. The rate of change in the proportion of aged-child ratio can similarly be expressed as:

$$\frac{dR(t)}{dt} = \frac{N_{65}\ (t)\ \{[d(t) + a_{15}\ (t) - d_{65}\ (t)] + [b_{65}\ (t) - b(t)]\}}{N_{15}\ (t)} \tag{20}$$

These new measures are capable of isolating the effects of fertility, mortality and also migration on population ageing. However, they presuppose the existence of a huge flow of data. Liao estimated the rate of change in ageing measures in Japan in 1988–89.[24] The difference between his estimated values and the observed values were found to be negligible. For example, the proportion aged 65 and above in Japan in 1988 was 0.11227. The loss rate and gain rate of the sub-population was 0.04172 and 0.07938 respectively. The estimated rate of change was 0.00379 against the observed rate at 0.00383.

CONCLUSION

In the foregoing analysis, attempts have been made to review the different measures of population ageing. Although the Proportions of Aged cannot be accepted as an exact measure of population ageing, this book uses ageing data based on this measure only. There are quite a few reasons why this was followed. First, because it is a convenient measure to calculate. Second, because this technique is easily comprehensible. Third, the internationally comparable ageing data for most countries is based on this method (e.g., United Nations data). Finally, because the preparation of alternative indices for so many countries over such long period of time is beyond the purview of the current research. Even then, a debate on ageing measures was needed to appreciate the relative strength and weaknesses of the available measures.

There may also be a need to develop a composite alternative index. An ESI, similar to the HDI may be useful. Again, to prepare such an index one needs to be certain about what variables to include. The studies on the aged have not yet produced enough materials to help reach such a consensus. A major objective of this book is to identify those variables, which might have a bearing on the status of the aged. In chapter five, attempts has been made to prepare such an index on the basis of NSS data on the aged in India.

NOTES AND REFERENCES

1. Holdger R. Stub, *The Social Consequences of Long Life*, C.C.Thomas, Springfield, 1982.
2. Mercedes B. Concepcion, 'Emerging Issues of Ageing in the ASEAN Region', in *Economic and Social Implications of Population Ageing*, Proceedings of the International Symposium on Population Structure and Development, Tokyo, 10–12 September 1987, United Nations, New York, 1988.
3. Usha S. Nayar, 'The Situation of Ageing: The Chip and the Old Block', in *Added Years of Life in Asia: Current Situation and Future Challenges*, Asian Population Studies Series No.141, (ST/ESCAP/1688), United Nations, Bangkok, 1996.
4. Paul Johnson and Jane Falkingham, *Ageing and Economic Welfare*, Sage Publications, London, 1992, p. 18.
5. S.H. Preston, C. Himes and M. Eggers, 'Demographic Conditions Responsible for Population Ageing', *Demography*, 26(4): 691–704, November 1989.
6. D.O. Cowgill, 'The Ageing of Populations and Societies', in *The Annals of the American Academy of Political and Social Science*, 415: 1–18, 1974.
7. Department of International and Economic and Social Affairs, United Nations, *Ageing and Urbanization*, Proceedings of the United Nations International Conference on Ageing Populations in the Context of Urbanization Sendai (Japan), 12–16 September 1988, ST/ESA/SER.R109, New York, 1991.
8. H.S. Shryock and J.S. Siegel, *The Methods and Materials of Demography*, condensed edition, Academic Press, New York, 1976.
9. M. Sivamurthy, 'Population Ageing and Demographic Dependency: A Global Analysis', *International Population Conference, Montreal, 24 August–1 September, 1993*, 3: 9–23, International Union for the Scientific Study of Population, Liege, Belgique, 1993.
10. E. Rosset, *Ageing Process of Population*, Pergamon Press, New York, 1964.
11. N. Ryder, 'Notes on Stationary Population', *Population Index*, 41: 3–28, 1975.
12. Toshi Kii, 'A New Index for Measuring Demographic Ageing', *The Gerontologist*, 22(4): 439–42, 1982.
13. C.R. Malaker and Roy S. Guha, *Reconstruction of Indian Life Tables for 1901–81 and Projections for 1981–2001*, Demography Research Unit, Indian Statistical Institute, Calcutta, 1986.
14. According to the Ryder's concept, 70 years would have been the cut-off point for preparing an ageing index in 1970. For that year, only 1.97 per cent of the total population was 70 plus.
15. This is an exact analogue used in the poverty analysis. The measure consists of identifying a critical level of income below which a person would be considered 'poor' and then computing the proportion of population that is poor.

16. A.K. Sen, 'Poverty: An Ordinal Approach to Measurement', *Econometrica*, 44, 1976.

17. Alaka Basu and Kaushik Basu, 'The Greying of Populations: Concepts and Measurement', *Demography India*, 1: 79–87, 1987.

18. Sen's P-index of poverty is given by the form: $P = H\{I + (1-I)\,G\}$ where H is the head-count index, I is the income gap ratio, and G is the Gini coefficient of the distribution of income among the poor.

19. Kuroda T. and P.M. Hauser, *Ageing of the Population of Japan and its Policy Implications*, Nihon University Population Research Institute, Research Paper 1, March, 1981.

20. See note 17.

21. National Sample Survey Organisation, India, *The Aged In India: A Socio-Economic Profile*, NNS 52nd Round, July 1995–June 1996, NSSO, Department of Statistics, Ministry of Planning and Programme Implementation, Government of India, Calcutta, 1998.

22. Toshi Kii, 'A New Index for Measuring Demographic Ageing', *The Gerontologist*, 22(4): 438–42, 1982.

23. As the index produced by different measures has widely dispersed values, the values have been standardised by their respective 1950 data. To be specific, data for all other years are percentages of 1950 data.

24. Tim Futing Liao, 'Measuring Population Ageing as a Function of Fertility, Mortality and Migration', *Journal of Cross-cultural Gerontology*, 11(1): 61–79, Kluwer Academic Publishers, The Netherlands, 1996.

CHAPTER FOUR

AGEING AND DEVELOPMENT

The link between ageing and development is wide ranging and researchers from almost all the social sciences have come forward with their own perspectives and biases on the matter. The concerns shown by these researchers helps us understand the question of population ageing in a much wider perspective. This chapter addresses the major social science linkages between ageing and development. However, in keeping with our objectives, it essentially centres around the issues relating to the integration of the elderly into the general mainstream of healthy and productive lives. To maintain clarity of thought and expression, the chapter avoids intricate intra-disciplinary technicalities and complex methodologies which have no connection with the current study.

AGEING AND ECONOMIC DEVELOPMENT

As explained in chapter two, population ageing is a part of demographic transition, and both demographic transition and population ageing are highly correlated. By corollary, therefore, the ageing of a population is a part of economic development. Notestein has called ageing a 'triumph of civilisation'[1] and, indeed, it is an important determinant of economic development. Ageing brings with it age-related changes in production, consumption and distribution. Productivity falls with the rise in the age of the workers. There is a tremendous shift towards unproductive consumption in the form of health care and finally a massive reallocation of resources from the young to the old in the form of old age social security benefits. These definitely are destabilising factors in economic development, however, family support as well as certain economic characteristics of the elderly act as shock absorbers against such destabilising consequences.

As also explained in chapter two, ageing is caused by a decline in fertility and an improvement in the mortality of the aged. Although experts differ on the cause and the mechanism of this demographic transition, it is observed that both of these are a result of economic development. Mortality improves when income grows and the costs of health care diminish. Remarkable improvements in the mortality of the aged have occurred through vast investments in life sciences, lower costs of medical services, better medical institutions, improvements in health conditions and higher standards of living.[2] In addition, there is an increased allocation of resources to support an extended life after retirement through public as well as private channels.[3] Although most of these opportunities were earlier only present in the developed countries, the developing countries of Asia too, despite the late start in economic development, have ensured that their people do not die as easily as before. Other developments are also closely associated with economic progress, such as, the desire for a long life; the efforts to prevent the loss of life; and the lust for freedom to minimise the uncertainties of life. These are the major objectives of economic development. Clearly, the desires and motives which have led to population ageing are the driving forces behind economic development.

There is a decline in fertility when economic development makes the cost of child caring and rearing high. There is a very high price attached to motherhood, both before and after the birth of children, as economic development makes women increasingly more useful and productive outside the home. As economic development proceeds, more human capital is needed per child and this makes child rearing very expensive. To be more precise, economic development means, among other things, an increase in consumption and the standard of living which expands the length of life, decreases infant mortality and reduces fertility. Moreover, economic development motivates physical movement and the spatial distribution of people and causes ageing in geographic-specific locations.

Interestingly, in the major economic models, ageing or any of the demographic parameters have been considered to be peripheral elements. For example, in the now famous neo-classical growth models, it was assumed that persons of different ages are alike in terms of their productivity and consumption.[4] Some of the later developments in theoretical economics like the life cycle models,[5] overlapping generations models,[6] human capital model,[7] macro-economic labour market models,[8] social interaction model,[9] economic growth models involving differential topology,[10] and the household production model[11] have all tried to investigate the dynamic paths of interaction between ageing and economy. However, a discussion of these highly technical models is beyond the scope of this book.

While population ageing constitutes a very important determinant of the macroeconomic performance of an economy, the diversity within the elderly is also equally important. To be more specific, it is very important to know which generation or birth cohort the different sections of the elderly represent. A small difference in date of birth can produce enormous differences in lifetime experiences. For example, those persons born around the World War I period have suffered a lot in their career: unemployment during the Great Depression of the 1930s, military service during World War II, rationing and food famines. Persons born 10 years later enjoyed better luck. The generations which are relatively free from such calamities are expected to have better health and savings than those affected by such medium-term disturbances. It is therefore, very important to recognise the cohort effect within ageing for a better understanding of the economic potential of the aged.

AGEING AND PRODUCTIVITY

Historically, the influence of the development theory in relation to older people has been particularly putting-off. The concept of development has generally been seen as a one way process: of efforts to increase productivity. This has had a pervasive effect on the thinking about older people in development as older people are usually regarded as economically unproductive. As older people have not been visible actors in the process of 'modernisation' they have come to be associated with traditional ways and the past, and factors inimical to growth. A British commission on population unhesitatingly wrote that,

> older people excel in experience, patience, in wisdom and breadth of view; the young are noted for energy, enterprise,

enthusiasm, the capacity to learn new things, to adapt themselves, to innovate. It thus seems possible that a society in which the proportion of young people is diminishing will become danger-ously unprogressive, falling behind other communities not only in technical efficiency and economic welfare, but in intellectual and artistic achievement as well.[12]

The changing age structure influences the size of the workforce. The participation rates of the elderly workforce are generally lower than those of workers in another age category. A decrease in the size of the active labour force may also reduce productivity. This influences the relative economic performance of people in different birth cohorts and the performance of the macroeconomy. There is very strong microeconomic evidence that suggests age to be an important deter-minant of productivity and remuneration. As the theory of human capital suggests, the productive contribution of a worker depends on three factors:

1. A combination of physical, mental and cultural inheritance which may be grouped together as *latent ability*;
2. deliberate enhancements of this ability through formal training and education; and,
3. less conscious enhancements acquired through work experience and on-the-job training.

The most important common determinant of work experience is age and most studies on age and wage find a positive relationship between the two.[13] If these theories of human capital formation are true, older workers should be more productive than younger workers as their age-related experience is greater. In such an event the relative expansion in the proportion of older workers, other things remaining unchanged, would indicate an increase in overall labour productivity and there-fore a positive stimulus to growth.[14] Despite the evidence on the posi-tive relationship between age and wage, the dominance of the elderly in the workforce may still reduce productivity, directly or indirectly, by raising industrial costs of production. The following are arguments and facts in favour of this hypothesis:

1. It is generally believed that elderly workers cannot adapt well to changing technology, management and other production rela-tionships in the same way workers in the younger age groups are

able to do. Most employers admit that the cost of training older workers is higher and the economic returns to training lower than is the case for younger workers. Thus, if the supply of young workers falls, it is possible that in the long run the technical efficiency of the workforce will fall too. Training and retraining of middle-aged and elderly workers cannot bring back efficiency, given the huge costs of such training and the technical efficiency being embodied in each generation of young workers.

2. The positive age-wage relationship is essentially an artefact of the employment contract rather than a representation of the marginal productivity of the workers, of different ages. It is now agreed that in order to secure the long-term loyalty of employees and to minimise the costs of labour turnover, firms often provide their senior workers with more than their market value. Therefore, by this logic, young workers are paid lower than their market worth.[15]

3. Under controlled laboratory conditions, psychologists observe that both physical and mental reactions decline from middle ages onwards.[16] However, such laboratory testing suffers a few limitations: (a) many of the laboratory tests have no relevance to actual work at employment; (b) improvements even within laboratory testing are possible; (c) while the results are true for average value, dispersion of data from the average was also high, that is, while on the average a 60-year old exhibited slower mental and physical reactions than a 40-year old, there were many elderly who exhibited reactions as good as the average youth.

4. Efficiency studies at the actual level of work show that for work that was carried out at an externally-set pace (e.g., production-line manufacturing), older workers are less efficient when compared to younger workers, though they were found to be as efficient as the young in skill, experience and motivation.[17]

5. While sexism is gradually diminishing from the employment sector everywhere in the world (evident from the increasing female participation in employment), ageism in employment has been sustained. Social characterisation still considers the young to be symbols of dynamism, efficiency and growth, and the old as inefficient and redundant. The respect and veneration extended to elders, a characteristic of Asian society, is also slowly dying out. Older people are considered to be slower, less adaptable and less productive than the young.

6. Older people suffer the most during times of recession. There is a strong incentive on the part of employers to retrench during a crisis,

not because they are unproductive but because their wages, which contain economic rent, are higher than those of the younger staff.

7. The elderly, who work during the post-retirement period, receive much less wages than what they were paid during primary employment. In Japan, most men opt for a 'second career' after retirement, sometimes with the same employer though more usually with a small employer, with a job involving much lower wages and benefits.[18] In many Indian universities, numerous teachers and senior staff accept, after retirement, a second employment as tabulators with much lower wages and no allied benefits. However, there are some incentives for the employer in employing them too. These workers tend to have lower rates of absenteeism and job mobility than the younger workers and are often seen to be more responsible thereby requiring less supervision.

8. As the workforce ages, unions are likely to shift their bargaining efforts away from the training and promotion of young workers, towards the income and pension preservation of middle-aged and older workers. The public choice voting models suggest that in democratic, participatory organisations policy goals tend to represent the interests of the dominant (age) groups. In this process, they are likely to secure resources disproportionate to their contribution to production.

9. Relative scarcity of young workers (a direct effect of the increase in the share of the elderly population) may encourage entry of new workers through official and unofficial immigration channels. Such immigration has its own costs and benefits on the national economy.

10. Habakkuk[19] suggested that incentives to innovate are strongest when population growth is slow and labour is scarce, since technical progress tends to be labour-saving. Simon[20] argues that technological progress depends on population growth, because a larger, denser and more rapidly expanding population experiences increasing economies of scale in both the production and the application of new technologies. It has also been suggested that the success of new technology depends on the existence of recently educated young people who hold the necessary dynamism and innovative spirit to support such change.[21] By implication, therefore, ageing and technological progress cannot go together.

11. It is suggested that pension should be made part of production costs. This view is gaining popularity in China.[22] If this happens,

although a part of the pension costs could be covered, it would make the economy less competitive and would make the elderly less attractive in the job market.

Though ageing and productivity are supposed to share an inverse relationship, concentrating only on paid work tends to ignore the valuable contribution that older people make in unpaid work in the informal sector (e.g., small-scale, self-employed activities and domestic work) and in the home. All over the world, older people often take on the prime responsibility of household management and child care so that younger adults can work outside the home. A number of skilled and experienced older people act as volunteers in schools, communities, religious institutions, businesses, health care and political organizations. Such activities, which make a significant con-tribution to their communities and nations, are often ignored in most economic calculations. It should be remembered that voluntary work contributes to around 8 to 14 per cent of the Gross Domestic Product, a major part of which comes from the elderly.[23]

AGEING AND SUPPLY OF LABOUR

The actual size of the labour force is determined by the sum of the individual labour supply decisions. In the face of increasing life expectancy, as indicated by the life cycle model, people would enjoy a longer time horizon vis-à-vis the lifetime allocation of consump-tion and income. Their expectation pattern would change and they could be moved to work longer in a given period and retire later in order to gain enough guaranteed lifetime income and save more by the age of retirement for future consumption. If, however, there exists some assured and stable system of social security, one need not work much in a given lifetime. In most developed countries, there is an unprecedented withdrawal of people in their 50s from the labour force. This is attributed to the rapid expansion of the social welfare system which provides viable alternatives to work.[24] Again, however, if income levels are low and consumption high in relation to income, one cannot plan much on lifetime labour schedule. More specifically, one needs to work even when physically limited by old age. This explains why elderly participation rates are so high in the developing countries. Tables 1.15 and 1.16 in chapter one present labour force participation rates among the elderly in different regions of the world and that of many countries of Asia.

There is, nevertheless, a general agreement among economists that population ageing affects supply of labour. As people move into old age they tend to undertake low-paying work.[25] To be more specific, people in their 50s and 60s, compared to those in their 30s and 40s, participate less in the workforce. This may be the result of three factors operating individually or collectively:

1. an increased frailty in old age;
2. restricted demand for the services of older workers on the part of employers;
3. a deliberate choice on the part of the elderly to opt for increased leisure at the expense of lost earnings.

The payment of pension is commonly considered to be a direct inducement to withdraw from the labour force as the system provides income in exchange for no work. Pension may also induce workers to accept low paying work in lieu of guaranteed income after retirement. The effect of pension on labour supply is not clear. It depends on the characteristics of individual and labour markets and availability of pension schemes, which vary from place to place. Furthermore, as the earlier section explained, average labour productivity declines after reaching a threshold level somewhere between the ages of 40 and 50.

However, the labour market adjusts itself to the ageing of a population. For instance, when the labour supply of aged workers falls, it creates scope for women and the youth to work. Full-time jobs outside the household improve the status of women in society. Moreover, it raises the wage elasticity of labour supply; keeps the male wage rates within limits. It, however, reduces the major source of elderly care at home. Full-time female workers also see a large family as a constraint on their movements outside the home.

AGEING AND CONSUMPTION

The reduction in the size of households which is accompanied by ageing sets in motion a cumulative mechanism which produces a reduction in total consumption. There is in fact a chain reaction: the reduction in the size of households prompts an increase in saving which in turn causes the weakening of effective demand, investment and finally in employment, income and consumption. However, we have no empirical studies to corroborate this hypothesis.

Ageing influences the structure of consumption. It produces a slow decline in the consumption of goods and services associated with childhood and a slow increase in the consumption of certain goods and services associated with advancing ages (a shift in the demand for a wheelchair from a pram, an increase in the demand for leisure and other services, dietary products, hearing aids, geriatric care etc.).

AGEING AND HOUSING

Housing in old age can be seen as the final phase of housing 'careers'; it is the succession of steps of dwellings occupied over a lifetime.[26] The most significant step is whether or not people ever attain home ownership. Home ownership provides security of occupancy, the prospect of lowering housing costs, and the means to buy more supportive accommodation during old age. Owners are unlikely to be pressured to move, while tenants face fewer costs in moving, they are more likely to be forced to move. Whether or not people become owners or public tenants depends on their circumstances and housing markets particularly during their critical, early adult years. A well-paid and secure job, and two incomes in one household, increases peoples' capacities to own a house during their old age. Having children increases preferences for buying slightly, all else being equal, while marital dissolution can cause people to relinquish home ownership. During the critical young adult years, potential buyers are affected heavily by the price of housing, interest rates, public subsidies and expectations for future price movements. A study in Australia shows that by the time individuals reach their mid-40s and mid-50s more than half of them own homes outright while one-third are purchasers. At ages 65–74, nearly four out of five are outright owners.[27]

In India, the 52nd Round of the NSSO study indicates that 63 per cent of rural and 58 per cent of urban elderly own some kind of property including housing. But only 43 per cent in rural areas and 40 per cent in urban areas enjoy decision-making roles with regard to these properties.[28] Andrews et al. found in their survey of the Philippines, that only 47 per cent of elderly respondents either owned their homes or lived in houses owned by their spouses, while 64 per cent of Malaysians had housing ownership tenures.[29] Home ownership was more common in rural areas than in urban areas. Fifty per cent (more or less) of the Asian elderly do not own any houses and are dependent on the houses owned or rented by their children and relatives. Due to overcrowding and lack of resources with urban administrators, houses in urban areas are hardly large enough to accommodate more than one nuclear family. So when adult sons get married, elderly parents find themselves short of living space. Housing costs prevent the urban elderly from living in independent dwelling units. In the developed world, when people experience major health problems and cannot manage their own house, most move into housing tenures or out of the private housing market into institutionalised homes.

Institutionalised homes for the aged are yet to take shape in most Asian countries. Around 0.8 to 0.9 per cent of elderly people in India are inmates at old age homes. Interestingly, these homes have more rural people staying in them, with more women as inmates than men.[30] There are few specialised institutions for the aged in most Asian countries and the level of institutionalisation is very low.

There is also a well-established pattern among the aged to move, on retirement, out of the larger cities and into the provincial towns and villages. This is combined with a general drift of retired people to areas with warmer climates, a drift which has created very distinct retirement enclaves, for instance Florida in the United States, the Gold Coast in Australia, a number of coastal towns in southern England and along the Mediterranean fringe of France. As shown in chapter five, there has been considerable movement of the elderly, all across Asia, into villages on retirement. The expensive cost of living and growing isolation from other members of the family induces the urban elderly to move to the villages in search of better community living. The geographical concentration of particular age groups means that there may be pronounced local age-related effects on the structure of demand.

Ageing may produce specific demands for certain types of housing. The emerging system of smaller families, compounded by rising divorce rates, increase in the number of widows and widowers and increasing incidence of solitary living among young adults, will reduce the demand for large housing. Mankiw and Weil predict that real housing prices will fall because of demographically induced changes in demand, where the elderly dominate.[31] The projected decline in housing prices occurs despite the increase in total population. It is a consequence of a decline in the rate of household formation. Borsch-Supan[32] argues rather controversially that increasing life expectancy will lead to a fall in the supply of houses being inherited by the young and this in turn will create an overall housing shortage. It may be mentioned that while age structure plays an important role in the long-run demand for housing, other important elements are availability and cost of loans, laws governing and regulating alternative forms of housing tenures, divorce rates etc.

AGEING AND HEALTH CARE COSTS

Different age groups in the population have widely different probabilities to sickness and medical needs.[33] Infants and old people are the groups with the highest incidence of sickness and hospitalisation. At ages above 50, sickness and hospitalisation rates are higher than in the infant age groups. For ages above 50, health care costs are substantially higher than all other age groups. This general pattern is true in the developed as well as in the developing countries.

In the developed countries, average health expenditures by people in the age group 65–79 are double the expenditures of all age groups and the difference is even higher among the very old.[34] O' Connel[35] finds, through a survey of seven OECD countries (USA, Japan, Italy, Austria, Canada, Finland and Greece), that age structure has a significant effect on per capita health care expenditures. Murthy and Ukpolo[36] also found the same results from the US time series data for 1960–87. Getzen[37] and Gerdtham et al.[38] however, failed to note any positive correlation between age structure and health care spending. Based on micro level data, Zweifel et al.[39] too found that ageing had no effect on individual health care expenditures. Their study, however, indicated that years remaining till death are an important determinant as most expenditure takes place during the last two years of life. In Japan, the health data for the National Health Insurance (NHI) plan shows that people aged 70 and above require 40 per cent more medical care than infants. Again as the proportions of the oldest among the old increase, expenditures for long-term care including institutional care and home care should rise. An OECD in-house research paper[40] confirms that it does.

A projection made by the OECD[41] shows that population ageing would explain 30 to 100 per cent of the increase in public expenditure in health care in seven industrialised countries between 1980 to 2025. In Canada, the increase in public expenditure on health between 1980 and 2025 will be 76.2 per cent, with 41.3 per cent due to population increase and 24.7 per cent due to ageing. In Finland, the increase for the same period will be 29.9 per cent, but the effect of demographic growth will be negative and the effect of ageing 30.3 per cent. Another study on the OECD countries including Japan finds that health care costs of the elderly are four times higher than the per capita health care spending by the non-elderly and that this accounts for 2.5 to 5 per cent of the GDP.[42] More importantly, the medical costs for the treatment of each disease differ widely with age. In the Japanese NHI plan, for instance, the cost per medical case for the infant age group was 7,265 yen in 1984 but was 33,194 yen for the elderly age group of above 70 years in the same year.[43] These differences in age-specific health care costs have a bearing on health care costs. As population ageing grows, health care costs rise more than proportionately. It is also interesting to note that although the medical expenditure for the whole population increases by 6.7 times between 1986 and 2025, while that of the elderly population rises by 10 times during the same period.[44] The share of national income required rises from 6.31 per cent in 1986 to 8.5 per cent in 2025.

No such data exists for India or any similar developing country in Asia. If this is the cost pattern on health care by the elderly, there will be a tremendous shift of resources. In addition to the financial resources, however, population ageing is likely to demand a great deal of human resources to cope with the rapid rise in the number of elderly patients who need intensive human care. These include the very old elderly, and bedridden and senile dementia patients. The supply of full-time housewives may not be sufficient to meet the needs of these dysfunctional elderly in the home. In most Asian countries these long-term care facilities cannot be met through regular market service providers. The provision of such services through community-based schemes will only add additional financial pressure on the future of Asia's economy.

Besides, Asian countries will have their own health peculiarities. As nations age, a shift in disease patterns, parallel to changing living and working conditions, becomes inevitable. These changes hit developing countries the hardest. Even as these countries continue to struggle against infectious diseases, malnutrition and complications from childbirth; they are faced with the rapid growth of non-communicable diseases such as cardiovascular diseases (CVD), cancer (particularly lung cancer), chronic obstructive pulmonary disease (COPD), musculoskeletal conditions (including osteoporosis), dementia, blindness and lesser visual impairments.[45] This 'double burden of disease' strains the already scarce resources to the limit. The shift from communicable to non-communicable diseases is fast occurring in most of developing Asia, where chronic illnesses such as heart disease, cancer and depression are quickly becoming the leading causes of death and disability. This trend will escalate over the next century. In 1995, 51 per cent of the global burden of disease in developing and newly industrialised countries was caused by non-communicable diseases, mental health disorders and injuries. By 2020, the burden of these diseases will rise to approximately 70 per cent. In India, some of the communicable diseases, particularly tuberculosis takes on a rampant form and effects people of all ages. There is also a resurgence of malaria, hepatitis, influenza and typhoid. When the aged are afflicted with these diseases, the pain, suffering and costs become higher when such diseases effect the non-elderly.

The Asian countries therefore require considerable expenditure on health care to pursue efficient and effective health care programmes to tackle both communicable and non-communicable diseases. While the United States spend around 14 per cent of its GDP on health, most Asian countries spend even less than 5 per cent of their GDP on health. In 1997, the health care expenditures of India, Thailand and Japan were 5.2, 5.7 and 7.1 per cent of the GDP respectively. Tables 4.1 and 4.2 give an account of the health care expenditures, as percentage of GDP, in several developed and Asian countries.

But the developing countries of Asia are yet to develop health care programmes for the aged, ageing not being a major issue. Most of these countries now aim at providing health care to all. Cost effectiveness of health care demands that priority be given to maternal and child health, as this may save more lives than any other alternative policy options. In the case of India, control of infectious and communicable disease like tuberculosis is also important. Interestingly, the incidence rate of tuberculosis among the elderly male population of India is the highest among the old. The tuberculosis incidence rate is 9.34 per 1000 elderly males, followed by 7.0 per 1000 in Middle-east Asian countries, 3.9 per 1000 in Sub-Saharan Africa and 3.6 per 1000 in China.

Table 4.1

National Health Expenditure of GDP, 1960–1997, in Developed Countries
(in percentage)

Countries	1960	1970	1980	1990	1997
Australia	4.9	5.7	7.3	8.2	8.4
Canada	5.4	7.0	7.2	9.2	9.2
France	4.2	5.8	7.6	8.9	9.6
Germany	4.8	6.3	8.8	8.7	10.7
Italy	3.6	5.2	7.0	8.1	7.6
Japan	3.0	4.6	6.5	6.1	7.2
South Korea	–	2.3	3.7	5.2	6.0
United Kingdom	3.9	4.5	5.6	6.0	6.8
United States	5.2	7.3	9.1	12.6	13.9

Source: Organisation for Economic Co-operation and Development (OECD), *OECD Health Data 1999: A Comparative Analysis of 29 Countries*, CD-ROM, Paris, OECD, 1999.

Table 4.2

Health Care Expenditures as Percentages of GDP in Several Asian Countries

Countries	Year	Total	Public Sector	Private Sector
Bangladesh	1995	2.4	1.2	1.3
	1997	4.9	2.3	2.6
Egypt	1995	3.7	1.6	2.1
	1997	3.7	1.0	2.7
India	1991	5.6	1.2	4.4
	1997	5.2	0.7	4.5
Indonesia	1994	1.8	0.7	1.2
	1997	1.7	0.6	1.1
Japan	1995	7.2	5.6	1.6
	1997	7.1	5.7	1.4
Philippines	1991	2.4	1.3	1.0
	1997	3.4	1.6	1.8
South Korea	1992	5.4	1.8	3.6
	1997	6.7	2.5	4.2
Thailand	1992	5.3	1.4	3.9
	1997	5.7	1.9	3.8

Sources: World Health Organization, *World Health Report 1998: Life in the 21st Century—A Vision for All*, Geneva, WHO, 1998 (for 1997 data); Edward Bos, Vivian Hon, Akiko Maed, Gnanaraj Chellaraj and Alexander Preker, *Health, Nutrition and Population Indicators: A Statistical Handbook*, World Bank, 1999.

In most developed countries including Japan, health care is subsidised. Japan like the US heavily subsidises its health care for the elderly, as also its long-term care insurance. Because of the prevalence of the health care insurance and huge subsidy on health sectors, an increase in household income would not raise the demand for health care much; this is evident from the low level of income elasticity of health care[46] in the developed countries. Income elasticity of health care is mostly less than or close to 1.[47] However, income elasticity for health care in the developing countries of Asia are much higher than 1. Russo estimates that the income elasticity of health care for Thailand was 1.85 in the 1988 socio-economic survey data.[48] His other studies show that elasticity was 1.65 for Indonesia[49] in 1987 and 1.65 for the Philippines[50] in 1985. This may be contrasted with the zero income elasticity of health care as estimated by Manning et al.[51] for USA on the basis of micro-level data for the period 1974–77. The policy makers of the developing countries of Asia need to take note of this. As economic development takes place, there would be increasing demand for health care in which the share of the elderly would be no less insignificant.

Health expenditure could become more difficult to control than it appears from the above narration. There are continuous technological advances, which are very expensive but are capable of prolonging the duration of human life. People are dying at later stages of their lives and in states of greater disrepair as both family and society need more resources to be able to care for such people.

AGEING AND CAPITAL FORMATION

Another important element in the link between ageing and development is the distribution of economic resources. By application of the life cycle model, an individual will accumulate resources during his prime working years through peak earnings and will then live off those savings during the later years of his life when his earnings move close to zero because of retirement or disability. This implies that an ageing population will contribute very little towards the savings of the country, as most of them are dependent on the realisation of past savings for livelihood. Though recent research supports the life cycle hypothesis that dissaving occurs in old age, this finding is not conclusive. Some longitudinal data shows that elderly people do not decumulate as they age.[52] Aaron points out that saving rates for the retired people are little below those aged 45–64 but much higher than those in the 25–44 age group.[53] Again, since consumption expenditure tends to fall in the old age bracket, many older people save from their annuity and pension income rather than reduce their accumulated wealth.[54]

PENSION AND CAPITAL FORMATION

Population ageing has considerable implications for the social security system. Most countries have a system of retirement pension. The developed countries have a universal pension system while the developing countries follow a much-truncated system for its organised sector workers. Such public provisions are generally seen as incentives for older people through their continued participation in the labour force. However, they are often considered to be a burden on the active population. Expenditure on unemployed young people constitutes an investment in human capital with positive effects on economic productivity, but expenditure on the old is no investment. It is fully used up in consumption. Expenditure on the old also imposes a burden on society through taxation. The present generation is taxed for the older generations. A growing aged population would require more such transfers and taxes. A minor adjustment in the fiscal set up may not be enough to accommodate the growing public pensions and other welfare measures needed for the aged. The huge intergenerational transfer, that may cause economic stagnation, carries within it the seeds for intergenerational tensions and conflicts of various interest groups.

In the USA, there were long debates on the long-term costs of public old age provisions. President Roosevelt wanted to have a large reserve fund to cover social security provisions, including those under the Old Age and Survivors Insurance. On the contrary, the industry was apprehensive that such accumulation might diminish consumer purchasing power with its adverse effect on capital markets.[55] A substantial amendment was made to introduce the pay-as-you-go system in lieu of the existing fully state-funded scheme. Much the same happened to the British system. Initially there were very few pensioners and rapid economic growth allowed the benefits to rise faster than the contributions. Such social security schemes were part of the government's counter-cyclical macroeconomic measures and they appeared to be benign and productive for the economy and society. Presently, however, with pensions typically consuming a half of the social security budget of the governments in the OECD countries, these public transfers are seen as obstacles to economic efficiency.

Feldstein[56] argued that the public pension system reduces the inducement to save during the working period. The overall rate of personal savings fall and other things remaining unchanged, this would increase the rate of interest. Borrowing becomes more expensive, investment falls and the long-term growth rate of the economy falls too. His exercises show that if there were no public pension scheme then the national income would have been higher than the actual value. The depressive effect on saving rates can be counteracted only by another tax on the working populations. Public pension schemes therefore depend heavily on additional taxes for financing as well as for macroeconomic adjustments that may be required in the process. Feldstein[57] contends elsewhere that social security pension schemes have a damaging impact on a country's long-term growth.

This view has been countered by the multigenerational planning horizon theory of Barro.[58] The fact that people make bequests is evidence enough that they derive some benefit from the well-being of future generations. In these circumstances, the gain of the present generation in being granted pension rights will be balanced by the tax liabilities of future generations, as they also secure these inheritances. Current generations will therefore find that they need to save less to finance their own old age, but need to save more in order to increase their bequest sufficiently to compensate successive generations for their tax liabilities. These two effects should cancel each other leaving the savings rate unchanged. However, with the future being so uncertain, no rational decision-maker will probably be able to get so much future data in his current decision-making. The individual discounts the future so heavily that, as Aaron[59] observes, future events have very little impact on current decision-making.

When looked at from the perspective of short horizon models, which obviously are more realistic, younger workers perceive social security contributions simply as a tax which reduces their consumption, but older workers consider themselves little richer as they approach retirement ages and increase their consumption slightly.

The aggregate effect on savings thus appears to be marginal. Again, the slow growth of the population that accompanies ageing lowers the required capital accumulation necessary to maintain the capital/labour ratio in the economy and so reduces the need for savings too. Once more, when there is domestic shortage of savings, the rate of interest moves up and this attracts foreign capital.[60]

The societal pension scheme also involves redistribution of resources from the current to the future generations. If the proportion of non-working elderly people to the working people rises, a large share of the national output, produced by the working population will have to be transferred to the retired population. This transfer which normally takes the form of private savings and social security systems, is effectively a redistribution of economic resources between generations from young to old. Such participation in a pension scheme is definitely a part of life cycle redistribution from the perspective of the individual. It is also a part of the intergenerational transfer of resources of the society.

AGEING AND INTERGENERATIONAL TENSIONS

The debate over intergenerational equity began in the USA following a social security tax hike and the adoption of cost-of-living index adjustments in the 1970s. The corporate world censured the social security welfare provisions as an intergenerational tax rather than an insurance programme. It was observed that more than 25 per cent of the US annual budgets were earmarked for the aged and Hudson had warned against the impending backlash towards such a trend.[61] Interestingly, one of the first indicators of an emerging backlash came in relation to defence spending. The 'greying of the budget' became so prominent that the commonly used metaphor of 'guns vs butter' was switched to 'guns vs canes' in economic textbooks.[62] The metaphor was conveniently modified into 'kids vs canes' in the debate on intergenerational equity. The famous corporate journal, *Forbes* commented in 1980 that the elderly were living well, not in poverty, as most believed. It wrote, 'The trouble is there are too many of them—God bless them'.[63] This corporate pessimism was reflected in the chairman's address to a group of shareholders of a giant corporate body: in future 'young and old will be pitted against each other in a fearful battle over the remains of a shrinking economy'.[64] *Forbes* reiterates in the final stage of the debate, 'it is part of the sorrowful lot of baby boom generation (those born between 1946 and 1964) that it will have to finance both its parents' retirement and a substantial portion of its own'.[65]

Samuel Preston elevated the corporate cynicism on elderly security provisions into a rich public debate on intergenerational equity though his presidential address before the Population Association of America in 1984. He makes a case for direct competition between the young and the old for society's humble resources: 'whereas expenditures on the elderly can be thought mainly as consumption, expenditures on the young are a combination of consumption and investment'.[66] He writes elsewhere that between 1970 and 1982, the incidence of poverty among the elderly in the US had fallen sharply while children under 14 showed increased incidence of poverty.[67] These divergent trends were essentially a result of social security programmes that favoured the aged. The funds for children's welfare were curtailed and the family was responsible for generating its own resources for the development and welfare of children, ironically at a time when the family itself was undergoing its own crisis through high and rising divorce rates. The elderly and the children competed with each other for scarce public funds. Interestingly, when the working age population is taxed to pay for the aged, their capacity to take care of the children diminishes, but it is the children who depend more on the working age population for their maintenance than the aged. Richman and Stagner maintain that in an ageing society, children are either a treasured resource or a forgotten minority.[68] Daniel Callahan proposed that limited resources should prompt policy makers to consider a health care rationing programme based on age.[69] Laslett states that an unfair burden was placed on the baby boom generation to support a growing ageing population.[70] Laurence Kotlikoff formulated the 'generational accounting' procedure to state that the later people are born, the more they will work for everyone else and the less for themselves.[71]

Longman[72] has argued that younger generations (incidentally those who belong to the baby-boom generation and have had tremendous luck in securing social security since birth) are in inevitable conflict with their elders. His estimates showed that the average net income and wealth of the young were lower than those of the elderly recipients. He suggested a rise in the normal age of retirement and a ceiling on the net income and wealth of the elderly for them to be entitled to public security. The concern for equity between the old and the young became so high that a pressure group, Americans for Generational Equity (AGE) came into direct electoral confrontation with the growing pressure group, American Association for the Retired Persons. Callahan[73] came up with convincing arguments for restricting health care facilities for the aged in order to introduce improved health care facilities for the aged and young alike.

Heller et al.[74] and the Organisation for Economic Co-operation and Development (OECD)[75] made detailed comparative studies of the financial effect of demographic change on social security systems in the developed countries. These studies demonstrate that population ageing would increase the cost of the public pension provision in all countries over the next few decades. There are other state expenditures on the aged too. As shown earlier, the financial implications of this steep age gradient in the use of health care services are considerable. The OECD report tells us that between 1980 and 2040, demographic change will lead to an 18 per cent reduction in the education budget (essentially because of the decline of children and the youth in the total population) and another 15 per cent reduction in family benefits in the 12 major member countries. During the same time, health expenditures will rise by 40 per cent and pension expenditure by almost 80 per cent. The social expenditure will rise by 30 per cent. The financing burden of this huge social expenditure will be very high. Schmahl[76] estimates that the average tax contribution rate will rise from 18.5 per cent to 41 per cent of wage costs from 1989 to 2030 in order to respond to the pension financing requirement of population ageing. In France, a similar rise in the contribution rate from 16.3 per cent in 1990 to around 40 per cent by 2040 has been projected.[77] Increase in social security taxes of such magnitude will create economic stagnation and unemployment and reduce the competitiveness of the economy.

Keyfitz[78] states that the rate of return from pension contributions for future generations will be negative. They will receive a sum much lower than their contributions. This makes the system unstable and there will be a growing incentive to abandon the entire social security system. Thompson writes,

> unless future generations of the young prove willing to pay taxes on a scale seen nowhere in the present century, the young adults of today cannot expect as they reach old age a treatment comparable to that which they are now giving the aged, let alone a return commensurate with their many times greater life time contributions.[79]

On the other side, it was opined that the intergenerational equity debate was deliberately planted to undermine the cross-class strengths of the old-age coalition and weaken the power of the elderly lobby.[80] Minkler and Robertson wrote, 'The rhetoric of young versus old was promulgated by an elite group of policy makers, academicians, and business leaders with a stake in remaking public images of the elderly in ways that would support decreased social spending'.[81] Binney and Estes believe that the intergenerational equity debate is a carefully crafted diversion that relieves the state of its responsibility towards human needs and permits large budgetary reallocations to the military and major tax cuts for the wealthy.[82] The arguments to the contrary view points are no less insignificant.

First, there are different needs at different stages of our lives. The demand for equity between the public expenditures on children and the elderly is not based on any sound principle of equity. It is also highly impractical. As Daniels[83] argues, to pit one age group against another is not only unfair but diverts our attention away from other inequities that may exist. In the words of Binstock, the current pre-occupation with equity between generations 'blinds us to inequities within age groups and throughout our society'.[84]

Second, the tensions that exist between generations are very different from the tensions that exist between different groups in any society. People always understand, through family experiences, that successive birth cohorts and generations are interdependent. The dismantling of social programmes for the old would mean dismantling of social programmes for the youth in their later lives.

Third, the elderly population in any country is highly heterogeneous. They are rich and poor, productive and non-productive, strong and weak, 'young old' and 'old old', conservative and liberal. Any blanket reduction in elderly welfare measures cannot be logically established.

Fourth, since each generation receives transfers from those that precede it and also gives transfers to those that follow, to reach accurate conclusions about equity between generations would require finding answers to some very difficult questions. The Generations United[85] raised the following questions:

◆ How should the economic and social investments made by previous generations be valued?
◆ Should part of what is spent on the elderly be counted as a return on their investments in younger generations?
◆ Should part of what is spent on children be considered an investment in the future productivity of society?

◆ How should investments made in research, conservation, environmental protection and defence be allocated across age groups? Unless we are able to provide adequate answers to these questions, no major conclusions can be drawn about equity generations.

Fifth, there is a misconception that public benefits directed towards the elderly represent only a one-way flow, from young to old and that reciprocity between generations does not exist. Such an approach only fuels misunderstanding among generations. Public policies should take note of the reciprocal relationship between the young and old generations. Many countries have already designed and enacted intergenerational policies, such as the Family and Medical Leave Act of 1993 in the US. Under this law, an employee can take time off from work to care for a sick child or a frail parent.

Finally, the intergenerational relationship is not a zero sum game. There is no reason to believe that resources directed toward one age group diminish the quality of life for another. It may be possible to make resources available for social sectors by cutting budgetary allocations in such areas as defence etc.

To sum up, the intergenerational equity question is gradually making its way into the political agenda of most countries of the world today. Intergenerational equity is definitely a goal which most societies aim for. However, to paraphrase Moody, intergenerational equity should not be viewed as a code word for 'smart politics' or 'sound public policy' or become the buzzword of politically correct language. Instead, it should become a means to keep the debate going, to keep the dialogue responsible and whenever possible, to guide us towards a better understanding of our social principles and towards wiser decisions in our personal lives.[86]

AGEING AND POLITICS

Not much research has been done on old age as a political identifier. The established political cleavages of class, caste, race and gender provide very little room for political division on age. For most countries, political issues have very little or no age dimension attached to them. But the absence of old age politics in the past should not be taken as a sign that it will not emerge again in the future. The demographic imperative of population ageing means that the electoral weight of people aged over 60 is rising. In India, in 1995, every eighth voter was aged 60 plus. Projections indicate that by 2025, every fifth voter will be an elderly and by 2050, every third voter will be a senior citizen.[87] If age-based politics does develop in the future, then the ageing of the population will turn into a powerful political resource. Already, in the USA and Canada, the elderly have received a good deal of attention on the campaign trail, and yet, in the realm of political science, it is still unclear as to what should be the appropriate 'classification' for the elderly. Clarifying this situation is important. Political candidates and party election strategists believe that the elderly have a significant impact not only on elections, but also on politics in general.

There has been considerable ageing among the voting age population, consisting roughly of persons aged 20 and above and their numbers are projected to rise even further in the future. Table 4.3 captures the current and projected trends in the MDRs, Asia, Japan, India and Thailand. In Japan today almost every fifth voting person is

Table 4.3
The Elderly in Voting Age Population in Some Regions/Countries, 1995, 2025 and 2050

(number in thousands)

Countries/ Regions	1995		2025		2050	
	Voting Age Population	Elderly (60 plus)	Voting Age Population	Elderly (60 plus)	Voting Age Population	Elderly (60 plus)
MDRs	862,316	215,693 (25.0)	958,400	337,074 (35.2)	916,518	376,516 (41.1)
Japan	96,893	18,265 (18.9)	98,616	39,909 (40.5)	85,152	39,430 (46.3)
India	513,348	67,177 (13.1)	922,778	168,133 (18.2)	1,130,707	323,856 (28.6)
Thailand	36,130	4,456 (12.3)	54,258	13,126 (24.2)	57,474	21,981 (38.2)
Asia	2,026,300	281,378 (13.9)	3,329,413	704,530 (21.2)	3,942,436	1,238,663 (31.4)

Source: Compiled and calculated from United Nations, *World Population Prospects: The 1998 Volumes I and II*, Sales No.E.99.XIII.8 and E.99.XIII.9, United Nations, New York, 2000.

Note: Figures in parenthesis indicate elderly voter as percentage of total voting population.

an elderly and 50 years from now, every second voter would be an aged person. This trend is almost the same for the developed countries. The countries of Asia, particularly India and Thailand, are only just catching up. The trend indicates an increasing potential for older voters to influence the political agenda of parties in these countries and the allocation of governmental resources. Moreover, there may be gender-based policies that may be affected by the accompanying more-than-proportionate growth of older females in the voting age population.

Voting Behaviour of the Aged

Voting behaviour is not the only dimension of political participation; it is also a fundamental aspect of examining the potential intergenerational conflict that could emerge as a response to the inequitable distribution of state resources by age. Clearly, the potential strength of voting participation depends on whether the attitudes of different age groups become crystallised around key issues that directly effect their own well-being vis-à-vis other age groups. Proponents of greater generational equity argue that there has been a significant redistribution of resources in favour of the old and at a cost to the young. Bengtson[88] identifies five elements in this redistribution:

1. The redistribution of resources in favour of the old was essentially due to the greater political influence and the effects of organised political lobbying on their behalf.
2. The economic status of the older persons has shown marked improvement.
3. Older persons have become better off as a group vis-à-vis the non-aged.
4. The flow of resources to children and other dependent population sub-groups has declined proportionately.
5. If these patterns continue in the future, there is a strong likelihood that this development will eventually lead to intergenerational conflict.

While it is true that more resources have flowed to the elderly as compared to the young, the existing literature does not confirm that the aged are being organised into a politically cohesive unit. Cumming and Henry have suggested the theory of disengagement.[89] When applied to political participation, the theory enabled political scientists to 'interpret the decline in voter turnout among the very old to reflect the onset of physical infirmities and a narrowing of psychological participation on the broader life of society as senility approaches.[90]

Wolfinger and Rosenstone however observe that 'ageing, by itself, produces not a decline but an increase in turnout'.[91] Greater voting rates among older Americans have been linked to the notion that patriotism develops in a life-cycle pattern. According to Robert Hudson and John Strate, the cost of entering the political system also decreases with age. As people age, they develop an increasing sense of attachment to the nation, and therefore, are more likely to participate in political activities such as voting.[92] In Indian electoral politics too, there is a huge turnout of elderly voters. These people, who have seen the nation through many ups and downs, are more committed and attached to it than the younger generation. Continual exposure to politics, as well as endless interactions with government institutions over a lifetime, equips individuals with the relevant skills and interests. Therefore, by the time individuals reach old age, voting becomes a tradition or a habit. The result is greater voter participation by the elderly.[93]

In a different context, higher electoral participation rates among those individuals aged 65 and above have been attributed to the generation effect. As time passes, successive cohorts become better educated. Education is a leading factor in determining whether or not an individual will vote. Relatively high levels of participation among individuals over the age of 65 are likely due to their membership in a 'younger,' more educated cohort. This would mean that an individual who is 70 years old in 2002 is more likely to vote than an individual who was 70 years old in 1950. It can thus be inferred from this hypothesis that political participation among the aged has tremendous potential to become more intense in the future.[94]

The growing levels of voter turnout among the elderly have often been linked with the concept of age consciousness, defined as the 'degree to which old people become aware of themselves as old'.[95] Applied to the study of politics, age consciousness can affect political attitudes of the elderly when political issues cause an individual's age to be highly relevant. The political analysis generally rejects the notion that older voters act as a cohesive voting block; they are 'swing voters,' and solely by virtue of their age, become more conservative in their later years.[96]

There has been considerable debate as to whether or not the elderly have become a self-conscious group with common interests and the ability to act as a political force. Many studies have asserted that 'the recognition that age identification, like class consciousness, partisan identification, ethnic identification, and sex identification, is potentially a potent force in the organisation of citizens and the mobilisation of political activity'.[97] Age may become a point around which organisations can be built and large numbers of people can be mobilised. There has been 'a dynamic movement of ageing consciousness that has developed in the last 5 years,' and the results have been an increasing number of voluntary associations for the elderly.[98] Despite the fact that these organisations are yet to develop a high level of cohesion, they signify a changing political orientation among the elderly. Many others, however, questioned the likelihood that the elderly operate as a pseudo-subculture.

There is also considerable agreement that persons tend to retain the general political orientations developed early on in adult life.[99] Researches also show that older persons tend to change their political attitudes in the same direction as the non-elderly.[100] A careful analysis of Indian electoral politics would show that there are hardly any age differences in party alliances. There has also been considerable evidence that age is not a major factor in determining attitudes towards major issues at the national level and that they have not crystallised for cohorts as they age.[101] In none of the developed countries, despite the intense debate on intergenerational equity, have older persons been found to vote distinctively on issues related to funding for children or other age groups in particular.[102]

The available evidence suggests that the growing population ageing in most western countries, although leading towards greater numbers of older persons and an ageing of the electorate, does not imply any direct link to the emergence of greater intergenerational conflict. However, the growing consciousness towards the 'senior voter' may be enough of a threat to their well-being to encourage the formation of a new generational consciousness and this may be reflected in the voting behaviour in future. Already in West Germany, studies indicate that strong age differences exist in party vote shares for two of the four main parties and that these differences have tended to persist over time.[103] Similar results are reported for Sweden. Binstock and Riemer envisage, in their essay on targeting the 'Senior Vote':

> if politicians believe in the commonly purveyed images of the aged as a potentially cohesive and decisive voting bloc, then they may be influenced by those beliefs in their allocation of

election campaign resources, in their public commitments to policy positions, and in their approaches to the adoption and implementation of policy. Regardless of whether there is an 'aged vote,' the belief that there is *may* importantly shape electoral campaign and public policy decisions.[104]

Facing the issues of allocation of resources and maintaining the unity among generations is one of the crucial challenges of the times ahead.

AGEING AND SOCIETY

Population ageing is a demographic process and this change has wide social repercussions. Nevertheless, sociology as a subject, studying the way that society functions and changes over time, has not been adequately receptive to the study of the elderly. Many grumble that 'sociology almost entirely neglects later life'.[105] But to understand the role of ageing in development, an understanding of the response of the family to the ageing process is of paramount importance. Families or households are those molecular units of society through which life continues from one generation to the next. A family shelters everyone, from the children to the old, from the unemployed to the most gainfully employed, from the sick to the healthy and from the male to the female. As population ages, the family too undergoes a transformation. Large families disintegrate into small families but the family as an institution continues to serve it's role more perfectly than any other institution. As yet, this institution has not abandoned any of its members wilfully. The family acts as a buffer and lessens the social and economic impact of ageing on society. Before we get into a discussion on the reactions of the family to the greying of populations, it will be interesting to review some sociological explanations about the consequences of the ageing process.

Some Sociological Premises on Ageing and Society

In traditional societies, the old are revered and respected; old age is treated as the golden age. Old people are believed to be the repositories of knowledge, wisdom, law and custom by virtue of their experience. Moreover, by being the titleholder of the family property, the elderly head exercised enormous control over the younger members of the family. This theory, that old people were revered and respected, however, has been challenged by Laslett[106] and Quadagno[107] through historical facts. Their findings show that in pre-industrial societies, many old people were dependent on the state for support, as they were not cared for adequately by their family members. There was no sign of respect and reverence towards the old by the young; the elderly were at the most tolerated.

There also exists a convergence theory of family structure. It believes that in largely rural traditional societies, families are essentially extended, either horizontally or vertically, whereas in modern industrialised societies, the independent nuclear family predominates. This theory believes that this is a natural progression of events as economic development expands. To quote Goode:

> Wherever the economic system expands through industrialization, family patterns change. Extended kinship ties weaken, lineage patterns dissolve, and a trend toward some form of the conjugal system generally begins to appear—that is, the nuclear family becomes a more independent kinship unit.[108]

One of the implications of this transition is a 'weakening of ties with the older generation'.[109] Apparently, this weakening of ties refers to the greater prevalence of separate living arrangements, as well as to a reduction in social interaction and financial, emotional and physical support for the older generation. Little research has been undertaken to confirm this hypothesis but popular faith has grown to believe that the dominating role of the aged in the family erodes with the advent of modernisation and urbanisation of society.

The spread of education, evolution of rational thinking, development of communication, growth of industries, introduction of the market system, popularisation of the consumerist culture—all have worked with each other to undermine the importance of the aged. People now recognise that knowledge can be acquired much faster through years of formal training than through experience. The concept of rational thinking has removed the elderly from their highly elitist status and put them on an equal footing with the rest of the adults in a modern society. The growth of industries has created job opportunities for the young and the development of communication has widened this scope further, often taking the young away from their homes in the process. The young are no longer dependent on the aged for a share of the family financial resources. The market system has brought with it a value mechanism based on competition. In this new market competition, there are hardly any areas where the elderly could beat the young. In the new consumerist culture, the old are just passive observers. In recognition of their inability to retain their supremacy in this fast changing world, the older people are increasingly choosing to disengage from competitive society and willingly retreat into a social and economic backwater of retirement.[110] Many try to refute the argument that a departure from the labour market can be a wilful disengagement from society, as today people are forced out of the labour market through inducements, regulations and threats.

Some sociological approaches are optimistic about the position of the elderly in modern society. They believe that the conditions of the aged have gone up significantly through the 20th century welfare legislation catering significantly to their needs; the share of the elderly in the national product has increased and they are now able to participate in society as fully entitled citizens. Such a view has come to be known as the liberal collectivist strand of sociological analysis.[111] Looked upon from the aspect of public policy, policy interventions are increasingly concerned with the elderly all over the world. Even then, the persistence of severe hardship and deprivation among the elderly and their existence under semi-moribund conditions in most parts of the world cast doubts over whether one should be optimistic about the status of the elderly today.

The structured dependency theory of old age argues that the problems of older people have been socially constructed through a complex network of welfare policies, retirement rules, legal restrictions and cultural norms.[112] The theory contends that, old age welfare policies are mere adjustment mechanisms for society to avoid some of its own crises, and are not for mitigating the mental and physical deterioration of the aged. To be specific, retirement systems control over-production in a capitalist society by reducing the size of the labour force. Population ageing works as a safety valve for the stabilisation of the entire economic system. The elderly bear the cost of an over-abundant labour supply. The theory, though fascinating, has ignored the historical evolution of old age policies.[113] It is hard to demonstrate that the majority of state policies on the aged have been developed to create a reserve army of unemployed labour force. At the same time, it is not known what the employers have gained through the continuance of retirement schemes.[114]

Changes in the Family Structure

Ageing brings about changes in the composition of family, both in structure and size. With rising life expectancy and decrease in infant mortality rates, it has become possible for three to four generations to live together in the same family. Where such a family structure has become achievable, the new and newer offspring have built-in-mechanisms to help them prosper and grow. It also allows family lineage and tradition to continue. However, such a system requires the young and productive members to bear all the economic and psychological stress and strain of the non-productive constituents. With diminishing fertility, the per capita cost of caring for the elderly in the family becomes high and this is a burden that lasts for long due to vast improvement in human life expectancy. As the elderly require more and more support with increase in age, the burden of caring too goes up. Another factor that is present in such families is that the young members, who also combine the role of caregivers for the elderly, are also growing old. Chapter one introduces the concept of Parent Support Ratio (PaSR) to indicate the number of family caregivers who are already old, or in the final stage before retirement, in the care of the very old elderly. In 1950, for the world as a whole, there were only 1.8 persons aged 50–64 years per the very old elderly (85 years and above); this ratio has now gone up to 4.3. The ratio is currently 8.8 in the MDRs. In Asian society, non-marketable care services are considered to be the responsibility of women who are now additionally burdened with prolonged aged care at home.[115] These women have been forced to reduce their own family size to take care of elderly parents. This phenomenon is quite common in Japan.

In view of the lopsided pattern of burden sharing within the family and the stress and strains that accompany that process, generational families are under constant structural pressure to disintegrate. There exists a natural instinct for living beings to develop their own conjugal home. Moody[116] suggests in this case the story of the baby bird who rides on her mother's back while the mother searches for food. One day the mother asks the baby bird, 'when I am old and frail, will you carry me on your back just as I am doing now?' 'Oh no, mother', replies the baby bird, 'I'll carry my own baby bird just as you're doing now'. The implication of this folklore is that there are limits to reciprocity. 'No matter what the older generation has done for the younger, each generation's primary obligation is transitive. That is, we repay the generosity of the preceding generation by giving in turn to our successors'.[117]

There already exist external pressures on the generational family. It is a widely accepted view that urbanisation and industrialisation create an isolated nuclear family[118] and that those modernisation forces prompt the creation of neo-local and nuclear residence.[119] Many internal problems arising from the mutligenerational mode of living are becoming public. The conflict between the mother and the daughter(s)-in-law is well known. In addition, there are enormous differences between generations with regard to food habits, clothes, modes of entertainment, use of time, bio-rhythm, susceptibility to different temperatures and, more generally, in the way of thinking and behaving. Elderly suicide rates are the highest in three generational households.[120] Despite all this, generational families continue to survive in most of Asia. While there are certain costs associated with intergenerational living, the benefits are no less important:

1. The family is the most specialised institution of non-marketable services.
2. There are deep cultural roots attached to living together with all the other family members.
3. The elderly members of the family often provide monetary support in a multigenerational setup and do many household chores like cooking, baby-sitting etc.
4. Very often the house where the multigenerational household lives is owned by the elderly head of the family.
5. A multigenerational family offers emotional dependence to both generations.
6. Elderly people are familiar with the nuances of cultural, social and religious life, which the younger generation is less inclined to master but cannot denounce altogether.

So long as the benefits are not outweighed by the costs, intergenerational living will survive. Also important here is the marketisation of household services. Today, many agencies which do household chores like baby-sitting etc., are coming up. In the West, long-term care is being efficiently provided by the private sector, a development which is taking shape in the developing countries of Asia too. Private institutions and nursing homes for the aged are also needed. These agencies are only waiting for the market demand for such services to be created.

Where families have already undergone the transformation into nuclear or conjugal units, the continuation of the ageing process is likely to cause them to either become two-person households for older couples or simply one person households of the elderly. It has been observed that when the elderly get older or more frail, or if one of the elderly couple dies, then in many cases the surviving elderly person either moves to another relative's house or invites other relatives to stay with them. Furthermore, mortality reductions favouring females more than the males, produce more female loners in old age. It is expected, that there will be many elderly women living alone, in isolation, with little financial and other support. A study of the US population tells us that after the age of 75, an older woman has a 20 per cent greater chance of living alone than living with a husband, and after the age of 85, the odds are 2:1 that she will live in a relative's household rather than with her spouse.[121] The picture would be no different in India or any other Asian country. At old ages, widows are more likely to be integrated into a kin network of mutual aid and support than before. If they are not, the only other option is their abandonment. In India, several widows are abandoned in the name of pilgrimage in the holy cities of Brindaban, Kashi etc.

Ageing and Women

As discussed in the earlier section, the family is the support base for the aged and women are the support base for the family.[122] Moreover, women are the dominant group among the elderly population today and will be even more so tomorrow. Any treatise on ageing and development becomes incomplete without a discussion on the role women play in the process. While women have distinct advantages over men in terms of life expectancy, this alone is not enough. Throughout their lives and in all societies, males and females play different roles, receive different rewards and experience different realities.

Women provide vital economic support for their families by working outside the home in the labour market. For over two-thirds of the world's families, women's labour is essential to economic survival; in one-third of the families, the women are the family's sole economic support. However, it is a well known fact that women, worldwide, receive considerably lower wages and benefits, including retirement benefits, than men. Second, women labour longer hours in the home than men. In villages, they are the main procurers of fuel and drinking water. With rapid deforestation, with the sources for these two essential requirements moving further away from human habitations, women need to walk for hours to fetch and carry water and firewood. These activities, in turn, adversely effect women's health. Moreover, the use of cheap chemical substitutes for fuelwood causes permanent damage to women's eyes and respiratory system. But who cares! While no woman ever expects any payment against such services, no attempt has been made to estimate the economic value of such activities either. Most women have very little access to personal leisure time which is most often the monopoly of men. Most men smoke and drink tea or liquor. They also spend considerable time playing cards and other games.

Third, women are the most frequent, stable and long-term caregivers in families. Even in Britain, three-quarters of those caring for dependent relatives are women.[123] The economic contributions of these caregivers are unrecognized, unrewarded, and neglected by society, thus perpetuating the life cycle of disadvantage for women. Women still bear the primary responsibility for child care and household care, and they also tend to be the primary caretakers for elderly relatives. While women's liability vis-á-vis child care has lessened as a result of lower fertility and spacing of children, the longevity of elderly relatives has added to their responsibility of caring during their prime working ages and even after retirement. In the past there were more females in households, but lower fertility means a jump in the caring burden. In developing countries with pervading poverty and malnutrition sickness is quite common. Therefore, men are important, as they are current or prospective breadwinners, and their early recovery becomes important too. They are nursed by the women of the house. If there is a school-going girl in the family, her movement outside the house is restricted since she provides care to the sick men. Conversely, when a woman becomes sick, there is a suitable system of caring for her in the traditional social setup as well. With the increasing participation of women in the labour force, conflicting demands and stress is being placed on them. Many women bear the quadruple burden of caring for children, the household, the elderly, their careers and themselves. The bulk of domestic and emotional labour still falls on women, irrespective of their employment status.

Despite this, girls and women are most often the victims of violence and neglect, including selective abortion of female foetuses, female infanticide, sexual exploitation, sexual abuse and rape, domestic violence and elder abuse. Girls and women have much less access to sources of political and societal influence and power. They also have much less access to education, property, paid employment, pension plans and other productive assets. As a result of these factors women make up the majority of the poor and very poor people all over the world. These gendered experiences culminate in later life.

While the process of getting old brings with it new experiences in a woman's life, it also introduces new risks and tensions. The gendered realities of old age are as discriminatory, exploitative and disquieting as they are elsewhere in women's lives. In the Asiatic scenario, a woman marries a man much senior to her. Such women, therefore, are more likely to be widowed and suffer from poverty in later life; their access to resources for care and sustenance is reduced, making them more vulnerable than before. The vulnerability becomes higher for those who have not acquired any human capital formation in the form of education; training and other skills needed to ensure an unencumbered life. The problem may be further compounded by failing health and other long-term chronic disabilities. An indigent and physically frail elderly widow is the most defenceless.[124] It has already been said elsewhere in this book that:

♦ There are fewer elderly women than men in the workforce.
♦ While having a spouse helps in leading a healthier life, older men are more likely than older women to be currently married.
♦ Although illiteracy among older persons has consistently declined, the incidence of illiteracy is higher among elderly females than males.
♦ As in the case of general life expectancy, women also live longer, healthier lives than men everywhere in the world, except in South Asia.

In addition, there is increasing evidence of elderly women being marginalised economically. They have lower pension incomes wherever the pension system exists because of their lower overall economic compensation in wages and salaries in the job market. Time off from work for childbearing also lowers the time spent by them earning a pensionable income. In addition, women, to a greater degree than men, have been engaged in housework, part-time work or unpaid family work. In most countries, the retirement age for women is about three to five years lower than that of men (see Appendix One).

Those women who do not participate in the labour force depend upon their husbands' pension schemes. Upon the death of their husbands, they receive the pension, though at a much reduced rate. The problems of divorced elderly women are much wider in scope since they are not allowed to use their former husbands' resources, including pension schemes. Women who remain single, doing unpaid work for the family, particularly taking care of the infirm and the disabled suffer from even more precarious economic conditions. In addition, because of a greater risk of widowhood, elderly women end up living in single person households, which are also economically disadvantageous.

With earlier retirement, a longer and healthier life, and the responsibility of bearing the burdens in the family, most women suffer from *social ageing,* defined as 'the process of relinquishing meaningful social functions, with the ensuing increased risk ... of becoming prematurely obsolete, senescent and estranged from society'.[125] These women might have been spared the ordeal of regular pregnancies and the hassle of caring and rearing too many children, but this has been in exchange for other less meaningful social functions.

AGEING AND DEPRIVATION

Though the drive to understand and tackle poverty now dominates development thinking, not much attention has been paid to comprehend the problem of poverty among the elderly population. Poverty is a major menace facing the elderly today. In the developing countries of Asia, the elderly are consistently and disproportionately among the poorest of the poor. Development analysts and policy makers have largely excluded older people from poverty debates, regarding them as economically unproductive. Not many efforts have been made to appreciate the development potential of the elderly. In the *World Development Report, 2000/2001*, which focussed on attacking world poverty, not a single section was on the elderly despite a suggestion to this effect in the debate that preceded the publication.

It is time to recognise that the impoverishment of older people is largely due to deprivation, discrimination and exploitation by powerful agencies, including the state, with regard to employment and ownership of land and other assets, which these people were subjected to since the early and formative years of their life. It is because of these reasons that they were also unable to secure significant human capital formation because of insipid state policies on education, employment and health care, as well as those based on gender.[126] An elderly *is* poor because he *was* poor. This structural weakness has been further heightened by the persistent exclusion of state support in old age.[127] There exists an urban bias in development in most of the Asian countries and this bias is reflected more in the organised sectors. So, the cohorts of today's elderly, who are not fortunate enough to have ever been absorbed in these sectors, have remained virtually untouched by state support policies. In return, however, they are required to fill the state treasury through various levies on commodities. Despite this, they are being denied access to public and private services, which in most cases are not even elder-friendly. Basic health and sanitation facilities, and housing and transportation networks are also inaccessible to them. The elderly are often deprived of access to bank loans and credit schemes as well as appropriate education, information and entertainment. They are also excluded from community decision-making processes. The elderly do not have the resources or physical and mental stamina to fight elections with others and so even the democratic decision-making process cannot benefit them. A system of reservations for the elderly in local self-governments would have been ideal. Lack of assets, isolation and physical weakness are the main elements which constitute the multidimensional disadvantages of the elderly today. Physical weakness, isolation, powerlessness and low self-esteem are all factors profoundly interconnected with age.[128] It is this exclusion, the effective distancing of older people from the mainstream of economic, social and political life, which creates the deepest levels of disadvantage. The problem of widows is not so much about a lower social status because of the loss of a husband, but more to do with their exclusion from the general mainstream of economic and social life. Through such exclusion, powerful and evil forces within civilised society can always take over the properties left to her by her deceased husband.

Old age is a situation in which people do not have much physical strength. Experts believe that we lose, on an average, 10 per cent of our body strength and ability every decade. This means that at age 80, half of our body strength has been lost and many people require outside support even for normal day-to-day activities. For doing outdoor work, we require more body strength and by implication, we need to be of a much lower age. Although the age 60 or 65 has been determined arbitrarily, most people lose the capacity to cope with the stress and strain of regular outside jobs around this age, when the body requires more rest and relaxation. However, in developing countries, people need to do multiple activities to earn a living even in their old age. Since obtaining employment is not easy for those with little marketable skills, many of the elderly are forced to accept hazardous jobs for their survival. The World Bank estimates that over 70 per cent of the world's older population relies on such 'informal' systems of security and that this percentage is certainly higher among the older populations in the developing countries.[129]

It is true that the vast majority of older people, whether co-residing with adult children or not, are supported and cared for by their family. Informal social networks and extended families provide the main source of care and support for the aged. But when families are trapped in endemic poverty, the younger generations have little scope to support their older relatives. Even co-residency is no guarantee of effective care, since many older people live with their families in a state of material and emotional neglect. So, not only does the personal lack of wealth, but also the poverty that exists within communities and families, threaten the elderly people equally.

A centralised system for income security, therefore, becomes very important for the aged. But the fact is that, in most developing countries, the scope for such systems is extremely limited. In practice, only a small minority of workers previously employed in the formal sector in urban areas, such as government staff and employees of large-scale public or private enterprises are fortunate to have social security. It is also quite problematic to seek old age pension for everybody. First, a large part of old age pensions are collected during peoples' earning period. It is not clear how and to what extent poorer informal workers can in fact contribute to such programmes. It is possible for the government to evaluate the feasibility of universal old age insurance for those who attain 30 years of age, where the premiums for informal sector people may be subsidised. Even then the government requires huge sums of money for such a subsidy. Second, in many less developed economies, the preconditions for secure, long-term private savings, such as stable markets and sound regulatory structures, do not exist. Third, because of the high moral hazards problem, private insuring companies may not be interested in such areas. Common people, because of ignorance and lack of awareness, may not be interested in such schemes either.

Till the time we are able to provide old age institutional support, support for the elderly should be made a part of wider poverty alleviation strategies. Any credible anti-poverty strategy should identify those elderly needing support, utilise their productive potential for their and their community's interests and support them through poverty eradication schemes in the most scientific, humane and transparent form. It may be useful to utilise the services of HelpAge International[130] and other similar NGOs.

CONCLUSION

Population ageing has many serious developmental linkages. It has the potential to jeopardise many economic calculations and planning strategies. Regrettably, the subject has received only peripheral attention from development theorists and policy makers. They all visualise ageing as a problem only in the very long run. This may not be true. Ageing has established itself as the most pressing problem in developed economies. The developing countries of Asia are not far behind either. However, we are not sure about the implications of population ageing. Most conclusions are still in the form of hypotheses. A detailed and careful economic analysis of population ageing is a pressing need of the day, else we may be tempted into unnecessary, inefficient and costly policy interventions.

NOTES AND REFERENCES

1. F.W. Notestein, *Some Demographic Aspects of Ageing*, Proceedings of the American Philosophical Society, pp. 38–45, Philadelphia, 1954.
2. S.H. Preston, 'Mortality Trends', *Annual Review of Sociology*, 3: 163–78, 1977.
3. J.B. Davies, 'Uncertain Lifetime, Consumption, and Dissaving in Retirement', *Journal of Political Economy*, 89(3): 561–77, 1981.
4. R.M. Solow, 'A Contribution to the Theory of Economic Growth', *Quarterly Journal of Economics*, 70(1): 65–94, 1956.
5. J. Tobin, 'Life Cycle Saving and Balanced Growth', in William Fellner (ed.), *Ten Economic Studies in the Tradition of Irving Fisher*, John Wiley, New York, 1967.
6. R. Lee, 'Age Structure, Intergenerational Transfers and Economic Growth: An Overview', in George Tapinos (ed.), *Revue Economique: Special Issue on Economic Demography*, Paris, 31(6): 1129–56, 1980.
7. D.W. Jorgenson and A. Pachon, 'The Accumulation of Human and Non-human Capital', in Modigliani and Hemming (eds), *The Determinants of National Saving and Wealth*, Macmillan, London, 1983.

8. R.B. Freeman, 'The Effect of Demographic Factors on Age-earnings Profiles', *Journal of Human Resources*, 14(3): 289–318, 1979.

9. G.S. Becker, 'A Theory of Social Interaction', *Journal of Political Economy*, 82(6): 1063–93, 1974.

10. J.P. Laitner, 'Stationary Equilibrium Transition Rules for an Overlapping Generations Model with Uncertainty', *Journal of Economic Theory*, 35(1): 83–108, 1985.

11. R. Pollock and M. Wachter, 'The Relevance of the Household Production Function and its Implications for Allocation of Time', *Journal of Political Economy*, 83(2): 255–77, 1975.

12. The Report of the Royal Commission on Population, page 121, HMSO, London, 1949.

13. G.S. Becker, *Human Capital*, National Bureau of Economic Research (NBER), New York, 1964.

14. J. Mincer, *Schooling, Experience and Earnings*, National Bureau of Economic Research (NBER), New York, 1974.

15. E.P. Lazear, 'Pensions and Deferred Benefits as Strategic Compensation', *Industrial Relations*, 29: 263–80, 1990.

16. P. Rabbit, 'Some Issues in Cognitive Gerontology and Their Implications for Social Policy', in W.J. van den Heuvel, R. Illsley, A. Jamieson and C.P. Knipscheer (eds), *Opportunities and Challenges in an Ageing Society*, pp. 233–74, North-Holland, Amsterdam, 1992.

17. A.T. Welford, *Ageing and Human Skill*, Oxford University Press, London, 1958.

18. L.G. Martin and N. Ogawa, 'The Effect of Cohort Size on Relative Wages in Japan', in R.D. Lee, W.B. Arthur and G. Rodgers (eds), *Economics of Changing Age Distributions in Developed Countries*, pp. 58–75, Oxford University Press, Oxford, 1988.

19. H.J. Habakkuk, *American and British Technology in the Nineteenth Century*, Cambridge University Press, Cambridge, 1962.

20. J.L. Simon, *The Ultimate Resource*, Princeton University Press, Princeton, 1981.

21. E. Van Imhoff, 'Age Structure, Education, and Transmission of Technical Change', *Journal of Population Economics*, 1: 167–81, 1988.

22. Li Baoku and Zhang Wenfan, 'Trend of Population Aging in China and the Strategy', *China Population Today*, April, 1998.

23. United Nations Volunteers, Expert Working Group Meeting on Volunteering and Social Development, United Nations Volunteers, New York, 1999.

24. D.O. Parsons, 'The Decline in Male Labour Force Participation', *Journal of Political Economy*, 88(1): 117–34, 1980.

25. J.F. Quinn and R.V. Burkhauser, 'Work and Retirement', in R.H. Binstock and L.K. George (eds), *Handbook of Ageing and the Social Science*, pp. 307–27, Academic Press, San Diego, 1990.

26. H. Kendig, 'A Life Course Perspective on Housing Attainment', in D. Myers (ed.), *Housing Demography: Linking Demographic Structures and Housing Choices*, pp. 133–56, University of Wisconsin Press, Madison, 1990.

27. J. Yates, 'Changing Directions in Australian Housing Policies: The End of Muddling Through', *Housing Studies*, 12(2): 265–77, 1997.

28. National Sample Survey Organisation (NSSO), *The Age in India: A Socio-economic Profile*, NSS 52nd Round, 1998.

29. G.R. Andrews A.J. Esterman, A.J. Braunack-Mayer and C.M. Rungie (eds), *Ageing in the Western Pacific—A Four Country Study*, World Health Organization, Western Pacific Reports and Studies No. 1, WHO Regional Office for the Western Pacific, 1986.

30. See note 28.

31. N.G. Mankiw and D. Weil, 'The Baby Boom, The Baby Bust and The Housing Market', *Regional Science and Urban Economics*, 19: 235–58, 1989.

32. A. Borsch-Supan, 'Ageing Population: Problems and Policy Options in the US and Germany', *Economic Policy*, 12: 104–39, 1991.

33. Gavin W. Jones, 'Population Growth and Health and Family Planning', in Warren C. Robinson (ed.), *Population and Development Planning*, Population Council, New York, 1975.

34. L. Tabah, 'The Economic and Social Consequence of Demographic Ageing', in *Economic and Social Implications of Population Ageing*, pp. 121–44, Proceedings of the International Symposium on Population Structure and Development, Tokyo, 10–12 September 1987, United Nations, New York, 1988.

35. Joan M. O' Connell, 'The Relationship between Health Expenditures and the Age Structure of the Population in OECD Countries', *Health Economics*, 5(6): 573–78, 1996.

36. N.R. Vasudeva Murthy and Victor Ukpolo, 'Aggregate Health Care Expenditures in the United States: New Results', *Applied Economics Letters*, 2: 419–21, 1994.

37. Thomas E. Getzen, 'Population Ageing and the Growth of Health Expenditures', *Journal of Gerontology*, 47(3): 98–104, 1992.

38. Ulf-G Gerdtham, Jes Sogaard, Fedrik Anderson and Bengt Jonsson, 'An Econometric Analysis of Health Expenditure: A Cross-section Study of OECD Countries', *Journal of Health Economics*, 11(1): 63–84, 1992.

39. Peter Zweifel, Stefan Felder and Markus Meiers, 'Ageing Population and Health Care Expenditure: A Red Herring?', *Health Economics*, 8(6): 485–96, 1999.

40. S.E. Jacobzone, E. Cambois, E. Chaplain and J. Robine, 'The Health of Older Persons in OECD Countries: Is it Improving Fast Enough to Compensate for Population Change?', Labour Market and Social Policy Occasional Papers No. 37, OECD, Paris, 1998.

41. *ibid.*

42. Gerad F. Anderson and Peter Sotir Hussey, 'Population Ageing: A Comparison Among Industrialised Countries', *Health Affairs*, 19(3): 191–203, 2000.

43. Naohiro Ogawa, 'Population Ageing and Medical Demand: The Case of Japan', in *Economic and Social Implications of Population Ageing*, Proceedings of the International Symposium on Population Structure and Development, Tokyo, 10–12 September 1987, Department of International Economic and Social Affairs (DIESA), United Nations, New York, 1988.

44. *ibid.*

45. World Health Organization (WHO), *World Health Report 1998: Life in the 21st Century—A Vision for All*, Geneva, WHO, 1998.

46. Income elasticity of health care refers to the change in the demand for health care followed by a change in income. It is a unit-free measure of this responsiveness and is calculated as the percentage change in the quantity demanded of health care goods and services divided by the percentage change in income. Income elasticity equal to one implies that the health care system

will grow proportionately with income and thus absorb a constant share of society resources. An income elasticity greater than unity implies the health care system will grow more than proportionately with income and absorb an increasing share of national income. An income elasticity less than unity implies the health care system will grow less than proportionately with income and claim a decreasing share of resources and output.

47. O' Connell (see note 35) finds the income elasticity to be less than one in OECD countries for panel data between 1975–90. Murthy and Ukpolo (see note 36) estimate the income elasticity of health care in USA between 1960–87 at 0.77.

48. Gerad Russo, Thamana Lekprichakul and Mathana Phanani Iramai, *Household Expenditures for Health Care in Thailand: Estimates from the 1988 Socio-economic Survey (SES)*, East–West Center, Program on Population, August, 1994.

49. Gerad Russo, Naohiro Ogawa, Wandaningsih and Nina Sarjunani, *Household Expenditures for Health Care in Indonesia: Estimates from the 1987 Socio-economic Survey (SUSENAS)*, Report Prepared for the Asian Development Bank, East-West Center, Program on Population, August, 1994.

50. Gerad Russo and Alejandro Herrin, The Determinants of Household Health Care Expenditures in the Philippines, East-West Center Working Paper, Population Series No. 68, 1993.

51. Willard G Manning, Joseph P. Newhouse, Naihua Duan, Emmett B. Keeler, Arleen Leibowitz and M. Susan Marquis, 'Health Insurance and the Demand for Medical Care: Evidence from a Randomized Experiment', *American Economic Review*, 77(3): 252–77, 1987.

52. S.F. Venti and D.A. Wise, 'Ageing, Moving and Housing Wealth', in D.A. Wise (ed.), *Issues in the Economics of Ageing*, pp. 13–32, National Bureau of Economic Research (NBER), University of Chicago Press, Chicago, 1989.

53. H.J. Aaron, B.P. Bosworth and G. Burtless, *Can America Afford to Grow Old?*, Brookings Institution, Washington D.C., 1989.

54. A. Borsch-Supan, 'Ageing Population: Problems and Policy Options in the US and Germany', *Economic Policy*, 12: 104–39, 1991.

55. J. Quadagno, *The Transformation of Old Age Security*, University of Chicago Press, Chicago, 1988.

56. M.S. Feldstein, 'Social Security and Private Savings: International Evidence in an Extended Life-cycle Model', in M.S. Feldstein and R.P. Inman (eds), *The Economics of Public Services*, Macmillan, London, 1977.

57. M.S. Feldstein, 'Social Security, Induced Retirement and Aggregate Capital Accumulation', *Journal of Political Economy*, 82: 905–26,1974.

58. R.J. Barro, *The Impact of Social Security on Private Saving: Evidence from the U.S. Time Series*, American Enterprise Institute, Washington, D.C., 1978.

59. H.J. Aaron, *Economic Effects of Social Security*, Brookings Institution, Washington D.C., 1982.

60. D.M. Cutler, J.M. Poterba, L.M. Sheiner and L.H. Summers, 'An Ageing Society: Opportunity or Challenge?', *Brookingss Papers on Economic Activity*, 1: 1–7, 1990.

61. R. Hudson, 'The Greying of the Federal Budget and Consequences for Old Age Policy', *The Gerontologist*, 18: 428–40, 1978.

62. R. Binstock, 'Policies on Ageing in the Post-war Era', in W. Crotty (ed.), *Post-Cold War Policies Vol.1 Domestic and Social*, Nelson-Hall, Chicago, 1992.

63. J. Flint, 'The Old Folks', *Forbes*, 18th February, pp. 51–65, 1980.

64. A. Ehrbar, 'The Wrong Solution', *Fortune*, 17th August, p. 118, 1980.
65. *Forbes*, 'The Truth about Social Security', *Forbes*, 6th December, p. 242, 1982.
66. S. Preston, 'Children and the Elderly in the Unites States', *Scientifc American*, 250: 44–49, 1984.
67. S.H. Preston, 'Children and the Elderly: Divergent Paths for America's Dependents', *Demography*, 21: 1435–57, 1984.
68. H. Richman and M. Stagner, 'Children in an Ageing Society: Treasured Resource or Forgotten Minority?', *Daedalus*, 115: 171–89, 1985.
69. D. Callahan, *Setting Limits: Medical Goals in an Ageing Society*, Simon and Schuster, New York, 1987.
70. P. Laslett, *Family Life and Illicit Love in Earlier Generations*, Cambridge University Press, Cambridge, 1977.
71. L. Kotlikoff, *Generational Accounting: Knowing Who Pays, and When, and for What We Spend*, Free Press, New York, 1992.
72. P. Longman, *Born to Pay: The New Politics of Ageing in America*, Houghton Mifflin, Boston, 1987.
73. See note 69.
74. P.S. Heller, R. Hemming and P.W. Kohnert, *Ageing and Social Expenditure in the Major Industrial Countries, 1980–2025*, International Monetary Fund, Occasional Paper 47, Washington D.C., 1987.
75. Organisation for Economic Co-operation and Development (OECD), *Ageing Populations: The Social Policy Implications*, Paris, OECD, 1988.
76. W. Schmahl, 'Demographic Change and Social Security', *Journal of Population Studies*, 3: 159–77, 1990.
77. L. Verniere, 'Retraites: L'urgence d'une reforme', *Economie et Statistique*, 233: 29–38, 1990.
78. N. Keyfitz, 'The Demographics of Unfunded Pensions', *European Journal of Population*, 1: 5–30, 1985.
79. D. Thompson, 'The Welfare State and Generation Conflict: Winners and Losers', in P. Johnson, C. Conrad and D. Thompson (eds), *Workers Versus Pensioners*, pp. 33–56, Manchester University Press, Manchester, 1989.
80. J. Myles and J. Quadagno (eds), *States, Labour Markets, and the Future of Old Age Policy*, Temple University Press, Philadelphia, 1993.
81. M. Minkler and A. Robertson, *Ageing and Society*, 11: 1–2, 1991.
82. E. Binney and Estes, 'The Retreat of the State and its Transfer of Responsibility: The Intergenerational War', *Intergenerational Journal Health Services*, 18: 83–96, 1988.
83. N. Daniels, 'Justice between Age Groups: Am I My Parents' Keeper?', *Millbank Memorial Fund Quarterly*, (summer), pp. 489–522, 1983.
84. R. Binstock, 'The Oldest Old: Fresh Perspective on Compassionate Ageing Revisited', *Millbank Memorial Fund Quarterly*, Health and Society, 63(2): 420–51, 1985.
85. Generations United, *The Common Stake: The Interdependence of Generations: A Policy Framework for an Ageing Society*, Washington D.C., 1992.
86. H. Moody, 'Ethical Dilemmas in Long-term Care', *Journal of Gerontological Social Work*, 5: 97–111, 1982.

87. The projections are based on the following demographic data for India. In India, 18 years is the entry point for the voter list. But with the age date for every single year not being available for future years, we have used the aged data for those 20 plus as proxy for the voting population.

Year	People Aged 20 plus (Voting age population)	People Aged 60 plus	Aged as a Percentage of Voting Age Population
1995	513,348	67,177	13.1
2025	922,778	168,133	18.2
2050	1130,707	323,856	28.6

Source: United Nations, 1999.

88. V.L. Bengtson, 'Ageing and the Problem of Generations: Prospects for a New Generational Contract', Paper presented at the United Nations International Conference on Ageing Populations in the Context of Family, October 1990, Kitakyushu, Japan.
89. Elaine Cumming and William E. Henry, Growing Old: The Process of Disengagement, Basic Books, New York, 1961.
90. Philip E. Converse and N. Richard, 'Non-voting among Young Adults in the United States', in William J. Crotty, Donald Freeman and Douglas S. Gattin (eds), Political Parties and Political Behavior, Second Edition, p. 445, Allyn and Bacon, Boston, 1971.
91. Raymond E. Wolfinger and Steven J. Rosenstone, Who Votes?, New Haven and Yale University Press, London, 1980.
92. Robert B. Hudson and John Strate, 'Ageing and Political Systems', in Handbook of Ageing and the Social Sciences, Second Edition, pp. 554–85, Van Nostrand Reinhold Company, New York, 1985.
93. See note 91; see also, Kent M. Jennings and Gregory B. Markus, 'Political Involvement in the Later Years: A Longitudinal Survey', American Journal of Political Science, 32(2): 302–16, 1988.
94. Neal E. Cutler, 'Demographic, Social-Psychological, and Political Factors in the Politics of Ageing: A Foundation for Research in Political Gerontology', American Political Science Review, 71: 1024,1977.
95. See note 94, p. 1024.
96. C. Campbell and John Strate, 'Are Old People Conservative?', The Gerontologist, 21(6): 581–91, 1981; see also, Hudson and Strate, Handbook of Ageing and the Social Sciences, pp. 554–85. (For full details see note 92.)
97. See note 94.
98. Henry J. Pratt, The Gray Lobby, The University of Chicago Press, Chicago and London, 1977.
99. R.M. Binstock, 'Old Voters and the 1992 Presidential Election', The Gerontologist, 32(5): 601–06, 1992.

100. S.J. Cutler and R.L. Kaufman, 'Cohort Changes in Political Attitudes: Tolerance of Ideological Nonconformity', *Public Opinion Quarterly*, 39(1): 63–81, 1975.

101. E.M. Douglas, W.P. Cleveland and G.L. Maddox, 'Political Attitudes, Ageing: A Cohort Analysis of Archival Data', *Journal of Gerontology*, 29(6): 1974.

102. G.C. Myers and E.M. Agree, Social and Political Implications of Population Ageing: Ageing of the Electorate, International Population Conference, Montreal 1992, International Union for the Scientific Study of Population, Belgium, 1993.

103. H. Rattinger, 'Demography and Federal Elections in Germany, 1953–1990 and Beyond', *Electoral Studies*, 11(3): 223–47, 1992.

104. Yosef Riemer and Robert Binstock, 'Campaigning for "The Senior Vote": A Case Study of Carter's 1976 Campaign', *The Gerontologist*, 18(6): 517, 1978.

105. S. Arber and J. Ginn, 'The Invisibility of Age: Gender and Class in Later Life', *Sociological Review*, 39: 260–91, 1991.

106. P. Laslett, *Family Life and Illicit Love in Earlier Generations*, Cambridge University Press, Cambridge, 1977.

107. J. Quadagno, *Ageing in Early Industrial Society*, Academic Press, New York, 1982.

108. William J. Goode, *World Revolution and Family Patterns*, Free Press of Glencoe, New York, 1963.

109. ibid.

110. E. Cumming and W. Henry, *Growing Old: the Process of Disengagement*, Basic Books, New York, 1961.

111. P. Johnson and J. Falkingham, *Ageing and Economic Welfare*, Sage Publications, London, 1992.

112. P. Townsend, 'The Structured Dependency of the Elderly: A Creation of Social Policy in the 20th Century', *Ageing and Society*, 1: 5–28, 1981.

113. R. Smith, 'The Structured Dependence of the Elderly as a Recent Development: Some Sceptical Historical Thoughts', *Ageing and Society*, 4: 409-28, 1984.

114. L. Hannah, *Inventing Retirement*, Cambridge University Press, Cambridge, 1986.

115. Graham Allan, *Family Life*, Basil Blackwell, London, 1985.

116. Harry Moody, *Ethics in an Ageing Society*, Johns Hopkins University Press, Baltimore, 1992.

117. ibid., pp. 229.

118. Talcott Parsons and Robert F. Bales, *Family, Socialization and Interaction Process*, Glencoe, New York, 1955.

119. William, J. Goode, *World Revolution and Family Patterns*, Free Press, New York, 1963.

120. M. Ueno, 'Suicide of the Elderly', *Medical Journal of Nihon University*, 40(10), Tokyo, 1981.

121. Jacob S. Siegel and Maria Davidson, 'Demographic and Socio-economic Aspects of Aging in the United States', *Current Population Reports: Population Estimates and Projections*, Special Studies Series 0–23, No. 138, Washington D.C., 1984.

122. Jane L. Menken, 'Age and Fertility: How Long Can You Wait?', *Demography*, 22(4): 469–83, New York, 1985.

123. The Economist. 'Those Who Care', The Economist, 17 May, London, 1986.

124. Martha Alter Chen and Jean Dreze, 'Widowhood and Well-being in Rural North India', in Monica Dasgupta, Lincoln C. Chen and T.N. Krishnan (eds),

Women's Health in India: Risk and Vulnerability, Oxford University Press, New Delhi, 1995.

125. Massimo, Livi Bacci 'Social and Biological Ageing: Contradictions of Development', *Population and Development Review*, 8(4): 771–81, 1982.

126. S. Neysmith and J. Edwardh, 'Economic Dependency in the 1980s: Its Impact on Third World's Elderly', *Ageing and Society*, 1(1), 1984.

127. A. De Haan, 'Social Exclusion: An Alternative Concept for the Study of Deprivation?', *IDS Bulletin*, 20(1), 1998.

128. R. Chambers, 'Poverty and Livelihoods: Whose Reality Counts?', *Environment and Urbanization*, 7(1),1995.

129. The World Bank, *Averting the Old Age Crisis*, Oxford University Press, Oxford, 1994.

130. HelpAge International, *Poverty and ageing: A Position Paper*, HelpAge International, London, 2000.

CHAPTER FIVE

STATUS OF THE AGED

Armed with an idea of what ageing means to development, this chapter investigates the status of the elderly in India. It also makes an assessment of the status of the elderly in other Asian countries on the basis of available evidence. Not many countries carry out national level surveys on the aged, however, now we do have significant data to permit a comparative understanding of the status of the aged. The earlier chapter discussed the probable impact of ageing on a developing economy. It was apprehended that rapid ageing accompanied by shrinking public resources and a transformation of the family support system could be difficult for the elderly, if not disastrous. This chapter gives an opportunity to delve into the real picture. It introduces the concept of Elderly Status Index, which helps in ascertaining whether the status of the elderly has changed over time. Also, it facilitates comparisons among different regions. The preparation of such an index requires similar data on the status of the elderly for those regions or time periods which need to be compared. If there is a world ageing survey, similar to the World Fertility Survey (WFS), it would be possible to make international comparisons through the Elderly Status Index. However, in the absence of such data the exercise has been restricted to the Indian states. Thanks to the 42nd and 52nd Round Surveys of the National Sample Survey Organisation (NSSO), we now have enough data on the aged in India to make the indices.

THE NATIONAL SAMPLE SURVEY:
SURVEY ON THE AGED

The National Sample Survey Organisation (NSSO), a division of the Department of Statistics operating within the Ministry of Planning and Programme Implementation is a nodal statistical agency of the Government of India. The NSSO gathers statistical data on various economic and social issues through carefully designed surveys throughout the country. The surveys are based on the finest principles of sampling applied to a highly heterogeneous society with wide and varied geographical coverage. The surveys on the aged were conducted along established guidelines through carefully chosen samples.

The NSSO, for the first time, conducted a survey on aged persons along with a survey on social consumption in its 42nd Round (July 1986 to June 1987). The survey was carried out to assess the nature and dimensions of the socio-economic problems of the aged. After a gap of a decade, the survey on social consumption was repeated in the 52nd Round (July 1995 to June 1996). In this survey, additional information on education and health were sought.

In the survey, data on the number of living children of the aged, their living arrangement, state of economic independence, number of dependants, persons supporting the aged, disability, chronic ailments, state of health and their familial roles in the household were collected. Information was also gathered on the routine activities of the elderly, retirement benefits, provisions for regular income etc.

The samples were chosen through a stratified two-stage design. The First Stage Units (FSUs) were census villages (panchayat ward in Kerala) in the rural sector and NSSO defined Urban Frame Survey blocks (UFS) for the urban areas. The second stage units are households in both the sectors.

A sample of 13,000 FSUs was selected as the central sample at the all India level and the individual state/union territories' sample was selected according to the relative size of rural and urban populations with double weightage for urban areas. The state level samples were drawn and analysed separately. The FSUs were selected through a circular systematic sample with equal probability. In the second stage, all the households in the selected FSUs were listed and 10 households chosen from there for the health care survey based on the following formula:

Composition	Number of Households (HHs) to be Selected
HHs with child aged less than one year	2
Remaining HHs with hospitalisation cases for last one year	2
Rest of HHs	6

Finally, 12,614 village/urban blocks with 120,942 households and 33,981 aged were surveyed for the whole country.

Elderly Status in India

Some major findings of the status of the elderly in India are as follows:

♦ There are more elderly in rural areas. There is also movement of the elderly from urban to rural areas.
♦ Old age dependency is higher in rural areas than in urban areas.
♦ The elderly are ageing.
♦ There are more females than males among the aged, and, in contrast to the general sex ratio, the elderly sex ratios are rising.
♦ The elderly are much less literate and educated than the general population.
♦ There are a considerable number of single elderly of whom a majority are widows. However, the proportions of widows is on the decline.
♦ About 94 per cent of the elderly in India have children surviving them but a large number of the elderly are without any children.
♦ The elderly generally live with their spouses/children and other relatives, however more and more elderly are now living without their children.
♦ The elderly are still working for a living in the absence of any suitable social security.
♦ As many as 70 per cent of the aged depend on others for their day-to-day maintenance. The situation is far worse for elderly females, 85 to 87 per cent of whom are dependent on others.

♦ By and large the elderly are still supported by their children. Interestingly, every sixth elderly is supported by his/her spouse.
♦ More elderly men than women are supported by their family.
♦ A majority of the elderly are not supported by any retirement benefits and the problem is compounded in rural areas.
♦ About 54 per cent of the aged own financial assets and housing, though many of them do not have any management rights or control over them.
♦ The prevalence of chronic diseases among the aged is quite high and it is higher still in urban areas. Problems of the joints and throat are the most common.
♦ The prevalence of disability among the aged is also very high.
♦ A great majority of the elderly participate in social and religious matters and in household chores, though a large number of them cannot participate in household activities.

RURAL–URBAN COMPOSITION OF THE ELDERLY

In chapter two, the section on population ageing and migration discusses why and how the elderly number more in the rural areas than in the urban areas. The 1991 census figures in India show that 25.7 per cent of the country's population stays in the urban areas while the remaining 74.3 per cent live in the villages. For the aged, a larger percentage (78.1 per cent) lives in villages. The same census tells us that 6.3 per cent of the urban population was in the 60 plus age bracket, while 7.6 per cent of the rural population was in the same age group. In the 1981 census, the aged constituted 5.4 per cent of the urban and 6.8 per cent of the rural population. The NSS surveys (43rd Round [1987–88], 50th Round [1993–94] and 52nd Round [1995–96]) have also made similar observations (see Table 5.1).

A similar pattern of rural–urban differences in the proportion of aged was evident in 1990 in China, Indonesia, Japan and the Republic of Korea and Thailand. The difference was particularly marked in Japan and the Republic of Korea.[1] Table 5.2 summarises the urban–rural characteristics of the Indian population and their elderly in all the states and union territories of India in 1991.

In all the states and union territories of India, except in West Bengal, Chandigarh, Delhi, Lakshadweep and Pondicherry, there is a higher concentration of the aged in the rural areas than in the urban areas. Things ought to have been different given the fact that the determinants

Table 5.1
Share of the Aged to the Total Population Obtained from NSS Surveys and
Population Censuses for Each Sex

Source	Year	Rural			Urban		
		Male	Female	Total	Male	Female	Total
Census	1981	6.8	6.8	6.8	5.1	5.8	5.4
Census	1991	7.8	7.4	7.6	6.2	6.6	6.3
NSS 43rd Round	1987–88	6.5	6.6	6.5	5.4	6.1	5.7
NSS 50th Round	1993–94	6.8	6.9	6.9	5.5	6.4	6.0
NSS 52nd Round	1995–96	5.5	5.9	5.7	4.7	5.3	5.0

Source: National Sample Survey Organisation (NSSO), *The Aged In India: A Socio-economic Profile*, NSS 52nd Round, July 1995–June 1996, NSSO, Department of Statistics, Ministry of Planning and Programme Implementation, Government of India, Calcutta, 1998.

Table 5.2
Percentage of the Total and the Elderly Population in India in the Rural Areas

States/Union Territories	Age	Total	Male	Female	Age	Total	Male	Female
Andhra Pradesh	All Ages	74.3	73.8	74.8	60 plus	78.1	78.4	77.8
Arunachal Pradesh	All Ages	73.1	72.9	73.3	60 plus	95.6	95.3	95.9
Assam	All Ages	88.9	88.4	89.5	60 plus	89.6	89.7	89.6
Bihar	All Ages	86.9	86.4	87.4	60 plus	89.7	89.6	89.8
Goa	All Ages	59.0	58.2	59.8	60 plus	63.8	63.2	64.4
Gujarat	All Ages	65.5	65.0	66.0	60 plus	70.2	70.1	70.3
Haryana	All Ages	75.4	75.4	75.3	60 plus	79.7	80.5	78.8
Himachal Pradesh	All Ages	91.3	90.6	92.0	60 plus	94.2	94.1	94.3
Karnataka	All Ages	69.1	68.6	69.6	60 plus	74.2	74.3	74.1
Kerala	All Ages	73.6	73.6	73.6	60 plus	74.3	75.3	73.4
Madhya Pradesh	All Ages	76.8	76.4	77.3	60 plus	81.3	81.3	81.4
Maharashtra	All Ages	61.3	60.1	62.6	60 plus	69.3	68.8	69.8

(continued)

Table 5.2
(Continued)

States/Union Territories	Age	Total	Male	Female	Age	Total	Male	Female
Manipur	All Ages	70.5	71.5	69.4	60 plus	72.5	72.7	72.2
Meghalaya	All Ages	81.4	81.0	81.9	60 plus	83.7	84.9	82.2
Mizoram	All Ages	53.9	54.2	53.6	60 plus	57.1	58.0	56.1
Nagaland	All Ages	82.8	84.4	84.3	60 plus	93.4	92.7	94.5
Orissa	All Ages	86.6	85.9	86.4	60 plus	90.5	90.2	90.7
Punjab	All Ages	70.5	70.2	70.7	60 plus	76.4	76.6	76.2
Rajasthan	All Ages	77.1	76.8	77.5	60 plus	80.8	81.1	80.4
Sikkim	All Ages	90.9	90.2	91.7	60 plus	94.0	94.0	94.0
Tamil Nadu	All Ages	65.8	65.6	66.1	60 plus	68.7	69.7	67.6
Tripura	All Ages	84.7	84.8	84.6	60 plus	84.8	86.1	83.5
Uttar Pradesh	All Ages	80.2	80.0	80.4	60 plus	84.5	84.6	84.4
West Bengal	All Ages	72.5	71.6	73.5	60 plus	70.3	69.1	71.5
Andaman & Nicobar	All Ages	73.3	72.5	74.2	60 plus	80.0	79.8	80.4
Chandigarh	All Ages	10.3	11.3	9.0	60 plus	7.4	8.1	6.6
Dadra and Nagar Haveli	All Ages	91.5	90.9	92.2	60 plus	92.9	92.5	93.3
Daman and Diu	All Ages	53.2	54.5	51.9	60 plus	45.0	46.9	43.7
Delhi	All Ages	10.1	10.2	9.9	60 plus	8.5	8.8	8.3
Lakshadweep	All Ages	43.7	43.3	44.1	60 plus	39.7	38.4	41.0
Pondicherry	All Ages	36.0	36.2	35.8	60 plus	34.3	36.3	32.4
India	All Ages	74.3	73.8	74.8	60 plus	78.1	78.4	77.8

Source: Census of India 1991, *Ageing Population of India: An Analysis of the 1991 Census Data*, Registrar General, India, New Delhi, 1999.

Table 5.3
Rural–Urban Differences in Fertility Indicators of India

Indicators	Rural			Urban		
	1981	1990	1993	1981	1990	1993
General Fertility Rate (GFR)	149.4	132.6	125.2	107.2	96.1	93.5
General Marital Fertility Rate (GMFR)	–	170.0	162.4	–	135.7	128.9
Total Fertility Rate (GFR)	4.8	4.1	3.8	3.3	2.8	2.8
Total Marital Fertility Rate (TMFR)	–	5.4	5.1	–	4.6	4.3
Gross Reproduction Rate (GRR)	2.3	2.0	1.8	1.6	1.3	1.3
Crude Birth Rate (CBR)	35.4$	31.6#	30.4	27.8$	24.7#	23.7

Source: Registrar General, India *Vital Rates of India, 1971 to 1996*, Based on the Sample Registration System (SRS), Office of the Registrar General of India, New Delhi, 1998.

Notes: $ indicates average of 1981–83; # indicates average of 1989–91.

of population ageing are stronger in the urban areas than in the rural areas. Given the urban bias prevalent in our developmental efforts, including those with regard to elderly care and living, many elderly people should have settled in urban areas. The Sample Registration System (SRS) data indicates that fertility rates are much lower in urban areas than in rural areas. The same is true for most Asian countries for which World Fertility Survey (WFS) data is available.[2] At the same time, urban life expectancy at birth is higher than the rural life expectancy. Table 5.3 provides rural–urban differences under the various fertility indicators of India, while Table 5.4 represents life expectancy at birth in rural and urban India for different years.

The factors underlying such a trend have not been fully identified yet. However, in continuation with what has been stated in chapter two, it may be reiterated that:

1. Laws and policies relating to accommodation in most developing countries including India have been structured to provide for nuclear families. Such a practice vitiates intergenerational commitments. As a result of overcrowding and the rising cost of living in urban areas, the elderly have been forced to live in rural areas away from their families, in loneliness, boredom and neglect which is compounded by the absence of children and other household members,

Table 5.4
Expectation of Life at Birth (in years) by Sex and Residence
from 1970–75 to 1991–95 in India

Period	Rural			Urban			Combined		
	Male	Female	Total	Male	Female	Total	Male	Female	Total
1970–75	48.9	47.1	48.0	58.8	59.2	58.9	50.5	49.0	49.7
1976–80	51.0	50.3	50.6	59.6	60.8	60.1	52.5	52.1	52.3
1981–85	54.0	53.6	53.7	61.6	64.1	62.8	55.4	55.7	55.5
1986–90	56.1	56.2	56.1	62.0	64.9	63.4	57.7	58.1	57.7
1991–95	58.5	59.3	58.9	64.5	67.3	65.9	59.7	60.9	60.3

Source: Registrar General, India, *Vital Rates of India, 1971 to 1996*, Based on the Sample Registration System (SRS), Office of the Registrar General of India, New Delhi, 1998.

the absence or death of a spouse and inadequate visits by relatives. However, for the rural economy, there is also the possibility of gain from the retirees' return migration to the villages. Such return has been fundamental to the spread of commercial agriculture and the transformation of the rural economy in parts of the Pacific and elsewhere,[3] where the villages have secured much-needed capital as well as the wide experiences of the elderly.[4] Other things remaining unchanged, ageing rural labour forces should promote the adoption of labour-saving technologies, as heads of households become increasingly unwilling or unable to undertake back-breaking agricultural tasks. All, however, will depend upon the potential of the local area for the introduction of either commercial agriculture or of new technologies.

2. Given the urban bias in our development efforts, villages provide very little job opportunities for the youth. The problem is much more acute for those who have had some education. This causes outmigration of the youth from the rural areas and the proportion of the aged in the population therefore rises.

3. A large number of people from the rural hinterland come to the urban areas for jobs with many of them staying on temporarily for the entire duration of their work. A great majority of them return to their villages on retirement.

4. There may also exist a higher degree of reporting errors on age by the rural population. Most aged people do not have birth registration documents and those who do, are often unable to locate them

because of poor record-keeping. There is also a tendency towards adding on ages ending in the digits zero and five. Since ages ending with zero appear to be chosen much more frequently as age estimates, this can lead to surplus of population in the age groups 60–64 and 70–74.[5] In addition, exaggeration of their ages by older persons frequently causes further errors. While these tendencies are present everywhere, village people tend to overstate their ages given that the aged are more respected in rural areas. With very little opportunities of a diversified pattern of life, they may feel aged despite not having attained the age marking their entry into the elderly age bracket.

5. There may also be a differential undercount of the aged. The Post Enumeration Checks for both 1981 and 1991 censuses indicated a higher than average net omission rate for aged females.[6]

The effects of the changing age structures are clearly reflected in the dependency ratios, or in the ratio of the potentially economically active population who are 15–59 years old vis-à-vis those who are assumed to be dependent, i.e., those 0–15 and 60 years of age and older. The dependency ratio is primarily a demographic index and it is well recognised that the old-age dependency ratio is higher for rural areas than urban areas. This means that the burden of the aged on the working population is higher in rural areas as compared to urban areas. Table 5.5 shows that this burden is rising with time. This, however, was not confirmed through NSS rounds on the aged. Table 5.6 gives some idea of the older age and youth dependency ratios for urban and rural areas of some countries of Asia.

Looking at the rural areas it is clear that Japan and the Republic of Korea are a class apart, with a very high proportion of the elderly

Table 5.5
Rural–Urban Differences in Old-age Dependency Ratio (per 1000) in India

Source	Year	Rural	Urban	Combined
Census	1981	94	71	89
Census	1991	111	88	103
NSS 43rd Round	1987–88	123	96	118
NSS 50th Round	1993–94	108	90	104
NSS 52nd Round	1995–96	92	74	87

Source: National Sample Survey Organisation (NSSO), *The Aged In India: A Socio-economic Profile*, NSS 52nd Round, July 1995–June 1996, NSSO, Department of Statistics, Ministry of Planning and Programme Implementation, Government of India, Calcutta, 1998.

Table 5.6
Old Age and Youth Dependency Ratios, by Urban and Rural Sector
in Some Asian Countries

	Rural		Urban	
Countries	Old Age Dependency Ratio	Youth Dependency Ratio	Old age Dependency Ratio	Youth Dependency Ratio
Japan (1995)	44.1	29.1	29.4	24.1
Republic of Korea (1995)	29.0	32.6	10.0	34.2
Brunei Darussalam (1991)	8.5	57.8	5.7	55.3
China (1990)	14.1	48.0	11.7	32.1
Indonesia (1995)	13.0	62.2	9.1	48.9
Malaysia (1991)	12.1	74.7	8.7	55.1
Philippines (1990)	10.5	80.7	8.7	63.2
Thailand (1990)	11.3	48.4	9.0	32.5
Cambodia (1996)	10.7	88.8	9.3	74.2
Laos PDR (1995)	11.8	–	9.7	–
Viet Nam (1992)	14.5	75.0	14.0	74.4
India (1991)*	67.0*	11.8*		

Sources: United Nations, *Demographic Yearbook, 1996*, Department of Economic and Social Affairs, ST/ESA/STAT/SER.R/27, Table 8, United Nations, New York. Also see *Demographic Yearbook: Historical Supplement 1948–1997 Series:R*, No.28/HS-CD Sales No.E/F99.XIII.12, United Nations, New York; 2002; United Nations 'A Demographic Perspective on Women in Development in Cambodia, Laos People's Democratic Republic, Myanmar and Viet Nam', Asian Population Studies Series No. 148, Economic and Social Commission for Asia and the Pacific, ST/ESCAP/1869, Tables 7 and 8, New York, 1998; Laos Census 1995: Country Report, Ventiane, 1997, National Statistical Centre, pp. 47–48; S.I. Rajan, U.S. Mishra and P. Sankara Sarma, *India's Elderly: Burden or Challenge?*, Sage Publications, New Delhi, 1999.

Note: The old age dependency ratio is the ratio of the population aged 60 years and older to the working population in the 15–59 years age bracket. Similarly, youth dependency is the ratio of the population younger than 15 years old to the working population 15–49 years old. The Indian data belongs to whole of the country, rural and urban combined.

relative to the numbers of economically active in that sector. There are considerably larger numbers of rural old relative to rural youth in Japan, while proportions in the Republic of Korea are virtually equal. In all the other countries, the pattern still consists of large proportions of youthful dependants, and ageing, as an economic burden, has not yet emerged as a significant issue. As might be expected, overall dependency in the urban areas is considerably lower than in the rural sector except in the cases of Brunei Darussalam and Viet Nam. Excluding Japan, there is also much less variation in the pattern of old-age dependency. Thus, ageing as a potential burden is found primarily in the rural sectors of the most developed economies of the region.

GENDER DIMENSION OF RURAL AGEING

The ageing of the rural sector also has a gender dimension attached to it. That women live longer than men is virtually a universal characteristic of human populations, even if there are certain exceptional areas where this is not the case. All the elderly populations in the countries under consideration, excluding Brunei Darussalam, follow this generalisation and have a greater proportion of women than men. India may also seem to be an exception if the 1991 Census is to be accepted. The following discussion however indicates that there was an underestimation in the 1991 Census. All the NSS rounds show that India is no exception and that it does have a greater proportion of women among the aged. The very high masculinity for urban areas in Cambodia is a direct result of the tragic events that occurred in the country during Pol Pot's regime which saw the virtual emptying of its cities. Men have been among the first to enter the urban sector with a return to more stable conditions. This trend has been most marked in the populations which have the highest longevity and greatest ageing: Japan and the Republic of Korea. There are fewer elderly men per elderly women in the rural sector of Japan when compared with the urban sector, while this situation is reversed in the Republic of Korea. The biggest difference, as far as the gender of the elderly populations is concerned, is found in Malaysia, the Philippines and Thailand. There, the elderly in the rural sector are much more balanced in terms of the sex ratio compared to the populations in the urban sector which are much more female dominant. This difference is essentially due to a greater incidence of return of male rural-to-urban migrants to the rural sector. This pattern should have been evident for Indonesia, where the phenomenon of male retirement migration back to the villages has been identified as being important,[7] though the data presented in Table 5.7 does not exhibit this clearly.

Table 5.7
Rural–Urban Sex Ratio (Male per 100 Females) of Populations 60 Years of Age
and Older for Selected Asian Countries

Country	Urban	Rural
Japan (1995)	77	74
Republic of Korea (1995)	64	69
Brunei Darussalam (1991)	101	122
China (1990)	95	89
Indonesia (1995)	85	87
Malaysia (1991)	83	95
Philippines (1990)	82	95
Thailand (1990)	79	96
Cambodia (1996)	248	75
Laos PDR (1995)	90	92
Viet Nam (1992)	70	77
India (1991)	104.1	108.4

Source: Same as Table 5.6.

As our discussion in this chapter and chapter two shows, there is a propensity for elderly males to move to urban areas on retirement. Elderly women, upon the death of their spouse, however, often move to urban areas to seek support from their families settled there. The elderly women can provide babysitting and other domestic services to their sons and daughters to help adult female members pursue urban employment. The demand for such elderly women becomes higher when there are few children to look after younger siblings. Interestingly, fertility in the major urban areas of Malaysia, the Philippines and Thailand is lower than in Indonesia. As a result, there are more elder siblings per family who can take care of younger siblings in Indonesia than anywhere else. This may explain why older women in Indonesia move less to the towns than their counterparts in Malaysia, the Philippines or Thailand.[8] However, this is still conjecture and more rigorous studies are necessary to establish the hypothesis.

AGEING AND THE RURAL ECONOMY

As Table 2.7 in chapter two shows, the Republic of Korea has a significantly large (and probably the largest in the region) proportion of the aged population in rural areas. However, the existence of such a large number of the elderly in rural areas (which may also imply an exodus of the surplus rural population to the cities) has caused no setback to development, either in the rural or the urban areas. To be precise, the standards of living have improved in both rural and urban areas. There has been no negative impact on the overall situation of food security at the national level. The conditions in the rural sector appear to have improved at the same time as the population has aged. This is not to say, of course, that conditions improved because the rural population aged. There could very well be localised pockets of deprivation because of the ageing of rural populations and the exodus of the younger, most productive members of those populations. However, the government policy for rural development was careful enough to ensure rural progress despite the ageing.[9]

The proportion of the elderly in the rural sector of Thailand rose from 6 per cent in 1980 to 8 per cent in 1990. This trend is similar to what happened in the rural sector of the Republic of Korea in the same demographic phase. With persistent decline in fertility, there is no doubt that the rural population in Thailand will grey more than ever before. In Thailand, the highest proportions of the elderly are seen in the central plains and in the north. These are precisely those areas where the decline in fertility began and from where it rapidly extended outwards during the 1970s. The north-east region remains an area of relatively high fertility; even then, the proportions of the aged here are not insignificant, essentially because of outmigration of the youth from these regions to Bangkok. Though the level of youth outmigration is high in the central plains and the north, there is a much larger flow of return migration of retirees from Bangkok.

A survey of the Mun River basin in Thailand found that, in 10 of the 11 provinces covered by the survey, 40 per cent or more of the economically active population in every district were migrant workers.[10] There was an overall bias towards males among the migrant workers from the region. This implies a growing feminisation of agricultural activities as well as an ageing of the labour force. The outmigration allowed some consolidation of landholdings on the better land and abandonment of more marginal holdings. Another national level survey indicates that over 40 per cent of the migrants to Bangkok, for example, had sent money back to their home areas.[11] In common with migration elsewhere, population movement from villages to towns initially acts as a support for the household economies in villages. The households receiving remittances are generally better off than those that do not. Given that most of the peasantry has access to land[12] and that there is intense circulation between rural and urban sectors, the Thai rural economy is unlikely to experience any negative impact vis-à-vis the greying of its rural population. However, unlike Korea, the rural population of Thailand is still rising and the net area under food production has declined over time. However, the Thai farmers have shifted to more intensive land-saving technology, and to more remunerative crops, wherever possible.[13] This has ensured a steady flow of food grains and other agricultural goods within rural areas. Where such opportunities did not exist, circulation to urban areas becomes an even more important means of ensuring rural food security. The incidence of poverty witnessed a marked decline in Thailand from almost 30 per cent in 1986 to less than 10 per cent in 1994.[14] Interestingly, the steepest declines in the incidence of poverty were in the north-east regions from where there was a constant flow of youth to the major cities and to Bangkok in particular.

In India, rural poverty has declined from 56.4 per cent during 1973–74 to 27.09 per cent during 1999–2000, according to the 55th Round of the Consumer Expenditure Survey of the NSS. Food grain production has gone up from 129.6 million tonnes during 1980–81 to 203 million tonnes during 1998–99. The rural share of the population has gone down from 80 per cent in the 1971 Census to 74.3 per cent in the 1991 Census. However, the country has reached its plateau insofar as the area devoted to food grain production is concerned. This thereby implies that all future progress in agriculture depends, to a great extent, on technological improvement. With the youth moving into the cities for their careers, the capital resources and skills of the elderly returned migrants could play a pivotal role in agricultural transformation in India. However, most rural areas lack infrastructure to motivate a significant flow of private investment; moreover, elderly care facilities are almost non-existent. Given this background, risk-averting middle-class retirees may be more tempted to keep their life's savings in urban financial investments rather than in highly uncertain agricultural investments.

In chapter two, in the section on population ageing and migration, it has been apprehended that the ageing of the rural population accompanied by the outmigration of the youthful cohorts of the population may cause depopulation of rural areas. In Japan today, such depopulation is a reality. Almost two-fifths of 'cities, towns and villages' are classified as 'Kasho', or severely depopulating areas. These areas account for virtually half of the land area of the country. In 1995, 20.5 per cent of Japan's population was aged 60 years and above: for those areas classified as Kasho, the equivalent figure was 33.2 per cent. The Kasho populations have become increasingly residual, gradually atrophying through mortality. With such a large number of the aged and a few youthful populations, the productivity per unit of land in Kasho areas is already lower than the rest of Japan. Although, one is not yet clear whether the emergence of the Kasho areas have any adverse effect on the Japanese economy, the fact remains that the overall food production index has been staggering at the same level for more than a decade and that the arable land area is declining in Japan.[15] However, there is no doubt that these Kasho areas are only pockets of relative deprivation in a prosperous country and that they should not be dismissed as typical Japanese phenomena. Rural depopulation is already visible in the Republic of Korea and perhaps in parts of China too. Labour shortages are already prevalent in the rural sectors of Malaysia and Thailand and these shortages are presently being met through migration from neighbouring countries, much of which is illegal.

It may, therefore, be seen that ageing increasingly appears to be a rural issue. The problem becomes more intense when younger family members move to the cities leaving behind the elderly to look after themselves. This is not to say that the elderly in urban areas do not face problems of isolation and loneliness, but the costs of providing basic support services for the elderly are likely to be greater and more difficult to implement in rural areas. In Japan, in 1990, 10 per cent of the elderly Japanese lived alone. In Kasho areas, the proportion of household heads of 65 years of age and above who lived alone in 1997 was 9.6 per cent; this is just double the proportion for non-Kasho areas. In India 4 to 5 per cent of the elderly, both in rural and urban areas, were living alone in 1995–96. In Thailand, 4.5 per cent of the elderly in rural and 3.5 per cent in urban areas lived on their own in 1990.

The decline in fertility throughout the Asian region means that there are fewer children available per person to look after the population when it becomes old. Urbanisation and the transition into industrial societies often weakens family ties, spatially if not emotionally, and residual rural populations without adequate welfare systems are likely to suffer relative if not absolute deprivation. Luckily, as our following discussions show, the familial system of care for the elderly has been maintained in most Asian countries. Very few of the elderly live on their own or without seeing their children on a regular basis. Even then, it is incumbent upon the government to ensure that ageing populations in isolated rural areas are adequately provided for, with services and care. There may be much to learn from the policies followed by Japan towards its Kasho areas for other countries in the region. The provision of basic medical services in Kasho areas over the recent past, for example, has outpaced that for the population as a whole.

AGEING OF THE AGED

The aged themselves are ageing everywhere in the world. In chapter one, a global picture of the ageing of the aged has been provided. The oldest of the old (80 years or older) in the world constituted 11 per cent of the aged in 1999. Their numbers will rise to 19 per cent by 2025. In the developed regions, this percentage almost doubles from 9 to 17 per cent. In Japan, the figure rises from 16 to 31 per cent, while in Thailand the oldest of the old increase from 10 to 21 per cent. The 1991 Indian Census data shows that about two-thirds of the elderly population belong in the 60–69 age group and about one-fourth of them in the 70–79 age group. The 'oldest' constitute 11.25 per cent of the old population. The census data indicates that the proportion of people in the age group of 60–69 has declined steadily from 1961 while the proportion of all other ten-year age groups has risen slowly. There was a marginal decline in the proportion of centenarians since 1961. The number of centenarians was 151,646 in 1981. The corresponding figures in 1971 and 1981 were 130,352 and 132,840 respectively. Table 5.8 shows the percentage distribution of those aged 60 and above (according to sex) since 1961.

There are several implications of such changes in the age composition of the aged:

1. Having survived several life-threatening situations through periods of high mortality and morbidity, the oldest among the old will therefore be subject to a higher incidence of morbidity and disability. This will have a serious impact on the country's health system, particularly public health. An OECD study[16] indicates that as the proportions of the oldest among the old rise, the demand for long-term health care rises. Long-term health care is still a low priority in the developing countries of Asia. But as ageing takes place within the aged, health policy makers can hardly ignore this element.

Table 5.8

Percentage Distribution of those Aged 60 and above by Sex, since 1961

Year	60-69			70-79			80-89			90-99			100 plus		
	M	F	T	M	F	T	M	F	T	M	F	T	M	F	T
1961	66.2	64.0	65.1	24.4	25.3	24.8	7.5	8.4	7.9	1.6	1.9	1.7	0.4	0.4	0.4
1971	66.0	64.8	65.4	24.8	24.9	24.8	7.3	8.1	7.7	1.6	1.8	1.7	0.3	0.3	0.4
1981	64.4	63.9	64.1	26.3	26.3	26.3	7.8	8.0	7.9	.3	1.5	1.4	0.3	0.3	0.3
1991	62.7	63.0	62.8	26.0	25.9	25.9	9.2	8.9	9.1	1.9	2.0	1.9	0.3	0.3	0.3
2021#	60.0	59.0	57.9	30.2	31.1	30.7	9.9*	12.9*	11.4*						

Source: Census of India 1991, *Ageing Population of India: An Analysis of the 1991 Census Data*, Registrar General, India, New Delhi, 1999. The data for 2021 was taken from L. Visaria and P. Visaria, *An analysis of Long Term Population Projections for States of India, 1991–2101*, (Mimeo), 1999.

Notes: M = Male; F = Female; T = Both sexes combined; # indicates projection data; * indicates data for those 80 plus.

2. As more and more people live beyond the retirement age, a larger burden is imposed on the public support system for pensions and other benefits. The family becomes more preoccupied with the care and support of the elderly, and this may cause considerable family tension, particularly when resources are diverted away from the younger generations.

FEMINISATION OF THE ELDERLY

According to the 1981 Census of India, there were 960 females for every 1000 males of age 60 and above. This number dropped to 930 in 1991. The NSS estimates on the other hand, show an upward trend. The trend is different for the rural and urban areas. Table 5.9 shows the rural–urban difference in sex ratio.

The sex ratio among the aged declined during the period 1987–88 and 1993–94 and rose during 1995–96 in the rural areas. In the urban areas, the sex ratio increased from 1,032 during 1987–88 to 960 during 1993–94 and then dropped to 1,043 during 1995–96. Table 5.10 shows the sex ratio among aged persons in selected countries.

There is no need to be perturbed over this feminisation trend among the aged. The sex ratio among the aged is generally favourable to women. The higher the level of economic development, the more favourable is the sex ratio towards the elderly. A perusal of Table 5.8 confirms this hypothesis. This is the global trend. According

Table 5.9
Rural–Urban Differences in Elderly Sex Ratio (Number of Females
per 1000 Males) in India

Source	Year	Rural	Urban	Combined
Census	1981	954	986	960
Census	1991	922	960	930
NSS 43rd Round	1987–88	971	1,032	983
NSS 50th Round	1993–94	963	1,060	984
NSS 52nd Round	1995–96	1,017	1,043	1,023

Source: National Statistical Survey Organisation (NSSO), *The Aged In India: A Socio-economic Profile*, NNS 52nd Round July 1995–June 1996, NSSO, Department of Statistics, Ministry of Planning and Programme Implementation, Government of India, Calcutta, 1998.

Table 5.10
Sex Ratio (Number of Females per 1000 Males) among Aged Persons
in Selected Countries

Countries	1950	1960	1970	1980	1990	2000	2050
India	1,112	987	949	969	1,033	1,086	1,095
Japan	1,263	1,201	1,224	1,341	1,346	1,290	1,230
Thailand	1,156	1,156	1,199	1,209	1,211	1,249	1,218
MDRs	1,356	1,416	1,463	1,470	1,493	1,415	1,277

Source: Compiled from United Nations, *World Population Prospects: The 1998 Revision, Vol. II: Sex and Age*, Population Division, Department of Economic and Social Affairs, New York, 1999.

to UN projections, in the year 2000, the elderly male population will constitute 7.1 per cent of the total male population while the corresponding figure for elderly females is 8.2 per cent. Women live longer than men do. The reason for this is purely biological.

A lower sex ratio in India further confirms the fact that elderly women in India are less favourably treated than their counterparts in relatively developed economies. Looking at regional variations, in 1991, the BIMARU (namely Bihar, Madhya Pradesh, Rajasthan and Uttar Pradesh) states in India had more than 5 million elderly females. Much against the global trend, elderly males exceeded elderly females in all these states. But in Kerala, Maharashtra, Andhra Pradesh, Karnataka and Gujarat, the elderly females outnumber the elderly males. The feminisation of the elderly, however natural it may be, results in several undesirable consequences:

1. The incidence of poverty among elderly women is generally very high, as a great majority of them are widows having very little access to the minimum requirements of a healthy life.
2. Although 'granny battering' is still an unknown concept in Asian society, elderly women are highly susceptible to verbal, physical and financial abuse from the younger members of their family.

THE SINGLE ELDERLY

Another peculiar feature of the aged in India is the heavy concentration of single persons in the widows and widowers category. A person generally depends on his/her family for support, love and care. This dependence grows during old age. Ironically, ageing and loneliness go together. Several interesting insights emerge from the NSS survey rounds of the aged in India. Table 5.11 shows the marital status of the aged in India.

A perusal of Table 5.11 reveals the following:

1. The proportions of single people (never married, widow, widower, divorced and separated) among the aged constituted 41.6 per cent in rural areas and 42.0 per cent in urban areas. This proportion is declining with time.
2. Over 60 per cent of aged females, in both urban and rural areas, are widowed. Here too, the proportion is declining. The proportion of widows dropped by 4 percentage points between 1993–94 and 1995–96. The proportion of widowers, however, showed no sign of change.
3. About 1 to 2 per cent of the aged never married.
4. Around 60 per cent of the aged are currently married and their proportion is rising.

The highest number of widows in India are seen in the state of Andhra Pradesh, followed by West Bengal and Assam. In all these states over 70 per cent of elderly females are widows. They live in pathetic conditions and are often subject to abuse. Three factors are responsible for such a high percentage of widowhood. First, women are at a much lower risk of death at the age of 60 than men. Second, widows generally do not remarry. Third, women marry men a few years senior to them and these higher aged men are therefore subject to a higher risk of dying. Interestingly, with the projected decline in mortality, the risk of widowhood will be lower in the future and this trend is already visible.

The NSS survey indicates that only 0.4 per cent of elderly females are divorced or separated. While this is certainly not an alarming figure, a large number of future elderly women will be divorced with a high proportion of marriages now ending in divorce. Divorced elderly women, unlike widows, have no claim on their late husbands' pension rights. If the divorce takes place at a later age, they may not even be able to earn enough to make provisions for their old age. In such situations divorced women are in a worse position than their widowed counterparts who atleast hold the pension rights of their late husbands.

Table 5.11
Marital Status of the Aged in India

		Rural				Urban			
		\\multicolumn{4}{c}{Marital Status}						
Sex	Source	Never Married	Currently Married	Divorced/ Separated	Widowed	Never Married	Currently Married	Widowed	Divorced/ Separated
Male	50th Round	1.7	77.2	0.4	20.7	1.9	79.4	18.4	0.3
	52nd Round	1.8	76.8	0.3	20.9	2.2	79.3	17.8	0.5
Female	50th Round	1.2	36.9	0.3	61.6	1.4	33.2	64.9	0.4
	52nd Round	1.1	40.1	0.4	40.8	1.3	37.3	60.9	0.4
Persons	50th Round	1.4	57.5	0.3	42.4	1.7	55.6	42.4	0.3
	52nd Round	1.5	58.3	0.3	39.8	1.8	57.9	39.8	0.4

Source: National Statistical Organisation (NSSO), *The Aged In India: A Socio-economic Profile,* NNS 52nd Round, July 1995–June 1996, NSSO, Department of Statistics, Ministry of Planning and Programme Implementation, Government of India, Calcutta, 1998.

LITERACY AMONG THE AGED

Literacy is one of the most powerful survival tools in today's world. It is next to impossible for a man to make a productive living without literacy. However, this was not the situation in the past when today's elderly were young. The facilities for education and schooling were quite limited. As a result, the level of literacy among the aged could not be high. A comparison of the literacy levels of the aged with the general population show the extent to which the elderly are lagging behind. Table 5.12 gives the comparison.

In India all persons aged 7 years and above, who can both read and write, and have an understanding of any language, are taken as literate in the census. With regard to elderly literacy, the following observations become very pertinent:

1. As expected, the general population is more literate than the elderly population.
2. The elderly urban population is more literate than the rural elderly.
3. Elderly males are more literate than elderly females.
4. The levels of literacy among the elderly have been rising since the 1961 Census.

In 1961 only the state of Kerala had elderly female literacy at above 15 per cent. Many states reported to have an elderly female literacy

Table 5.12
Literacy among the Aged and General Population in India

Source	Residence	Elderly Population		General Population	
		Male	Female	Male	Female
1961 Census	Total	29.18	4.30	34.46	12.96
	Rural	24.36	2.28	29.09	8.55
	Urban	55.89	15.82	57.49	34.51
1981 Census	Total	34.79	7.89	46.89	24.82
	Rural	28.74	4.44	40.79	17.96
	Urban	60.03	21.82	65.83	47.82
1991 Census	Total	40.62	12.68	52.75	32.17
	Rural	33.65	7.51	47.07	24.85
	Urban	65.97	30.76	68.76	53.85

Source: Registrar General, India, *Census of India, 1961, Census of India 1981* and *Census of India 1991*, Ministry of Home Affairs, New Delhi, 1992.
Note: The Census of India 1971 had no data on the literacy of elderly people.

level of below 5 per cent. But in 1991, Goa, Kerala, Mizoram, Chandigarh, Delhi and Pondicherry had elderly female literacy of above 25 per cent. The states of Arunachal Pradesh and Rajasthan still have elderly female literacy at below 5 per cent.

For all literate persons, the census collects information on the highest educational level attained by literate persons. Table 5.13 give the percentage distribution of the literate population aged 60 years and above by level of education for India as available from the 1981 and 1991 censuses.

From Table 5.13 it can be seen that the proportion of graduates and those at a higher educational level among the elderly literates has increased from 2.76 per cent in 1981 to 4.51 per cent in 1991. The majority of the elderly literates had primary and below primary level of education. About 20 per cent of the elderly male literates and 10 per cent of the elderly female literates had passed matriculation and higher levels of education.

The following policy implications emerge from the foregoing discussion on literacy among the aged:

1. A great majority of the elderly in the country are illiterate and therefore enjoy a very low status in society. Respect towards elders is eroded considerably when the younger generations notice the great disparity between their level of education and that of their seniors.
2. The government policy formulations on the elderly need to take into account the wide differences in the educational levels among the aged. With increasing levels of education among the aged, new demands for public services and social security may emerge. The organisation of the elderly into a powerful pressure group may not be ruled out.

LIVING ARRANGEMENTS OF THE ELDERLY

Households in developing countries are vital institutions for the well-being of the elderly. In the final years of their life, the elderly often experience a decrease in physical functioning, and tend to acquire physical ailments and disabilities that make it difficult for them to carry out their day-to-day activities. They become essentially dependent on others for their financial, physical and emotional support. This is true everywhere but less so in places where well developed public institutions and market agencies have become sensitive to the needs of the elderly, and more where institutional support outside

Table 5.13
Percentage Distribution of Literate Population Aged 60 and above by the Level of Education, India, 1981 and 1991

Level of Education	Year	Total			Rural			Urban		
		Total	Male	Female	Total	Male	Female	Total	Male	Female
Literate	1981	100.0	100.0	100.0	100.0	100.0	100.0	100.0	100.0	100.0
	1991	100.0	100.0	100.0	100.0	100.0	100.0	100.0	100.0	100.0
Below Primary (Non-formal)	1981	5.36	5.22	6.01	6.48	6.34	7.44	3.48	2.99	4.84
	1991	3.48	3.39	3.80	4.42	4.26	5.22	2.02	1.77	2.59
Below Primary (Formal)	1981	32.71	31.54	38.10	39.41	38.15	47.97	21.41	18.33	30.00
	1991	25.03	24.27	27.64	30.87	30.02	35.01	15.99	13.60	21.34
Primary	1981	34.43	33.60	38.23	36.18	36.21	36.01	31.48	28.40	40.05
	1991	36.59	34.89	42.46	39.80	38.75	44.89	31.63	27.72	40.39
Middle	1981	13.57	14.14	10.94	11.85	12.65	6.43	16.46	17.11	14.63
	1991	16.56	17.00	15.04	15.29	16.26	10.57	18.53	18.38	18.86
Matriculation/Secondary	1981	8.93	9.90	4.46	4.26	4.69	1.28	16.81	20.31	7.07
	1991	10.87	12.09	6.68	6.33	7.13	2.45	17.90	21.30	10.29
Higher Secondary	1981	1.61	1.82	0.67	0.67	0.74	0.18	3.20	3.96	1.08
	1991	2.18	2.44	1.27	1.17	1.31	0.50	3.74	4.55	1.94
Non-technical diploma	1981	0.12	0.12	0.14	0.11	0.11	0.10	0.16	0.15	0.17
	1991	0.29	0.27	0.34	0.27	0.28	0.25	0.30	0.26	0.41
Technical Diploma	1981	0.51	0.52	0.44	0.37	0.36	0.41	0.74	0.84	0.46
	1991	0.49	0.50	0.47	0.33	0.31	0.40	0.74	0.84	0.53
Graduate and above	1981	2.76	3.14	1.01	0.68	0.75	0.18	6.27	7.91	1.69
	1991	4.51	5.15	2.30	1.51	1.68	0.71	9.14	11.59	3.66

Source: Registrar General, India, Census of India, 1991, Ageing Population of India, An Analysis of 1991 Census Data, New Delhi, 1999.

the family has not grown adequately. Households also serve as very satisfactory agencies for the distribution of economic and other goods among its members.[17] The family also allocates different roles for its members, maintaining a balance between the different kin and age groups in such a way that they all reflect and contribute to the fundamental structure of the society as a whole.[18] In many cultural settings, the family sets the norms for a reciprocal relationship between the young and the old.[19]

Several studies have been undertaken to investigate the nature of living arrangements in developing countries. Most of these studies have been carried out in East and South-east Asian nations, and some in Latin America and African countries. No proper investigations have however been conducted on the living arrangements of the elderly. In this sense, the NSSO findings can help in further analysis and scrutiny of the subject. The most consistent findings from this research, including the NSSO survey, are that older adults rarely live alone and usually reside with a spouse and/or adult child. The NSSO findings have been summarised in Tables 5.14 and 5.15, while census

Table 5.14
Proportion of Aged Persons by Number of Surviving Children

Area	Sex	Source	Zero	One	Two	One or More
						Number of Surviving Children
Rural	Male	NSS 42nd Round 1986–87	7.4	–	–	92.6
		NSS 52nd Round 1995–96	5.5	6.1	10.5	94.5
	Female	NSS 42nd Round 1986–87	5.6	–	–12.0	94.4
		NSS 52nd Round 1995–96	6.2	8.1		93.8
	Total	NSS 42nd Round 1986–87	6.7	–	–11.3	93.3
		NSS 52nd Round 1995–96	5.8	7.1		94.2
Urban	Male	NSS 42nd Round 1986–87	8.3	–	–	91.7
		NSS 52nd Round 1995–96	5.3	7.1	11.2	94.7
	Female	NSS 42nd Round 1986–87	6.9	–	–	93.1
		NSS 52nd Round 1995–96	6.5	8.7	11.1	93.5
	Total	NSS 42nd Round 1986–87	7.7	–	–	92.3
		NSS 52nd Round 1995–96	5.9	7.9	11.2	94.1
Total		NSS 52nd Round 1995–96	5.8	7.3	11.2	94.2

Source: National Sample Survey Organisation (NSSO), *The Aged In India: A Socioeconomic Profile*, NNS 52nd Round, July 1995–June 1996, NSSO, Department of Statistics, Ministry of Planning and Programme Implementation, Government of India, Calcutta, 1998.

Note: Numbers in table indicate percentage.

Table 5.15
Living Arrangements of the Elderly in India

Living Arrangement	Rural			Urban		
	Male	Female	Total	Male	Female	Total
Alone	2.5	6.1	4.3	3.0	6.0	4.5
	(12.4)	(1.4)	(8.0)	(9.5)	(0.8)	(5.9)
With spouse	13.7	7.7	10.7	10.3	5.7	8.0
With spouse and other members	61.3	31.3	46.2	64.8	29.7	46.9
(2+3)	75.0	39.0	56.9	75.1	35.4	54.9
	(45.1)	(25.1)	(37.0)	(44.9)	(21.5)	(35.3)
With children	17.0	48.1	33.1	17.8	51.2	34.9
	(36.8)	(66.0)	(48.6)	(39.6)	(67.3)	(51.0)
With other relations/non-relations	3.8	5.9	4.8	3.5	6.5	5.1
	(5.7)	(7.4)	(6.2)	(5.6)	(10.0)	(7.4)
Total	100.0	100.0	100.0	100.0	100.0	100.0

Source: National Sample Survey Organisation (NSSO), *The Aged In India: A Socio-economic Profile*, NNS 52nd Round, July 1995–June 1996, NSSO, Department of Statistics, Ministry of Planning & Programme Implementation, Government of India, Calcutta, 1998.

Notes: The figures in brackets indicate the findings of the NSS 42nd Round, 1986–87. Numbers in table indicate percentage.

and other survey data for Thailand, the Philippines, Indonesia, Sri Lanka, Singapore, Taiwan, Vietnam, Korea and Japan and South Korea are presented in Table 5.16. The tables confirm that the extended, multigenerational family is a resilient feature of Asian society. The percentage of elderly living with children ranged from 67 per cent in Indonesia to 85 per cent in Singapore, barring Japan and South Korea where the percentages have fallen below 50. However, this proportion was still much higher than that of the multigenerational living arrangements in developed countries. A World Bank report indicates that only 7, 12 and 13 per cent of the elderly live with their children in Australia, the Netherlands and the United States respectively.[20]

Interestingly, the proportions of the elderly living with children are falling all over in Asia (see Table 5.16). A study of rural China for a long time period shows that in the 1930s there were no elderly living in simple conjugal units, but by 1995, 30 per cent of them were living in such households. The proportions of the elderly living in multigenerational households dropped from 86 to 60 per cent between the same time period.[21] In 1996, only 15 per cent of elderly

Table 5.16
Percentage of Co-residence of Elderly Aged 60 and Over in Selected Asian Countries

Country	Year	Total			Men			Women		
		Living Alone	Living only with Spouse	Living with any Child	Living Alone	Living only with Spouse	Living with any Child	Living Alone	Living only with Spouse	Living with any Child
Thailand	1986	4	7	77	–	9	77	5	5	77
	1990	6	–	77	–	–	78	6	–	76
	1994	4	12	73	–	15	73	5	9	73
	1995	4	12	71	–	15	73	6	10	70
Philippines	1986	3	5	74	–	11	72	5	9	–
	1988	4	10	68	–	–	68	–	–	–
	1996	6	8	69	–	9	72	7	7	67
Singapore	1986	2	3	88	–	–	–	–	–	–
	1995	3	6	85	–	–	–	–	–	–
Indonesia	1990	4	–	67	–	–	–	–	–	–
Sri Lanka	1990	3	–	84	–	–	–	–	–	–
Viet Nam	1996	7	13	74	–	–	–	–	–	–
	1997	5	5	82	–	–	–	–	–	–
Japan	1970	–	–	–	–	–	68	–	7	70
	1990	–	–	–	3	18	–	7	7	–
Korea	1984	–	–	78	–	36	49	–	16	–
	1994	–	–	47	6	–	–	15	–	51

Source: A. Mason, Sang-Hyop Lee and Gerard Russo, Population Momentum and Population Ageing in Asia and Near-east Countries, Population Series No. 107, February 2001.

men and women in Japan mentioned children as a source of income, down from 30 per cent in 1981.[22]

The Indian data is very surprising. While 94 per cent of the aged have children, only 33 to 34 per cent live with their children; this was in 1995–96. In the 1986–87 survey periods, 49 to 51 per cent of the aged were living with their children. The 1995–96 NSS survey shows that 94 per cent of the elderly had atleast one surviving child. The rural–urban differences are negligible with regard to the proportion of elderly living with surviving children. However, these were marginally higher for males than for females. Between the 42nd and 52nd Rounds, there have been some improvements with regard to the proportion of aged persons whose children are still living. The improvement is prominent for males, while the proportion remained the same for females.

The Indian data shows that around 58 per cent of the elderly are currently married and that almost all of them live with their spouses. The older males are more likely than the older females to live with a spouse. In the rural areas, over 60 per cent of the elderly males live with their spouses and other family members, but only one-third of the elderly females enjoy this privilege. The male-female gap in the living arrangement vis-à-vis spouses and other family members is higher in the urban areas. The gender differential in the living arrangement of the elderly is primarily because of the higher incidence of widowhood among elderly females than among elderly males. Around 10 per cent of aged people stay with their spouses. This percentage is lower in urban than in rural areas. About 5 per cent of the elderly live with their friends and relations and around 4 per cent of them alone. The elderly, living as inmates in old-age homes, constitute 0.8 to 0.9 per cent of the total elderly population in India. Interestingly, the living arrangement of the elderly underwent a favourable change between the 42nd and 52nd Round surveys of the NSSO. The proportions of the elderly living alone dropped from 5.9 per cent to 4.5 per cent in urban areas, and from 8.0 per cent to 4.3 per cent in rural areas. At the same time, the proportions of elderly females living alone shot up dramatically: from 0.8 per cent to 6 per cent in urban areas and from 1.4 per cent to 6.1 per cent in urban areas. The proportion of the aged living with their spouses also went up significantly from 37 per cent to the current 57 per cent in rural areas, and from 35 per cent to 55 per cent in urban areas.

It has been stated that the levels of parent–child co-residence are inversely related to socio-economic development.[23] Without being biased towards such hypothesis, it can be argued that socio-economic development introduces an economic element in all decision-making processes. Already, today, in the Asian situation, the parent–child co-residence is beneficial to both parent and child. The older adults receive the social, financial and health support they require from the younger generation in exchange for looking after the younger children or the home while the other adults are away. Also, the house where everyone lives very often belongs to the elderly parents and expensive living costs may not allow children to live seperately. However, these calculations may not hold much water in the future. The expectations and preferences of today's working-age adults suggest that the economics of multigenerational living will not be a likeable proposition in the future. In 1997, only 8 per cent of South Korean women of childbearing age indicated that they wished to live with their children when they grew old.[24] In the Philippines, where the actual proportion of the elderly living with their children has not declined much, fewer working-age adults wish to live with their children in the future.[25]

Most of Indian society, except Kerala in the south, is patrilineal i.e., the male dominates the ownership of resources and presides over family decision-making. Women leave their parental home and move to their husband's house after marriage. Older adults generally live with the family of a married son. If they do not have a son, they prefer to move into a relative's house rather than live with their married daughters. The Chinese system appears to be very similar. In contrast, in some of the South-east Asian countries like Cambodia[26] and Thailand, the elderly couples prefer to live with their unmarried daughters. In Thailand, there is a preference for living with the youngest daughter who is not likely to be married.[27] Although the pattern of co-residence should have bearing on the nature and level of support provided to older adults, a comparative analysis of the implications of the two systems is not yet available.

Bongaarts and Zimmer[28] reconstructed the demographic data of households for 43 developing countries, including 11 Asian countries that participated in the Demographic and Health Survey (DHS) programme between 1990 and 1998, to analyse the pattern of living arrangements of the elderly. The findings do corroborate with data from India and other countries on the living arrangements of the elderly. To be more specific, the study shows that most older adults tend to live in large households and that they are likely to be living with an adult child, who is more likely to be male than female. It also finds that on average, nearly one out of 10 older adults lives alone, and that the probability of living alone is greater for older women than men. Women are much less likely to live with a spouse in the household, while a slightly greater proportion of older women than men live with adult children. The programme also noted a weakening of extended family links in conjunction with socio-economic development.

There is an inverse relationship between the educational levels of the elderly and their living arrangements with adult children: where levels of education are higher, older adults live in smaller households, with fewer children and other adults, and are more likely to be alone. The reasons for this are: (a) older adults with higher levels of schooling have more skills and are therefore generally better able to care for themselves; (b) the better-educated older adults have a stronger preference for privacy than the poor and least educated. Conversely, where education is lower, older adults own fewer resources. They are, therefore, more dependent on adult children, especially the male offspring, who are more likely to control household resources than female members, who in general move to another house after marriage. It is also likely that cultural taboos make them stay away from their sons' residence.

ECONOMIC ACTIVITIES OF THE ELDERLY

According to the 1991 Census, there were 22.2 million elderly workers in India. Of these, 17.8 million were males and 4.4 million females. This implies that 39.1 per cent of the total elderly population were workers as against 37.5 per cent for the total population. The elderly male workforce participation rate was 60.5 per cent while it was 16.1 per cent for females compared to 51.6 per cent for males and 22.3 per cent for females in the all ages' category. In the rural areas, the elderly workforce participation rate is larger than the all ages' population. The urban elderly, however, participate in the workforce little less than the general population. The female workforce participation for the aged category is lower everywhere as compared to the all ages' population. In India, even people in the age group 80 plus participate in the workforce. Table 5.17 sums up the workforce participation rate for the elderly and the general population.

Table 5.17
Work Participation Rate for the Elderly and General Population
in India, 1991 (in percentage)

Category	Total			Rural			Urban		
	Total	Male	Female	Total	Male	Female	Total	Male	Female
Elderly	39.1	60.5	16.1	43.1	65.4	19.0	25.0	42.9	6.3
General	37.5	51.6	22.3	40.0	52.5	26.7	30.2	48.9	9.2
60–69 Age Category	46.9	71.4	20.8	51.7	77.1	24.4	30.0	50.7	8.0
70–79 Age Category	28.8	47.0	9.2	31.9	51.2	10.8	17.8	31.3	3.7
80 plus Age Category	19.3	31.7	5.7	20.9	33.5	6.7	13.4	24.7	2.6

Source: Registrar General, India, Census of India, 1991, Ageing Population of India, An Analysis of 1991 Census Data, New Delhi, 1999.

The elderly workforce participation rates for nine major states of India are as follows: Uttar Pradesh (45 per cent), Bihar (42.4 per cent), Maharashtra (39 per cent), Madhya Pradesh (46.1 per cent), Andhra Pradesh (43.4 per cent), Tamil Nadu (39.9 per cent), West Bengal (30.8 per cent), Karnataka (37.3 per cent) and Rajasthan (36.4 per cent). Andhra Pradesh has the highest female workforce participation rate (24.2 per cent) among the elderly and West Bengal the lowest (6.5 per cent).

Table 5.18 gives the percentage distribution of main workers aged 60 plus by industrial category, sex and residence.

About 78 per cent of the elderly workforce is engaged in agricultural activities. In the case of female workers, this figure is over 84 per cent. As there is no age limit in self-employed agriculture, people continue to work on their farms and allied enterprises even after 60 years of age. In the absence of any social security in the agricultural sector, the elderly fare badly and this is especially true for female workers. Even in the non-agricultural sectors, there is some social security only in the organised sector, which, however, constitutes only a tiny part of the economy. The problem is most acute in the informal or unorganised sector. The census data however does not clarify the kind of jobs the elderly are engaged in. Most of the elderly workers (92.6 per cent) were main workers and not marginal workers. In the urban areas, the elderly are generally engaged in

Table 5.18
Percentage Distribution of Main Workers Aged 60 plus by Industrial Category, Sex and Residence

Category	Total			Rural			Urban		
	Total	Male	Female	Total	Male	Female	Total	Male	Female
Cultivators	55.9	58.6	40.3	63.4	66.9	44.0	12.9	13.3	9.7
Agricultural Labourers	22.4	18.6	44.1	24.6	20.5	46.7	9.8	8.3	22.4
Livestock, Fisheries etc.	1.6	1.7	1.3	1.5	1.6	1.3	2.0	2.0	1.6
Mining and Quarrying	0.2	0.2	0.1	0.2	0.2	0.1	0.5	0.5	0.3
Household Industry	2.4	2.3	3.2	2.1	2.0	2.5	4.5	4.0	8.7
Non-household Industry	3.9	4.2	2.2	1.8	2.0	1.2	15.8	16.4	10.2
Construction	1.0	1.1	0.4	0.5	0.6	0.1	4.0	4.2	2.2
Trade and Commerce	6.6	7.1	3.5	2.8	3.0	1.9	28.2	29.6	16.7
Transport, Storage Communication	0.9	1.1	0.1	0.3	0.4	0.0	4.3	4.7	0.8
Other Services	5.0	5.1	4.8	2.8	2.9	2.1	18.1	16.9	27.4
Total	100.0	100.0	100.0	100.0	100.0	100.0	100.0	100.0	100.0

Source: Census of India, 1991, same as Table 5.17.

work requiring considerable use of manual labour. Census data on the class of worker status indicates that over 75 per cent of workers in the main category are either employees or single workers (see Table 5.19). Being uneducated and not adequately skilled, they have to be satisfied with low wages, insecurity of work and unhealthy working conditions.

Economic Dependence of the Elderly

The National Sample Survey (52nd Round, 1995–96) collected data on the economic dependence of the elderly in India. It discovered that as many as 70 per cent of the aged had to depend on others for their livelihood. The situation was worse for elderly females. Over 85 per cent were found to be dependent, partially or fully on others. The elderly males fared little better with 49 to 52 per cent of them not dependent on others. While the situation was slightly better in the urban areas than the national average, the rural elderly virtually are at the mercy of others. Among the elderly rural males, 48.5 per cent claimed that they were not dependent on others, 18 per cent claimed they were partially dependent on others and 31.3 per cent claimed they were fully dependent on others. In the case of elderly rural females, 70.6 per cent were fully dependent on others, 14.6 per cent were partially dependent on others and only 12.1 per cent said that they were not dependent on others. In the urban areas, 51.5 per cent of the elderly males claimed that they were not dependent on others, 29.7 per cent said they were fully dependent on others and 16.9 per cent said they were partially dependent on others. In the case of urban females, 75.7 per cent were fully dependent on others, 11 per cent were partially dependent on others and 11.5 per cent were not dependent on others. Table 5.20 summarises the state of elderly economic independence.

In West Bengal, over 88.3 per cent of rural females and 85.1 per cent of urban females were fully dependent on others. These figures are the highest among all the states. Regrettably, in Kerala, which has the highest proportion of elderly in India and has several social security schemes, 73.6 per cent of rural females and 76 per cent of urban females are fully dependent on others. Even economically impoverished states of Bihar and Uttar Pradesh seem to have better status for the elderly based on the NSS data.

Table 5.19
Percentage Distribution of Elderly Workers by Class of Worker Status

Residence	Employer			Employee			Single Worker			Family Worker		
	Total	Male	Female	Total	Male	Female	Total	Male	Female	Total	Male	Female
Total	17.4	18.4	8.8	42.3	41.6	48.2	33.6	33.6	33.6	6.7	6.4	9.4
Rural	14.8	15.5	9.1	38.4	38.1	41.2	37.5	37.8	35.4	9.3	8.7	14.3
Urban	19.5	20.6	8.6	45.3	44.3	54.9	30.6	30.5	31.8	4.7	4.7	4.8

Source: Census of India, 1991, same as Table 5.17.

Table 5.20
Percentage Distribution of Elderly Persons by State of Economic Independence for Each Sex

Sex	Rural				Urban			
	Not Dependent on Others	Partially Dependent on Others	Fully Dependent on Others	Total	Not Dependent on Others	Partially Dependent on Others	Fully Dependent on Others	Total
Male	48.5	18.0	31.3	100.0	51.5	16.9	29.7	100.0
Female	12.1	14.6	70.6	100.0	11.5	11.0	75.7	100.0
Total	30.1	16.3	51.1	100.0	31.1	13.9	53.2	100.0

Source: National Sample Survey Organisation (NSSO), *The Aged In India: A Socio-economic Profile*, NNS 52nd Round July, 1995–June 1996, NSSO, Department of Statistics, Ministry of Planning and Programme Implementation, Government of India, Calcutta, 1998.

ECONOMIC SUPPORT TO THE ELDERLY

The NSS data provides details about those people who support the economically dependent elderly—children, grandchildren, spouse and others. In India as a whole, over 75 per cent of the economically dependent elderly are supported by their children and grandchildren. This does indicate the almost total reliance on the family in the case of the elderly, who are not economically independent. To be specific, children support 71.1 per cent of the rural elderly and 70.8 per cent of the urban elderly. The grandchildren support 5 per cent of the rural elderly and 5.4 per cent of the urban elderly. The share of the spouse was 13.8 per cent in rural and 15.2 per cent in urban areas. The share of 'others' which ironically includes the government among many others is only 5.9 per cent in urban and 6.9 per cent in rural areas. Table 5.21 summarises the NSS findings about the elderly economic support providers.

The ESCAP study indicates that the picture is almost similar in China, Indonesia and Thailand, with children providing bulk of the support to the elderly.[29] While families continue to support the elderly, the extent and adequacy of that support is unknown. Very little is known about intra-household resource allocation, which may not always favour the elderly. This makes it difficult to assess the relative living standards of the elderly and the evidence on this subject in India and other developing countries in Asia is very scarce. Also important is the relative position of the different categories within the elderly. A few

Table 5.21
Percentage Distribution of Economically Dependent
Aged Persons by Category of Persons Supporting

Sex	Rural				Urban			
	Spouse	Own Children	Grand-children	Others	Spouse	Own Children	Grand-children	Others
Male	11.3	76.6	5.0	7.1	10.5	79.2	5.4	4.9
Female	15.9	71.7	5.2	7.2	18.2	72.3	5.6	6.7
Total	14.2	73.5	5.2	7.1	15.6	72.8	5.5	6.1

Source: National Sample Survey Organisation (NSSO), *The Aged In India: A Socio-economic Profile*, NNS 52nd Round, July 1995–June 1996, NSSO, Department of Statistics, Ministry of Planning and Programme Implementation, Government of India, Calcutta, 1998.

attempts to deal with these issues have produced evidence that certain groups among the elderly are particularly vulnerable, especially widows.[30] Table 5.21 shows that 'own children' discriminate between father and mother with regard to old age support. This is true in both rural and urban areas. While this percentage is not significant yet, the informal safety nets are not always dependable and are by no means adequate, even under the best circumstances. The poor are especially vulnerable since their main source of income during old age, their children, are also likely to be poor and thus unable to provide more than limited support. At the same time, there are reasons to believe that family support systems will come under increasing strain as income and life expectancy rises, especially in urban areas. As mentioned earlier, economic growth and intergenerational support are generally inversely related. In the developed countries, co-residence rates and intergenerational support were much higher prior to the rapid growth of incomes during the last few decades. The determinants of these changing social relationships are very complex and go beyond the purview of this book, but demographics are certainly influential. As fewer children must support parents for longer periods of time, the per capita cost of 'parent caring' is high. The tremendous jump in health care costs, unaccompanied by suitable development of health insurance schemes, multiples the burden on children. Finally, the mechanisms for enforcing these social contracts are not always very effective. Community control has become very weak. Many governments have come forward with legislations, making children support to the elderly mandatory. Singapore passed a law to this effect in 1982. In China, under the Penal Code of 1980, children can be imprisoned for neglecting their parents. Indian laws are not any less progressive (see the section ahead). Even then, some children will choose not to fulfil the implicit obligation to care for their elderly parents.

In the United States for example, more than three-fourths of the elderly lived in multigenerational households at the beginning of this century. Today, this ratio is closer to 20 per cent. In Japan, two-thirds of young married women expected support in their old age from their children in 1950. By 1988, this figure had dropped to 20 per cent.

SOCIAL SECURITY FOR THE ELDERLY

The Indian constitution in Article 41 recognises the needs of the elderly and enjoins upon the state, the responsibility of making effective provisions for public assistance in the case of old age along with the unemployed, sick and disabled. While the welfare of the aged is a state subject, the nodal responsibility of the aged is vested with the Ministry of Welfare of the union government. Under section 20(1) of the Hindu Adoption and Maintenance Act, 1956, the aged and infirm parent, if unable to maintain himself or herself, is entitled to maintenance. Muslim law imposes an obligation to maintain needy parents, subject to certain circumstances. The Code of Criminal Procedure, 1973 (Section 125 [1][d]) makes it obligatory for a person with sufficient means to support his father and/or mother unable to maintain himself or herself.

Public policies in the area of old age income support take three general forms in India. The first, retirement benefits, are given to formal sector employees. These are supplemented by the second kind, voluntary old age insurance schemes, encouraged through tax exemptions. Finally, there are direct government transfers to the needy aged persons. Table 5.22 summarises the main schemes, their statutory coverage, sources of financing and eligibility conditions.

In India, only the retired employees of the public sector enjoy old age social security. At the end of March 1996, there were 19.43 million public sector employees (comprising 3.37 million in the central government, 7.41 million in the state governments and another 6.46 million in the quasi-governments). The combined coverage in these schemes is less than 10 per cent of the labour force. This is a low figure, but fairly typical of countries at a similar income level.[31] As in other poor countries, such low coverage is due to a very large agricultural population as well as an informal sector that bypasses taxes and social insurance contributions.

Participation in voluntary insurance-linked savings schemes is even more limited. Ironically, a part of formal sector employees, who enjoy retirement benefits, join such programmes to supplement old age incomes as well as to save money on taxes. Many households at the bottom of the income distribution system in India are too poor to save for their old age. Available resources are needed for survival demands. Even those with some surplus resources, are unwilling to subscribe savings instruments that require a commitment of several decades. Instead, these people prefer to use the surplus resources for self-insurance against emergencies or perhaps in short-term investments that increase their own productivity or the productivity of their children. People with comfortable surplus resources prefer to keep their money in the bank and other short-term savings instruments.

Table 5.22
Government-sponsored Schemes for Old Age Income Security in India

Retirement Benefits for Formal Sector Employees

Programme	Legal Coverage	Effective Coverage	Financing
Employees' Provident Fund	Employees in firms with more than 20 employees (extends to 177 types of establishments).	About 5.8 per cent of the labour force.	Employer and employee contributions.
Employees' Pension Fund	Same as above with some exemptions.	About 5.4 per cent of the labour force.	Employer, government contributions.
Government Employees Pension Scheme	Central and state government employees.	About 3.5 per cent of the labour force.	State or central government budgets.
Government Employees Provident Fund	Central and state government employees.	Same.	Employee contributions.
Special Provident Funds	Certain occupations and employees in Jammu and Kashmir.	About 0.5 per cent of the labour force.	Employer and employee contributions.
Gratuity under Gratuity Act, 1972 (15 days wage per year of service subject to a maximum of Rs 350,000).	All formal sector employees.	About 10 per cent of workforce.	Employers, including government as employers.
Employees Deposit Linked Insurance (EDLI)	All formal sector employees.	About 10 per cent of workforce.	Employers and government.

Self-purchased Old Age Insurance Schemes

Public Provident Fund	All individuals.	About 0.8 per cent of the labour force.	Contributions.
Superannuation Plans	All employees.	About 0.2 per cent of the labour force.	Contributions.

(continued)

Table 5.22
(continued)

Programme	Legal Coverage	Effective Coverage	Financing
Personal Pensions	All individuals.	About 0.2 per cent of the labour force.	Purchase of annuity-like products.
Social Old Age Supports for the Needy			
State Level Social Assistance	Varies by state.	Varies by state.	State budgets.
National Old Age Pension Scheme	Destitute persons over the age of 65.	About 15–20 per cent of population over the age of 65.	Central budget.

Source: World Bank, Finance And Private Sector Development, *India: The Challenge of Old Age Income Security*, Mimeo, April 5, 2001.

The reluctance to join old age insurance schemes is due to high transaction costs; poor service of insurance agencies and the rates of return which do not compensate for loss of liquidity. Also, there is a general lack of awareness of the need to insure the risks of survival and longevity. In India, the tax incentives do not encourage people to purchase pension plans. However, most developed countries do use the tax system to encourage participation in pension plans. In some countries, such as the United States and Ireland, this has resulted in private pension coverage of more than half of the labour force. It is also one of the largest tax expenditures in these countries.

For the needy and destitute elderly, several social security schemes operate, both at the central and the state level. Most provinces in the Indian federation have some kind of 'means–tested' pension for older citizens. However, eligibility rules are often complicated and benefit levels vary significantly across states. While in Kerala around 20 per cent of the aged have some access to certain kinds of pension,[32] in the other provinces only 10 to 15 per cent of the elderly hold this privilege. Pension levels also vary across states from Rs 55 to Rs 300 per month with an average in the range of Rs 75. Since 1995, the central government has supplemented this with the National Old Age Pension Scheme (NOAPS).[33] This programme pays Rs 75 per month to destitute persons aged 65 and above. It is administered by the central government but implemented by the state governments. The centre allocates resources to each state who, through its existing eligibility criteria, determines the number of recipients. One estimate suggests that only 10 per cent of the elderly population in India is served by this scheme.[34] In March 1999, the government introduced an 'in kind assistance scheme' called Annapurna which provides 10 kg of rice or wheat per month to the destitute elderly (the details of the programmes are given in Appendix Two at the end of this book). In its maiden appearance, the programme supported 0.66 million people. It intends to reach more destitute elderly in the next few years. In addition to the central government expenditure, each state also spends on social assistance programmes for the elderly from its own budget. Combining the central and state level programmes, a World Bank report estimates that only 0.08 per cent of the GDP is spent on old age security.[35] In addition, the Ministry of Welfare of the central government supports 'day activity centers', managed by private voluntary agencies for the elderly. Many elderly secure assistance from charitable non-governmental organizations (NGOs), who along with several religious groups operate few old age homes. However, not much information exists on either the benefits or the beneficiaries of such charitable old age schemes.

While the final impact of old age security programmes is not known, several limitations have already become visible:

1. There is no consensus yet on the cut-off age for entry into old age. Some states use 60 years as the cut-off, while many others stipulate 65 years, which in fact is the entry point into old age for the national programme.

2. Recent incidence analyses of other poverty programmes in India found that many are not effective in reaching the poor.[36] The same is likely to be true for social assistance targeted towards the elderly. Unfortunately, data on these programmes is very limited.

3. The take up rates of such programmes in many states is very low, though some states have attained 100 per cent take up rates on paper. Very often, potential recipients are not aware of such programmes. Some case studies mention high transaction costs and other obstacles in the application process that have prevented individuals from receiving benefits. In other cases, local authorities hold no interest and manipulate the programmes to please themselves and their political bosses.[37] In addition, administrative inefficiency

and bureaucratic paraphernalia keeps many of its potential users away from the scheme. Jain mentions that payment delays can range from one month to one year depending on the state.[38]

4. The prevalence of such government support programmes, albeit unsatisfactorily, may make children shy away from supporting their aged parents. There is some evidence from other countries that public transfers are partially offset by reductions in private transfers. Cox and Jimenez find that for every dollar in public transfers to the elderly in Peru, private transfers are reduced by 37 cents.[39]

The NSS 52nd Survey, 1995–96, collected some valuable information on the retirement benefits received by the elderly. The benefits are summarised in Table 5.23.

The NSS Survey indicates that 79 per cent of the elderly (who were ever engaged in wage/salaried jobs or as casual labour) in the rural areas and 35 per cent in the urban areas did not receive any benefit in the event of their retirement. In rural areas, every sixth aged person who retired from some kind of employment received a pension whereas in the urban areas, every second person was fortunate to receive a pension.

Governments everywhere in the world have come to provide old age security to their citizens. Many Asian countries offer some type of support programme for the elderly, although coverage is often restricted to narrow population groups such as civil servants or employees of large enterprises. An ILO report shows that while Malaysia, Singapore and Japan have programmes with close to universal coverage, India's performance in providing cash benefits to the aged, disabled and survivals is quite dismal compared to other major Asian countries.[40] (See Table 5.24.)

OWNERSHIP AND MANAGEMENT OF PROPERTY AND FINANCIAL ASSETS BY THE ELDERLY

An important indicator of elderly status is the possession and control of wealth. The NSS 52nd Survey reveals a lot of interesting information on the ownership and control of financial assets and property. The findings of the survey are summarised in Table 5.25.

About 54 per cent of the aged had some kind of financial assets during 1995–96. Around 58 to 63 per cent owned property. Not all who have either financial assets or property are involved in their

Table 5.23

Percentage Distribution of Aged Persons (Who Were Ever Engaged in Wage/Salaried Jobs or as Casual Labour) by Category of Retirement Benefits

Sex	Rural				Urban			
	Pension Only	Pension with Other Benefits	No Pension but with Other Benefits	No Benefits	Pension Only	Pension with Other Benefits	No pension but with Other Benefits	No Benefits
Male	9.9	15.7	6.9	67.5	17.1	37.2	18.9	26.8
Female	2.6	1.8	2.8	92.8	0.5	15.3	9.8	67.4
Total	6.7	9.3	5.0	79.0	15.1	32.8	17.1	35.0

Source: National Sample Survey Organisation (NSSO), *The Aged In India: A socio-economic Profile*, NSS 52nd Round, July 1995– June 1996, NSSO, Department of Statistics, Ministry of Planning and Programme Implementation, Government of India, Calcutta, 1998.

Table 5.24
Coverage of Schemes Providing Cash Benefits to the Aged,
Disabled and/or Survivals, 1992

Country	Percentage of Population	Coverage of Scheme	Special Scheme
Japan	100	National Pension Scheme: All residents aged 20–59 years. Voluntary coverage for residents aged 60–64 years and citizens residing abroad aged 20–64 years.	Public employees, private school teachers, agriculture, fishery and forest sector.
Singapore	100	Employed persons earning more than $ 50 a month. Also some self-employed workers.	Public workers.
South Korea	25.9	Employers and employees in work place of more than five persons.	Public employees, private school teachers, military personnel.
Philippines	52.6	All private employees 60 or less. House helpers and self employed earning at least 1,000 pesos a month.	Public employees, military personnel.
Thailand	–	Employees of firms with 10 or more workers. Voluntary coverage for the self-employed.	Civil servants, private school teachers.
Indonesia	6.9	Employees of firms with 10 or more workers or establishments with a pay roll of Rs 1 million or more a month.	Public employees, military personnel.
India	0.9	Employees of establishments with 20 or more employees in 177 categories of industries.	Public employees, railway, coal miners.

(continued)

Table 5.24
(Continued)

Country	Percentage of Population	Coverage of Scheme	Special Scheme
Bangladesh	0.0	None	Public employees.
Malaysia	95.6	Mandatory coverage for private sector employees, non-pensionable public sectors employees and foreign workers. Voluntary coverage for domestic workers, self-employed and pensionable public sector employees.	
China	21.1	Employees in state-run enterprises. Private, collective and foreign invested companies depend on local government regulations.	Government and party employees, cultural, scientific and educational institutions.

Source: International Labour Organization (ILO), World Labour Report, ILO, Geneva, 1995; Also see, Social Security Administration, *Social Security Programs Throughtout the World,* Washington D.C., 1999.

management as well. Around 37 to 38 per cent of the aged had financial assets and were also involved in taking decisions vis-à-vis converting them from one form to another. In the case of property, the proportion was 43 per cent in rural areas and 40 per cent in urban areas.

HEALTH STATUS OF THE ELDERLY

Health problems increase with age. Elderly people are more likely to have major health concerns than the rest of the population. In a developing country, elderly health takes on an extra dimension as most of the aged have survived several bouts of ill-health during periods of mass epidemics and communicable diseases. Interestingly, they have also become immune to the communicable diseases structure.

Table 5.25
Percentage of Aged Persons with Financial Assets/Property

Sex	Rural				Urban			
	Own Financial Assets	Having Financial Assets and Managing Them	Own Property	Having Property and Managing Them	Own Financial Assets	Having Financial Assets and Managing them	Own Property	Having Property and Managing Them
Male	69.5	56.9	80.4	65.1	70.2	58.1	74.2	60.5
Female	39.1	17.7	45.6	20.6	37.6	18.15	42.0	20.6
Total	54.2	37.2	62.9	42.7	53.5	37.9	57.8	40.1

Source: National Sample Survey Organisation (NSSO), *The Aged In India: A Socio-economic Profile,* NSS 52nd Round, July 1995–June 1996, NSSO, Department of Statistics, Ministry of Planning and Programme Implementation, Government of India, Calcutta, 1998.

In contrast to general health, where infections are still the leading causes of death, the leading cause of death in old age in India is cardiovascular disease (CVD).[41] This is a disease emanating from an urban lifestyle, which crudely speaking, might give the impression that the elderly are well fed at least in the old age bracket. Under-nutrition is also common in this population.[42] Elderly people in low socio-economic groups, in urban slums or among those living alone, are at a higher risk of poor dietary intake.[43] It is well known that socio-economic status and health are intimately related. All over the world, it is the poor of all ages who suffer more disabilities and early deaths, and the very poor who suffer the most. With each step up the socio-economic ladder, people live longer, healthier lives.[44] In recent years, the gap between the rich and the poor and subsequent inequal-ities in health status has been increasing in all parts of the world.[45] Failure to address this problem will have serious consequences for the global economy and social order, as well as for individual societies and people of all ages.

The 52nd Round of the NSS collected considerable data on old age morbidity, with particular stress on chronic diseases. While the NSS data linking age and health status are not available yet, an Economic and Social Commission for Asia and the Pacific (ESCAP) and United Nations sponsored study reveals many interesting insights from sur-veys in China, Indonesia and Thailand.[46] In China and Thailand, the young elderly have had a better health status than the old elderly, aged 70 years. In Indonesia, the rural elderly enjoyed a better health status than their urban counterparts and the rural elderly aged 70 and above reported better health than the new entrants into the elderly fraternity. With regard to the difficulties encountered in per-forming day-to-day activities, an overwhelming majority of the elderly said that they did not face much difficulty. There were no significant rural-urban or sex differences here either.

Table 5.26 provides a clear picture of the chronic diseases from which aged people in India suffered the most.

The prevalence of chronic diseases among the aged was in general seen to be very high. Chronic diseases in complicated health areas were higher in the urban areas. This was found in the ESCAP study too. This is quite natural in surveys where health problems are eval-uated through self-assessment of respondents. In the urban areas, health facilities are better and one is capable of diagnosing the disease. This is often not done in rural places. In India, problems of the joints and throat happened to be the most severe diseases for the

Table 5.26
Percentage of Aged Persons Reporting a Chronic Disease by Sex

Type of Disease	Rural Male	Rural Female	Rural Total	Urban Male	Urban Female	Urban Total
Cough	25.0	19.5	22.2	17.9	14.2	16.0
Piles	3.3	1.6	2.4	3.2	1.8	2.5
Joints Problem	36.3	40.4	38.4	28.5	39.3	34.0
High/Low B.P	10.8	10.5	10.6	20.0	25.1	22.6
Heart Disease	3.4	2.7	3.0	6.8	5.3	6.1
Urinary Problem	3.8	2.3	3.1	4.9	2.4	3.6
Diabetes	3.6	2.8	3.2	8.5	6.6	7.5
Cancer	0.2	0.3	0.3	0.2	0.4	0.3
Any of the above	52.7	51.4	52.0	52.8	56.0	54.5

Source: National Sample Survey Organisation (NSSO), *The Aged In India: A Socio-economic Profile*, NSS 52nd Round, July 1995–June 1996, NSSO, Department of Statistics, Ministry of Planning and Programme Implementation, Government of India, Calcutta, 1998.

aged. Blood pressure problems came next. Lifestyle diseases like heart disease, urinary infections and diabetes appeared to have taken considerable place in the suffering pattern of the people. In China, high blood pressure appears to be the major problem of the elderly, followed by heart problem, asthma, arthritis and back pain. High blood pressure, heart disease and diabetes are much more common in urban areas than in rural areas. While high blood pressure is common to the younger elderly and males, the reverse holds true for heart disease. Diabetes is higher among the young elderly and females. Interestingly, a rural setting was no protection from arthritis and asthma for the elderly; these problems were more common in the rural areas.[47] In Indonesia too, high blood pressure is the most serious health problem with the elderly; every fifth elderly is down with this health problem. Very interestingly, high blood pressure is much more a rural problem than an urban one, and more so for females than males. Though high blood pressure is a major problem, heart disease is not. Arthritis, ulcers, back pain, diabetes and asthma are the other chronic diseases (in order of their importance) plaguing the elderly.[48] In Thailand, blood pressure is the most serious problem, followed by neural disorders. The older elderly suffer from more disorders and diseases than the young elderly, and women tend to suffer from more chronic diseases than men. Ulcers were the only exception, which the men were more prone to. One resean for this could be that elderly men had irregular eating habits.[49] While self-assessment studies of health by the elderly shed important light, health is a highly specialised area with a wide knowledge gap existing between common people and professionals. Surveys which are not accompanied by any medical tests through trained professionals might not provide a true picture.

In 1996, the number of elderly suffering from hypertension was nearly nine million. An almost equal number of the elderly were down with coronary heart disease, another urban lifestyle disease in that year. The prevalence rate in urban areas was three times that of rural areas.[50] Among other urban diseases, diabetes and strokes played havoc with the health of the elderly. An estimated five million were diabetic and the prevalence rates were two-and-half times more for the urban elderly than their rural counterparts. The crude prevalence rate of strokes is estimated at about 200 per 100,000 persons. Although a stroke is not a great killer these days, it still is one of the major causes of old age disability.[51] The number of older persons with cancer in 1996 was 0.35 million. Interestingly, the prevalence of cancer is the same among the rural and urban aged. Another point of concern is that cancer is more rampant among elderly females than males. In contrast to the developed countries where breast, colorectal and lung cancers are more prevalent, in developing countries, cancers of the stomach, breast and cervix predominate. Cervical cancer is very common in the developing/rural setting. A primary cause of this cancer is genital infection with the human papilloma virus (HPV); early initiation into childbearing and frequent pregnancies are considered to be the major cause.[52] Although death from communicable and infectious diseases has fallen among the elderly, some of the former killer diseases like tuberculosis (TB) have returned as serious ailments among the aged. The suffering of TB patients has multiplied through the many side effects of anti-tuberculosis therapy.[53] There are reports that HIV/AIDS infection among Indian elderly is not insignificant; it could be as high as 11 per cent in the 50 plus age category among total HIV infected cases.[54] This is a disturbing trend as HIV incidence is generally high among the middle-age groups.

From the resource utilisation point of view, there is a significant difference between morbidity among the aged and the rest of the population. An elderly person takes longer to recover from the same disease as compared to a younger person. Most of the diseases suffered by the elderly are chronic in nature. Treatment of the elderly in hospitals and nursing homes blocks scarce health resources for considerable amounts of time. The principles of elementary health economics suggest that such long confinement cases be treated at home.

Disability among the Aged

Table 5.27 gives the prevalence rate of physical disability among the aged by type.

The prevalence of disability among the aged is also very high. After the age of 30, a person's functional ability declines and various forms of disability creep in. There are generally four forms of physical disability. *Visual disability* is the lack of the ability to execute tasks requiring adequate visual acuity. These include (*a*) those who do not have any light perception on both eyes; and, (*b*) those who have light perception but cannot correctly count fingers of a hand even with visual aids from a distance of 3m in good daylight. *Hearing disability* is the inability to hear properly without hearing aids. *Speech disability*

Table 5.27
Prevalence Rate of Physical Disability among the
Aged by Type for Each Sex (in percentage)

	Visual Disability	Hearing Disability	Speech Disability	Locomotor	Amnesia/ Senility	Any Disability
Rural Male	24.9	13.9	3.2	10.7	9.6	38.0
Rural Female	29.1	15.6	3.8	11.5	11.3	42.5
Rural Person	27.0	14.8	3.5	11.1	10.5	40.2
Urban Male	22.5	11.1	2.9	8.0	6.1	33.3
Urban Female	36.0	13.2	3.4	9.4	8.0	36.7
Urban Person	24.3	12.2	3.2	8.7	7.0	35.0

Source: National Sample Survey Organisation (NSSO), *The Aged In India: A Socio-economic Profile*, NSS 52nd Round, July 1995–June 1996, NSSO, Department of Statistics, Ministry of Planning and Programme Implementation, Government of India, Calcutta, 1998.

is the person's inability to speak properly. These include people (a) who cannot speak; (b) who can speak only a few words with loss of voice; and (c) who can speak but suffer from speech defects like stammering, nasal voice, hoarse voice, discordant voice, articulation defects etc. *Locomotor disability* is a person's inability to move themselves and other objects because of amputation, paralysis, deformity and dysfunction of joints. Persons with physical deformities in other parts of their body other than hands and legs are also included in this category. In addition to these disabilities, people with mental dysfunctions are termed amnesic/senile. Disabilities relating to sight and hearing are generally age related; other types of disabilities may occur through diseases. Some of the locomotor disabilities are brought about by strokes; a weakening musculo- skeletal system can cause osteoarthritis which may hinder movement. Lack of adequate nutrition in old age or before helps accelerate the disability process for many people. The problem is aggravated for those who are already disabled through birth complications, polio etc.

The findings from the NSS 52nd Round are quite revealing (see Table 5.27). Around 40 per cent of the rural aged and 35 per cent of the urban aged suffer physical disabilities. Visual disability was mentioned by about 24–27 per cent of the aged; half of these people also suffered hearing disabilities. The females suffered from more disabilities than the males and a rural lifestyle did not ensure better physical well-being. Visual disability had the highest incidence; failing eyesight is concomitant with ageing. The NFHS data shows that blindness is highest among the elderly and lowest among children. The same pattern is found in most other Asian countries. The total number of blind persons among the older population was around 11 million in 1996. The most common cause (around 80 per cent) for blindness is cataract,[55] followed by uncorrected refractive errors, glaucoma and corneal opacity, trachoma and Vitamin A deficiency. Women suffer from eyesight related problems more because of: (a) problems encountered during pregnancy; (b) use of hazardous fuel during cooking etc.; (c) needlework; (d) diabetes, glaucoma and metabolic disorders; (e) a diet deficient in Vitamin C and E; (f) excessive exposure to ultraviolet rays; and (g) severe diarrhoea etc. The consequences of blindness are not limited to physical disability, but move beyond to envelope the economic, social and psychological domains of the effected individual's life. The monetary burden of these individuals would be enormous for the nation to bear.

Nearly 12 to 15 per cent of older people are said to have a hearing impairment, in both urban and rural areas. A study, however, indicates that the percentage could be as high as 60.[56] The hearing impairment creates a gap between the elderly and others and is often the cause of embarrassment and misunderstanding. There are many hearing aids in the market but these are usually expensive to maintain too. Locomotor disabilities usually are a result of paralysis, dysfunction of limbs, amputation or dystrophy of joints. The curtailment of physical movement has implications for the caregivers and the type of care required.

About 10 per cent of the aged have difficulty in moving about in addition to amnesia or senility. Studies indicate that in 1996 around 4 million suffered from some form of mental illness.[57] The risk of mental illness/senile dementia increases with age. Among the late age mental disorders, Alzheimer's disease, depression, late paraphrenia and dementia are quite common. Neurotic disorders, though less common are also becoming popular. Interestingly, suicide rates rise with age among the elderly. Prakash[58] reports that the rate of suicide in the 50 plus age group is around 12 per 100,000 compared to only 7 for the general population. There is a general tendency within the family to suppress a suicide case. While it is difficult to manipulate young age suicides, such manoeuvring over old age suicides is much easier; every third suicide among the elderly is not reported.[59] Physical diseases of a painful and incurable nature are prominent among the 'causes' of such suicides. Economic misfortune and difficulty also lead the elderly towards self-destructive behaviour. Interestingly, many more people are held back from attempting suicide through certain inbuilt cultural, religious, ethical and familial deterrents, known as 'suicide counters'.[60]

The disabled elderly require more intense support than the elderly suffering from a chronic illness. Moreover, they also require some infrastructure in the form of wheelchairs, and housing that is constructed in such a way to allow the use of such facilities. Both the sick and the disabled elderly need constant care and nursing. In an extended family network, the existence of a large army of unemployed women does not allow caring/nursing to become a point of concern. However, with the break down of extended families and with increasing participation of women in activities outside the home, the caring and nursing of elderly at home might pose a problem in future years.

Health Facilities for the Elderly in India

The elderly do not enjoy any specific government sponsored health care programmes in India as yet. The Indian health care system represents a unique dualistic structure combining a wide variety of traditional medicine along with government sponsored western-style hospital systems. The private sector dominates both the finance and delivery of health care in India. About 75 per cent of all financing comes from households' out-of-pocket payments and much of their spending is directed toward private outpatient services. Only the central government employees and a part of the state government employees are covered through government health schemes. Now the retired central government pensioners can participate in the Central Government Health Scheme facilities. Industrial workers are subject to Employees State Insurance programmes. So far the state owned General Insurance Corporation and its subsidiaries were the sole health insurance agency in India, though recently, some private sector insurance firms have also entered the Indian health insurance business. The public sector Life Insurance Corporation has the Asha Deep Policy which gives insurance cover on malignant cancer, coronary artery disease involving bypass surgery, paralysis or renal failure of both kidneys. The nationalised Unit Trust of India has the Senior Citizen Unit Plan, an investment-cum-health insurance scheme under which residents between 21 to 55 years can join for lifetime coverage of hospitalisation after 61 years of age. However, none of these health insurance schemes could make a dent in the Indian health sector because of: (a) lack of awareness of the uncertainty element in health and the importance of health insurance in this regard; (b) high premium on insurance; (c) heavy exclusion clauses on coverage; (d) bureaucratic delays in the disbursement of expenditures; and (e) lack of interest on the part of the insurance provider, the scheme not being a profitable one owing to a severe 'moral hazard' problem.

Compared to India, Thailand has developed a better health system network for its elderly. The Japanese health care system for the aged is one of the best in the world. Here we present some salient features of the health care systems for the aged in these two countries. This will help us understand what India needs to do to establish a suitable health care structure for the elderly in the country. Thailand's public health system consists of a three-tier delivery system consisting of (a) village health stations; (b) community (district) hospitals; and

(c) provincial hospitals providing extensive outpatient and inpatient services. The rural health services are mainly provided by public sector agencies working under the Ministry of Public Health. The health system in the country is administered by the government. The private sector health services operate mainly in the urban areas. But unlike India, around 60 per cent of the Thai population is covered by some type of health insurance.[61] In Thailand there are four main categories of publicly sponsored insurance schemes:

1. **Free Health Care to the Poor, Elderly and School Children:** This scheme is 'means-tested' for low-income households. The beneficiaries have free access to district and sub-district hospitals through a referral system. In 1996, 36 per cent of the country's population including 3.5 million elderly were covered by the scheme.
2. **Public Insurance for Public Sector Employees:** This has a Civil Servant and State Enterprises Medical Benefit Scheme financed fully through tax revenue. All public sector employees including their spouses, parents and upto three children under the age of 18 years are covered under this scheme. Government retirees enjoy this benefit right into old age. Nearly 11 per cent of the country's population is covered by this scheme.
3. **Social Security Scheme for Private Sector Employees:** This covers private sector employees in firms with more than 10 employees. Social security is financed through contributions received from the employers, employees and the government. The private sectors are allowed to have their own privately sponsored scheme.
4. **Health Card Programmes:** This is a voluntary programme mainly targeting low-income households. The annual premium is 1,000 baht per household upto a maximum of 5 persons; the government provides a matching amount of premium.

Japan follows a system of universal coverage achieved through a patchwork of more than 5,000 independent insurance plans, which are generally employment-based and funded through premium contributions from employee, employers and the government. There are no private health insurances and the entire population is covered through these public schemes. Three basic types of plans are in operation:

1. Society Managed Health Insurance (SMHI) plans and Mutual Aid Associations (MAAs) for large employers in the private and public sector, where premiums are split between employer and employees.

2. Government Managed Health Insurance (GMHI) that covers the employees of small enterprises. It is partially subsidised by the government and there is a co-payment charged for the actual users.
3. The Citizens' Health Insurance (CHI) which covers the self-employed and retirees and is based within local committees through local governments with a 50 per cent government subsidy.

Every scheme receives a government subsidy and in addition, the premium structures are designed to generate cross-subsidiaries from the rich to the poor and young to the old. Effective from 1st April 2000, Japan has instituted a mandatory long-term care insurance programme (Kaigo Hoken) for the elderly. This scheme requires everyone aged 40 years and older to contribute premium payments to the national insurance pool. For workers aged 40–64, the programme provides services in the event of disability. Their mandatory premium payments can be viewed as a wage tax and is very similar to the US Medicare programme. The governments contribute 50 per cent of the costs of the programme with 25 per cent from the national govern-ment, 12.5 per cent from prefectures and 12.5 per cent from municipal governments. The beneficiaries, mostly the frail elderly, will pay a 10 per cent co-payment at the point of service for nursing care. A monthly premium is deducted from the pension payments of those aged 65 years and above.

SOCIAL ACTIVITIES OF THE ELDERLY

Participation in social, household and religious activities is essential for the well-being of all ages. Connecting with family members, friends, neighbours, work colleagues and community groups brings happiness to all. In older ages this is more important, since older people are more likely to lose loved ones and friends and are there-fore more vulnerable to loneliness, social isolation and the availability of a 'smaller social pool.' Social isolation in old age is linked to a decline in both physical and mental capacities and an increase in health damaging behaviours such as excessive alcohol consumption and physical inactivity. In Japan, older people who reported a lack of social contact were 1.5 times more likely to die within the next three years than those with higher social support. In the USA, studies have shown that older people with high levels of social support especially from family members were more likely to recover from hip surgery and successfully adjust to the onset of a chronic illness.[62]

Around 75 per cent of the aged participated in social matters, 80 to 83 per cent in religious matters and about 78 per cent in household chores. While in percentage terms this information may not be very alarming, around 12 to 15 million elderly cannot participate in house-hold activities. In most societies, older men are less likely than older women to enjoy a supportive social network. In some cultures, older women who are widowed are systematically excluded from main-stream society or even rejected by their community. Maybe because of the rejection of widows in Indian society, elderly male participation rates in social activities are higher than that of their female counter-parts. Also, physical disabilities among the old aged women restricts the movement of women outside the home. Table 5.28 gives the percentage of aged persons participating in social activities.

ELDERLY STATUS INDEX

In chapter three, we stressed the need for developing an Elderly Status Index (ESI). A properly constructed index can guide us about the changing status of the elderly with changing time and with respect to other regions. From the aforementioned analysis of the demographic

Table 5.28
Percentage of Aged Persons Participating in Social Activities

Sex	Rural			Urban		
	Social Matters	Religious Matters	Household Chores	Social Matters	Religious Matters	Household Chores
Male	81.4	83.9	78.3	80.6	86.2	77.2
Female	67.8	76.9	77.0	70.7	80.8	78.2
Total	74.6	80.3	77.6	75.6	83.4	77.7

Source: National Sample Survey Organisation (NSSO), *The Aged In India: A Socio-economic Profile*, NSS 52nd Round July 1995–June 1996, NSSO, Department of Statistics, Ministry of Planning and Programme Implementation, Government of India, Calcutta, 1998.

characteristics of the elderly, it appears that the status of the elderly can be judged from the combined role of the following factors:

1. Life expectancy at age 60
2. Literacy
3. Living arrangements
4. Economic independence
5. Retirement benefits
6. Ownership and control of wealth
7. Health status
8. Social interaction

For the **Elderly Health Index**, measures of healthy life expectancy have been used for a number of years. By incorporating estimates of mortality and functional disability the health expectancy indicator provides a measure of disability-free life expectancy that can be compared with total life expectancy to understand a population's general state of health. Most studies on health expectancy have been carried out for Western Europe, North America and Australia. Few studies for health expectancy exist for non-western countries for lack of data. For India, no studies have been conducted to estimate this active life expectancy. To calculate healthy life expectancy we need a life table as well as data on ADL (Activities of Daily Living) or IADL (Instrumental Activities of Daily Living). ADL includes activities such as bathing, eating, dressing, toiletting, walking etc. IADL includes shopping for personal items, cooking, managing money, telephoning etc. But this data does not exist for India and we therefore, cannot estimate our health index meaningfully.

While making the ESI, one has to convert each of the demographic characteristics into an index. An index may be defined as,

$$\text{Index} = (\text{Actual Value} - \text{minimum value})/(\text{Maximum value} - \text{minimum value})$$

The Elderly Status Index (ESI) is a simple average of these indices.

THE ELDERLY STATUS INDEX FOR INDIA

There is no data on healthy life expectancy for Indian states, and no attempt has been made to include health factors while determining the ESI apart from life expectancy at 60. The living arrangement of the elderly could also be ignored, with only 4 per cent of them living alone in India and there being not much interstate difference.

The ESI has been estimated for all the major states of India for which NSS 52nd Round data is available. A perusal of Table 5.29, indicates that the elderly are most well placed in Himachal Pradesh, followed by Punjab, and Jammu & Kashmir. The elderly status is lowest in Assam, preceded by Karnataka. The index shows that in the urban areas, the elderly in Kerala enjoy a slightly better status than their counterparts in West Bengal. The procedure for estimating the ESI for two states is given in the endnotes.[63] If data for healthy life expectancy were available, the index would have been very comprehensive. Although health status (particularly the morbidity aspect of health) could not be satisfactorily represented in the index, life expectancy at 60 does satisfactorily represent mortality patterns of the aged. When comparable data is created, such an index may be prepared for countries of any region. This requires a comprehensive survey over a specific geographic area. It may be possible for SAARC or ASEAN to undertake such a survey among its member nations. Table 5.30 sums up the ESI for major Indian states.

Table 5.29
Maximum and Minimum Values of
Elderly Status Indicators among the Indian States

Indicators	Maximum Value	Minimum Value	Difference
Life Expectancy at 60	20.8 (Punjab)	14.7 years (Assam)	6.1
Literacy	64.55 (Kerala)	14.62 (Rajasthan)	49.93
Economic Independence (Urban)	49.8 (Himachal Pradesh)	21.7 (Assam)	28.1
Retirement Benefit (Urban)	87.5 (Haryana)	33.4 (Karnataka)	54.1
Wealth (Urban)	78.0 (Himachal Pradesh)	29.9 (Andhra Pradesh)	48.1
Social Interaction (Urban)	95.1 (Himachal Pradesh)	56.5 (Assam)	38.6

Source: Census of India 1991, *Ageing Population of India: An Analysis of the 1991 Census Data*, Registrar General, India, New Delhi, 1999; National Sample Survey Organisation (NSSO), *The Aged In India: A Socio-economic Profile*, NSS 52nd Round, July 1995–June 1996, NSSO, Department of Statistics, Ministry of Planning and Programme Implementation, Government of India, Calcutta, 1998

Table 5.30
Elderly Status Index (ESI) for the Major Indian States

State	Life Expectancy Index	Literacy Index	Economic Independence Index	Retirement Benefit Index	Wealth Index	Social Interaction Index	Sum of Six Indices	Elderly Status Index	Rank
Andhra Pradesh	0.033	0.103	0.548	0.484	0.000	0.653	1.821	0.304	XIV
Assam	0.000	0.290	0.000	0.906	0.069	0.000	1.265	0.211	XVII
Bihar	0.311	0.112	0.260	0.510	0.324	0.508	2.025	0.338	XI
Gujarat	0.082	0.351	0.060	0.543	0.279	0.598	1.913	0.319	XIII
Haryana	0.541	0.048	0.324	1.000	0.326	0.832	3.071	0.512	IV
Himachal Pradesh	0.443	0.072	1.000	0.871	1.000	1.000	4.386	0.731	I
Jammu & Kashmir	NA	NA	0.377	0.364	0.146	0.694	1.581	0.527	III
Karnataka	0.295	0.281	0.249	0.000	0.062	0.541	1.428	0.238	XVI
Kerala	0.770	1.000	0.164	0.107	0.110	0.282	2.433	0.406	V
Madhya Pradesh	0.049	0.097	0.495	0.477	0.304	0.650	2.072	0.345	IX
Maharashtra	0.426	0.330	0.363	0.614	0.212	0.075	2.02	0.337	XII
Orissa	0.180	0.270	0.121	0.636	0.139	0.453	1.799	0.300	XV
Punjab	1.000	0.101	0.310	0.591	0.326	0.891	3.219	0.537	II
Rajasthan	0.131	0.000	0.306	0.858	0.227	0.681	2.203	0.367	VIII
Tamil Nadu	0.115	0.382	0.402	0.510	0.081	0.575	2.065	0.344	X
Uttar Pradesh	0.098	0.106	0.171	0.841	0.464	0.746	2.426	0.404	VI
West Bengal	0.148	0.517	0.299	0.784	0.154	0.440	2.342	0.390	VII

Source: Estimated by the author.

CONCLUSION

Certainly, there is now enough evidence of a growing incidence of low levels of well-being among the aged in Asia, particularly for India for which enough data is currently available. The Asian media contains frequent reports which suggest that the time-honoured traditions of caring for parents during their old age are breaking down to the extent that abandonment of old people has become a significant social problem. In fact, this problem often takes on such gigantic proportions that laws are amended to make it compulsory for children to support their elderly parents. The old Chinese saying that 'an elderly person is like unto a treasure at home' is no longer taken seriously. Many younger Asians now prefer to live alone and deeply resent having to make the effort to support and care for their elderly parents. There are also indications that the elderly are less well off economically than the other adult population owing to their inability to earn a living.

However, the current view is that there is an inverse relationship between modernisation, urbanisation and industrialisation in society and that the status accorded to the aged,[64] cannot be supported from the analysis of data from India and other Asian countries. There are reasons to believe that the decline in family support with urbanisation has been exaggerated and in most Asian countries, family relationships are still intact. Certainly there is a general lower incidence of the elderly living with their children and grandchildren. This, however, should not be viewed as a negative development. It may be interpreted as the desire of the elderly for greater autonomy and freedom. As Heisel points out, 'social development does not necessarily result in a worsened situation for the aged'.[65] The aged today are simply temporary victims of demographic and economic transition. As economic development takes place and demographic factors adjust accordingly, the conditions of the aged may improve. Currently, they are in transition from high levels of well-being based on family support systems to high levels of well-being in which institutional support is a major component. There is only an intervening period of low, average levels of well-being in which emerging governmental support is not sufficient to counterbalance reduction in family-based support. This is what Palmore and Manton[66] predicted in 1974: 'early stages of economic development correspond to the relative decrement of resources held by the aged, but in economically advanced nations, entitlements such as pension plans begin to redress the previous losses incurred.'

NOTES AND REFERENCES

1. See chapter two. Table 2.28 presents the composition of the rural and urban elderly in several countries of South, South-east and East Asia. Table 2.27 shows that there are more elderly outside the 30-km and above radii of the major cities in Japan than in the centre of the city.
2. See chapter two, Table 2.29.
3. J. Connell, 'Copper, Cocoa and Cash: Terminal, Temporary and Circular Mobility in Siwai, North Solomon's', in M. Chapman and R.M. Prothero (eds), *Circulation in Population Movement: Substance and Concepts from the Melanesian Case*, pp. 119–48, Routledge and Kegan Paul, London, 1985.
4. N. Long and B. Roberts, *Miners, Peasants and Entrepreneurs: Regional Development in the Central Highlands of Peru*, Cambridge University Press, Cambridge, 1984.
5. Douglas C. Ewbank, *Age Misreporting and Age-Selective Underenumeration: Sources, Patterns and Consequences for Demographic Analysis*, National Academy Press, Washington, D.C., 1981.
6. Pravin Visaria, 'Demographics of Ageing in India', *Economic and Political Weekly*, 36(22), June 2, 2001.
7. G. Hugo 'Ageing in Indonesia: A Neglected Area of Policy Concern', in D.R. Phillips (ed.), *Ageing in South East Asia*, pp. 207–230, Arnold, London, 1992.
8. R. Skeldon, 'Rural-to-Urban Migration and its Implications for Poverty Alleviation', *Asia-Pacific Population Journal*, 12(1): 3–16, 1997.
9. R. Skeldon, *Ageing of Rural Populations in South-East and East Asia*, SD Dimensions, Sustainable Development Department, Food and Agriculture Organization of the United Nations (FAO), April 1999.
10. Royal Thai Government, Royal Irrigation Department, 'Mun River Basin Water Resources Development Master Plan: Final Technical Report', Thailand, 1995.
11. National Statistical Office, Office of the Prime Minister, 'Thailand Report of the Migration Survey 1994', Bangkok, 1997.
12. P. Pasuk and C. Baker, *Thailand: Economy and Politics*, Oxford University Press, Kuala Lumpur, 1995.
13. FAO, Thailand, World Food Summit Follow-up, draft strategy for national agricultural development, Horizon 2000, Rome, 1996.
14. P.G. Warr, 'Thailand', in R.H. McLeod and R. Garnaut (eds), *East Asia in Crisis: From Being A Miracle To Needing One?*, pp. 49–65, Routledge, London, 1998.
15. FAO, *Yearbook: Production*, Volume 51, 1997, Rome, FAO Statistics Series No. 142, 1998.
16. S.E. Jacobzone, Cambois, E. Chaplain and J. Robine, *The Health of Older Persons in OECD Countries: Is it Improving Fast Enough to Compensate for Population Change?*, Labour Market and Social Policy Occasional Papers No. 37, OECD, Paris, 1998.

17. Arland Thornon, Ming-Cheng Chnag and Te-Hsiung Sun, 'Social and Economic Change, Intergenerational Relationships, and Family Formation in Taiwan', *Demography*, 21(4): 475–99, 1984.

18. John B. Casterline, 'Differences in Living Arrangements in Four Asian Countries: The Interplay of Constraints and Preferences, Comparative Study of the Elderly in Asia, Research Report No. 91–10. Population Studies Center, University of Michigan, Ann Arbor, 1991.

19. L.G. Martin, 'The Status of South Asia's Growing Elderly Population', *Journal of Cross-cultural Gerontology*, 5: 93–117, 1990.

20. World Bank, *Averting the Old Age Crisis*, World Bank, Washington, D.C., 1994.

21. D. Benjamin, L. Brandt and Scott Rozelle, 'Ageing, Well-being and Social Security in Rural Northern China', in C.Y. Cyrus Chu and Ronald Lee (eds), *Population and Economic Change in East Asia*, A supplement to *Population and Development Review*, 26: 89–116, 2000.

22. Ogawa Naohiro and Robert D. Retherford, 'Shifting Costs of Caring for the Elderly Back to Families in Japan', *Population and Development Review*, 23(1): 59–74, 1997.

23. M.M.B. Asis, D. Domingo, J. Knodel and K. Mehta. 'Living Arrangements in Four Asian Countries: A Comparative Perspective', *Journal of Cross-cultural Gerontology*, 10: 145–62, 1995.

24. Hung-Tak Lee, 'Family Welfare and Reproductive Health: The Korean Experience', Paper presented at KIHASA/UNFPA seminar on Population and Development Policies in Low Fertility Countries, Institute for Health and Social Affairs (KIHASA), Seoul, Korea, 1998.

25. Jose N. Natividad and Grace T. Cruz, 'Patterns in Living Arrangements and Familial Support for the Elderly in the Philippines', *Asia-Pacific Population Journal*, 12(4): 17–34, 1997.

26. Zimmer Zachary, and Sovan Kiry Kim, 'Living Arrangements and Socio-demographic Conditions of Older Adults in Cambodia', Working Papers No. 157, Population Council, New York, 2002.

27. John Knodel, Napaporn Chayovan and Siriwan Siriboon, 'Family Support and Living Arrangements of Thai Elderly', *Asia-Pacific Population Journal*, 12(4): 51–68, 1992.

28. John Bongaarts and Zachary Zimmer, 'Living Arrangements of Older Adults in the Developing World: An Analysis of DHS Household Surveys', Working Papers No. 148, Population Council, New York, 2001.

29. *ibid*.

30. J. Dreze and P.V. Srinivasan, 'Widowhood and Poverty in Rural India: Some Inferences from Household Survey Data', *Journal of Development Economics*, 54: 217–34, 1997.

31. R. Palacios and M. Pallares, 'International Patterns of Pension Provision', Pension Reform Primer Working Paper Series, World Bank, 2000.

32. S.M. Dev, 'Social Security in the Unorganised Sector: Lessons from the Experiences of Kerala and Tamil Nadu States', *Indian Journal of Labour Economics*, 37(4), 1994.

33. Government of India, *National Social Assistance Programme (NSAP): Guidelines*, Ministry of Rural Areas and Employment, Department of Rural Development, Delhi. 1995.

34. S.I. Rajan, 'Social Assistance for Poor Elderly: How effective?', *Economic and Political Weekly*, 36(8), February 24, 2001.
35. World Bank, Finance and Private Sector Development, 'India: The Challenge of Old Age Income Security', Mimeo, April 5, 2001.
36. World Bank, *India: Macroeconomic Update*, World Bank, Washington D.C., 1998.
37. T.S. Sankaran, 'Social Assistance: Evidence and Policy Issues', in van Ginneken (ed.), *Social Security for All Indians*, Oxford University Press, Delhi, 1998.
38. S. Jain, 'Basic Social Security in India', in Wouter (ed.), *Social Security for the Excluded Majority*, International Labour Office, Geneva, 1999.
39. D. Cox and E. Jimenez, 'Social Security and Private Transfers in Developing Countries: The Case of Peru', *World Bank Economic Review*, 6(1): 155–70, World Bank, 1992.
40. International Labour Office (ILO), *World Labour Report*, ILO, Geneva, 1995.
41. S. Guha Roy, 'Morbidity Related Epidemiological Determinants in Indian Aged: An Overview', in C.R. Ramachandran & B. Shah, (eds), *Public Health Implications of Ageing in India*, pp. 114–25, Indian Council of Medical Research, New Delhi, 1994.
42. M. Srivatsava, U. Kapil, V. Kumar, A.B. Dey, K.M. Nagarkar and G. Sekaran, 'Knowledge, Attitude and Practices Regarding Nutrition in Patients Attending Geriatric Clinic at the AIIMS', in V. Kumar, (ed.), *Ageing-Indian Perspective and Global Scenario: All India Institute of Medical Sciences*, pp. 407–09, All India Institute of Medical Sciences, New Delhi, 1996.
43. A. Wadhwa, M. Sabharwal and S. Sharma, 'Nutritional Status of the Elderly', *Indian Journal of Medical Research*, 107: 340–48, 1997.
44. R.G. Wilkinson, *Unhealthy Societies: The Affliction of Inequality*, Routledge, London, 1996.
45. J.W. Lynch, G.D. Smith, G.A. Kaplan and J.S. House, 'Income Inequality and Mortality: Importance to Health of Individual Income, Psychosocial Environment and Material Conditions', *British Medical Journal*, 320: 1200–04, 2000.
46. ESCAP, United Nations, *The Family and Older Persons in China, Indonesia and Thailand*, Asian Population Studies Series No. 152, New York, 1999.
47. Peng Du, 'Survey on Family Structure and the Elderly in China', in ESCAP, United Nations (ed.), *The Family and Older Persons in China, Indonesia and Thailand*, Asian Population Studies Series No. 152, New York, 1999.
48. M.D. Wirakartakusumah, 'Household Structure and Elderly in Indonesia', in ESCAP, United Nations (ed.), *The Family and Older Persons in China, Indonesia and Thailand*, Asian Population Studies Series No. 152, New York, 1999.
49. M. Wongsith and Siriwan Siriboon, 'Household Structure and Care for the Elderly in Thailand', ESCAP, United Nations (ed.), *The Family and Older Persons in China, Indonesia and Thailand*, Asian Population Studies Series No. 152, New York, 1999.
50. B. Shah and A.K. Prabhakar, 'Chronic Morbidity Profile among Elderly', *Indian Journal of Medical Research*, 106: 265–72, 1997.
51. P.M. Dalal, 'Strokes in the Elderly: Prevalence, Risk Factors and the Strategies for Prevention', *Indian Journal of Medical Research*, 106: 352–32, 1997.

52. S. Rama Rao and John W. Townsend, 'Health Needs of Elderly Indian Women: An Emerging Issue', in Maithreyi Krishnaraj, Ratna M. Sudarshan and Abusaleh Shariff (eds), *Gender, Population and Development*, Oxford University Press, New Delhi, 1998.

53. A.B. Dey and D. Chaudhury, 'Infections in the Elderly', *Indian Journal of Medical Research*, 106: 273–85, 1997.

54. I.J. Prakash, *Ageing in India*, World Health Organization, 1999.

55. S.K. Angra, G.V.S. Murthy, S.K. Gupta and V. Angra, 'Cataract Related Blindness in India and its Social Implications', *Indian Journal of Medical Research*, 106: 312–24, 1997.

56. S.K. Kacker, 'Hearing Impairment in the Aged', *Indian Journal of Medical Research*, 106: 333–39, 1997.

57. A. Venkoba Rao, 'Psychiatric Morbidity in the Aged', *Indian Journal of Medical Research*, 106: 361–69, 1997.

58. I.J. Prakash, *Ageing in India*, World Health Organization (in-house publication), 1999.

59. *ibid*.

60. A. Venkoba Rao, 'Suicide in the Elderly', *Indian Journal of Social Psychiatry*, 1: 3–10, 1985.

61. Dow Mongkolsmai, 'Private Health Sector Growth and Social Security Insurance in Thailand', in William Newbrander (ed.), *Private Health Sector in Asia: Issues and Implications*, pp. 83–107, Wiley, New York, 1997.

62. World Health Organization (WHO), *Active Ageing: From Evidence to Action*, WHO, Geneva, 2001.

63. Life expectancy at 60 Index: Kerala = 19.4–14.7/6.1 = 0.770; West Bengal = 15.6–14.7/6.1 = 0.148. Elderly Literacy Index: Kerala = 64.55–14.62/49.93 = 1.00; West Bengal = 40.43–14.62/49.93 = 0.517. Economic Independence Index: Kerala = 26.3–21.7/28.1 = 0.164; West Bengal = 30.1–21.7/28.1 = 0.299. Retirement Benefit Index: Kerala = 39.2–33.4/54.1 = 0.107; West Bengal = 75.8–33.4/54.1 = 0.784. Elderly Wealth Index: Kerala = 35.2–29.9/48.1 = 0.110; West Bengal = 37.3–29.9/ 48.1 = 0.154. Social Interaction Index: Kerala = 67.4–56.5/38.6 = 0.282; West Bengal = 73.5–56.5/ 38.6 = 0.440.

64. D.O. Cowgirl and L.D. Holmes (eds), *Ageing and Modernisation*. Appleton-Century-Crofts, New York, 1972.

65. M.A. Heisel, 'Aging in the Context of Population Policies in Developing Countries', *Population Bulletin of the United States*, 17: 54, United Nations Publications, 1984.

66. E. Palmore and K. Manton, 'Modernisation and the Status of the Aged: International Correlation', *Journal of Gerontology*, 29: 205–10, 1974.

CHAPTER SIX

Graceful Ageing

As population ageing continues, Asian governments will face a variety of challenges. As discussed in chapter four, problems are apprehended everywhere from stagnating economic growth to inter-generational conflict. The issues are many and some of them are deeply rooted in the structure of the society and economy. There is no policy that can change the present condition of the aged overnight. The developing countries of Asia will have to work very hard to sensitise their systems to the needs of a rapidly changing demographic age structure. Changes are required everywhere, in order to create an environment in which people of all ages and sex can live happily. The task is enormous and the policy interventions needed are many. Most Asian countries are in their infancy vis-à-vis formulation of elderly policy programmes. Their governments must, therefore, redirect their efforts to plan and implement elderly policies and programmes that are pragmatic, efficient and geared towards growth and equity. They will have to develop better legal structures, financial markets and administrative mechanisms to create an environment where elderly-friendly programmes can be implemented, in addition to protecting and supporting old family values. However, given the pace of population ageing in Asia, policy makers need to act fast.

The aim of development is to improve the well-being of the entire population on the basis of its full participation in the process of development and an equitable distribution of the benefits that are generated in the process. The development process must enhance human dignity and ensure equity among all age groups in the sharing of society's resources, rights and responsibilities. Individuals, regardless of age, sex or creed, should contribute according to their abilities and be served according to their needs. In this context,if economic growth, productive employment, social justice and human solidarity are fundamental and indivisible elements of development; so is the preservation and recognition of cultural identity. The various problems of the aged can find their real solution under conditions of peace, security, cessation of arms and a reallocation of defence expenditure for the economic and social development of the elderly. The developmental and humanitarian problems of the aged can best find their solution under conditions where tyranny and oppression, colonialism, racism, and discrimination based on race, sex or religion, do not prevail, and where respect for human rights reigns.

An important objective of socio-economic development is an age-integrated society, in which age discrimination and involuntary segregation is eliminated and in which solidarity and mutual support among generations is encouraged. Ageing is a lifelong process and should be recognised as such. The preparation of the entire population for later stages of life should be an integral part of social policies and encompass physical, psychological, cultural, religious, spiritual, economic, health and other factors. Ageing, in addition to being a symbol of experience and wisdom, can also bring human beings closer to personal fulfilment, according to their beliefs and aspirations.

AGEING AWARENESS

The primary task of any ageing policy intervention is to recognise the importance of aged persons in human life and to understand the ageing process. Recognition of the authority, wisdom, dignity and self-control that comes with a lifetime of experience has been a usual aspect of the respect shown to the aged throughout history. These values are, however, often neglected in some societies and older persons are unreasonably accused of being a drain on the economy, with their increasing demands for health and support services. Although healthy ageing is becoming an increasingly important issue for older persons, the public focus on maintaining the aged has sometimes fostered a negative image of ageing. Older women, by being shown as weak and dependent, are particularly affected. But the fact remains that,

the human race is characterised by a long childhood and by a long old age. Throughout history this has enabled older persons to educate the younger and pass on values to them; this role has ensured man's survival and progress. The presence of the elderly in the family home, the neighbourhood and in all forms of social life still teaches an irreplaceable lesson of humanity. Not only by his life, but indeed by his death, the older person teaches us all a lesson. Through grief the survivors come to understand that the dead do continue to participate in the human community, by the results of their labour, the works and institutions they leave behind them, and the memory of their words and deeds. This may encourage us to regard our own death with greater serenity and to grow more fully aware of the responsibilities toward future generations.[1]

Older people have spent a long life on this earth. A reinterpretation of their life stories provides us with an opportunity to examine our lives in retrospect, to correct some of our past mistakes, to get closer to the truth and to achieve a different understanding of the sense and value of our past actions. This should help us all to achieve the urgently needed reorientation of history. The spiritual, cultural and socio-economic contributions of the aged are valuable to society and should be so recognised and promoted further.

The task before policy makers is to enhance the public recognition of the authority, wisdom, productiveness and other important contri-butions of older persons. They need to create the framework in which there is an individual and collective responsibility to recognise past and present contributions of older persons, seeking to counter-act preconceived biases and myths, and to consequently treat older persons with respect and gratitude, dignity and sensitivity. Viet Nam is one of the few countries in the world to have an ordinance on the aged. It clearly defines the status of the aged in society, the care and respect they deserve and the role of government and society. (The ordinance has been included in Appendix Five of the book.) While many different words have been used in favour of the aged in semi-nar reports and conference resolutions, including those of national governments and United Nations, the same words take on a different meaning and impetus when converted into a statute. A perusal of the

Indian laws on the aged (as summarised in Appendix Two) show that 'old age' was an afterthought inclusion in laws meant for other sub-sections of the community. Such a perfunctory approach may not suffice. A positive view of ageing is an integral aspect of the International Plan of Action on Ageing 2002. The media can play a formidable role in portraying the elderly beyond stereotypes and in illuminating the full diversity of humankind. The Plan of Action on Ageing also recognises media as 'the harbingers of change' and expresses the hope that it can be the guiding factor in fostering the role of older persons in development strategies, including in rural areas. Mass media should be encouraged to promote images that highlight the wisdom, strengths, contributions, courage and resourcefulness of older women and men, including older persons with disabilities. In addition, educators should recognise and include in their courses, the contributions made by older persons. All these should form a part of educational courses in the formative years of students' careers. Also needed is the avoidance of ageism in the workplace, whether the public or the private sector. Here too, the media can be an important watchdog.

PROMOTE GRACEFUL AGEING

If ageing is to be a positive experience, longer life must be accompanied by continuing opportunities for life sustenance, self-esteem and freedom.[2] Life sustenance means the provision of basic needs during old age; self-esteem demands respect for the elderly from all institutions of civil society; and freedom is the ability to choose and be free from servitudes of dependence and ill health. Once the people in a country are able to secure these core values in their old age, they can be said to be 'ageing gracefully.' **Graceful ageing** is a process of optimising opportunities for physical, social and mental well-being throughout life, in order to ensure a healthy, independent, quality life in older age. The World Health Organization (WHO) has termed this process 'active ageing' since the late 1990s. Other international organisations, academic circles and governmental groups (including the G8, the Organisation for Economic Co-operation and Development [OECD], the International Labour Organization [ILO] and the Commission of the European Communities [CEC]) are also using 'active ageing', primarily to express the idea of continuing involvement in socially productive activities and meaningful work. Though the word 'active' implies continuing involvement in all facets of life and not just the ability to be physically active, it may send wrong signals both to the aged and others. The older people who are either ill or are physically restricted due to disabilities may feel ignored by a term that appears to be demanding immediate action from them, though when interpreted broadly, these people are active contributors to their families, peers, communities and nations. Others may feel that the aged need to be active to be supported. We use the term 'graceful ageing' to recognise the process with core values of life.

Graceful ageing allows older people to optimise their potential for independence, good health and productivity while providing them with adequate protection and care from the family, the community and the state. In this approach, apart from the aged themselves, there are three additional players: family, community and state. All of them have specific responsibilities towards the aged under the coordination of the state. The aged themselves are also required to behave in a manner that is conducive to a healthy life. The approach is based on recognition of the human rights of older people and the United Nations principles of independence, participation, dignity, care and self-fulfilment. It shifts strategic planning away from a 'needs-based' approach (which assumes that older people are passive targets) to a 'rights-based' participatory approach that recognises the rights of older people to equality of opportunity and treatment in all aspects of life. Potentially, when the family, the community and the state support the aged in their pursuit of graceful living, their own quality of life improves. More specifically, when the state comes up with suitable health, labour market, employment, education and social policies to support graceful ageing, the aged will be able to contribute more to general mainstream life. If they remain well, the society's cost in maintaining them through medical treatment and care systems will lower. The cost of parent caring will fall and this in turn will promote intergenerational integration too. This approach believes in the dictum that 'prevention is better than cure.' It seeks to remove old age related health and associate problems before they become a threat. Studies indicate that a $1 investment in measures to encourage moderate physical activity among the aged leads to a saving of $ 3.2 in medical costs alone.[3] In the United States, the decline in disability rates between 1982 and 1994 were responsible for a saving of health care resources to the tune of $17.3 billion in 1994.[4]

SELF-SUPPORT BY THE AGED

It is true that with age, persons lose their body strength. It is however also possible to make good this loss through regular exercise and physical activity. For example, a fit 70-year-old person's physical performance can be equal to the performance of an unfit 30-year-old person. Some intellectual capacities such as reaction time, learning speed and memory are also lost. However, these losses can be compensated for through gains in wisdom, knowledge and experience. Often, a decline in cognitive functioning is triggered by negligence through lack of practice, behavioural dysfunction such as alcohol use and psychosocial factors such as lack of motivation, lack of confidence, isolation and depression, rather than due to ageing. Genetic factors and heredity are also important elements in the health of an individual. The physical, social and economic environment in which people live also has an impact on individual health. However, the final player on individual health is the person himself. For most people, living a disease- and disability-free old age depends on the ability to be flexible and adaptable. Most people remain flexible in their old age and it is these people who have a sense of control, a positive attitude and a belief in their ability to succeed. Older people do not differ significantly from younger people in their ability to cope. It is a wrong notion that old people cannot adjust to lifestyle changes. For graceful ageing to succeed, elderly persons ought to engage themselves in appropriate physical activity and household chores, participate in religious, social and community activities, eat healthy food, avoid tobacco, alcohol and drugs, and use medications wisely. These few precautions in older ages can prevent disease and functional decline, extend longevity and enhance one's quality of life. At the same time, religious adherence to self-care by the elderly may not ensure graceful ageing if the spontaneous support from family and state is lacking. What is needed is an environment in which the aged can live and die gracefully. In this section, we suggest some do's and dont's for the elderly that are necessary for graceful ageing.

PHYSICAL ACTIVITY

Participation in regular, moderate physical activity can delay functional decline and reduce the risk of chronic diseases in both healthy and chronically ill older people. Regular, moderate physical activity reduces the risk of cardiac death by 20 to 25 per cent among people with established heart disease.[5] It can substantially reduce the severity of disabilities associated with heart disease and other chronic illnesses.[6] It also improves mental health and often promotes social interaction. Being active can help older people maintain their day-to-day activities as independently as possible for the longest period of time. There are also economic benefits associated with being physically active for older people. Medical costs are substantially lower for older people who are active.[7] However, despite all these benefits, a high proportion of older people in most countries lead sedentary lives. Populations with low incomes, and older people with disabilities are the most likely to be inactive. Policies and programmes should encourage sedentary older people to become more physically active and provide them with opportunities to do so. Providing safe areas for walking is particularly important as well as support for culturally appropriate community activities that are organised and led by the older people themselves. Professional advice to 'go from doing nothing to doing something' and physical rehabilitation programmes that help older people recover from mobility problems are both effective and cost-efficient. In addition, since many older people are also engaged in strenuous physical work and chores which may hasten disabilities and cause injuries, they require support in the form of health promotion efforts directed at providing relief from repetitive, strenuous tasks and through adjustments to unsafe physical activity at work.

Household Chores, Community Participation

The elderly should engage themselves in household chores like household management, cooking, cleaning, gardening, pet caring, child care and baby-sitting, shopping etc., without straining themselves. Participation in such activities will make them physically active and keep their minds occupied. Moreover, such activities will give them a sense of belonging to the place where they stay. If living with their children and their families, the latter would be benefit from such spontaneous activities of elderly parents. At the least, such younger adults can go to work without being concerned about the children at home. The usefulness of the aged in the family will rise and ease the intergenerational tensions in the family.

It is also necessary that the elderly entertain themselves adequately through reading, listening to music, watching television etc. Even playing cards, chess and similar indoor games is useful. If the elderly are talented or interested in any of the performing arts or literature (like singing, playing musical instruments, painting etc.), they should continue to nurture that talent, irrespective of its marketable worth. It would also be beneficial for the elderly to either continue or take up a vocation, whether remunerative or not. Such activities, which are not boring and monotonous, will help keep the elderly physically and mentally alert.

As mentioned earlier, old age is a period of loss, where, one loses many things of life, including loved ones. One must develop adequate mental strength to face such trauma and be active despite such happenings. Many experts believe that participation in religious and spiritual activities are useful in controlling the body and mind. Involvement in community and social activities have a similar effect. Older people who actively participate in social and community activities have lower disability rates. They can cope with chronic ailments quicker and increase their lifespan. In all countries, a number of skilled and experienced older people act as volunteers in schools, communities, religious institutions, businesses, and health and political organisations. Such activities should be encouraged as voluntary work benefits older people by increasing their social interactions and mental well-being while making a significant contribution to their communities and nations at the same time.

Healthy Eating

Malnutrition in older adults includes both undernutrition in poorer households and excess calorie consumption in richer households. Malnutrition can be caused by a number of factors: limited access to food, tooth loss, socio-economic hardships, emergency situations, lack of nutritional knowledge and information, poor food choices (e.g., eating high fat foods), disease and subsequent medication, social isolation, cognitive or physical disability that inhibit one's ability to buy food and prepare it, and a lack of physical activity. With advancing age, certain nutrients are not easily absorbed into the body and energy requirements are reduced due to a decline in the basal metabolic rate. Therefore, it is especially important for older people to eat a variety of nutrient-rich foods that are culturally acceptable and regionally available at affordable prices. Excess calorie consumption greatly increases an older person's risk for chronic diseases and disabilities. Obesity and a high-fat diet are highly related to diabetes, cardiovascular disease, high blood pressure, arthritis and some cancers. Insufficient calcium and Vitamin D intake can result in loss of bone density in older age and an increase in painful, costly and debilitating bone fractures, especially in older women.

Reducing Smoking

Middle-aged and older adults who smoke are more likely than non-smokers to suffer from serious disabilities and die prematurely of smoking-related diseases. Smoking may also decrease the effect of needed medications. Exposure to passive smoking can also have a negative effect on older people's health, especially if they suffer from asthma or other respiratory problems. Most smokers start young and are quickly addicted to the nicotine in the tobacco. Therefore, attempts to prevent children and youth from starting to smoke must be a primary objective in any tobacco control strategy. At the same time, it is possible to reduce the demand for tobacco among adults through comprehensive actions such as raising taxation on all tobacco-related products and restrictions on their advertising. Studies have shown that tobacco control is highly cost-effective in low- and middle-income countries. In China, for example, conservative estimates suggest that a 10 per cent increase in tobacco taxes would reduce consumption by 5 per cent and increase overall revenue by 5 per cent. This increased revenue would be sufficient to finance a package of essential health care services for one-third of China's poorest citizens.[8] It is never too late to quit smoking. Quitting at an older age can substantially reduce the risk of heart attack, stroke and lung cancer.

Alcohol Overuse

While older people tend to consume less alcohol than younger people, the metabolism changes that accompany ageing increases their susceptibility to alcohol-related diseases, including malnutrition, liver disease and peptic ulcers. Older people also have a greater chance of suffering alcohol-related falls and injuries, as well as dementia and other potential hazards that result from mixing alcohol and medication. Treatment services for alcohol problems should be available to older people as well as younger people. According to a recent WHO review of the literature, there is evidence that alcohol use at very low levels (upto one drink a day) may offer some degree of protection against coronary heart disease and stroke for people age 45 and over. However, in terms of overall excess mortality, the adverse effects of drinking outweigh any protection against coronary heart disease, even in high risk populations.[9]

Unnecessary Medication

Because older people often suffer from chronic health problems, they are more likely than younger people to need and use medication: traditional, over-the-counter and prescribed. In most countries, older people with low incomes have little or no access to insurance for medication. As a result, many either go without medicines or spend an inappropriately large part of their meagre incomes on drugs. In contrast, in wealthier countries, medication is sometimes over-prescribed to older people (especially to older women). Adverse drug-related illnesses and falls are significant causes of personal suffering and costly preventable hospital admissions.[10] As the population ages, the demand will continue to rise for medications that are used to delay and treat chronic diseases, alleviate pain and improve quality of life. There is call for a renewed effort to increase affordable access to essential, safe medications and to better ensure the appropriate, cost-effective use of current and new drugs. Partners in this effort should include governments, health workers, traditional healers, the pharmaceutical industry, employers and organisations representing older people.

Self-protection Measures

The elderly must also take appropriate measures to adequately safeguard themselves from common dangers. A will is a sensible and practical safeguard for the elderly. Carefully designed through knowledgeable and trustworthy people, it may not be time consuming and expensive. If a person dies intestate (without making a will) what usually ensues is an expensive and laborious process to determine the legal heirs/successors. The spouses, particularly elderly widows, are usually the major victims of such imprudence; the legal beneficiaries receive less than the actual share. In due course what's left of the estate of the deceased may not be distributed as the person had wished. It is erroneously believed that in the absence of a will everything automatically goes to the wife or husband of the deceased. In fact, if there are children or relatives, only a portion of the estate passes to the spouse. The rest is shared equally amongst the children or relatives. In some unfortunate cases, a husband or wife may even be forced to sell the family home to pay relatives the money they are entitled to by law.

It is also a good idea for the elderly to ensure security at home, rather than regret the loss of valuables and then undergo uncertain and expensive legal and bureaucratic procedures to secure them. A comprehensive householders' insurance is a good idea. Some of the additional precautions that may be taken are:

For security at home:

♦ Never leave your doors open or unlocked.
♦ Secure the front and back doors with metal gates.
♦ Never open the door to strangers.

While on the street, the elderly should:

♦ Leave valuables at home.
♦ Never carry more cash needed.
♦ Never walk in deserted or dark areas alone.
♦ Carry handbags close to the body.
♦ Keep change in purse or wallet and credit cards and notes in an inside pocket, never in the back pocket of trousers.
♦ Stay calm and co-operate with the police if robbed in the street. Don't try to fight back, as you may get hurt. Be observant in order to give maximum information to the police.

While using public transport the elderly should:

♦ Avoid waiting at deserted terminals, wait in well-lit areas.
♦ Stand close to others who are waiting for the transport.
♦ In a bus or train, be aware of people who look or act suspiciously, raise an alarm if need be.

- ◆ If transport is partially empty, sit as close to the driver as possible.
- ◆ When arriving at your destination, take note of who leaves with you.
- ◆ If being followed, rush to nearest building and ask for help.

While driving the elderly should:

- ◆ Make sure that car is in good driveable condition.
- ◆ Keep all belongings in the car boot.
- ◆ Keep car doors locked and windows closed while driving.
- ◆ Park the car in a well-lit area at night.
- ◆ Never pick up hitch-hikers.
- ◆ Beware of strangers who may approach you at traffic lights.
- ◆ If followed or threatened, honk continually and if necessary seek help.

Some other safety precautions include:

- ◆ Ask for help in danger and always wait for help to arrive.
- ◆ Beware of pickpockets, bag-snatchers in shopping malls.
- ◆ Do not keep wallet or purse in a visible place or back pocket.
- ◆ Don't travel with much money; always have an escort when this is absolutely essential.
- ◆ Keep emergency telephone numbers close at hand.

While the aged are expected to follow the guidelines and precautions essential for a healthy and secure life, the list is neither on exhaustive nor a foolproof way to good health. There is also no guarantee that the aged will follow these guidelines. It therefore becomes imperative that the community and the government come forward with new ideas to motivate the aged into following these guidelines. It is they who have to create an environment in which such guidelines could be followed without any problem. The tasks before the community and the government therefore include:

- ◆ To develop culturally appropriate, population-based guidelines for self-support of the elderly men and women for graceful ageing.
- ◆ To make use of the strengths and abilities of the older people while helping them build self-efficacy and confidence, to help them cope and set realistic goals.

- To provide the elderly with accessible, pleasant and affordable opportunities for physical activity (safe walking areas and parks) and support groups that promote regular, moderate exercise.
- To educate the elderly about healthy eating by providing them with information specifying the nutritional needs of older people and by suggesting measures to improve oral health among older people.
- To take comprehensive actions to assist older people quit smoking.
- To reduce the misuse of alcohol and drugs and to discourage the practice of inappropriate prescription of drugs for the elderly.
- To provide incentives and training for health and social service professionals to counsel and guide older people in positive self-care and healthy lifestyle practices.
- To reduce the risk of social isolation by supporting community empowerment and mutual aid groups, traditional societies, peer outreach, neighbourhood visits and family caregivers.
- To recognise and support the importance of mental health and spirituality in older ages.
- To take older people along in prevention and education efforts to reduce the spread of HIV/AIDS.

FAMILY SUPPORT

As we saw in chapter five, in most Asian societies, the elderly live in extended multigenerational households and rely primarily on their adult children for financial support and personal care. It is the family members and neighbours who provide the bulk of the support and care to older adults who need assistance. However, these traditional families are now showing signs of breaking up due to demographic, economic and social change. In countries where fertility has declined, the elderly have fewer adult children to provide them with support and care. Many of these children have moved away from their homes because of their jobs. Women are now entering the workforce in increasing numbers and therefore have less time than they did in the past to spend on caring for elderly family members. It is also apprehended that the provision of state support for the elderly reduces the propensity of children to support their parents. Though, it is not clear how quickly or to what extent these pressures will undermine traditional family systems, a study of East Asia's low fertility countries shows that by 2050 a fully functioning family support system will be able to meet only about one-half of the retirement needs of the elderly.[11]

Even then, there is no replacement for the family as a source of support for the elderly. The aged do not have the resources or the ability to support themselves. The state, even in developed countries, does not have the necessary resources to follow up on old age caring programmes infinitely. Signs of intergenerational tensions for whatever little that has been done for the elderly are evident. But families must be supported, motivated and encouraged if they are to continue to provide care and support to the elderly without becoming over-burdened in the process. The family can be an important partner even when the state is able to evolve an elaborate system of support for the elderly.[12] Some of the measures that can be suggested to motivate family support systems towards the aged in the future are:

♦ Several Asian governments have adopted policies to encourage family care for the elderly. In Singapore, India and China among others, children are now legally responsible for the support of their elderly parents. The ordinance on the elderly in Vietnam clearly specifies the role the family is expected to play in protecting the elderly. The statutory obligation of the family to support their aged members is very important to instil confidence in the minds of the elderly. Also important are supportive measures that promote the family support system.

♦ There should be information, education and communication programmes to convey the message that family ties are the most powerful built-in support mechanism and any effort to undermine the family system could be disastrous.

♦ Fiscal support to families supporting the aged is also a good idea. The Malaysian government provides such families with tax incentives for elderly care. In countries like India, where only a handful of people pay income tax, such a system could mean a good beginning, although it may not have universal impact. Some other preferential treatments like relaxation of land reform regulations, preferences in state allotment of housing, permits and licenses to individuals can be extended to those who support the aged in the family. In countries where moral hazards pose a big problem, these schemes are faced with problems of effective implementation. Some East and South-east Asian countries are subsidising adult care and other support services for the elderly within the family network. Malaysia and Singapore have revised their public housing policies to accommodate multigenerational living arrangements.

♦ Very often family members, some of whom are already old, fall ill due to continuous stress, both at work and at home. The provision of visiting nurses, home care, peer support programmes, rehabilitation services, assistive devices, respite care and elderly day care is important to enable family members to continue to provide for older people.

♦ In many countries family care without compensation to caregivers is resulting in new economic and social strains. The cost to women in particular, who continue to provide the majority of informal care, is enormous. Female caregivers face losses on two fronts: loss of income (present and future) by being irregular in the job market; and, physical and emotional stress from balancing work and household obligations. The situation becomes even more demanding for women with careers, children and elder care responsibilities. The burden is compounded if the elderly become disabled.

♦ The caregiving families need training, social security coverage, help with housing adjustments to look after disabled elderly.

GOVERNMENT SUPPORT IN GRACEFUL AGEING

Graceful ageing requires elderly-friendly and supportive economic, physical and social environments. In most developing countries of Asia, the setting in which the elderly live is critical and entails interventions on the part of the government and the community. Graceful ageing demands a health care system that emphasises health promotion, disease prevention and the provision of cost-effective, equitable and dignified long-term care. Again, such health systems can function effectively only if the economic, physical and social settings are made favourable to elderly life sustenance, freedom and choice. The economic environment becomes conducive to graceful ageing if the elderly have access to work and income and social protection that takes care of their basic needs. The physical environment is geared towards graceful ageing if the elderly have adequate barrier-free housing (explained later), transportation and other physical requirements of life, whether in urban or rural areas. Social surroundings are conducive to graceful living if the elderly have access to information and knowledge without discrimination, are not subject to any abuse and have the freedom to choose when to end their lives. As the governments in developing countries lack the resources, organisational skills and capacities to unearth the changing requirements of elderly life, international cooperation can play a focal role here. If countries could divert resources from military ventures, a lot of the existing human scarcity could be met easily. Among all others sections of society, the elderly too would benefit from such a positive approach towards life.

HEALTH POLICY SUPPORT FOR GRACEFUL AGEING

Maintaining a healthy lifestyle is the responsibility of individuals; the responsibility of the government is to create a supportive environment that enables the advancement of health and well-being into old age. To promote graceful ageing, the government health policy must take a life course perspective that converges on health promotion, disease prevention, equitable access to primary health care and a balanced approach to long-term care. Health promotion is the process of motivating and enabling people to take control of, and improve their own health. Disease prevention activities include both primary prevention activities to prevent and manage non-communicable diseases and injury; and, secondary prevention activities for taking necessary steps for the early detection of chronic diseases. These activities help reduce the risk of painful and costly disabilities.

Long-term care has been defined by the WHO as,

the system of activities undertaken by informal caregivers (family, friends and/or neighbours) and/or professionals (health and social services) to ensure that a person who is not fully capable of self-care can maintain the highest possible quality of life, according to his or her individual preferences, with the greatest possible degree of independence, autonomy, participation, personal fulfilment and human dignity.

Thus, long-term care includes both informal and formal support systems. The latter may include a broad range of community and public health care, primary care, palliative care and rehabilitation services, as well as institutional care in supportive housing, nursing homes, hospices, etc., and treatments to halt or reverse the course of disease and disability. Mental health services should also be an integral part of long-term care. The under-diagnosis of mental illness, particularly of depression in older people is increasingly being recognised. However, suicide rates among older people suggest the need for even more recognition and action. Health and social services need to be integrated, equitable and cost-effective, and at the same time, strike a balance among self-support, family and state support.

The health care systems must be professionalised and made sensitive to the special needs of the elderly. They must take note of older people's strengths and empower them to maintain even small measures of independence when they are ill or frail. The paternalistic attitude of health care providers can have a devastating effect on the self-esteem and independence of older people. Equity of access and cost-effectiveness are key concerns for health systems. In many countries older people who are poor and who live in rural areas have limited or no access to health care. A decline in public support towards primary health care services in many areas has increased the financial and intergenerational strain on older people and their families. When health and social services are available and accessible, lack of coordination among the service providers often causes duplication and delays. These factors combined with ineffective care delivery and the inappropriate use of high-cost technologies are the main drivers of the escalating health care costs. Also, because of very little local level research into health care needs the health sector is virtually ruled by multinational drug companies. Often the cost of health care is too high for the elderly to bear. This has become a matter of great concern with the current globalisation movement through WTO avenues.

Many developing countries in Asia, are confronting the double burden of fighting emerging and re-emerging communicable diseases like HIV/AIDS, tuberculosis and malaria, and the increasing threat of non-communicable lifestyle diseases. The elderly too are affected by this new trend of epidemiological transition. Older persons also experience institutional, financial, physical, psychological and legal obstacles vis-à-vis health care services. They require special geriatric care and palliative care,[13] especially those suffering from painful or incurable illnesses or diseases. Older people may also encounter age discrimination and age-related disability discrimination in the provision of services because their treatment may be perceived as less essential than the treatment of younger persons. In addition, there is a tremendous need to integrate effective care for older persons with physical, mental, social, spiritual and environmental conditions.

Older persons also run the risk of HIV/AIDS infection. Since they already suffer from other immunodeficiency syndromes, the diagnoses of such diseases becomes difficult. Regrettably, the AIDS awareness programmes rarely address the aged. As a result, many of them, including their old caregivers may not be aware of how to protect them from the AIDS virus. The primary task, therefore, is to collect HIV/AIDS data to assess the extent of HIV/AIDS infection in older persons. It might be necessary to bring old people within the network of AIDS awareness programmes. Luckily, the problem is not that acute in the Asian countries yet. However, this should not be a reason for complacency.

There is an urgent need worldwide to expand educational opportunities in the field of geriatrics and gerontology for all health professionals who work with older persons. There is also a need to expand educational programmes on health and older persons for professionals in the social service sector. Informal caregivers also need access to information and basic training on how to care for older persons. Though it is not an easy task, if some of the inherent weaknesses in health care systems could be removed, if people could be protected from preventable disabilities, and if a suitable scheme of health care financing could be evolved, universal access to health care for the elderly would be a possibility. Some of the specific policies that may be needed to attain these broad goals are:

♦ Although the incidence of poverty is declining, the cohorts of today's elderly remain victims of its intensity having suffered it in their early years. The damage done to them may still be undone through a safe and nutritionally adequate supply of food and drinking water.

♦ Health policy makers should provide every region with a specific nutritional chart for older persons, based on local food and cultural habits. The general public including older people and caregivers should be educated about it. It should be remembered that the general health of people is under threat from the emergence of fast food.

♦ The elderly require affordable dental services to prevent and treat disorders that can impede eating and cause malnutrition.

♦ To foster better health and disease prevention, adult immunization programmes should be used wherever possible as a preventive measure.

- Efforts should be made to utilise technologies such as telemedicine, wherever available, and distance learning to reduce geographical and logistical limitations in access to health care in rural areas.
- Traditional medicine may be included in primary health care programmes where appropriate and beneficial. Older healers who are knowledgeable about traditional and complementary medicines should be supported and their roles as teachers encouraged.
- Specialised gerontological services should be developed and their activities coordinated with primary health care and social care services. At the same time, the concept of palliative care should be promoted and integrated into the comprehensive health care plan.
- Regulatory mechanisms should be developed at appropriate levels to set appropriate standards of health care and rehabilitation for older persons.
- Public health and prevention strategies should be revised to reflect local epidemiology. Information on the prevention and the risks of HIV/AIDS should meet the needs of older persons.
- Professional education in gerontology and geriatrics should be expanded. To begin with, gerontology could be made a compulsory subject in graduate courses in medicine and nursing.

MENTAL PROBLEMS

Mental health problems among the aged are a leading cause of disability and reduced quality of life. Though mental health problems are not an inevitable outcome of growing old, a significant proportion of the elderly do suffer from them. Losses and life changes often lead to any array of mental health disorders, which, if not properly diagnosed, can lead to inappropriate, expensive, painful and clinically unnecessary institutionalisation. Strategies to cope with such diseases include medication, psychosocial support, cognitive training programmes, training for caregivers (both family members and professionals) and specific structures of inpatient care. The following are areas where specific attention is still needed:

- Efforts should be made to help persons who are mentally infirm to live in their own homes for as long as possible and to respond to their health needs. Households with elderly members suffering from mental sickness should be trained to develop a comprehensive continuum of services to prevent unnecessary institutionalisation.

♦ Elderly persons with mental disorders are generally very sensitive. They need to be handled with care and dignity, and the services and facilities for their treatment and rehabilitation ought to be very safe and secure. When the patients are discharged from hospitals, they must be reintegrated into society through special psychosocial therapy programmes.

♦ The precise reasons for mental disorders among the elderly are still not known. Research on these disorders should be undertaken on a multidisciplinary basis to guide patients, health professionals and carergivers further.

♦ The NGOs in the health sector should promote public information vis-à-vis the symptoms, treatment, consequences and prognosis of mental diseases. The health system should provide ongoing training to health care professionals in the detection and assessment of all mental disorders.

DISABILITY

The incidence of impairment and disability increases with age. Women are particularly vulnerable to disability in old age due to gender differences in life expectancy and disease susceptibility, and gender inequalities suffered over a lifetime. The effects of impairment and disability are often exacerbated by negative labels about persons with disabilities. This often results in lowered expectations of their abilities and in social policies which do not allow such people to realise their full potential. Enabling interventions and environments supportive of all older persons are essential to promote independence and empower older persons with disabilities to participate fully in all aspects of society. The ageing of persons with cognitive disabilities is a factor that should be considered in planning and decision-making processes. Some of the specific programmes that may be tried are:

♦ Gender specific targets should accompany improvements in the health status of older people and the reduction of disabilities and premature mortality, so that the feminisation of the disabled elderly can be halted.

♦ It is necessary to create 'age-friendly' standards and environments that help prevent the onset or worsening of disabilities.

Some changes like improved roads, superior traffic management and transportation, and the promotion of barrier-free housing (introduced later in this chapter) both in private and public houses, can prevent injuries by protecting older pedestrians. Making walking safe, implementing fall prevention programmes, eliminating hazardous situations in the home and providing safety advice will all help. Implementation and reinforcement of national and international safety standards can also prevent injuries at all ages.

♦ Also important are rehabilitation services, effective assistive devices like corrective eyeglasses, cost-effective treatments that reduce disabilities (such as cataract removal and hip replacement therapy) and availability of essential safe medications to older people with low incomes.

♦ Employers are generally reluctant to employ people with disabilities. This reluctance is more if the disabled are aged too. Employers, therefore, need both education and motivation to employ older persons with disabilities who remain productive and capable of paid or volunteer work.

♦ Education and mass awareness also play an important role here. Community-based programmes should be organised to provide education on causes of disabilities and information on how to prevent or manage them through life. The establishment of self-help organisations of older persons with disabilities and their caregivers is very useful.

Financing of Health Care During Old Age

In view of the growing health care needs of the elderly and the accompanying financing problems, there is an emergent need for the spread of health insurance in the developing countries of Asia. Only this can provide a strong, effective demand for health care, which generates a ready source of revenue for service providers. Health insurance provides protection against the risk of medical expenses by allowing the insured to share that risk with other members of the group. At any time, insured individuals faced with adverse health and associated medical expenses will receive payment either directly or indirectly from a common financial pool. That financial pool is supported by all members of the group through taxes or premium contributions. Since all members contribute but few claim benefits, the pool remains financially solvent. Since contributors in the scheme claim the financial resources of the scheme in a more or less random fashion, the risk is spread over many individuals and is substantially lower than that faced by an individual in financial isolation.

However, neither a purely privatised health system relying on unfettered competition nor a purely public system is likely to generate optimal efficiency and equity. The private health insurance providers in the developing countries have so far not taken many initiatives in the health insurance business because of prevailing 'moral hazards'. Many people often make claims based on bills and documents which are illegitimately designed and prepared. So some systems need to be reworked where the existing problems can be tackled. To begin with the health insurance scheme can be made compulsory for all past and present formal sector employees where a premium structure could generate a cross-subsidy from them with a built-in cross-subsidy from the present to the past employees and from the young to the old. Once made successful, the scheme should be extended to all households under various programmes. The government could act as the facilitator and rule-maker to limit the inefficiencies of competition. It should keep the insuring public informed about competing health insurers and caregivers. If possible, the government should grade the various health care providers and health insurers using some transparent criteria, so that common people who lack 'perfect knowledge' about market conditions in the health sector are not deceived in the name of competition. To ensure equity in the provision of health care services, the government may look into the feasibility of cross-subsidy in favour of the poorer households. The private care providers may also be asked to follow a similar price structure. Among the Asian countries, Japan has a system of universal health insurance, while the Philippines is attempting to achieve universal health insurance coverage by 2010. In Thailand, 59 per cent of the population is currently covered by some type of health insurance.

ECONOMIC SUPPORT FOR GRACEFUL AGEING

Many older people in the developing countries of Asia do not have sufficient and regular sources of income. Industrialisation and labour market mobility is threatening much of the traditional work of older people, particularly in rural areas. The most defenceless are those with no assets, little or no savings, no pension or social security and families with low or uncertain incomes. While those without children or family members run the risk of homelessness and destitution, an uncertain income could have an adverse impact on the health and general well-being of the elderly. While younger people can hope to earn an income in the future and keep themselves functional, the poorly placed elderly have nothing to look forward to but despair. Studies have shown that physical capacities of older people with low incomes could be one-third of the physical strengths of those with high incomes.[14]

Ironically, older people in less developed countries are driven by necessity to continue to earn a living even after retirement, while in developed countries there is a tendency for the aged to seek early retirement. This trend is also evident in the formal sectors of the developing countries. In fact, there is said to be an inverse relationship between economic development and workers retiring at younger ages. In Asia too, the estimated median age of retirement for men has been declining over time. Early retirement is often caused by personal factors: accumulation of enough personal wealth to last through old age; and, ill health. An economic downturn in the economy and a decrease in the mandatory retirement age also causes elderly people to lose their jobs. Studies in many developed countries show that expanding pension and social security programmes tend to encourage early retirement. Private companies in Asia have also encouraged older workers to retire early through several compensation packages.

There is an increasing recognition of the need to support the active and productive contributions of older people through paid, unpaid and voluntary work. The ground reality today is that people are being forced to retire early through lowered mandatory retirement ages, the objective being to create more jobs for younger people. The aged, however, suffer a lower standard of living during their retirement years because of this policy of early retirement. Experience has shown that the use of early retirement to create jobs for the unemployed has not been an effective solution.[15] Economic development also declines because of the loss of human capital through early retirement. Retirement ages were generally based on health status and life expectancy at the time when they were initially fixed. Many countries have improved their health status since, but there has not been any corresponding upward revision in the retirement ages. Many countries still have lower retirement ages for women despite the fact that women generally live longer than men and may spend more years in old age without employment or a spouse to provide them with financial support.

Although global attention has recently focused more on poverty eradication targets and policies, older persons in many countries still tend to be excluded from these policies and programmes. Where poverty is endemic, persons who survive a lifetime of poverty often face an old age of deepening poverty. For women, institutional biases in social protection systems, in particular those based on uninterrupted work histories, contribute further to the feminisation of poverty. Gender inequalities and disparities in economic power sharing, unequal distribution of unremunerated work between women and men, lack of technological and financial support for women's entrepreneurship, unequal access to, and control over capital, particularly land and credit and access to labour markets, as well as all harmful traditional and customary practices have constrained women's economic empowerment and exacerbated the feminisation of poverty. In many societies, female-headed households, including divorced or separated, unmarried women and widows are at particular risk of poverty.

Thus, graceful ageing policies must intersect with the poverty eradication and employment protection policies for the elderly. Older persons should be enabled to continue with income generating work for as long as they want, and for as long as they are able to do so productively. There is a need to increase awareness in the workplace of the benefits of maintaining an ageing workforce. To do this, employment opportunities must be raised. The policy makers must place employment growth at the heart of macroeconomic policies, by ensuring that labour market policies do not hinder high rates of growth in production and employment, for the benefit of persons of all ages. Given here are the aspects that should be considered in existing and new policies:

♦ Policies must allow older persons to continue working for as long as they want to and are able to do so. This may require either an increase in the mandatory retirement age or the elimination of such a system. It may also be necessary to abolish the rigid seniority-based wage system. Such flexible employment options will automatically make the elderly more attractive in the job market. The policies must also promote a realistic portrait of older workers' skills and abilities by correcting damaging stereotypes about older workers or job candidates. Also important is the removal of disincentives to working beyond the retirement age by ensuring that acquired pension rights, disability benefit rights and health benefits are not effected by delayed retirement age.

◆ All the incentives to retire early must be withdrawn. With early retirement more resources are spent in supporting the extended period of retirement. The introduction of a sliding pension scale, whereby those who retire early receive lower monthly benefits than those who retire late, may be useful.

◆ Elderly workers should be retrained in the use of modern technology. This will allow older men and women to learn new skills and take up new occupations, and cope with technological changes in the workplace.

◆ Self-employment initiatives among older persons should be promoted, by encouraging small and micro-enterprise development and ensuring access to credit for older persons, without any discrimination, particularly gender discrimination.

◆ Older persons already engaged in informal sector activities should be given assistance by improving their income, productivity and working conditions.

◆ New work arrangements and innovative workplace practices aimed at sustaining working capacity and accommodating the needs of workers as they age through employee assistance programmes should be promoted. Older workers could be allowed to work from home, unless their presence at the workplace is essential for technological reasons. What is necessary is the productivity and not the adherence to old-fashioned regulations.

◆ Special social protection measures are required to address the feminisation of poverty, in particular among older women. Older persons with disabilities are also at greater risk of poverty than others. If old age pension programmes cannot be initiated for all, nations should atleast not delay the planning of old age pension programmes for poor widows and disabled older men and women. This may require huge sums of money and most developing nations of Asia would not have the required resources. The state could, thus, develop a special fund for poverty eradication among the underprivileged through tax free donations from business houses, individuals and NGOs. International cooperation from multilateral agencies and developed nations could also be sought. NGOs and business houses could be encouraged to establish elderly villages in each district of the country so as to gainfully accommodate the elderly destitute, both men and women.

SOCIAL SECURITY AND PENSION POLICIES

In the developing countries of Asia, families still provide the majority of support to older people. In addition, the elderly also have some informal service transfers and personal savings to bank upon during old age, however, this support is usually inadequate. Social insurance programmes are minimal. To complicate the matter further, the practice of co-residency among several generations is declining. In such a situation, there is a crying need for mechanisms that can provide social protection to older people who are unable to earn a living and are alone and vulnerable. The government and civil society will have to develop and implement policies aimed at ensuring that all persons have adequate economic and social protection during old age. The women and others engaged in the informal sector deserve more serious attention. It may also be necessary to introduce programmes to promote employment of low-skilled older workers.

As mentioned earlier, while Japan, Singapore and Malaysia have large-scale programmes with close to universal coverage, in most countries this coverage is restricted to narrow population groups. The state expenditure on social security is also very low in most countries of Asia. Where most European countries spend over 30 to 40 per cent of their budgets on social security, the proportion is only 1or 2 per cent of public expenditure in most of the developing countries of Asia. This proportion is only 8 per cent for the economically advanced South Korea. Publicly funded pension programmes offer two important advantages. First, they provide an economic safety net for those elderly who might otherwise experience severe economic difficulty. Second, in the absence of public programmes, people will need to save, and in an imperfect capital market there are high risks associated with the return on such savings. When they save, market demand falls and this reduces the growth potential of the economy. Third, the disabled, sick, unskilled and other economically vulnerable sections of society will have very little saving to bank upon in the future. Fourth, public social security programmes take care of cases of unusual longevity experienced by some people who may not be able to then adjust this with their lifetime savings.

Public social security programmes entail their own set of risks too. The first is the most obvious, the fiscal cost. Most developing countries of Asia do not have resources to fund universal public pension schemes. Second, providing wide coverage may entail enormous administrative hurdles. It is extremely difficult to collect pension payments in sectors where there are large numbers of agricultural, self-employed, casual, domestic and informal-sector workers and where labour turnover is high and documentation weak.[16] Third, huge access to large pension reserves often tempts the government to use the money for 'politically viable' but economically unwise investments or pursue large-scale public infrastructure projects without adequate scrutiny of potential risk and return.[17] Fourth, there is also a possibility that an increase in public transfers will result in a reduction of private transfers, leaving the recipient only slightly better off. Fifth, there is some evidence that public funded benefits may lead to a reduction in labour supply or savings. Sixth, public pension programmes that are not carefully designed will prove to be unsustainable as the numbers of the elderly increase relative to the working-age (and tax paying) population. Finally, if the social assistance benefits are high and relative to those paid through the basic pension, there will be little incentive to participate in the latter programme.

With the cost of public funded pension schemes rising over and above the expected benefits, governments will have to have newer ideas on pension reforms. It is apprehended that a country like Japan may not be able to continue its existing pension schemes. In India, between 1995 and 2000, the central government pension bill alone almost doubled as a share of national income. In the fiscal year 2000–01, it consumed more than 15 per cent of the central government's tax revenues. The increase in pension expenditure on provincial civil servants is even more dramatic. In present value terms, the 'pension debt' has now reached almost one-third of the Gross Domestic Product (GDP). It is time to recognise that some dependence on the market is necessary to make the pension scheme viable. In this regard, the suggestion of the Old Age Social and Income Security (OASIS) project in India is innovative and deserves scrutiny. The primary goal of the initiative was to promote voluntary participation of the vast informal sector in a cost-effective private pension system. The crux of the OASIS proposal is to establish a system based on privately managed, individual accounts with low costs and widespread accessibility. The scheme proposes to rely on a limited number of private asset managers each offering three investment portfolio options to individual savers. The three options range from a more conservative portfolio with greater weightage to government bonds, to a more aggressive, equity-based portfolio. The scheme proposes to select managers for the fund through a competitive bidding process. Low administrative costs would be one of the criterions for the selection of managers. The government would facilitate access to the system through its network to keep costs at a minimum. A new entity, the Indian Pensions Authority would be created and would select the asset managers.

However, whatever be the form of the pension structure, the government would have to ensure the integrity, sustainability, solvency and transparency of the pension scheme, so that the elderly would not have to suffer in their old age. It should take measures to counteract the effects of hyperinflation on pension and take into account the living standards of older persons. The government could establish a regulatory framework for private and supplementary pension. The government and civil society could also provide advice and counselling services for older persons with regard to social protection/social security.

Till such time a suitable pension scheme is not achieved, people will have to reduce their current consumption patterns to save for their future. Policy makers have with them several options to encourage workers to save towards retirement. One priority is to ensure that the nation's financial institutions provide attractive and secure long-term investment opportunities. The second is to control the rate of inflation so that money saved today will retain its value in the future. The third is to provide tax incentives for pension related savings.

PHYSICAL ENVIRONMENT FOR GRACEFUL AGEING

The physical environments in which the elderly live should not be inimical to their life sustenance, self-esteem and freedom. If their mobility is restricted both inside and outside their home, if they are denied fresh air to breathe and if they are isolated from their friends and relatives, ageing cannot be graceful. Safe and adequate housing is therefore very important for the well-being of older adults. The elderly who live in unsafe or polluted areas are less likely to move around and therefore more prone to isolation and depression which would reduce their fitness. This in turn would increase society's expenditure on health care and support for these elderly. Even inappropriate housing which constrains movement can be detrimental to the well-being of the elderly. For the elderly in the rural areas, who are deprived from most basic facilities of life and subject to more diseases, a hazardous physical environment could lead to incapacitating and painful injuries among the aged. Injuries from falls, fires and traffic accidents are the most common. Injuries resulting from road accidents tend to be higher for elderly age groups than any other age groups.[18] The consequences of injuries sustained in older ages are more critical than among younger people. Older people experience more disability, longer hospital stays, extended periods of rehabilitation, a higher risk of dying and a higher risk of subsequent dependency. Often, in medical emergencies, it is difficult to rescue older people, particularly females. Even if they are rescued, finding shelter and food is difficult, especially for older widows. It thus becomes imperative for the community and the government to ensure that the physical environment is free from such obstacles, to allow the elderly to age gracefully.

This is definitely a difficult task given the huge responsibilities and resource obligations, however, if the policy makers are sensitive to some of these suggestions, the difficulties of the current cohort of elderly could be eased and the future elderly can hope for an environment tailored to suit their needs.

Housing

Safe and satisfactory living accommodation and amenable physical surroundings are vital for the well-being of human beings, and there is no doubt that housing affects the quality of life of any age group in any country. Suitable housing is even more important for the elderly, for whom a majority of activities revolve around the four walls of their homes. In addition, close proximity to family members, services and support helps provide the elderly with positive social interaction and freedom from isolation. However, in the developing countries of Asia, rapid demographic ageing is taking place in the context of continuing urbanisation, and a growing number of the aged in urban areas now lack affordable housing and services. At the same time, a large number of people are also ageing in isolation in the rural areas, rather than in the traditional environment of an extended family. Left alone, these people are often without any adequate transportation or support system. Today, housing developments are typically designed to meet the requirements of young people who apart from being physically fit can also use the regular transport system.

Despite all this, many older persons continue to live in houses that they are unable to maintain even after their children have moved out or after the death of a spouse. Worldwide, there is an increasing trend for older people to live alone. Older women are often poorer, and may be forced to live in shelters that are inadequate and unsafe. In many developing countries, the proportion of the elderly living in slums and shanty towns is rising rapidly due to the paucity of resources and over-urbanisation of many cities. Older people living in these settlements run a high risk of social isolation and ill health.

Improvisations to the home, the provision of practical domestic aids to enable daily living and appropriately designed household equipment can make life easier for those elderly people whose mobility is restricted or who are otherwise disabled. It is also important that older persons are provided, wherever possible, with the freedom to choose where they live, a factor that needs to be built into elderly policies and programmes. All these are contingent upon the development of age-integrated communities which are able to coordinate multi-sectoral efforts to support the continued integration of older persons with their families and communities and encourage investment in local infrastructure, such as transportation, health, sanitation and security, designed to support multigenerational communities. Listed here are some crucial requirements of the elderly that need to be addressed in elderly programmes and policies:

♦ The need for safe, usable, affordable and accessible public housing for older persons. The government could plan models of elderly housing projects in each district, linking affordable housing with social support services to ensure the integration of living arrangements, long-term care and opportunities for social interaction. The houses could be rented or sold only to aged people. In the event of the death of an elderly person, ownership or tenancy ought to be automatically transferred to the spouse but in no case would it be transferred to children who are earning. In case of a crisis, the government could buy back the house at an appropriate rate with due compensation to the owner or his/her legal inheritor.

♦ The need for timely and effective information and advice on housing options for older persons, their families and caregivers.

♦ All public buildings and spaces must be made accessible to the elderly and the disabled.

♦ Promotion of barrier-free housing, based on improvements in housing and environmental design to promote independent living by taking into account the needs of older persons, particularly those with disabilities. Barrier-free housing meets the need for shared and multigenerational co-residence through special design of housing and public space. It is also much safer and more inhabitable for longer periods of time for very old persons living without younger family members. Research indicates that such appropriate houses for older people can be made with the simplest and most readily available raw materials and with no great technological input. 'Old fashioned' materials, such as wood, mud, tile and thatch could be as effective as contemporary materials. While use of materials would depend on climate, geology, supply routes and other variables, the general recommendations are as follows:

♦ Avoid double storey buildings, and avoid steps and stairs, but, if different levels are unavoidable, use gentle ramps.
♦ Storage space that is frequently used should be at heights between 2' and 6' (60 and 180 cm.).
♦ Avoid low-down storage in kitchens; after the age of 60 people may no longer be able to bend easily.
♦ Make arrangements for strong handles where stooping is unavoidable (e.g., latrines).
♦ Fix strong handles to walls near beds and seats.
♦ Avoid slippery or shiny floors and use non-slip surfaces leading to ramps and kitchens.
♦ Make doors wide enough for two people to pass through side by side.
♦ Ensure wheelchair width for bathroom and toilet doors.
♦ The housing plan should ensure good lighting, both natural and artificial.
♦ Have built-in furniture, that would ensure more space in the house and facilitate the movement of wheel chairs.
♦ For economy purposes, simple colour wash on exposed unplastered brick walls can be made pleasant with the addition of pictures and flowers.
♦ All locks, fasteners, plugs and latches must be within reach for a person who can no longer bend.
♦ For security reasons good locks on doors and windows, and also peepholes on doors are essential.

The government should encourage such age-friendly and accessible barrier-free housing designs through easy loans. Existing housing may also be altered on the basis of these guidelines.

The government should encourage the promotion of old age homes for the destitute and frail elderly as such homes will help reduce hospital occupancy rates. Many developed countries have established supportive housing for single older people. Such housing accommodates single, frail elderly with some support services without nursing care. Studies have shown that the use of supportive housing is a cost-effective alternative to inappropriate nursing home placements.[19]

Transportation

The elderly encounter manifold problems vis-à-vis traffic and transport. Their movements are restricted by the several dangers present on roads today. Transportation is all the more problematic in rural areas. Roads are often inaccessable, and public transport few and far in between. The concept of graceful ageing requires that the rules governing traffic be adapted to suit older people. This can be done through the regular spread of traffic education, traffic governance, maintenance of street lamps and traffic signals at all crossings, imposition of speed limits near human settlements, discarding of old traffic-unsafe vehicles, special buses for the elderly and the disabled etc. The following may also be useful:

♦ Increasing the availability of efficient public transportation services in rural and urban areas.
♦ Facilitating the growth of both public and private alternative forms of transport in urban areas, such as neighbourhood-based businesses and services.
♦ Encouraging the training and assessment of older drivers, the design of safer roadways and the development of new kinds of vehicles that cater to the needs of older persons and persons with disabilities.

SUPPORT FOR RURAL ELDERLY

As we have seen in earlier chapters, most of the ageing population lives in rural than urban areas of most developing countries of Asia. In fact, 60 per cent of the world's elderly stay in rural areas. Owing to the exodus of young adults to urban areas for education and jobs, the older people are often left behind without traditional family support and at times even without adequate financial resources. Other support services are often few if not negligible for most of the elderly in rural areas. The rural aged are also unable to support themselves since they lack the physical strength to continue agriculture work. Older women in rural areas are worse hit since their roles are restricted to non-remunerative work and they are dependent on others for their support and survival. Rural areas also have different disease patterns than urban areas, with more incidences of malaria, snake bites, and water-borne diseases. Policies and programmes for food security and agricultural production must therefore take into account the implications of rural ageing. Older farmers need support in the form of access to credit schemes and training in new techniques of farming to ensure that their livelihoods and food production remains viable.

Graceful ageing in rural areas is contingent upon improving the living conditions and infrastructure in rural areas. This requires a comprehensive strategy of rural development including a shift in the urban bias towards developmental efforts. Some specific measures that can ameliorate the unsatisfactory conditions of the rural elderly are:

♦ The development of local financial services including microcredit schemes and microfinance institutions in under-served rural areas to encourage investment in agriculture and small-scale industry. Many of the elderly return from urban areas with their retirement funds and urban skills. It would be useful if these resources could be used for furthering gains in rural areas.

♦ Many of the rural elderly need adult education, training and retraining, both on improved farming techniques and technologies, as well as on agro-based small-scale industries.

♦ With very limited economic opportunities in rural areas, the government must develop some workable system of social protection and social security measures for older persons in rural and remote areas. With more deprivation among elderly women, the government must ensure that their economic needs are given prior consideration along with those of the destitute and disabled elderly.

♦ Most Asian villages, though weak in financial and technological resources, abound in traditional rural and community support mechanisms. Such mechanisms should be facilitated and strengthened for the mutual benefit of different generations. The elderly have the knowledge and experience and enough free time to support the functioning of local village governments. To allow elderly participation in village-level local self-governments, seats should be reserved for them.

SUPPORT FOR THE MIGRANT ELDERLY

Just as the rural elderly are deprived of basic support systems, many of the elderly who migrate to urban areas to join their sons and relatives often experience similar problems. They may not have prior experience of living in small urban shanties and slums. They may find the urban lifestyle, culture, and language alien to them. It is there-fore necessary to integrate such older migrants into the communities around them through supportive social networks including economic and health security. The Action Plan for Ageing recommends the following actions:

♦ Develop community-based measures, to prevent or offset the negative consequences of urbanisation, such as establishment of centres for older persons.
♦ Encourage housing design that promotes intergenerational living, wherever culturally appropriate and desired.
♦ Assist families to share accommodation with older family members who desire it.
♦ Develop policies and programmes that facilitate, as appropriate and consistent with national laws, the integration of older migrants into the social, cultural, political and economic life of countries of destination (and) that encourage respect for them.
♦ Remove language and cultural barriers when providing public services to older migrants.

EMERGENCY SITUATIONS

In emergency situations, such as natural disasters, armed conflict and foreign occupation, and other emergencies, older people are highly vulnerable. They may be immobile because of chronic diseases or disability and therefore cannot save themselves from manmade or natural disasters. Even in the event that they are rescued by others, they may still be isolated from their family and friends and thus unable to find food, shelter and health care. Governments and humanitarian relief agencies should recognise that while older persons need special attention during such catastrophes, they can also make a positive contribution in emergencies as caregivers and by helping in rehabilitation and reconstruction activities. Some of the specific measures that need to be taken in an emergency situation include the following:

♦ Older persons in situations of internal displacement should be assisted in accordance with established international norms. This may require information about their location and identity in emergency situations and inclusion of their potential and peculiarities in needs assessment reports to plan rescue and relief operations more effectively. The relief agency personnel must be trained in physical and health issues specific to older persons and of ways to adapt to the requirements of the elderly. These agencies should assist older persons to re-establish family and social ties, and address their post-traumatic stress. It may also be necessary for them to prevent financial exploitation of older persons by frauds masquerading as relief staff. The older refugees from different cultural backgrounds who grow old in new and unfamiliar surroundings are often in special need of social networks and extra support. The government must ensure that such people have physical access to these services.

♦ Many older persons have some skills and expertise in different fields. For example, many elderly women can cook or take care of children in relief camps, while elderly men can take effective part in education, communication and conflict resolution. Such individual skills should be properly assessed and the aged should be made active partners wherever possible.

♦ Older persons need assistance to re-establish economic self-sufficiency. This can be achieved through rehabilitation projects, including income generation, educational programmes and occupational activities, taking into account the special needs of older women. Many of them would require legal advice and information to recover their land and other productive and personal assets.

♦ Equally important is the enhancement of international cooperation to countries affected by natural disasters, other emergencies and post-conflict situations in ways that would be supportive of recovery and long-term development.

SOCIAL SETTING FOR GRACEFUL AGEING

Through a peaceful resolution to the growing tensions between generations, by creating opportunities for education and lifelong learning, by ensuring protection from violence and abuse, and by creating a supportive environment that ensures honourable death in old age, the state can prepare a social milieu that is necessary to enhance health, independence and productivity among older ages. Exposure to intergenerational tensions, illiteracy and lack of education, elder abuse, and the prolonged wait for peace from the excruciating pain of a terminal disease in old age greatly increases the risks, tensions and indignity of elderly life.

Peaceful Resolution to Intergenerational Tensions

Solidarity between generations is fundamental for the achievement of a society with room for all ages. Solidarity is also a major prerequisite for social cohesion and the foundation for a formal public welfare and informal care system. At the family and community level, intergenerational ties can be valuable for everyone. To appreciate its importance, Simon de Beauvoir[20] cites the case of a farmer who could not accommodate his frail father at the dining table. Sent to the barn, the old man eats his meal out of a trough. One day the man finds his own son playing in the barnyard with some wood. When asked what he was doing, the boy replied, 'Oh father, I am building a trough for you to eat when you get old, like grandfather.' That evening the old man was brought back at the dining table. The implication here is that there may be a very high price to pay if efforts are not made to strengthen intergenerational ties. After all, when we look at the aged and gear specific policies toward them, we are looking at our future selves. To quote Moody, 'we need to take the whole life cycle into account in thinking about justice across generations'.[21] Despite geographic mobility and other pressures of contemporary life that can keep people apart, a great majority of people in all cultures maintain close relations with their families throughout their lives. These relationships work in both directions, with the elderly often making significant contributions, both financially and, crucially, in the education and care of grandchildren and other kin. All sectors of society, including governments, should aim to strengthen these ties. Nevertheless, it is important to recognise that living with younger generations is not always the preferred or best option for older persons.

To strengthen the solidarity between generations through equity and reciprocity, some explicit measures need to be taken. They are:

♦ The young generation should be taught about ageing through public education. They should be taught to approach ageing as an issue of concern for the entire society. It may also be necessary to provide intergenerational activities in schools to teach young people about graceful ageing. Intergenerational learning bridges the gap between generations, enhances the transmission of cultural values and promotes the worth of all ages. Studies have shown that young people who learn with older people have a more positive and realistic attitude towards the older generation.

♦ Policy makers will have to work hard to foster intergenerational solidarity and promote social cohesion. Unnecessary policy biases towards the older generations should be avoided. Initiatives must be developed to promote mutual, productive exchanges between generations. Focusing on older persons as a societal resource is a key element for social development.

♦ In local communities, efforts should be on to maximise opportunities for maintaining and improving intergenerational relations, by facilitating meetings for all age groups and avoiding generational segregation.

♦ It is equally important to have more information on the advantages and disadvantages of different living arrangements for older persons, including familial co-residence and independent living in different cultures and settings. Also important is to study the problems of caregivers who are overburdened with the responsibilities of parenting their own children as also their grandchildren.

Education and Literacy

Education is crucial for an active and fulfiling life. All over Asia, striking disparities in literacy rates between men and women, between the young and the old continue to exist. As stated earlier, in India and in many other countries of Asia, older women and men make up a large proportion of the illiterate and those with lower levels of education. Low levels of education and illiteracy are associated with low productivity and unemployment which increase the risk of disease, disability and death among older people. Education in early life combined with opportunities for lifelong learning can give older people the cognitive skills and awareness they need to adapt and stay independent. Employment problems of older workers are often more rooted in their relatively low literacy skills than in their ages. If older adults are to remain engaged in meaningful and productive activities, there is a need to encourage continuous training in the workplace and lifelong learning opportunities in the community. Like younger people, older citizens also need to be trained in new technologies, in agriculture, small-scale industries and electronic communication. Studies have shown that through self-directed learning, increased practice and physical adjustments, aged people can compensate for visual acuity, hearing and short-term memory and remain creative and flexible. With their experience, wisdom and self-discipline, they can, in fact, be more productive than many others.

However, the following must be considered while making adult literacy policies and programmes:

♦ It is very important that the government sets targets for improvement in the levels of adult literacy for the next 10 years and works hard to attain these targets through equitable access to basic and continuing education for all adults, especially for women. The elderly would also need numerical and technological skills, including computer training to live independently, productively and happily. In these areas, policy makers should fully utilise the potential and expertise of older persons and encourage older volunteers to offer their skills.

♦ Policy makers would need to ensure that the benefits of new technologies, especially information and communication technologies are available to all, taking into account the needs of older women. It may be necessary to raise the awareness of employers' and workers' organisations vis-à-vis the value of retraining older workers, particularly women.

♦ Policy makers and educational experts would have to develop and disseminate user-friendly information to assist older persons so that they are able to respond effectively to the technological demands of everyday life. They should encourage the design of computer technology and print and audio materials that take account of the changes in the physical abilities and visual capacities of older persons. Also important is further research to better determine the relationship between training and productivity so as to clearly demonstrate to both employers and employees the benefits of continuous training and education of older persons.

♦ Last but not the least, opportunities should be created within educational programmes for the exchange of knowledge and experience between generations, including the use of new technologies. Older persons should act as mentors, mediators and advisors in such programmes. Also important here is the promotion of traditional and non-traditional multigenerational, mutual assistance activities in the family, the neighbourhood and the community with a clear gender perspective.

Neglect, Abuse and Violence

Older people are increasingly running the risk of neglect, abuse and violence, both in times of war and peace. In times of violence, the elderly are often easy targets as they are usually the custodians of family wealth and personal wealth and are unable to resist or fight hooligans. In peace time too, older people who are frail or live alone may be particularly vulnerable to theft, assault and robbery. However, the most common form of violence against older people is 'elder abuse' committed by caregivers within or outside the family. The incidences of 'granny battering' are showing an overwhelming increase. According to the International Network for the Prevention of Elder Abuse, elder abuse is 'a single or repeated act, or lack of appropriate action occurring within any relationship where there is an expectation of trust which causes harm or distress to an older person.' It includes physical, sexual, psychological and financial abuse, as well as neglect, and occurs in families at all economic levels. It is likely to escalate in societies experiencing economic upheaval and social disorganisation, a period when overall crime and exploitation tends to increase. It is a violation of human rights and a significant cause of injury, illness, lost productivity, isolation and despair. However, elder abuse is particularly under-reported in all cultures because of shame and fear.

The process of ageing brings with it a decline in the ability to heal. The aged who are the victims of abuse are often not able to fully recover, physically or emotionally, from the trauma suffered. The impact of the trauma is worsened as they are unable to tell others about the incidents for fear of the act being repeated more violently.

Older women face a greater risk of physical and psychological abuse due to discriminatory societal attitudes. Some harmful traditional and customary practices result in abuse and violence directed at older women, often exacerbated by poverty and lack of access to legal protection. Women are also subject to sexual exploitation.

Domestic and societal violence and abuse against older people is a matter of justice, and communities must work together to prevent such abuse, consumer fraud and crimes against older persons. Confronting and reducing this violence requires a multicultural, multidisciplinary approach involving all sections of the community. Sustained efforts to increase public awareness of the problem and to shift values that perpetuate gender inequities and ageist attitudes are also required. Some measures that may help ease the crisis are suggested below:

♦ All elder abuse, whether physical, psychological or financial, and/or the neglect of elders should be recognised as major crimes, and the offenders and perpetrators of these heinous activities must be prosecuted within the quickest possible time frame. The laws should fix the time limit within which such trials must end. Prolonged trials seldom benefit the aged.

♦ It may be necessary to train the police, health and social service providers, spiritual leaders, advocacy organisations and groups of older people in how to tackle the problems of elder abuse effectively. The government should encourage cooperation between the government and civil society, including NGOs, in addressing elder abuse by developing community initiatives. Establishment of services for victims of abuse and rehabilitation arrangements for abusers should be a part of such initiatives. Health and social service professionals as well as the general public should be asked to report suspected elder abuse.

♦ Also important are the laws that can protect widows from the theft of property and other possessions and from charges of witchcraft. If possible, widowhood rites that are harmful to the health and well-being of women should be abolished, even if they are against religious practices.

♦ Harmful traditional practices involving older persons should be banned.

♦ The government and civil society should strive to educate the general public on elder abuse, its various characteristics and causes using media and other awareness-raising campaigns. Common people and the elderly should also be educated about the safeguards under the law against consumer fraud and all other elder abuses.

♦ The government and civil society should promote further research into the causes, nature, extent, seriousness and consequences of all forms of violence against older women and men, and widely disseminate findings of the research and studies.

Right to Honourable Death

Anthony Trollope in his novel, *The Fixed Period*, talks about a fictitious island in which all citizens aged 67 or older are deposited in a place called 'necropolis' by the younger members. Here they are required to spend one year in deep thought and peaceful reflection before being chloroformed and cremated. This is intended to avoid the imbecility and weakness of human life when taken beyond its fitting limits and to dignify death with honour and glory. While there may be several debates over how to accomplish this, there is no doubt that everyone must have the right to die peacefully and honourably. The old elderly who are living with painful terminal diseases are often kept technically alive using modern medicine and technology with no resulting increase in the quality of care. Many patients do not wish to live in an artificially sustained environment, either through ventilators or even heart-lung machines. Not only does the family and society bear a huge cost in such cases, but the patients also suffer tremendously. There is a need to question how long this process of living with a terminal illness can continue. Just because medical science can do something does not make such a condition ethical or desirable. Neither the law nor medical ethics requires that 'everything be done' to keep a person alive. Insistence, against the patient's wishes, that death be postponed by every means available is contrary to law and practice. It is also cruel and inhumane.

In this context, *The Fixed Period* shows us a peaceful way out. The right to honourable death must be recognised under law. Countries may think in terms of euthanasia and assisted suicide for the 'too old elderly' suffering from terminal disease, but the laws must ensure that this process is voluntary and that the elderly patient, the family, the doctors and the state concur to this form of death, without being biased at any stage.

The Netherlands, Belgium and the state of Oregon in the United States, permit euthanasia or assisted suicide by the elderly suffering from painful terminal diseases. Oregon permits assisted suicide.[22] The Netherlands and Belgium permit both euthanasia and assisted suicide.[23] In 1995, Australia's Northern Territory approved a euthanasia bill.[24] It went into effect in 1996 but was overturned by the Australian parliament in 1997. In 1997, Colombia's Supreme Court ruled that penalties for mercy killing should be removed.[25] However the ruling does not go into effect until guidelines, still to be drafted, are approved by the Colombian Congress. In the Hesse state of Germany, mercy killing is allowed for coma patients when approved by a guardianship court.[26]

However, the use of euthanasia and assisted suicide in these few places have given rise to many misgivings about the law. It is felt that too much power then lies with doctors and often the assisted suicide/euthanasia is anything but voluntary. The British House of Lords recently recommended no change to the law on euthanasia after an extensive enquiry. It is worth quoting from the debates in the House of Lords:

We concluded that it was virtually impossible to ensure that all acts of euthanasia were truly voluntary and that any liberalisation of the law in the United Kingdom could not be abused. We were also concerned that vulnerable people—the elderly, lonely, sick or distressed—would feel pressure, whether real or imagined, to request early death.[27]

In fact, there exists a middle path, that of creative and compassionate caring. Meticulous research in palliative medicine has in recent years shown that virtually all unpleasant symptoms experienced in the process of terminal illness can be either relieved or substantially alleviated by techniques already available. This method has found practical expression in the hospice movement, which has enabled patients' symptoms to be managed either at home or in the context of a caring in-patient facility. Hospice care is the appropriate solution to reducing the acute care treatment of dying patients. Hospice care is appropriate for relieving symptoms in the terminally ill, because the patient's disease is truly not curable and further curative treatment is futile (not effective) and likely to result in further distress to the patient.

However, whatever may be the mode of treatment, the task of policy makers is to ensure that all people have a right to an honourable death, with due respect to their cultural values. Policy makers, thus, must endorse policies which enable people to choose, whenever possible, where they want to die and the people they want around them, as free from distress and pain as possible.

International Cooperation

The ageing of the population is a global phenomenon that demands international cooperation to settle many of the issues that an individual country by itself cannot accomplish. The developing countries of Asia are overwhelmingly troubled by the lack of resources, ideas and their implementation. In an increasingly connected world, failure to deal with rapid ageing and its implications in a rational way, in any part of the world, has socio-economic and political consequences everywhere. Unless the benefits of globalisation are extended to all countries, a growing number of people will remain marginalised. Globalisation should be fully inclusive and equitable, and there is a strong need for international support to the developing countries to help them respond effectively to those challenges and opportunities.

International agencies must come forward to end poverty in the world as a first step towards globalisation. Huge resources are wasted in the name of global security. Conservative estimates suggest that if only 5 per cent of the money spent on such activities be curtailed and diverted towards poverty reduction, the world would be more secure than before. The amount of food that developed countries destroy to maintain the 'remunerative price,' if retained, could have ended international poverty. With more food intake, the productivity of countries suffering from poverty would increase and they in turn would have a higher purchasing power to absorb products from developed countries. If another 5 per cent of the defence budgets could be curtailed and money channelised into the developing nations, the much needed resources to initiate and maintain social security and health insurance for the marginalised sections of the elderly population could be procured. Most developing nations today are undergoing structural economic reforms under pressure from developed nations and multilateral agencies. When such pressure evidently works, why not pressurise them further to reduce social and economic inequality through pragmatic programmes? Studies confirm that reduction in inequality can raise effective demand and ease the other pressures of life. Also important is an international consensus for a speedy, comprehensive, equitable and concerted effort to solve the debt problems of developing countries.

To ensure graceful ageing, some of the specific ways in which international cooperation may be needed are as follows:

♦ International financial institutions and development banks should recognise older persons as development resources, and their lending and grants practices to the developing countries should be a part of that recognition.
♦ Efforts should be on to mobilise funds from the United Nations sources for the development and implementation of programmes for the integration of the aged into society.
♦ Support from the international community and international development agencies for organisations that specifically promote training and capacity building on ageing in developing countries is extremely important.
♦ There is a need to encourage and promote comprehensive, diversified and specialised research on ageing in all countries, particularly in developing countries. Also important is the evolution of a satisfactory system of exchange of such findings.

CONCLUSION

It is not an easy task to develop and implement effective strategies that foster graceful ageing. It also may not be possible to secure all the conditions necessary for graceful ageing at a given time. Any such strategy must acknowledge the uncertainty surrounding both demographic and economic trends. Capacities for implementing programmes also vary widely and political considerations may rule out otherwise attractive options. Despite these difficulties, the civil society and the government must work concertedly to evolve a situation where ageing is really recognised and identified as a 'triumph of civilisation'.

NOTES AND REFERENCES

1. International Plan of Action on Ageing, Vienna, can be accessed at http://www. un.org/esa/socdev/ageing/ageipaa.htm
2. Three core principles of economic development suggested by Denis Goulet.

3. U.S. Centers for Disease Control and WHO, Report from a Workshop on the Economic Benefits of Physical Activity/Burden of Physical Inactivity, Asheville, North Carolina, 1999.

4. B. Singer and K. Manton, *The Effects of Health Changes on Projections of Health Service needs for the Elderly Population of the United States*, Proceedings of the National Academy of Sciences, 23: 321–35, 1998.

5. C.N. Merz and J.S. Forrester, 'The Secondary Prevention of Coronary Heart Disease,' *American Journal of Medicine*, 102: 573–80, 1997.

6. U.S. Preventive Services Task Force, *Guide to Clinical Preventive Services*, Williams and Wilkins, Baltimore, 1996.

7. R.L. Heikkinen, *Growing Older. Staying Well. Ageing and Physical Activity in Everyday Life*, World Health Organization, Geneva, 1988.

8. World Bank, *Curbing the Epidemic: Governments and the Economics of Tobacco Control*, World Bank, Washington, 1999.

9. D.H. Jernigan, M. Monteiro, R. Room and S. Saxena, 'Towards a Global Alcohol Policy: Alcohol, Public Health and the Role of WHO,' *Bulletin of the World Health Organization*, 78(4), 2000.

10. J.H. Gurwitz and J. Avorn 'The Ambiguous Relationship between Ageing and Adverse Drug Reactions,' *Annals of Internal Medicine*, 114(11): 956–66, 1991.

11. Ronald Lee, Andrew Mason and Tim Miller, 'From Transfers to Individual Responsibility: Implications for Saving and Capital Accumulation in Taiwan and the United States,' Paper presented at the annual meeting of the Population Association of America, San Diego, California, 2000.

12. World Health Organization (WHO), *Home Based and Long-term Care, Home Care Issues and Evidence*, World Health Organisation, Geneva,1999.

13. Palliative care is active, total care of patients whose disease is not responsive to curative treatment. This is done by controlling pain and other symptoms of the disease and offering psychological, social and spiritual support to patients and their families.

14. J.M. Guralnick and G. Kaplan, 'Predictors of Healthy Ageing: Prospective Evidence from the Almeda County Study,' *American Journal of Public Health*, 79: 703–8, 1989.

15. Organisation for Economic Cooperation and Development (OECD), *Maintaining Prosperity in an Ageing Society*, OECD, Paris, 1998.

16. Clive Bailey, '*Coverage under Social Security Pension Schemes*,' Paper prepared for Tripartite Regional Consultation with Asian countries, Bangkok, International Labor Office (ILO), Social Security Department, Geneva, 1997.

17. World Bank, *Averting the Old Age Crisis*, World Bank, Washington, D.C. 1994.

18. J.M. Lilley, Arie T. Chilvers, 'Accidents involving Older People: A Review of the Literature,' *Age and Ageing*, 24: 346–65, 1995

19. N. Gnaedinger, 'Supportive Housing for Seniors in the New Millennium: A Position Paper,' *Seniors' Housing Update*, Gerontology Research Centre, Simon Fraser University, 9(1): 1–11, 1999.

20. S. de Beauvoir, *The Coming of Age*, Putnam, New York, 1972.

21. Moody, H., *Ethics in an Ageing Society*, Johns Hopkins University Press, Baltimore, 1992.

22. Oregon's 'Death with Dignity Act' (ORS 127.800–897) was passed in November 1994 and went into effect in 1997.

23. Although both euthanasia and assisted suicide had been widely practiced in the Netherlands, they remained technically illegal until the passage of a bill for the 'Review of cases of termination of life on request and assistance with suicide' was approved in April 2001. Belgium's law was passed on May 16, 2002.

24. 'Rights of the Terminally Ill Act,' Northern Territory of Australia (1996).

25. Republic of Colombia Constitutional Court, Sentence # c-239/97, Ref. Expedient # D-1490, May 20, 1997.

26. Associated Press story 7/27/98.

27. Speech to the House of Lords on 9 May 1994 by Lord Walton, the Chairman, Select Committee on Medical Ethics.

THE STATUTORY RETIREMENT AGE

The Statutory Retirement Age (SRA) is the legal age at retirement. It is in practice in government employment, although private employers are also required to adhere to the SRA. However, in unorganised sectors the SRA has very little meaning. Even then, the data on SRA reflects the mood of policy makers vis-à-vis the social response to the progress of ageing.

The SRA is generally higher in the MDRs than in the LDRs. It is often lower for women than for men. Theoretically, the SRA should be linked with life expectancy at birth. However, in practice the SRA rarely revised with rise in life expectancy. There is also pressure on the policy makers to revise the SRA by decreasing it to accommodate the increasing flow of the unemployed. In some developed countries like the USA, there is, for all practical purposes, no fixed retirement age. Workers are allowed to work till they are considered to be physically and mentally fit.

Currently, the SRA varies anywhere between the ages of 40 and 67. Solomon Islands have the lowest retirement age at 40. There is no other country in the world where the superannuating age is lower than 50. Denmark, Iceland and Norway have the highest retirement ages in the world at 67 for both men and women. There are many countries (about one-third of the globe) where women retire at an earlier age. In Table A.1, we present the SRA for different countries of the world.

Japan and Cyprus have the highest SRA in Asia; 65 years for both men and women. In Israel, the SRA for men is 65 years while for women it is 60. Lebanon has a SRA of 64 years for both men

Table A.1
Statutory Retirement Age in Different Countries of the World

Africa

Country	SRA for Males	SRA for Females	Country	SRA for Males	SRA for Females
Burundi	55	55	Kenya	55	55
Mauritius	60	60	Madagascar	60	55
Mozambique	55	55	Seychelles	63	63
Uganda	55	55	Zambia	50	50
Zimbabwe	60	60	Central African	55	50
Cameroon	60	60	DR Congo	63	60
Congo	55	55	Sao Tome	62	57
Gabon	60	60	Morocco	60	60
Guinea(E)	60	60	South Africa	65	60
Algeria	60	55	Burkina Faso	55	55
Sudan	55	55	Gambia	55	55
Swaziland	50	50	Liberia	60	60
Cape Verde	65	60	Niger	60	60
Ghana	60	60	Sierra Leone	60	60
Mali	55	55			
Nigeria	60	60			

Asia

Country	SRA for Males	SRA for Females	Country	SRA for Males	SRA for Females
China	60	55	South Korea	60	60
Afghanistan	60	55	Iran	60	55
Japan	65	65			
India	55	55			

(continued)

Table A.1
(Continued)

Country	SRA for Males	SRA for Females	Country	SRA for Males	SRA for Females	Country	SRA for Males	SRA for Females
Kazakhstan	61	56	Kyrgyzstan	60	55	Nepal	60	55
Pakistan	60	55	Sri Lanka	55	50	Turkmenistan	60	55
Uzbekistan	60	55	Indonesia	55	55	Malaysia	55	55
Philippines	60	60	Singapore	55	55	Viet Nam	60	55
Armenia	60	55	Bahrain	60	55	Cyprus	65	65
Georgia	60	55	Iraq	60	55	Israel	65	60
Jordan	60	55	Kuwait	50	50	Lebanon	64	64
Oman	60	55	Saudi Arabia	60	60	Syria	60	60
Turkey	55	50						
			Europe					
Belarus	60	55	Bulgaria	60	55	Czech	60	53–57
Hungary	60	60	Poland	65	60	Moldova	60	55
Romania	60	55	Russia	60	55	Slovakia	60	53–57
Ukraine	60	55	Denmark	67	67	Estonia	65	60
Finland	65	65	Iceland	67	67	Ireland	66	66
Latvia	60	60	Lithuania	62	60	Norway	67	67
Sweden	65	65	UK	65	60	Albania	60	55
Andorra	65	65	Croatia	60	55	Greece	65	60
Italy	65	60	Malta	61	60	Portugal	65	65
Spain	65	65	Slovenia	63	58	Austria	65	60

(continued)

Table A.1
(Continued)

Country	SRA for Males	SRA for Females	Country	SRA for Males	SRA for Females	Country	SRA for Males	SRA for Females
Belgium	65	61	France	60	60	Germany	63	63
Luxembourg	65	65	Monaco	65	65	Netherlands	65	65
Switzerland	65	62						

Latin America and the Caribbean								
Antigua and Barbuda	60	60	Bahamas	65	65	Barbados	65	65
Cuba	60	55	Dominica	60	60	Dominican Republic	60	60
Grenada	60	60	Jamaica	65	60	Puerto Rico	65	65
Trinidad & Tobago	60	60	Belize	60	60	Costa Rica	63	61
El Salvador	60	55	Guatemala	60	60	Honduras	65	60
Mexico	65	65	Nicaragua	60	60	Panama	62	57
Argentina	65	60	Bolivia	55	50	Brazil	65	60
Chile	65	60	Colombia	60	55	Ecuador	55	55
Paraguay	60	60	Peru	65	65	Uruguay	60	60

North America								
Canada	65	65	USA	65	65			

(continued)

Table A.1
(Continued)

Oceania

Country	SRA for Males	SRA for Females	Country	SRA for Males	SRA for Females	Country	SRA for Males	SRA for Females
American Samoa	65	65	Australia	65	61	Fiji	55	55
Guam	65	65	Kiribati	50	50	Micronesia	60	60
New Zealand	65	65	Papua New Guinea	55	55	Solomon Islands	40	40
Vanuatu	55	55	Palau	60	55	N. Mariana Islands	65	65

Source: United States Bureau of the Census, International Programs Center, International Data Base; International Labour Office (ILO), *Estimates and Projections of the Economically Active Population, 1950–2010*, 4th edition, ILO, Geneva, 1996; *Social Security Programs Around the World – 1997*, Washington, D.C., United States Social Security Administration.

and women. In 19 out of 33 Asian nations for which data could be collected, the SRA is lower for women than for men, about five years lower for women.

In India, the retirement age for government employees was 58 years till May 1998. This was raised to 60 years following the belated acceptance of the Fifth Central Pay Commission. Even now the retirement age in the state of Kerala is 55 years because of massive educated unemployment among the youth in the state. The state of Rajasthan had raised its retirement age as well but could not maintain the limit because of public pressure.

APPENDIX TWO

POLICIES AND PROGRAMMES ON THE AGED IN INDIA

CONSTITUTIONAL PROVISIONS

♦ Article 41 of the Indian constitution deals with the state's role in providing social security to the aged. According to this article,

the State shall, within the limits of its economic capacity and development, make effective provision for securing the right to work, to education and to public assistance in case of unemployment, OLD AGE, sickness and disablement and in other cases of undeserved want.

♦ In the Constitution of India, Entry 24 in List III of Schedule VII deals with the *'Welfare of Labour, including conditions of work, provident funds, liability for workmen's compensation, invalidity and old age pension and maternity benefits'.*

♦ Item No. 9 of the State List and Item Nos 20, 23 and 24 of the Concurrent List relate to old age pension, social security and social insurance, and economic and social planning.

♦ The right of parents without any means to be supported by their children having sufficient means has been recognised by the Section 125(1)(d) of the Code of Criminal Procedure 1973 (details of the provision are given here), and Section 20(3) of the Hindu Adoption and Maintenance Act, 1956.

CODE OF CRIMINAL PROCEDURE 1973

Order for Maintenance of Wives, Children and Parents

125. Order for maintenance of wives, children and parents—

(1) If any person having sufficient means neglects or refuses to maintain—

   (a) his wife, unable to maintain herself, or
   (b) his legitimate or illegitimate minor child, whether married or not, unable to maintain itself, or
   (c) his legitimate or illegitimate child (not being a married daughter) who has attained majority, here such child is by reason of any physical or mental abnormality or injury unable to maintain itself, or
   (d) his father or mother, unable to maintain himself or herself,

   a Magistrate of the first class may, upon proof of such neglect or refusal, order such person to take a monthly allowance for the maintenance of his wife or such child, father or mother, at such monthly rate not exceeding five hundred rupees in the whole, as such Magistrate thinks fit, and to pay the same to such person as the Magistrate may from time to time direct:

   Provided that the Magistrate may order the father of a minor female child referred to in clause (b) to make such allowance, until she attains her majority, if the Magistrate is satisfied that the husband of such minor female child, if married, is not possessed of sufficient means.

Explanation

   (a) "minor" means a person who, under the provisions of the Indian Majority Act, 1875(9 of 1875) is deemed not to have attained his majority;
   (b) "wife" includes a woman who has been divorced by, or has obtained a divorce from, her husband and has not remarried.

(2) Such allowance shall be payable from the date of the order, or, if so ordered, from the date of the application for maintenance.

(3) If any person so ordered fails without sufficient cause to comply with the order, any such Magistrate may, for every breach of the order, issue a warrant for levying the amount due in the manner provided for levying fines, and may sentence such person, for the whole or any part of each month's allowance remaining unpaid after the execution of the warrant, to imprisonment for a term which may extend to one month or until payment if sooner made:

Provided that no warrant shall be issued for the recovery of any amount due under this section unless application be made to the Court to levy such amount within a period of one year from the date on which it became due.

126. Procedure—

(1) Proceedings under section 125 may be taken against any person in any district–

(a) where he is,

(2) All evidence in such proceedings shall be taken in the presence of the person against whom an order for payment of maintenance is proposed to be made, or, when his personal attendance is dispensed with in the presence of his pleader, and shall be recorded in the manner prescribed for summons-cases:

Provided that if the Magistrate is satisfied that the person against whom an order for payment of maintenance is proposed to be made is wilfully avoiding service, or wilfully neglecting to attend the Court, the Magistrate may proceed to hear and determine the case ex parte and any order so made may be set aside for good cause shown on an application made within three months from the date thereof subject to such terms including terms as to payment of costs to the opposite party as the Magistrate may think just and proper.

(3) The Court in dealing with applications under section 125 shall have power to make such order as to costs as may be just.

127. Alteration in allowance—

(1) On proof of a change in the circumstances of any person, receiving, under section 125 a monthly allowance, or ordered under the

same section to pay a monthly allowance to his wife, child, father or mother, as the case may be, the Magistrate may make such alteration in the allowance as he thinks fit:

Provided that if he increase the allowance, the monthly rate of five hundred rupees in the whole shall not be exceeded.

(2) *Where it appears to the Magistrate that, in consequence of any decision of a competent Civil Court, any order made under section 125 should be cancelled or varied, he shall cancel the order or, as the case may be, vary the same accordingly.*

(4) *At the time of making any decree for the recovery of any maintenance or dowry by any person, to whom a monthly allowance has been ordered to be paid under section 125, the Civil Court shall take into account the sum which has been paid to, or recovered by, such person as monthly allowance in pursuance of the said order.*

128. *Enforcement of order of maintenance—*

A copy of the order of maintenance shall be given without payment to the person in whose favour it is made, or to his guardian, if any, or to the person to whom the allowance is to be paid; and such order may be enforced by any Magistrate in any place where the person against whom it is made may be, on such Magistrate being satisfied as to the identity of the parties and the non-payment of the allowance due.

LEGAL ARRANGEMENTS MADE BY THE INDIAN STATES TO PROTECT THE ELDERLY

♦ The Himachal Pradesh Assembly passed a Parents Maintenance Bill in 1996 wherein a simple procedure was introduced for parents being ignored by their children to be given maintenance. In addition to making elderly care obligatory for errant wards not taking care of their aged parents, the Bill aims at simplifying the procedure by authorising the sub-divisional officer (civil) for fixing maintenance and additional commissioner as the appellate authority so that the decision can be taken and cases disposed of promptly bringing justice and relief to older persons without loss of time. The Bill is waiting ascent of the president of India.

♦ The Government of Maharashtra has also prepared a similar Bill. The Government of Goa also proposes to initiate action and introduce the Parents Maintenance Bill.

NATIONAL POLICY ON OLDER PERSONS

The Government of India announced a National Policy on Older Persons (NPOP) in January 1999. This policy provides a broad framework for inter-sectoral collaboration and cooperation, both within the government as well as between government and non-governmental agencies. In particular, the policy has identified a number of areas of intervention:

♦ To encourage individuals to make provisions for their own, as well as their spouse's old age.
♦ To encourage families to take care of the older members of their family.
♦ To enable and support voluntary and non-governmental organisations to supplement the care provided by the family, with greater emphasis on non-institutional care.
♦ To provide care and protection to the vulnerable elderly especially widows, the frail, handicapped, abused and destitute elderly.
♦ To provide health care facilities specially suited to the elderly.
♦ To promote research and training facilities to train geriatric caregivers and service providers for the elderly.
♦ To continually evaluate and upgrade existing services and programmes for older people.
♦ To facilitate and strengthen inter-sectoral partnerships in the field.
♦ To create awareness regarding elderly persons to develop themselves into fully independent citizens.

To facilitate the implementation of the policy, the participation of panchayati raj institutions (PRI), state governments and different departments of the Government of India is envisaged with coordinating responsibility resting with the Ministry of Social Justice and Empowerment.

NATIONAL COUNCIL FOR OLDER PERSONS

A National Council for Older Persons (NCOP) has been constituted by the Ministry of Social Justice and Empowerment to operationalise the NPOP. The basic objectives of the NCOP are:

♦ To advise the government on policies and programmes for older persons.
♦ To provide feedback to the government on the implementation of the NPOP as well as on specific programme initiatives for older persons.
♦ To advocate the best interests of older persons.
♦ To provide a nodal point at the national level for redressing the grievances of older persons which are of an individual nature.
♦ To provide lobby for concessions, rebates and discounts for older persons both with the government as well as with the corporate sector.
♦ To represent the collective opinion of older persons to the government.
♦ To suggest steps to make old age productive and interesting.
♦ To suggest measures to enhance the quality of intergenerational relationships.
♦ To undertake any other work or activity in the best interest of older persons.

There are 39 members in the council. A seven-member working group has also been constituted from amongst the members of the NCOP. The working group has so far held two meetings to discuss ways and means to achieve its objectives.

Aadhar

The Ministry of Social Justice and Empowerment has commissioned Aadhar to be a part of the secretariat of the NCOP. It is being coordinated by the Agewell Foundation. Aadhar is an initiative in the direction of empowering the elderly population of India to find satisfactory solutions to their problems as through the coordination of voluntary efforts and administrative initiatives. Since its inception in December 1999, Aadhar has been attending to requests for intervention from all over the country, by the ministry and various other government agencies and functionaries. Aadhar has so far received 3,027 suggestions, complaints and grievances from individuals/organisations out of which 2,981 had been processed up to 30th September 2000. In addition to the regular activities, Aadhar has initiated a process of identification for setting up voluntary action groups in all 578 districts of the country for better implementation of ideas and to provide for older persons effectively at the local level. So far over 27,438 NGOs, voluntary organisations and old age homes covering 578 districts of the country have been contacted. Information has been sought in order to identify committed individuals from these areas, from legal, medical and social fields. Simultaneously, all the district collectors have also been contacted with a request for their participation and support in the task. The district administration is being requested to verify the selected applicants and after verification, local voluntary action groups consisting of 15 to 20 members would be appointed in each district.

National Policy on Older Persons: Plan of Action, 2000–2005

To implement the NPOP, several ministries of the Government of India have adopted specific plans of action for 2000–2005 with the intention of making a difference in the lives of senior citizens. A plan of action is a document with endless possibilities, which do not confine or restrict actions for its implementation. The policies being adopted by the different ministries are as follows.

Ministry of Social Justice and Empowerment

- The Ministry of Social Justice and Empowerment will function as the nodal ministry.
- Concerned ministries will be asked to nominate a nodal officer for the NPOP.
- An inter-ministerial committee will be set up by the ministry to coordinate the implementation of the NPOP.
- Publicity of the NPOP will be a continuous process so that the underlying principles and features remain in constant public focus.
- State governments will be requested to identify a nodal department to coordinate and monitor the implementation of the policy.
- The setting up of a National Association of Older Persons will be facilitated.
- Every three years a detailed review document will be prepared on the implementation of the NPOP.

♦ Voluntary organisations in the field of ageing will be promoted, assisted and encouraged to raise their own resources.
♦ Grants will be given for the construction and maintenance of old age homes in urban, semi-urban and rural areas.
♦ A Senior Citizens Welfare Fund will be set up at the centre.
♦ The instruments providing for old age social and income security for unorganised sector workers will be developed as recommended by the OASIS Committee.
♦ The concept of active ageing will be promoted.
♦ Trusts and charities will be approached to provide services to older persons.
♦ Non-institutional forms of care, inside as well as outside the home, will be promoted in order to strengthen the capacity of families to smoothly discharge their caring responsibilities.
♦ Panchayati raj institutions (PRIs) will be assisted to provide institutional and non-institutional services to older persons.
♦ Facilities will be provided for the training and orientation of workers and volunteers in organisations providing services to the elderly.
♦ Research on ageing issues will be promoted.
♦ Assistance will be given for setting up resource centres on ageing in different parts of the country.
♦ Professional associations of gerontologists will be encouraged to strengthen research activity, disseminate research findings and provide a platform for dialogue.
♦ Websites on older persons will be encouraged. Internet service providers will be requested to give rebates on tariffs to older persons.
♦ State governments will be requested to issue a multi-purpose identity card to senior citizens.

Ministry of Health and Family Welfare

♦ Affordable health services will be made available to older persons, heavily subsidised for the poor and a graded system of user charges for others.
♦ The development of health insurance will be given high priority.
♦ The health insurance sector will be given relief and concessions to enlarge the base of coverage and make the schemes affordable.
♦ The primary health care system will be strengthened to be able to meet effectively the health care needs of older persons.

- Trusts, charitable societies and voluntary agencies providing health care to older persons will be promoted, encouraged and assisted by way of grants, relief, land at subsidised rates and other concessions.
- Facilities for testing and treating visual impairment, hearing impairment, dental and locomotion problems will be considerably expanded.
- Treatment facilities for chronic, terminal and degenerative diseases will be expanded.
- Public hospitals will be directed to provide separate OPD counters for older persons.
- Medical social workers in hospitals will be given the right orientation on how to care for elderly patients in hospitals.
- The setting up of welfare funds in hospitals to provide for free treatment and medicines to the poor elderly patients will be facilitated.
- Geriatric beds/wards will be provided in public hospitals.
- Hospices will be set up to cater to the needs of the chronically/terminally ill, aged patients.
- Mobile health services will be organised to reach out to the elderly, particularly women, the poor and the infirm in rural and urban areas.
- Societies, which can enrol volunteers, raise funds, mobilise and hire manpower to provide health care at home in the case of immobile older persons will be established.
- Medical colleges will be assisted to provide facilities for specialisation in geriatric medicine.
- Training courses in nursing care will include courses in geriatric care.
- Medical and paramedical personnel will be given training and orientation on morbidity patterns of the elderly and their treatment and rehabilitation.
- Mental health services will be strengthened and expanded to increase their accessibility and use.
- The concept of healthy ageing—physical and mental, and its practice through preventive health care, will be vigorously promoted. The preparation and dissemination of educational material on healthy ageing will be assisted.
- A special campaign on healthy ageing will be launched.
- The existing knowledge base on the health of older persons, both men and women, will be strengthened through further research.

♦ The medical fraternity will be encouraged to set up geriatric care societies at the national, state and district level.
♦ Associations of older persons and retired medical professionals will be encouraged to organise mobile health awareness and health check-ups.

Ministry of Finance

♦ Issues connected with better returns from pension and provident fund accumulations will be examined so that employees can get more benefits.
♦ Pension schemes will be devised to reach out to self-employed and other persons currently not covered by pension.
♦ The insurance, mutual funds and banking sector will be encouraged to play a big role in promoting long-term savings for old age.
♦ Taxation policies will take cognisance of the heavy liabilities on older persons to meet their survival, health and other needs during old age.
♦ Schemes proposed by different ministries for the well-being of older persons will be sympathetically considered and adequate budgetary provisions will be made.
♦ Pre-budget consultations made with different groups will include consultations with organisations representing the interests of older persons.
♦ The proposed Welfare Fund for Senior Citizens will be provided tax relief.

Ministry of Rural Development and Employment

♦ The non-contributory pension scheme for older persons will be progressively expanded to reach all elderly persons living below the poverty line.
♦ The system of disbursement of pensions will be streamlined and a strict watch kept to prevent delays and abuses.
♦ The possibility of providing old persons, living below the poverty line, a fixed quantum of foodgrains at a heavily subsidised price or free of cost.
♦ Poverty alleviation schemes of the ministry will show sensitivity to older persons.
♦ Public rural housing schemes for older persons will include subsidised housing programmes.

Ministry of Urban Affairs and Employment

♦ Town planners and architects will be sensitised to the needs of older persons for a comfortable and safe home, neighbourhood and city.
♦ The ministry will help remove physical barriers to mobility and provide easy and safe accessibility to public places.
♦ Common causes of accidents inside the home and outside, places where they most commonly occur, types of injuries that are caused and ways to prevent them will be identified.
♦ Guidelines for the design and construction of old age homes and day care centres to make them lively places for group living will be developed.
♦ In multi-storied housing without elevators, preference will be given to older persons in the allotment of flats on the ground floor.
♦ Older persons will be given easy access to loans with easy repayment schedules.
♦ Roads, footpaths, road and street crossings will be modified to ensure safe movement of older persons.
♦ Every housing colony will be required to have a multi-purpose centre for older persons.
♦ Flats for older persons with common service facilities for meals, laundry, common rooms, rest rooms and guestrooms will be encouraged.
♦ Norms will be laid down to check noise and other forms of pollution.
♦ Older persons will be given special consideration over matters relating to transfer of property, property tax and others.
♦ The tenancy legislation will be reviewed so that the rights to occupancy of older persons are restored speedily.
♦ State governments will be requested to earmark and allot lands at concessional rates to trusts, charities etc. for the construction of old age homes in urban and semi-urban areas.

Ministry of Human Resource Development

♦ Discrimination against older persons in the matter of availing opportunities for education, training and orientation will be removed.
♦ Budgetary allocation will be made for educational programmes meant for older persons.

♦ Open universities/departments of continuing education of universities will be encouraged to develop and offer continuing education packages relevant and useful for older persons.
♦ The curriculum at different stages of education will include course material on older persons to encourage values of caring towards the old.
♦ The departments of social sciences in universities will be requested to include courses on ageing in their curriculum and encourage students to take up research on ageing at the M.Phil. and Ph.D. level.
♦ Corporate bodies, banks, trusts and foundations will be approached to set up centres devoted to the study of ageing.
♦ Libraries of universities, research institutions and others academic and cultural bodies will be requested to permit older persons to utilise their facilities.
♦ Interactive programmes between associations of older persons and schools will be promoted.

Ministry of Labour

♦ Coverage of establishments in which workers are entitled to contributory provident fund, pension and other retirement benefits will be progressively increased.
♦ Pre-retirement counselling programmes will be promoted and assisted.
♦ Organisations will be assisted to provide career guidance, training, placement and support services to older persons.
♦ Trade unions will be encouraged to promote the cause of older workers.
♦ The National Commission on Labour will be requested to give its recommendations on older workers.
♦ The National Labour Institute will include older workers in its programme of activities.

Ministry of Personnel, Public Grievances and Pensions

♦ The system of settlement of pension/provident fund/gratuity and other retirement benefits will be characterised by fairness, transparency, accountability and promptness.
♦ Training programmes of officers of central and all India services will contain modules, which will sensitise them to older persons.

- Institutes of public administration will seek the help of experts in the field for suggestions on implementation, coordination and monitoring of NPOP.
- All organisations giving pensions to superannuated workers will be directed to create a grievance cell under a senior officer.

Ministry of Law, Justice and Company Affairs

- Steps will be taken to simplify the adequacy of current provisions granting rights to parents with no support from their children, provide speedy relief, lay down the machinery for processing cases and define the rights, obligations and circumstances in such cases in a comprehensive manner.
- State legislation will be modified so that older parents unable to maintain themselves do not face abandonment and acute neglect.
- Legal aid services to older persons will be expanded.
- Legal advice and helpline services will be provided to older persons to protect them from abuse, fraud and coercion in connection with property rights.
- A provision will be made in the Indian Penal Code (IPC) to protect older persons from domestic violence, both physical and psychological.
- Judicial authorities will be sensitised to the problems faced by older persons and urged to provide speedy disposal of their cases.

Ministry of Home Affairs

- Police departments will be directed to pay special attention to the security of life and property of older persons.
- Information will be provided to senior citizens' and residents' welfare associations on the precautions necessary to ensure the safety of the elderly in the neighbourhood.
- Importance of maintaining close contacts with friends and neighbours and sharing information on security matters will be stressed.
- The National Crime Records Bureau will compile and publish in its annual publications, *Crime in India* and *Suicides and Accidental Deaths in India*, data on victims aged 60 and above.
- The registrar general and census commissioner will include questions on older persons in the decennial census operations.

Ministry of Information and Broadcasting

♦ Subjects concerning older persons will be identified, programmes produced and time allocated for their broadcast.
♦ The concept of active ageing will be promoted.
♦ Programmes will target older persons in order to help them enrich and update their own knowledge, and also pass on more effectively the socio-cultural heritage to their grandchildren.
♦ Interaction between media and persons active in the field of ageing will be facilitated.
♦ Organisations concerned about ageing issues will be requested to institute awards for the best reporting on ageing in print, radio and television in English and the regional languages.

Ministry of Communications

♦ High priority will be given to providing telephone connections to senior citizens.
♦ Immediate action will be taken in the matter of transfer of telephones and redressal of faults.
♦ Telephone advisory bodies will include a nominee from the NCOP.
♦ Telephone tariff concessions in the case of domestic use will be considered.
♦ Postal authorities will issue, every year, on the National Day for Older Persons a commemorative postage stamp.
♦ Messages relating to older persons will be printed on inland letters, aerogramme, and other items of postal stationery.

Ministry of Railways

♦ Fare concession will be given by the railways to senior citizens in all classes.
♦ The railway authorities will provide better services to senior citizens at booking counters, railway platforms, waiting rooms and during the journey.
♦ Allotment of lower berths, availability of wheel chairs and easy access to retiring rooms will be ensured for older persons.

♦ Senior citizens will be provided protection from harassment by coolies and anti-social elements.
♦ A senior officer will be nominated by the railways for speedy redressal of the grievances of older persons.

Ministry of Agriculture

♦ Older persons will be provided gratuitous relief during natural calamities.
♦ The Relief Code will specifically mention the special provisions for relief and rehabilitation of older persons.

Ministry of Surface Transport

♦ State road transport authorities will consider giving fare concessions to senior citizens.
♦ Buses will be designed in such a way so as to provide easy entrance and exit, and safety to the elderly.
♦ Buses will have seats reserved for the elderly.

Ministry of Civil Aviation

♦ The airlines will consider the facilities they can provide to senior citizens to make their travel comfortable.
♦ The airlines will be requested to lower the age of entitlement to fare concessions in the case of women.

Ministry of Petroleum and Natural Gas

♦ Senior citizens will be given high priority in the allotment of gas connections for domestic use.
♦ Complaints of senior citizens will be attended to on a priority basis.

Ministry of Food and Consumer Affairs

♦ The public distribution system will reach out to cover all older persons below the poverty line and issue ration cards promptly.

♦ Ration card holders above the age of 60 will be given priority in fair price shops for issue of ration, etc.
♦ Older persons will be made aware of their rights as consumers and the redressal mechanisms available to them.
♦ Priority will be given to the disposal of applications and complaints of older persons.

Ministry of Science and Technology

♦ Research on ageing will be recognised as a priority area. Funding support will be provided for research.
♦ Development of aids and appliances for use by older persons will be encouraged.

Ministry of Parliamentary Affairs

♦ Sensitisation programmes on issues concerning older persons will be organised for Members of Parliament.
♦ Programmes and measures for the well-being of older persons in developing and developed countries will be made available.

Ministry of Planning

♦ The Planning Commission will sanction outlays for schemes on older persons.
♦ The National Sample Survey Organisation (NSSO) will generate data on older persons.
♦ Special surveys on older persons will be conducted at periodic intervals.

Ministry of Industry

♦ Manufacture of user friendly items for senior citizens will be encouraged.

NATIONAL LEVEL
PROGRAMMES ON THE AGED IN INDIA

Old Age Social and Income Security (OASIS)

As a result of the growing concern for old age social and income security due to changes in demographic, social and traditional structures, the Social Defence Bureau had commissioned the National Project titled Old Age Social and Income Security (OASIS). An eight-member expert committee headed by Dr S.A. Dave, former chairman of the Unit of Trust of India was nominated to examine policy questions connected with old age. The OASIS expert committee was mandated to make concrete recommendations for the immediate actions that the Government of India could take, so that every young worker could build enough savings during his/her working life, which would serve as a shield against poverty in their old age and reduce the burden on the state. The need for this arose because of lack of adequate instruments available to enable the unorganised sector to provide for their future old age. The final report of the OASIS project has been accepted by this ministry and has been presented to the prime minister by the minister of state for social justice and empowerment. The Social Defence Bureau is taking the necessary action for the implementation of the recommendations of the report. The report also contains detailed recommendations for enhancing the coverage, improving the rate of returns and for bringing about a qualitative improvement in the customer service of Public Provident Fund, the Employees Provident Fund, the Annuity Plans of the LIC, UTI, etc. Meanwhile, Phase II of the project is looking at the pension and gratuity schemes of the central government and old age pension provided under the National Social Assistance Programme (NSAP). At the core of the second phase of project OASIS however, lies the designing of a new, fully-funded, contributory pension programme for the balance (uncovered) workers, including casual/contract workers, self-employed workers, farmers etc.

Integrated Programme for Older Persons

An Integrated Programme for Older Persons has been formulated by revising the earlier scheme of assistance to voluntary organisations for programmes relating to the welfare of the aged. The programme hopes to:

1. Reinforce and strengthen the ability and commitment of the family to provide care for older persons.
2. Foster amiable multigenerational relationships.
3. Generate greater awareness on issues pertaining to older persons and enhance measures to address these issues.
4. Popularise the concept of Life Long Preparation for Old Age at the individual level as well as at the societal level.
5. Facilitate productive ageing.
6. Promote health care, and fulfil the housing and income security needs of older persons.
7. Provide care to the destitute elderly.
8. Strengthen capabilities on issues pertaining to older persons of local bodies/state governments, NGOs and academic/research and other institutions.

Under this scheme financial assistance of upto 90 per cent of the project cost is provided to NGOs for establishing and maintaining old age homes, day-care centres, mobile Medicare units and to provide non-institutional services to older persons. The scheme has been made flexible so as to meet the diverse needs of older persons including reinforcement and strengthening of the family, awareness generation on issues pertaining to older persons, popularisation of the concept of lifelong preparation for old age, facilitating productive ageing, etc. As many as 733 old age homes/day-care centres/mobile Medicare units are operational under the scheme. Realising the importance of strengthening the partnership between the young and the old a collaborative project has been launched under this scheme with the Nehru Yuvak Kendra Sangathan under which 100 new day-care centres for older persons have been established in different parts of the country.

Scheme of Assistance for Construction of Old Age Homes

The scheme of assistance to panchayati raj institutions/voluntary organisations/self-help groups for construction of old age homes/multi-service centres for older persons has been revised to enhance the one time construction grant for old age homes/multi-service centres. The scheme aims at providing a financial grant for the construction of old age home or service centres for older persons. Registered societies, public trusts or charitable companies, or registered self-help groups of older persons in addition to panchayati raj institutions (PRIs) are eligible to receive assistance under this scheme. Since its inception three years ago, as many as 59 old age homes have been constructed in different parts of the country under this scheme. Recently, the scheme has been revised to enhance the one-time construction grant for old age homes/multi-service centres from Rs 500,000 to Rs 3,000,000 to eligible organisations.

National Old Age Pension Scheme (NOAP)

Under the National Old Age Pension Scheme (NOAP), central assistance is available on fulfilment of the following criteria: (a) the age of the applicant (male or female) should be 65 years or more; (b) the applicant must be a destitute in the sense that he/she has no regular means of subsistence from his/her own source of income or through financial support from family members or other sources. The amount of old age pension is Rs 75 per month. This scheme is implemented in the state and union territories through panchayats and municipalities. Both panchayats and municipalities are encouraged to involve voluntary agencies as much as possible in helping the destitute elderly for whom this scheme is intended. (*Ministry of Rural Areas and Employment, NSAP Guidelines for State Governments.*)

Old Age and Widow Pension in Maharashtra

Under the Sanjay Gandhi Niradhar Anudan Yojana, an individual (female 60 years or above and males 65 years or above) can get Rs 100 per month if he/she has no source of income. If a woman is a widow and has one or more under age children then she is eligible for a pension of Rs 250 per month. Under the Indira Gandhi Bhumihin Vrudh Sheth-Majdoor Sahayay Yojana, an individual (female 60 years or above and male 65 years or above) gets Rs 100 per month. The beneficiary of this scheme must be a destitute and from a rural area.

Widow Pension in Karnataka

The pension amount is Rs 75 per month. Age is no bar.

Widow Pension in West Bengal

The pension amount is Rs 150 per month for widows below poverty line. There is no age bar. Table A.2 gives the old age pension amounts offered by different states.

Table A.2
Old Age Pension amounts Given by Different States

Name of the State	Current amount of Pension (Rs p.m.)	Minimum Age of Eligibility (in years)
Andhra Pradesh	75	65
Arunachal Pradesh	150	60
Assam	60	65 (males)
		60 (females)
Bihar	100	60
Gujarat	200	60 to 65
	275	65 plus
Haryana	100	60
Himachal Pradesh	150	60
Jammu & Kashmir	125	60
Karnataka	100	65
Kerala	110	65
Madhya Pradesh	150	60 (males)
		50 (females)
Maharashtra	100	65 (males)
		60 (females)
Mizoram	100	65 (males)
		60 (females)
Orissa	100	65
Punjab	200	65 (males)
		60 (females)
Rajasthan	200	58 (males)
	300	55 (females)
Tamil Nadu	150	60
Uttar Pradesh	125	60
West Bengal	300	60
Chandigarh	200	65 (males)
		60 (females)
Delhi	200	60

Source: HelpAge India, *Senior Citizen's Guide*, HelpAge India, New Delhi, 2001. Also available online at http://www.helpageindia.com/guide.html.

Widow Pension in Kerala

Widow pension is Rs 110 per month. The person must be a destitute and her income per year must be below Rs 12,000. Age is no bar.

Annapurna

A new scheme called 'ANNAPURNA' has been recently initiated by the Government of India under which free food grains upto 10 kg per month will be provided to such destitute older persons who are otherwise eligible for old age pension under the National Old Age Pension Scheme but are not receiving it and whose sons are not residing with them. However, the scheme is yet to be implemented.

Pension and Family Pension

For central government employees
The revision of pension/family pension approved by the central government based on the 5th Pay Commission, is given here:

(1) **Pension:** People who retired from service as on 1 January 1996, will receive their pension at 50 per cent of their basic pay. Pension for people who retired before 1 January 1996 will be fixed based on 50 per cent of the minimum of the new scale applicable in place of the old scale, in which they retire. A special provision has been made for people who retire before completing 10 months of service after 1 January 1999, i.e., before 30 September 1996 and have opted to come over to the revised scales of pay. They are eligible to weightage at 40 per cent on the existing basic pay for arriving at average pay fixation of pension.

(2) **Family Pension:** Family pension for people who retire from service as on 1 January 1996 will be fixed at 30 per cent of the pay drawn by the deceased employee based on the new pension formula subject to his having put in 33 years of service. Family pension of people who retired before 1 January 1996 will be fixed at 30 per cent of the pay drawn by the deceased employee based on the new pension formula subject to his having put in 33 years of service.

For central government employees who have been permanently absorbed in public sector undertakings/autonomous bodies.

(1) **Pension:** Where the government servants, on permanent absorption into the public sector undertakings/autonomous bodies, continue to draw pension separately from the government, the pension of such absorbees will be updated in terms of these orders. In cases where the government servants have drawn one-time lump sum terminal benefits equal to 100 per cent of their pensions and have become entitled to the restoration of one-third commuted portion of pension as per the Supreme Court judgement dated 15 December 1995, their cases will not be covered by these orders.

(2) **Family Pension:** In cases where there is no permanent absorption into public sector undertakings/autonomous bodies, the terms of absorption permit grant of family pension under the CCS (Pension) Rules, 1972 or the corresponding rules applicable to railway employees/members of all India services. The family pension being drawn by family pensioners will be updated in accordance with these orders.

Dearness Relief (DR)

The Grant of Dearness Relief to central government pensioners/family pensioners as serving employees—revised rates effective from 1 January 1999.

Central government employees who had drawn a lump sum payment on absorption in a Public Sector Unit (PSU)/autonomous body and have become entitled to restoration of one third commuted portion of pension as well as revision of the restored amount in terms of this department's OM No. 4/59/97–P&PW (D) dated 14 July 1998, will also be entitled to the payment of DR as applicable to serving employees on the restored amount of one-third commuted portion of pension with effect from 1 January 1999. The following categories of Contributory Provident Fund (CPF) beneficiaries who are in receipt of ex-gratia payment in terms of this department's OM No. 45/52/97–P&PW (E) dated 16 December 1997 will be paid a DR as applicable with effect from 1 January 1999: (a) the widows and dependent children of the deceased CPF beneficiary who had retired from service prior to 1 January 1986, or who had died while in service prior to 1 January 1986, and are in receipt of ex-gratia payment of Rs 605 p.m;

(*b*) central government employees who had retired on CPF benefits before 18.11.1960 and are in receipt of an ex-gratia payment of Rs 654, Rs 703 and Rs 695; (*c*) central government employees who had retired on CPF benefits between the period 18 November 1960 to 1 December 1985 and are in receipt of an ex-gratia at Rs 600 with effect from 1 November 1997.

Gratuity

The conditions for securing gratuity for central government employees are as follows:

♦ A minimum of 5 years qualifying service and eligibility to receive service gratuity/pension is essential to get this one-time lump sum benefit.
♦ The retirement gratuity is calculated at the rate of one-fourth of the month's basic pay plus the DA last drawn before retirement for each completed six-monthly period of qualifying service.
♦ There is no minimum limit for the amount of gratuity. The maximum retirement gratuity payable is over 16 times the basic pay limited to Rs 350,000.

Taxation

♦ **Income Tax Rebate (Section 88B of Finance Act, 1992):** This provision provides a rebate on income tax to senior citizens. The rebate is available in the case of a resident individual (he/she may be an ordinary resident or an non-ordinary resident; he/she may be an Indian citizen or a foreign citizen) who has attained the age of 65 years at any time during the relevant previous year. From the assessment year 1998–99, tax rebate under Section 88B shall be: (*a*) the amount of income-tax before giving any rebate under Sections 88, 88B and 89(1); or (*b*) Rs 10,000 or 40 per cent whichever is less. The rebate will be available from the assessment year 1998–99, even if the gross total income is above Rs 20,000. *(Ministry of Finance, Income Tax Act, 1961.)*
♦ **Deduction in respect of medical insurance premia (Sec. 80D):** An assessee is entitled to a deduction of up to Rs 15,000 with effect from the assessment year 2000–01 where the assessee or his/her spouse, or dependent parents or any member of the family is a

senior citizen, (i.e., one who is at least 65 years of age at any time during the previous year), and the medical insurance premium is paid to effect or keep in force an insurance in relation to him or her.

♦ Section 80DDB has been inserted to provide for a separate deduction to a resident assessee being an individual or a Hindu undivided family member for expenditure incurred for medical treatment for the individual himself or his dependent relative in respect of disease or ailments which may be specified in the rules. The deduction shall be limited to Rs 40,000. However, where the expenditure incurred is in respect of the assessee or his dependent relative or any member of a Hindu undivided family of the assessee and who is a senior citizen (i.e., one who is at least 65 years of age at any time during the previous year), a fixed deduction of Rs 60,000 will be available. *(Ministry of Finance, Finance Bill, 1999.)*

Inusurance Schemes

Jeevan Dhara: This pension plan is for those individuals who are self-employed, artists, technicians, in business, and professionals, since they cannot enjoy any 'Pension' benefit after they retire, compared to state/central government employees who are endowed with 'Pension' benefits. Age range at entry: 18 to 65 years. The minimum annuity per month is Rs 100.

Jeevan Akshay: This pension plan provides lifelong pension and a lump sum death benefit as also a survival benefit at the end of 7 years under certain terms and conditions. The minimum age at entry is 50 years. The minimum purchase price is Rs 10,000, in multiples of Rs 100 thereafter. Back dating is not permitted in this scheme. Jeevan Akshay Policies will not be issued under the Married Women's Property Act (MWP), 1874. This annuity cannot be assigned.

Jeevan Suraksha: Jeevan Suraksha is available under three different categories to suit individual needs: (*a*) pension with life cover; (*b*) pension without life cover; and, (*c*) pension with endowment type. Contributions under Jeevan Suraksha upto Rs 10,000 p.a. will be eligible for tax exemption under Section 80 CCC(1) of the Income Tax Act, 1961. Commuted value upto 25 per cent as allowed under the plan is free of tax.

Bima Nivesh: Bima Nivesh is a short-term, single-premium life insurance scheme that also provides safety, liquidity, attractive returns and tax benefits. The salient features of the scheme are: The minimum age for entry is 35 years and the maximum age is 65 years (for a 10-year term), and 70 years (for a 5-year term). Contributions are eligible for tax exemption under Section 88 of the IT Act. No medical examination is required; only a simple declaration of good health needs to be submitted.

Senior Citizens Unit Plan (SCUP): The Senior Citizens Unit Plan is a scheme under which one has to make a one time investment depending on one's age and have the benefit of medical treatment for self and spouse at select hospitals on completion of 58 years of age. The SCUP has special arrangements with the New India Assurance Co. Ltd. (NIAC) under an exclusive medical insurance cover whereby the bills from the hospitals in connection with all medical treatment by you are settled directly by NIAC upto the prescribed limit. People in the age group of 18–54 years can join this scheme. The person may be a resident or non-resident Indian. The person will be entitled for a medical insurance cover of Rs 250,000 after he/she attains the age of 58 years. This insurance cover is available for both the citizen and his/her spouse. After the age of 61 years both of them are eligible for a cover of Rs 500,000 after adjusting any claims made earlier. The citizen can avail medical treatment in any of the hospitals under this scheme. The trust will call for all details about recent photograph, signature and address of the member and the spouse as soon as the member attains the age of 54 years so as to prepare an identity card cum log book, for the member and the spouse.

Medical Insurance Scheme: The Medical Insurance Scheme known as Mediclaim is available to persons between the ages of 5 years and 75 years. Earlier, the sum insured varied from Rs 15,000 to Rs 300,000 and the premium varied from Rs 175 to Rs 5,770 per person per annum depending upon the different slabs of sum insured and different age groups. However, w.e.f. 1st November 1999, these limits on benefits and premium rates have since been revised. The sum insured now varies from Rs 15,000 to Rs 500,000 and the premium varies from Rs 175 to Rs 12,450 per person per annum depending upon the different slabs of sum insured and different age groups. The policy is now available to persons between the ages of 5 years and 80 years. The cover provides for reimbursement of medical expenses incurred by an individual towards hospitalisation/domiciliary hospitalisation for any illness, injury or disease contracted or sustained during the period of insurance.

Group Medical Insurance Scheme: The group Mediclaim policy is available to any group/association/institution/corporate body of more than 100 persons provided it has a central administration point. The policy covers reimbursement of hospitalisation and/or domiciliary hospitalisation expenses only for illnesses/diseases contracted or injury sustained by the insured person. The basic policy under this scheme is Mediclaim. This policy is also available to persons between the ages of 5 years and 80 years. The sum insured varies from Rs 15,000 to Rs 500,000 and premium varies from Rs 175 to Rs 12,450 per person per annum depending upon the different slabs of sum insured and different age groups.

Jan Arogya: This scheme is primarily meant for the larger segment of the population who cannot afford the high cost of medical treatment. The limit of cover per person is Rs 5,000 per annum and it provides for reimbursement of medical expenses incurred by an individual towards hospitalisation/domiciliary hospitalisation for any illness, injury or disease contracted or sustained during the period of insurance. The age limit for this scheme is 70 years.

Varistha Pension Bima Yojana: The old-age pension scheme of the LIC, called the Varistha Pension Bima Yojana was launched by the Indian prime minister on 14th July, 2003. It will provide a minimum pension of Rs 250 a month and a maximum of Rs 2,000 a month to people over 55 years of age who opt for the scheme.

For the minimum pension, a lump sum payment of Rs 33,335 has to be made while for the Rs 2,000 scheme Rs 266,665 has to paid (the figure has been revised downwards from the earlier amount of Rs 277,490). There is no upper age limit for availing of the scheme and in the event of the death of the pensioner, the purchase price will be returned to the nominee.

The assured rate of return worked out by the LIC is 9 per cent per annum. In case the LIC earns lower returns on the corpus of the scheme, the government would step in to make up the shortfall.

Private Pensions Plans: Private insurance companies like ICICI Prudential Life, HDFC Standard Life, ING Vysys Life and Aviva Life have also launched their prulife pension plans. Details may be seen in the following websites:

http://www.iciciprulife.com/creative/blankproduct.jsp?
productid=8
http://www.hdfcinsurance.com/InsuranceProducts/Personal
Pension.htm
http://www.canbankindia.com/personal/insurance/pension
plusmain.htm)

Travel

By Road

Specific elder friendly programmes vis-à-vis road travel followed in different states of India may be summed up as follows:

1. **Delhi:** A 50 per cent discount on travel fare on Delhi Transport Corporation (DTC) buses is offered to senior citizens who are 65 years old. This discount is only applicable on the Monthly Pass. The Automobile Association of Upper India (AAUI) has extended a life membership to all its senior citizen members (above 65 years of age) at a concessional fees of Rs 1,500. For new members, the overall life membership fees will be Rs 1,500 + Rs 200, i.e., Rs 1,700, which will include an entrance fees of Rs 200 as against Rs 5,000 + Rs 500, i.e., Rs 5,500.
2. **Tamil Nadu:** In all Tamil Nadu Transport Corporation buses, two seats in the front are reserved exclusively for old people and the handicapped.
3. **Maharashtra:** The BEST buses in Mumbai as such offer no concessions to the elderly. However, senior citizens can enter buses from front. The Maharashtra State Road Transport Corporation (MSRTC) buses provide a 50 per cent concession if a person is 65 years of age or above and has an election identity card or a tehsildar certificate. Local trains in Mumbai have around eight to 10 seats reserved for senior citizens in one of the compartments.
4. **Chandigarh:** Senior citizens pass holders get a 50 per cent travel concession for travelling in city buses in Chandigarh.
5. **Punjab:** Elderly women above 60 years of age enjoy free travel in the state of Punjab.
6. **Rajasthan:** The Rajasthan State Road Transport Corporation (RSRTC) provides a 25 per cent concession to people 65 years of age and above.
7. **Kerala:** Free passes are provided to the elderly who are also freedom fighters to travel in the fast and express buses.

By Train

Specific elder friendly programmes vis-á-vis travel by train include the following:

♦ The Indian railways offer a 30 per cent concession to citizens who have reached 65 years of age in all classes and trains including the

Rajadhani/Shatabdi trains. *[Vide office memo of Government of India, Ministry of Railway by Telemax/Post Copy Issued on 27.07.1998. No. TCII/2066/95/Sr. Citizens/Policy. Reference S.No. 42 of Annexure to Rule 101 of IRCA Coaching Tariff No. 24, Part I (Vol.II) regarding concession to Senior Citizens]*

♦ The Indian railways also provides a 30 per cent concession in all classes and trains including Rajdhani/Shatabdi trains for females who have attained 60 years of age. (Announced in parliament by the railway minister.)

♦ In Tamil Nadu and West Bengal, the lower berth is also provided to senior citizens on request. Table B.2 shows the special provisions offered to the elderly in other categories.

Table B.2
Provision for Other Categories

Categories	Concession	
	I Class	II/Sleeper Class
For Cancer, T.B./Lupas Valgaris, Non-infectious Leprosy and Thalassemia patients travelling alone or with an escort (for both)	75%	75%
For heart patients travelling alone or with an escort for heart surgery (for both)	75%	75%
For orthopaedically handicapped/ paraplegic travelling alone or with an escort for any purpose (for both)	75% in II, Sl, I, AC, CC & AC 3-T and 50% in AC 2-T & AC I	
For blind persons, mentally retarded persons travelling alone or with an escort for any purpose (for both)	75%	75%
For deaf and dumb persons (both afflictions together in the same person) travelling for any purpose.	50%	50%

Source: IRCA, *Coaching Tariff*, 24 (25), Part-I (Vol. II), Ministry of Railway; HelpAge India, *Senior Citizen's Guide*, HelpAge India, New Delhi, 2001. Also available at http://www.helpageindia.com/guide.html

By Air

Specific elderly friendly programmes followed by different airlines vis-à-vis air travel are as follows:

- **Indian Airlines:** A 50 per cent discount (in normal rupees) on adult fare is offered for travel on Indian Airlines domestic flights only to senior citizens who have attained the age of 65 years. This discount is applicable to the economy class only. For a permanent identity card two recent stamp size photographs, and for a one-time journey, one passport size photograph is required.

- **Sahara India Airlines:** A 50 per cent discount on basic fare is offered to senior citizens for travel on Sahara India Airlines (SIAL) domestic flights. This discount extends to those elderly who have attained the age of 62 years. The discount is applicable in economy class only.

- **Jet Airways:** A 50 per cent discount is offered to senior citizens of 65 years of age on basic fare for travel on Jet Airways domestic flights. This discount is applicable in economy class only.

SPECIAL COUNTERS FOR THE AGED

Railway Ticket Booking

Separate reservation counters are earmarked for senior citizens at various Passenger Reservation System (PRS) centres if the average demand per shift is more than 120 tickets. The position is reviewed from time to time for continuity of this facility.

Income Tax Return

- Separate counters are marked for senior citizens at the time of filing of income tax returns.
- On the spot assessment is offered.
- A person must be 65 years of age or above as on 31st March of the assessment year, must be a pensioner and should be present in person to access this privilege. (*Directorate of Income Tax, Government of India.*)

Bills Payments

- Priority is given to senior citizens for payment of electricity/telephone bills as well as in hospitals in Chandigarh and Haryana.

◆ In Punjab, the government gives priority to senior citizens over matters of paying electricity/telephone bills, reservation of bus seats and separate OPDs in hospitals.
◆ In Gujarat, all civil hospitals have separate counters for registration and also separate queues for the elderly.
◆ In Delhi, a separate counter has been opened to help senior citizens submit property tax bills.

Old Age Homes

There are currently 728 old age homes in India. Detailed information on 547 homes is available. Out of these, 325 homes are free, while 95 of them are run on a pay and stay basis; about 116 of the homes are both free as well as offering pay and stay facilities; and, 11 homes offer no such information. A total of 278 old age homes all over the country are for the sick and 101 exclusively for women. Kerala has 124 old age homes, the maximum number in any state. (*Directory of Old Age Homes in India*, HelpAge India, 1998.)

Health Care

Some of the health care programmes for the aged followed in different states are:

1. **Delhi:** Sunday clinics at various hospitals in Delhi exist to enable senior citizens get medical care easily. The aim is to provide OPD services/facilities even on Sundays in hospitals under the Delhi government so that the older patients' caregivers can also accompany them without having to take leave from their work-place. The following hospitals have Sunday clinics (9.00 am to 1.00 pm): Lal Bahadur Shastri Hospital, Rao Tulla Ram Hospital, Jag Jivan Ram Hospital, Dr. N.C. Joshi Hospital, Lok Nayak Jai Prakash Narain Hospital, Deen Dayal Upadhyay Hospital, Guru Teg Bahadur Hospital, Sanjay Gandhi Memorial Hospital, Aruna Asaf Ali Hospital, Maulana Azad Medical College, Ram Manohar Lohia Hospital. These hospitals also have separate counters for senior citizens for medicines and the OPD. All India Institute of Medical Sciences (AIIMS) conducts a geriatric clinic every Friday at 2.00 PM in the Medicine OPD (2nd Floor, Room No. 15). (Directorate of Health, Government of N.C.T. of Delhi.)

2. **Tamil Nadu:** There are geriatric wards and an OPD in the government hospital in Chennai; a geriatric OPD in the Government general hospital in Madurai; and, a geriatric care clinic/hospital run by the Lions Club in Coimbatore.

3. **Maharashtra:** Under the District Blindness Control Scheme the state pays Rs 600 per Intra Ocular Lens (IOL) operation. In a few municipal hospitals there are geriatric wards with an OPD, once in a week, in the afternoons. They have separate queues for the elderly.

4. **Andhra Pradesh:** Only widows are entitled to health care benefits which include free registration at government hospitals and free treatment for TB, leprosy etc., to a very limited extent.

5. **Gujarat:** Free Intra Ocular Lens (IOL) is given to the elderly (60 years and above) for cataract surgery.

6. **Kerala:** In government hospitals, in Trivandrum, there is a geriatric ward with 12 beds (eight for males and four for females) and free treatment is provided to old people whose income is below Rs 300 per month. The Medical College Hospital in Trivandrum has an Out Patient Wing on every Monday from 10.30 AM to 12.00 noon for senior citizens. The District Blindness Society under the chairmanship of the collector and with the support of the Health Services Department offers a detection of cataract facility and further action for older persons.

OTHER INITITATIVES FOR THE AGED

Telephone

A telephone connection is being given on priority to senior citizens 65 years of age and above. They shall be entitled to register a demand for one telephone connection in their names. The telephones thus provided shall be transferable only in the name of spouse, if alive, after death of the subscriber as a general category telephone and subsequent transfers shall be governed by prevailing telephone transfer rules.

Helpline

On the initiative and with the financial assistance of the Ministry of Social Justice and Empowerment, Agewell Foundation, an NGO of Delhi, has started a helpline for older persons. A centre named

AADHAR is also being set up with the financial assistance of the
Ministry of Social Justice and Empowerment to receive and process
the representations/petitions of older persons pertaining to their various problems and to take follow up action thereon.

Expeditious Disposal of Court Cases

The Supreme Court has advised the chief justice of all the high courts
in the country to accord priority to cases involving older persons and
ensure their expeditious disposal. The Mumbai high court has
announced that it would give out-of-turn priority to hearing and disposal of petitions wherein litigants have crossed 65 years of age. The
high court decision would also be applicable to its benches at Goa,
Aurangabad and Nagpur besides the subordinate courts in the state.
It would extend to all the matters, including civil or criminal, pending
in any court of law.

Mobile Medicare Unit Programme

HelpAge India provides basic essential medicare to the door steps of
the needy and underprivileged elderly in India through its Mobile
Medicare Unit (MMU) Programme operating in the places shown in
Table B.3.

In addition, HelpAge India has provided about 80 MMUs to grass-
root NGOs for similar services.

Table B.3
The MMU Programme in India

Cities	MMU's	Cities	MMU's	Cities	MMU's	Cities	MMU's
Delhi/ Gurgaon	2 plus planned	Nagpur	1	Hyderabad	1	Bhadohi	1
Mumbai	2	Lucknow	1	Ahmedabad	1	Bhubaneswar	1
Calcutta	2	Jammu	1	Pune	1	Paradeep	1
Chennai	1	Faridabad	1	Chandigarh	1	Bikaner	1
Bangalore	1	Jaipur	planned	Coimbatore	planned	Bhopal	planned

BANKING

Most banks in India provide a slight enhanced rate of interest for savings maintained by the elderly. The Indusind Bank Ltd. has also launched a Senior Citizens Scheme—an investment option that gives high returns with assured security.

MAGAZINES FOR THE ELDERLY

There are two magazines specifically designed for the elderly: *Dignity Dialogue* by Dignity Foundation and *Senior Heritage Selections* by Heritage Medical Centre. Both *Dignity Dialogue* and *Senior Heritage Selections* are a refreshing social contribution and restore some balance to the otherwise distorted view society tends to have of old age. The publications deal with a wide spectrum of issues, starting from the indignity of elder abuse to alternative medicine, to some philosophy and some inspirational material. Moreover, they provide a forum for the elderly to express their opinions and creativity.

RECOMMENDATIONS AT THE WORLD ASSEMBLIES ON AGEING

RECOMMENDATIONS AT THE WORLD ASSEMBLY ON AGEING AT VIENNA, AUSTRIA, 1982

(Approved by the United Nations General Assembly in 1982 vide resolution 37/51 and in 1991 under resolution 46/91)

HEALTH CARE AND NUTRITION

Recommendation 1

Care designed to alleviate the handicaps, re-educate remaining functions, relieve pain, maintain the lucidity, comfort and dignity of the affected and help them to re-orient their hopes and plans, particularly in the case of the elderly, are just as important as curative treatment.

Recommendation 2

The care of elderly persons should go beyond disease orientation and should involve their total well-being, taking into account the interdependence of the physical, mental, social, spiritual and environmental factors. Health care should therefore involve the health and social sectors and the family in improving the quality of life of older persons. Health efforts, in particular primary health care as a strategy, should be directed at enabling the elderly to lead independent lives in their own family and community for as long as possible instead of being excluded and cut off from all activities of society.

There is no doubt that, with advancing age, pathological conditions increase in frequency. Furthermore, the living conditions of the elderly make them more prone to risk factors that might have adverse effects on their health (e.g., social isolation and accidents)—factors that can be modified to a great extent. Research and practical experience have demonstrated that health maintenance in the elderly is possible and that diseases do not need to be essential components of ageing.

Recommendation 3

Early diagnosis and appropriate treatment is required, as well as preventive measures, to reduce disabilities and diseases of the ageing.

Recommendation 4

Particular attention should be given to providing health care to the very old, and to those who are incapacitated in their daily lives. This is particularly true when they are suffering from mental disorders or from failure to adapt to the environment; mental disorders could often be prevented or modified by means that do not require placement of the affected in institutions, such as training and supporting the family and volunteers by professional workers, promoting ambulant mental health care, welfare work, day-care and measures aimed at the prevention of social isolation.

Some sectors of the ageing, and especially the very old, will nevertheless continue to be vulnerable. Because they may be among the least mobile, this group is particularly in need of primary care from facilities located close to their residences and/or communities. The concept of primary health care incorporates the use of existing health and social services personnel, with the assistance of community health officers trained in simple techniques of caring for the elderly.

Early diagnosis and treatment are of prime importance in the prevention of mental illness in older people. Special efforts need to be taken to assist older persons who have mental health problems or who are at high risk in this respect.

Where hospital care is needed, application of the skills of geriatric medicine enables a patient's total condition to be assessed and, through the work of a multidisciplinary team, a programme of treatment and rehabilitation to be devised, which is geared to an early return to the community and the provision there of any necessary continuing care. All patients should receive in proper time any form of intensive treatment which they require, with a view to preventing complications and functional failure leading to permanent invalidity and premature death.

Recommendation 5

Attentive care for the terminally ill, dialogue with them and support for their close relatives at the time of loss and later require special efforts which go beyond normal medical practice. Health practitioners should aspire to provide such care. The need for these special efforts must be known and understood by those providing medical care and by the families of the terminally ill and by the terminally ill themselves. Bearing these needs in mind, exchange of information about relevant experiences and practices found in a number of cultures should be encouraged.

A proper balance between the role of institutions and that of the family in providing health care for the elderly—based on recognition of the family and the immediate community as elements in a well-balanced system of care—is important.

Existing social services and health-care systems for the ageing are becoming increasingly expensive. Means of halting or reversing this trend and of developing social systems together with primary health care services need to be considered, in the spirit of the Declaration of Alma-Ata.

Recommendation 6

The trend towards increased costs of social services and health-care systems should be offset through closer co-ordination between social welfare and health care services both at the national and community levels. For example, measures need to be taken to increase collaboration between personnel working in the two sectors and to provide them with interdisciplinary training. These systems should, however, be developed, taking into account the role of the family and community—which should remain the interrelated key elements in a well-balanced system of care. All this must be done without detriment to the standard of medical and social care of the elderly.

Those who give most direct care to the elderly are often the least trained, or have insufficient training for their purpose. To maintain the well-being and independence of the elderly through self-care, health promotion, prevention of disease and disability requires new orientation and skills, among the elderly themselves, as well as their families, and health and social welfare workers in the local communities.

Recommendation 7

The population at large should be informed in regard to dealing with the elderly who require care. The elderly themselves should be educated in self-care:

- ◆ those who work with the elderly at home, or in institutions, should receive basic training for their tasks, with particular emphasis on participation of the elderly and their families, and collaboration between workers in health and welfare fields at various levels;
- ◆ practitioners and students in the human care professions (e.g., medicine, nursing, social welfare etc.) should be trained in principles and skills in the relevant areas of gerontology, geriatrics, psychogeriatrics and geriatric nursing.

All too often, old age is an age of no consent. Decisions affecting ageing citizens are frequently made without the participation of the citizens themselves. This applies particularly to those who are very old, frail or disabled. Such people should be served by flexible systems of care that give them a choice as to the type of amenities and the kind of care they receive.

Recommendation 8

The control of the lives of the ageing should not be left solely to health, social service and other caring personnel, since ageing people themselves usually know best what is needed and how it should be carried out.

Recommendation 9

Participation of the aged in the development of health care and the functioning of health services should be encouraged.

A fundamental principle in the care of the elderly should be to enable them to lead independent lives in the community for as long as possible.

Recommendation 10

Health and health-allied services should be developed to the fullest extent possible in the community. These services should include a broad range of ambulatory services such as day-care centres, out-patient clinics, day hospitals, medical and nursing care and domestic services. Emergency services should be always available. Institutional care should always be appropriate to the needs of the elderly. Inappropriate use of beds in health care facilities should be avoided. In particular, those not mentally ill should not be placed in mental hospitals. Health screening and counselling should be offered through geriatric clinics, neighbourhood health centres or community sites where older persons congregate. The necessary health infrastructure and specialised staff to provide thorough and complete geriatric care should be made available. In the case of institutional care, alienation through isolation of the aged from society should be avoided inter alia by further encouraging the involvement of family members and volunteers.

Nutritional problems, such as deficient quantity and inappropriate constituents, are encountered among the poor and underprivileged elderly in both the developed and the developing countries. Accidents are also a major risk area for the elderly. The alleviation of these problems may require a multi-sectoral approach.

Recommendation 11

The promotion of health, the prevention of disease and the maintaining of functional capacities among elderly persons should be actively pursued. For this purpose, an assessment of the physical, psychological and social needs of the group concerned is a prerequisite. Such an assessment would enhance the prevention of disability, early diagnosis and rehabilitation.

Recommendation 12

Adequate, appropriate and sufficient nutrition, particularly the adequate intake of protein, minerals and vitamins, is essential to the well-being of the elderly. Poor nutrition is exacerbated by poverty, isolation, maldistribution of food, and poor eating habits, including those due to dental problems. Therefore special attention should be paid to:

♦ Improvement of the availability of sufficient foodstuffs to the elderly through appropriate schemes and encouraging the aged in rural areas to play an active role in food production;
♦ a fair and equitable distribution of food, wealth, resources and technology;
♦ education of the public, including the elderly, in correct nutrition and eating habits, both in urban and rural areas;
♦ provision of health and dental services for early detection of mal-nutrition and improvement of mastication;
♦ studies of the nutritional status of the elderly at the community level, including steps to correct any unsatisfactory local conditions;
♦ extension of research into the role of nutritional factors in the ageing process to communities in developing countries.

Recommendation 13

Efforts should be intensified to develop home care to provide high quality health and social services in the quantity necessary so that older persons are enabled to remain in their own communities and to live as independently as possible for as long as possible. Home care should not be viewed as an alternative to institutional care: rather, the two are complementary to each other and should so link into the delivery system that older persons can receive the best care appropriate to their needs at the least cost.

Special support must be given to home care services, by providing them with sufficient medical, paramedical, nursing and technical facilities of the required standard to limit the need for hospitalisation.

Recommendation 14

A very important question concerns the possibilities of preventing or at least postponing the negative functional consequences of ageing. Many lifestyle factors may have their most pronounced effects during old age when the reserve capacity usually is lower.

The health of the ageing is fundamentally conditioned by their previous health and, therefore, lifelong health care starting with young age is of paramount importance; this includes preventive health, nutrition, exercise, the avoidance of health-harming habits and attention to environmental factors, and this care should be continued.

Recommendation 15

The health hazards of cumulative noxious substances—including radioactive and trace elements and other pollution—assume a greater importance as lifespan increases and should, therefore, be the subject of special attention and investigation throughout the entire lifespan.

Governments should promote the safe handling of such materials in use, and move rapidly to ensure that waste materials from such use are permanently and safely removed from man's biosphere.

Recommendation 16

As avoidable accidents represent a substantial cost both in human suffering and in resources, priority should be given to measures to prevent accidents in the home, on the road, and those precipitated by treatable medical conditions or by inappropriate use of medication.

Recommendation 17

International exchange and research co-operation should be promoted in carrying out epidemiological studies of local patterns of health and diseases and their consequences together with investigating the validity of different care delivery systems, including self-care, and home care by nurses, and in particular of ways of achieving optimum programme effectiveness; also investigating the demands for various types of care and developing means of coping with them paying particular attention to comparative studies regarding the achievement of objectives and relative cost-effectiveness; and gathering data on the physical, mental and social profiles of ageing individuals in various social and cultural contexts, including attention to the special problems of access to services in rural and remote areas, in order to provide a sound basis for future actions.

PROTECTION OF ELDERLY CONSUMERS

Recommendation 18

Governments should:

♦ Ensure that food and household products, installations and equipment conform to standards of safety that take into account the vulnerability of the aged;
♦ encourage the safe use of medications, household chemicals and other products by requiring manufacturers to indicate necessary warnings and instructions for use;
♦ facilitate the availability of medications, hearing aids, dentures, glasses and other prosthetics to the elderly so that they can prolong their activities and independence;
♦ restrain the intensive promotion and other marketing techniques primarily aimed at exploiting the meagre resources of the elderly.

HOUSING

Recommendation 19

Housing for the elderly must be viewed as more than mere shelter. In addition to the physical, it has psychological and social significance, which should be taken into account. To release the aged from dependence on others, national housing policies should pursue the following goals:

- Helping the aged to continue to live in their own homes as long as possible, provision being made for restoration and development and, where feasible and appropriate, the remodelling and improvement of homes and their adaptation to match the ability of the aged to get to and from them and use the facilities;
- planning and introducing—under a housing policy that also provides for public financing and agreements with the private sector— housing for the aged of various types to suit the status and degree of self-sufficiency of the aged themselves, in accordance with local traditional and customs;
- co-ordinating policies on housing with those concerned, with community services (social, health, cultural, leisure, communications) so as to secure, whenever possible, an especially favourable position for housing the aged vis-à-vis dwellings for the population at large;
- evolve and apply special policies and measures, and make arrangements so as to allow the aged to move about and to protect them from traffic hazards;
- such a policy should, in turn, form part of the broader policy of support for the least well off sectors of the population.

Recommendation 20

Urban rebuilding and development planning and law should pay special attention to the problems of the ageing, assisting in securing their social integration.

Recommendation 21

National governments should be encouraged to adopt housing policies that take into account the needs of the elderly and the socially disadvantaged. A living environment designed to support the functional capacities of this group and the socially disadvantaged should be an integral part of national guidelines for human settlement policies and action.

Recommendation 22

Special attention should be paid to environmental problems and to designing a living environment that would take into account the functional capacity of the elderly and facilitate mobility and communication through the provision of adequate means of transport.

The living environment should be designed, with support from governments, local authorities and non-governmental organisations, so as to enable elderly people to continue to live, if they so wish, in locations that are familiar to them, where their involvement in the community may be of long standing and where they will have the opportunity to lead a rich, normal and secure life.

Recommendation 23

The growing incidence of crime in some countries against the elderly victimises not only those directly involved, but the many older persons who become afraid to leave their homes. Efforts should be directed to law enforcement agencies and the elderly to increase their awareness of the extent and impact of crime against older persons.

Recommendation 24

Whenever possible, the ageing should be involved in housing policies and programmes for the elderly population.

FAMILY

The family, regardless of its form or organisation, is recognised as a fundamental unit of society. With increasing longevity, four- and five-generation families are becoming common throughout the world. The changes in the status of women, however, have reduced their traditional role as caretakers of older family members; it is necessary to enable the family as a whole, including its male members, to take over and share the burden of help in and by the family. Women are entering and remaining in the labour force for longer periods of time. Many who have completed their child-rearing roles become caught between the desire and need to work and earn an income and the responsibility of caring for elderly parents or grandparents.

Recommendation 25

As the family is recognised as a fundamental unit of society, efforts should be made to support, protect and strengthen it in agreement with each society's system of cultural values and in responding to the needs of its ageing members. Governments should promote social policies encouraging the maintenance of family solidarity among generations, with all members of the family participating. The role and contribution of the non-governmental organisations in strengthening the family as a unit should also be stressed at all levels.

Recommendation 26

Appropriate support from the wider community, available when and where it is needed, can make a crucial difference to the willingness and ability of families to continue to care for elderly relatives. Planning and provision of services should take full account of the needs of those carers.

There is ample evidence of the high esteem in which older people are held in developing countries. Trends towards increasing industrialisation and urbanisation and greater mobility of the labour force indicate, however, that the traditional concept of the role of the elderly in the family is undergoing major change. Worldwide, the overall responsibility of the family to provide the traditional care and support needs of the ageing is diminishing.

Recommendation 27

Ways to ensure continuity of the vital role of the family and the dignity, status and security of the ageing, taking into account all the internal and international events which might influence this status of security, are issues that deserve careful consideration and action by governments and non-governmental organisations. Recognising the predominance of older women, and the relatively greater numbers of widows than widowers throughout the world, particular consideration should he given to the special needs and roles of this group.

Recommendation 28

Governments are urged to adopt an age/family-integrated approach to planning and development, which would recognise the special needs and characteristics of older persons and their families. Older persons should be included in the governmental and other decision-making processes in the political, social, cultural and educational areas among others, and children should be encouraged to support their parents.

Recommendation 29

Governments and non-governmental bodies should be encouraged to establish social services to support the whole family when there are elderly people at home and to implement measures especially for low-income families who wish to keep elderly people at home.

SOCIAL WELFARE

Social welfare services can be instruments of national policy and should have, as their goal, the maximising of the social functioning of the ageing. They should be community-based and provide a broad range of preventive, remedial and developmental services for the ageing, to enable them to lead as independent a life as possible in their own home and in their community, remaining active and useful citizens.

In relation to elderly migrants appropriate measures should be taken to provide social welfare services in accordance with their ethnic, cultural, linguistic and other characteristics.

Recommendation 30

Social welfare services should have as their goal the creation, promotion and maintenance of active and useful roles for the elderly for as long as possible in and for the community.

In many countries where resources are scarce, there is a general lack of organised social welfare services, particularly in the rural areas. Although the role of governments in providing such services is paramount, the contribution of non-governmental organisations is also of great importance.

In traditional societies, old people have always enjoyed a privileged position based on respect, consideration, status and authority. But this is starting to be upset under the influence of modern trends and that privileged position is now being questioned. It is therefore time to become aware of these changes and on that basis to define national ageing policies that would avoid some of the problems concerning the elderly faced by some developed countries.

Recommendation 31

Existing formal and informal organisations should consider the particular needs of the ageing and allow for them in their programmes and future planning. The important role that co-operatives can play in providing services in this area should be recognised and encouraged. Such co-operatives could also benefit from the participation of elderly people as full members or consultants. A partnership should be formed between governments and non-governmental organisations designed to ensure a comprehensive, integrated, co-ordinated and multi-purpose approach to meeting the social welfare needs of the elderly.

Recommendation 32

The involvement of young people—in providing services and care and in participating in activities for and with the elderly—should be encouraged, with a view to promoting intergenerational ties. Mutual self-help among the able and active elderly should be stimulated to the extent possible, as should the assistance this group can provide to its less fortunate peers, and the involvement of the elderly in informal part-time occupations.

Recommendation 33

Governments should endeavour to reduce or eliminate fiscal or other constraints on informal and voluntary activities, and eliminate or relax regulations, which hinder or discourage part-time work, mutual self-help and the use of volunteers alongside professional staff in providing social services or in institutions for the elderly.

Recommendation 34

Whenever institutionalisation is necessary or inevitable for elderly persons, the utmost effort must be made to ensure a quality of institutional life corresponding to normal conditions in their communities, with full respect for their dignity, beliefs, needs, interests and privacy; States should be encouraged to define minimum standards to ensure higher quality of institutional care.

Recommendation 35

In order to facilitate mutual help among the elderly and let their voices be heard, governments and non-governmental bodies should encourage the establishment and free initiative of groups and movements of elderly persons and also give other age groups opportunities for training in, and information on, the support of the elderly.

INCOME SECURITY AND EMPLOYMENT

Major differences exist between the developed and the developing countries and particularly between urban, industrialised and rural, agrarian economies—with regard to the achievement of policy goals related to income security and employment. Many developed countries have achieved universal coverage through generalised social security schemes. For the developing countries, where many if not the majority of persons live at subsistence levels, income security is an issue of concern for all age groups. In several of these countries, the social security programmes launched tend to offer limited coverage; in the rural areas, where in many cases most of the population lives, there is little or no coverage. Furthermore, particular attention should be paid, in social security and social programmes, to the circumstances of the elderly women whose income is generally lower than men's and whose employment has often been broken up by maternity and family responsibilities. In the long term, policies should be directed towards providing social insurance for women in their own right.

Recommendation 36

Governments should take appropriate action to ensure to all older persons an appropriate minimum income, and should develop their economies to benefit all the population. To this end, they should:

- ♦ Create or develop social security schemes based on the principle of universal coverage for older people. Where this is not feasible, other approaches should be tried, such as payment of benefits in kind, or direct assistance to families and local co-operative institutions;
- ♦ ensure that the minimum benefits will be enough to meet the essential needs of the elderly and guarantee their independence. Whether or not social security payments are calculated taking into account previous income, efforts should be made to maintain their purchasing power. Ways should be explored to protect the savings of the elderly against the effects of inflation. In determining the age at which pensions are payable, due account should be taken of the age of retirement, changes in the national demographic structure and of the national economic capacity. At the same time, efforts should be made to achieve continuous economic growth;
- ♦ in social security systems, make it possible for women as well as men to acquire their own rights;
- ♦ within the social security system and if necessary by other means, respond to the special needs of income security for older workers who are unemployed or those who are incapable of working;
- ♦ other possibilities of making available supplementary retirement income and incentives to develop new means of personal savings for the elderly should be explored.

Broadly related to the issues of income security are the dual issues of the right to work and the right to retire. In most areas of the world, efforts by older persons to participate in work and economic activities which will satisfy their need to contribute to the life of the community and benefit society as a whole meet with difficulties. Age discrimination is prevalent: many older workers are unable to remain in the labour force or to re-enter it because of age prejudice. In some countries this situation tends to impact women more severely. The integration of the aged into the machinery of development affects both the urban and rural population groups.

Recommendation 37

Governments should facilitate the participation of older persons in the economic life of the society. For that purpose:

♦ Appropriate measures should be taken, in collaboration with employers' and workers' organisations, to ensure to the maximum extent possible that older workers can continue to work under satisfactory conditions and enjoy security of employment;
♦ governments should eliminate discrimination in the labour market and ensure equality of treatment in professional life. Negative stereotypes about older workers exist among some employers. Governments should take steps to educate employers and employment counsellors about the capabilities of older workers, which remain quite high in most occupations. Older workers should also enjoy equal access to orientation, training and placement facilities and services;
♦ measures should be taken to assist older persons to find or return to independent employment by creating new employment possibilities and facilitating training or retraining. The right of older workers to employment should be based on ability to perform the work rather than chronological age;
♦ despite the significant unemployment problems facing many nations, in particular with regard to young people, the retirement age for employees should not be lowered except on a voluntary basis.

Recommendation 38

Older workers, like all other workers, should enjoy satisfactory working conditions and environment. Where necessary, measures should be taken to prevent industrial and agricultural accidents and occupational diseases. Working conditions and the working environment, as well as the scheduling and organisation of work, should take into account the characteristics of older workers.

Recommendation 39

Proper protection for workers, which permits better follow-up for people of advanced age, comes about through a better knowledge of occupational diseases. This necessarily entails training medical staff in occupational medicine.

Similarly, pre-retirement medical checks would allow the effects of occupational disease upon the individual to be detected and appropriate steps to be planned.

Recommendation 40

Governments should take or encourage measures that will ensure a smooth and gradual transition from active working life to retirement, and in addition make the age of entitlement to a pension more flexible. Such measures would include pre-retirement courses and lightening the workload during the last years of the working life, for example by modifying the conditions of work and the working environment of the work organisation and by promoting a gradual reduction of work-time.

Recommendation 41

Governments should apply internationally adopted standards concerning older workers; particularly those embodied in Recommendation 162 of the International Labour Organization. In addition, at the international level, approaches and guidelines concerning the special needs of these workers should continue to be developed.

Recommendation 42

In the light of ILO Convention No. 157 concerning maintenance of social security rights, measures should be taken, particularly through bilateral or multilateral conventions, to guarantee to legitimate migrant workers full social coverage in the receiving country as well as maintenance of social security rights acquired, especially regarding pensions, if they return to their country of origin. Similarly, migrant workers returning to their countries should be afforded special conditions facilitating their reintegration, particularly with regard to housing.

Recommendation 43

As far as possible, groups of refugees accepted by a country should include elderly persons as well as adults and children, and efforts should be made to keep family groups intact and to ensure that appropriate housing and services are provided.

EDUCATION

The scientific and technological revolutions of the 20th century have led to a knowledge and information 'explosion'. The continuing and expanding nature of these revolutions has given rise also to accelerated social change. In many of the worlds societies, the elderly still serve as the transmitters of information, knowledge, tradition and spiritual values: this important tradition should not be lost.

Recommendation 44

Educational programmes featuring the elderly as the teachers and transmitters of knowledge, culture and spiritual values should be developed.

In many instances, the knowledge explosion is resulting in information obsolescence, with, in turn, implications of social obsolescence. These changes suggest that the educational structures of society must be expanded to respond to the educational needs of an entire lifespan. Such an approach to education would suggest the need for continuous adult education, including preparation for ageing and the creative use of time. In addition, it is important that the ageing, along with the other age groups, have access to basic literacy education, as well as to all education facilities available in the community.

Recommendation 45

As a basic human right, education must be made available without discrimination against the elderly. Educational policies should reflect the principle of the right to education of the ageing, through the appropriate allocation of resources and in suitable education programmes. Care should be taken to adapt educational methods to the capacities of the elderly, so that they may participate equitably in and profit from any education provided. The need for continuing adult education at all levels should be recognised and encouraged. Consideration should be given to the idea of university education for the elderly.

There is also a need to educate the general public with regard to the ageing process. Such education must start at an early age in order that ageing should be fully understood as a natural process. The importance of the role of the mass media in this respect cannot be overstated.

Recommendation 46

A co-ordinated effort by the mass media should be undertaken to highlight the positive aspects of the ageing process and of the ageing themselves. This effort should cover, among other things:

♦ The present situation of the aged, in particular in rural areas of developed and developing countries, with a view to identifying and responding to their real needs;
♦ the effects of migration (both internal and international) on the relative ageing of populations of rural areas, and its effects on agricultural production and living conditions in these areas;
♦ methods to develop job opportunities for and adapt conditions of work to older workers. This would include developing or furnishing simple equipment and tools which would help those with limited physical strength to accomplish their assigned tasks;
♦ surveys of the role of education and ageing in various cultures and societies.

Recommendation 47

In accordance with the concept of lifelong education promulgated by the United Nations Educational, Scientific and Cultural Organization

(UNESCO), informal, community-based and recreation-oriented programmes for the ageing should be promoted in order to help them develop a sense of self-reliance and community responsibility. Such programmes should enjoy the support of national governments and international organisations.

Recommendation 48

Governments and international organisations should support pro-grammes aimed at providing the elderly with easier physical access to cultural institutions (museums, theatres, opera houses, concert halls, cinemas etc.) in order to encourage their greater participation in leisure activities and the creative use of their time. Furthermore, cultural centres should be asked to organise for, and with, the elderly workshops in such fields as handicrafts, fine arts and music, where the elderly can play an active role both as audience and participants.

Recommendation 49

Governments and international organisations concerned with the problems of ageing should initiate programmes aimed at educating the general public with regard to the ageing process and the ageing. Such activities should start from early childhood and continue through all levels of the formal school system. The role and involvement of min-istries of education in this respect should be strengthened in encour-aging and facilitating the inclusion of ageing in curricula, as an aspect of normal development and education for the life of individuals begin-ning with the youngest age, so leading to greater knowledge of the subject and to possible positive change in the stereotypical attitudes to ageing of present generations. Non-formal channels and the mass media should also be used to develop such programmes. The mass media should also be used as a means of promoting the participation of the aged in social, cultural and educational activities within the community; conversely, the aged or their representatives should be involved in formulating and designing these activities.

Recommendation 50

Where stereotypes of the ageing person exist, efforts by the media, educational institutions, governments, non-governmental organisations and the ageing themselves should be devoted to overcoming the stereotyping of older persons as always manifesting physical and psychological disabilities, incapable of functioning independently and having neither role nor status in society. These efforts are necessary for achieving an age-integrated society.

Recommendation 51

Comprehensive information on all aspects of their lives should be made available to the ageing in a clear and understandable form.

Recommendation 52

Full use should also be made of opportunities existing for technical co-operation between developed and developing countries in the field of ageing.

DATA COLLECTION AND ANALYSIS

Data concerning the older sector of the population—collected through censuses, surveys or vital statistics systems—are essential for the formulation, application and evaluation of policies and programmes for the elderly and for ensuring their integration in the development process.

Governments and organisations that are in a position to do so should develop an information base, which would be more specific than the 'sixty-and-over' one now in use and which would be of help in planning the development of and solving problems concerning the elderly. The base could cover social, age, functional and economic classifications, among others.

Household sample and other surveys and other sources of demographic and related socio-economic statistics provide important data for use in formulating and implementing policies and programmes for the elderly.

All countries that so request should be provided with the technical assistance needed to develop or improve databases relating to their elderly and the services and institutions that concern them. The assistance should cover training and research in methodologies for collecting, processing and analysing data.

Recommendation 52

Data concerning the ageing could be developed along the line of a codification system, which will give national governments information, tabulated by sex, age, income levels, living arrangements, health status and degree of self-care, among others. Such data could be collected through the census, micro or pilot census or representative surveys. Governments are urged to allocate resources for that purpose.

Recommendation 53

Governments and institutions concerned should establish or improve existing information exchange facilities, such as databanks in the field of ageing.

TRAINING AND EDUCATION

The dramatic increase in the number and proportion of older adults calls for a significant increase in training. A dual approach is needed: an international programme for training concomitant with national and regional training programmes that are particularly relevant to conditions in the countries and regions concerned. The needs of the elderly, as well as the implications of the ageing of the population for development, need to be taken into account in developing education and training policies and programmes for all ages, especially the younger generation.

Recommendation 54

Education and training programmes should be interdisciplinary in nature, as ageing and the ageing of the population is a multidisciplinary issue. Education and training in the various aspects of ageing and the ageing of the population should not be restricted to high levels of specialisation, but should be made available at all levels. Efforts should be made to regulate the training skills and educational requirements for different functions in the field of ageing.

The exchange of skills, knowledge and experience among countries with similar or comparable structures and composition, or having historical, cultural, linguistic or other links, with respect to their ageing population would be a particularly fertile form of international co-operation. Besides the transfer of specific skills and technologies, the exchange of experience regarding the wide array of practices relating to ageing could also constitute an area for technical co-operation among developing countries. In regions, which include both developed, and developing countries side by side, the rich opportunities for mutual learning and co-operation in training and research should be vigorously explored.

Recommendation 55

Intergovernmental and non-governmental organisations should take the necessary measures to develop trained personnel in the field of ageing, and should strengthen their efforts to disseminate information on ageing, and particularly to the ageing themselves.

Recommendation 56

Retirees' and elderly people's organisations should be involved in planning and carrying out such exchanges of information.

Recommendation 57

The implementation of several recommendations will require trained personnel in the field of ageing. Practical training centres should be promoted and encouraged, where appropriate facilities already exist, to train such personnel, especially from developing countries, who would in their turn train others. These centres would also provide updating and refresher courses and act as a practical bridge between and among developed and developing regions; they would be linked with appropriate United Nations agencies and facilities.

Recommendation 58

At national, regional and international levels, extra attention should be given to research and study undertaken in support of integrating the problems of ageing in planning and policy formulation and management.

Recommendation 59

Training in all aspects of gerontology and geriatrics should be encouraged and given due prominence at all levels in all educational programmes. Governments and competent authorities are called upon to encourage new or existing institutions to pay special attention to appropriate training in gerontology and geriatrics.

RESEARCH

The Plan of Action gives high priority to research related to developmental and humanitarian aspects of ageing. Research activities are instrumental in formulating, evaluating and implementing policies and programmes: (a) as to the implications of the ageing of the population for development; and, (b) as to the needs of the ageing. Research into the social, economic and health aspects of ageing should be encouraged to achieve efficient uses of resources, improvement in social and health measures, including the prevention of functional decline, age-related disabilities, illness and poverty, and co-ordination of the services involved in the care of the ageing.

The knowledge obtained by research provides scientific backing for a sounder basis for effective societal planning as well as for improving the well-being of the elderly. Further research is required, e.g. (a) to narrow the wide gaps in knowledge about ageing and about the particular needs of the ageing; and (b) to enable resources provided for the ageing to be used more effectively. There should be emphasis on the continuum of research from the discovery of new knowledge to its vigorous and more rapid application and transfer of technological knowledge with due consideration of cultural and social diversity.

Recommendation 60

Research should be conducted into the developmental and humanitarian aspects of ageing at local, national, regional and global levels. Research should be encouraged particularly in the biological, mental and social fields. Issues of basic and applied research of universal interest to all societies include:

- The role of genetic and environmental factors;
- the impact of biological, medical, cultural, societal and behavioural factors on ageing;
- the influence of economic and demographic factors (including migration) on societal planning;
- the use of skills, expertise, knowledge and cultural potential of the ageing;
- the postponement of negative functional consequences of ageing;
- health and social services for the ageing as well as studies of co-ordinated programmes;
- training and education.

Such research should be generally planned and carried out by researchers closely acquainted with national and regional conditions, being granted the independence necessary for innovation and diffusion. States, intergovernmental organisations and non-governmental organisations should carry out more research and studies on the developmental and humanitarian aspects of ageing, co-operate in this field and exchange their findings in order to provide a logical basis for policies related to ageing in general.

Recommendation 61

States, intergovernmental organisations and non-governmental organisations should encourage the establishment of institutions specialising in the teaching of gerontology, geriatrics and geriatric psychology in countries where such institutions do not exist.

Recommendation 62

International exchange and research co-operation as well as data collection should be promoted in all fields having a bearing on ageing, in order to provide a rational basis for future social policies and action. Special emphasis should be placed on comparative and cross-cultural studies on ageing. Interdisciplinary approaches should be stressed.

POLITICAL DECLARATION OF THE SECOND WORLD ASSEMBLY ON AGEING IN MADRID, SPAIN

12 APRIL 2002

Article 1

We, the representatives of Governments meeting at this Second World Assembly on Ageing in Madrid, Spain, have decided to adopt an International Plan of Action on Ageing 2002 to respond to the opportunities and challenges of population ageing in the twenty-first century and promote the development of a society for all ages. In the context of this Plan of Action, we are committed to actions at all levels, including national and international levels, on three priority directions: older persons and development; advancing health and well being into old age; and, ensuring enabling and supportive environments.

Article 2

We celebrate rising life expectancy in many regions of the world as one of humanity's major achievements. We recognize that the world is experiencing an unprecedented demographic transformation and that by 2050 the number of persons aged 60 years and over will increase from 600 million to almost 2,000 million and the proportion of persons aged 60 years and over is expected to double from 10 per cent to 21 per cent. The increase will be greatest and most rapid in developing countries where the older population is expected to quadruple during the next 50 years. This demographic transformation challenges all our societies to promote increased opportunities, in particular for older persons to realize their potential to participate fully in all aspects of life.

Article 3

We reiterate the commitments made by our heads of State and Governments in major UN conferences and summits and their follow-up processes, and in the Millennium Declaration, with respect to the promotion of international and national environments that will foster a society for all ages. We furthermore reaffirm the Principles and Recommendations for Action of the International Plan of Action on Ageing endorsed by the United Nations General Assembly in 1982 and the United Nations Principles for Older Persons adopted by the General Assembly in 1991, which provided guidance in areas of independence, participation, care, self-fulfillment and dignity.

3. bis: We emphasize that in order to complement national efforts to fully implement the International Plan of Action on Ageing 2002, enhanced international cooperation is essential. We therefore, encourage the international community to further promote cooperation among all actors involved.

Article 4 (former 5) deleted.

Article 5 (former 2)

We reaffirm the commitment to spare no effort to promote democracy, strengthen the rule of law, promote gender equality, as well as to promote and protect human rights and fundamental freedoms, including the right to development. We commit ourselves to eliminate all forms of discrimination, including age discrimination. We also recognize that persons, as they age, should enjoy a life of fulfillment, health, security and active participation in the economic, social, cultural and political life of their societies. We are determined to enhance the recognition of the dignity of older persons, and to eliminate all forms of neglect, abuse and violence.

Article 5 bis deleted.

Article 6

The modern world has unprecedented wealth and technological capacity and has presented extraordinary opportunities: to empower men and women to reach old age in better health, and with more fully realized well-being; to seek the full inclusion and participation of older persons in societies; to enable older persons to contribute more effectively to their communities and to the development of their societies; and to steadily improve care and support for older persons as they need it. We recognize that concerted action is required to transform the opportunities and the quality of life of men and women as they age and to ensure the sustainability of their support systems, thus building the foundation for a society for all ages. When ageing is embraced as an achievement, the reliance on human skills, experiences and resources of the higher age groups is naturally recognized as an asset in the growth of mature, fully integrated, humane societies.

6 bis: At the same time, considerable obstacles to further integration and full participation in the global economy remain for developing countries, in particular the least developed countries, as well as for some countries with economies in transition. Unless the benefits of social and economic development are extended to all countries, a growing number of people, particularly older persons in all countries and even entire regions will remain marginalized from the global economy. For this reason we recognize the importance of placing ageing in development agendas, as well as strategies for the eradication of poverty and in seeking to achieve the full participation in the global economy of all developing countries.

Article 7 (former 11) deleted.

Article 8 (former 7)

We commit ourselves to the task of effectively incorporating ageing within social and economic strategies, policies and action while recognizing that specific policies will vary according to conditions within each country. We recognize the need to mainstream a gender perspective into all policies and programmes to take account of the needs and experiences of older women and men.

new 8 bis: We commit ourselves to protect and assist older persons in situations of armed conflict and foreign occupation.

Article 9 (former 8) deleted.

Article 10 (former 12)

The potential of older persons is a powerful basis for future development. This enables society to rely increasingly on the skills, experience and wisdom of older persons, not only to take the lead in their own betterment but also to participate actively in that of society as a whole.

new 10 bis: We emphasize the importance of international research on ageing and age related issues, as an important instrument for the formulation of policies on ageing, based on reliable and harmonized indicators developed by, inter alia, national and international statistical organizations.

Article 11 (new)

The expectations of older persons and the economic needs of society demand that older persons be able to participate in the economic, political, social and cultural life of their societies. Older persons should have the opportunity to work for as long as they wish and are able to, in satisfying and productive work, continuing to have access to education and training programs. The empowerment of older persons and the promotion of their full participation, are essential elements for active ageing. For older persons, appropriate sustainable social support should be provided.

Article 12

We stress the primary responsibility of governments in promoting, providing and ensuring access to basic social services, bearing in mind specific needs of older persons. To this end we need to work together with local authorities, civil society, including non-governmental organizations, private sector, volunteers and voluntary organizations, older persons themselves and associations for and of older persons, as well as families and communities.

new 12 bis: We recognize the need to achieve progressively the full realization of the right of everyone to the enjoyment of the highest attainable standard of physical and mental health. We reaffirm that the attainment of the highest possible level of health is a most important worldwide social goal, whose realization requires action of many other social and economic sectors in addition to the health sector. We commit ourselves to provide older persons with universal and equal access to healthcare and services including physical and mental health services and we recognize that the growing needs of an ageing population require additional policies, in particular care and treatment, the promotion of healthy lifestyles and supportive environments. We shall promote independence, accessibility and the empowerment of older persons to participate fully in all aspects of society. We recognize the contribution of older persons to development in their role as caregivers.

Article 13 (new)

We recognize the important role played by families, volunteers, communities, older persons organizations and other community-based organizations in providing support and informal care to older persons in addition to services provided by Governments.

Article 14

We recognize the need to strengthen solidarity among generations, and intergenerational partnerships, keeping in mind the particular needs of both older and younger ones, and encourage mutually responsive relationships between generations.

Article 15 (former 9)

Governments have the primary responsibility to provide leadership on ageing matters and on the implementation of the International Plan of Action on Ageing 2002 but effective collaboration between national and local governments, international agencies, older persons themselves and their organisations, other parts of civil society, including non-governmental organisations, and the private sector is essential. The implementation of the International Plan of Action on Ageing 2002 will require the partnership and involvement of many stakeholders: professional organisations; corporations; workers and workers organisations; co-operatives; research, academic, and other educational and religious institutions; and the media.

Article 16 (new)

We underline the important role of the United Nations system, including the regional commissions in assisting the Governments, at their request, in the implementation, follow-up and national monitoring of the International Plan of Action on Ageing 2002, taking into account the differences in economic, social and demographic conditions existing among countries and regions.

Article 17 (former 15)

We invite all people in all countries from every sector of society, individually and collectively, to join in our dedication to a shared vision of equality for persons of all ages.

MAJOR CHRONIC CONDITIONS AFFECTING OLDER PEOPLE WORLDWIDE

Table A.4
Major Chronic Conditions Affecting Older People Worldwide

Broad Disease Pattern	Examples
Cardiovascular Diseases	Coronary Heart Disease
Hypertension	
Stroke	
Diabetes	
Cancer	
Chronic Obstructive Pulmonary Disease	
Musculoskeletal Conditions	Arthritis and Osteoporosis
Mental Health Conditions	Dementia and Depression
Blindness and Visual Impairment	

Source: WHO, *Life in the 21st Century: A Vision For All*, World Health Report, World Health Organization, Geneva, 1998.

Note: The causes of disability in older age are the same for both women and men, although women are more likely to report musculoskeletal problems.

ORDINANCE ON ELDERLY PEOPLE IN VIET NAM

No.23/2000/PL-UBTVQH10 of April 28, 2000

When they were younger, today's elderly people had the task of giving birth to, bringing up and educating children about dignity, and they still play an important role in families and the society. Caring for the material and spiritual needs of elderly persons and continuously promoting their role are the responsibilities of families, the State and the entire society, which reflect the fine nature, morality and traditions of our nation;

Pursuant to the 1992 Constitution of the Socialist Republic of Vietnam;

Pursuant to the Resolution of the Xth National Assembly, sixth session, on its 2000 legislative program;

This Ordinance provides for the support of and care for, as well as the promotion of, the role of elderly people.

CHAPTER I: GENERAL PROVISIONS

Article 1

Elderly people covered by this Ordinance are citizens of the Socialist Republic of Vietnam aged 60 or older.

Article 2

Elderly people are rendered support and care, and have their role promoted by families, the State and society according to the provisions of law. All citizens must respect the elderly and they have the obligation to help elderly people.

Article 3

It is the prime responsibility of the families of elderly people to support them. Elderly people who are lonely, have no one to support them and have no source of income shall be assisted by the State and society.

Article 4

The State shall adopt appropriate policies of caring for the health, improving the material and spiritual life of elderly people, creating conditions for them to lead a healthy, cheerful as well as useful life, and at the same time, promoting their role in the cause of building and defending the Fatherland.

Article 5

The People's Committees at all levels shall work out plans on caring for elderly people; they shall organize and mobilize society's contributions in order to create conditions to care for, and promote the role of, elderly people.

Article 6

The State, society and families have the responsibility to educate young generations to show their gratitude to and respect for elderly people, and look after them.

Article 7

Elderly people must set a good example in fostering their own ethical qualities and in observing the law, and educating young generations in preserving and developing the nation's fine traditions.

Article 8

The organization of establishments for the care of the elderly must be based on practical situations and the demand for such care, and be in accordance with the provisions of the law.

CHAPTER II: SUPPORTING AND CARING FOR ELDERLY PEOPLE

Article 9

Supporting elderly people means providing economic assistance for, looking after, and spiritually encouraging them and respecting their legitimate aspirations so as to ensure their basic demands for meals, clothing, housing, travel, health, study, culture, information and personal communication.

Those who have the obligation to support elderly people are the latter's spouses, biological children and grandchildren.

Those who have the supporting obligation must not decline this obligation.

Article 10

Those who have the obligation to support the elderly must, depending on their circumstances, arrange living places suitable for maintaining the health and psychological conditions of elderly people.

Those who have the obligation to support the elderly must pay for the cost of medical treatment when their elders get sick, or burial when they die.

All acts of maltreatment or forcing elderly persons to perform excessive work are strictly forbidden.

Article 11

Those who have the obligation to support the elderly but are not in a position to attend directly to elderly people may authorize individuals or service organizations to do so, but with the consent of the elderly people concerned.

The authorized individuals or service organizations shall have to fulfil their commitments to those who authorized them to take care of the elderly people concerned.

Elderly people may request a change in the individuals or service organizations authorized to take care of them, if these individuals or service organizations fail to fulfil their duties.

Article 12

Elderly people who are lonely, without any support and without any source of income shall be entitled to:

♦ Social allowance or being cared for at social relief establishments;
♦ free medical examination and treatment;
♦ when they die, the commune/ward or district township (hereinafter collectively referred to as the commune-level People's Committees) or the social relief establishments must organize their burial and bear the costs thereof.

Article 13

The elderly are given priority in medical examination and treatment, and when seeking public transport, recreation and entertainment.

Article 14

The elderly are given primary health care at their place of residence. The commune-level health stations shall, depending on concrete local conditions, monitor, manage and directly look after the health of elderly persons, and organize periodic health check-ups for them, the funding for which shall be provided by the local budget.

When elderly people who are disabled, lonely and without support get sick but are unable to go for medical examination and treatment at designated places, the heads of the commune-level health stations shall send medical workers to give medical examination and treatment to them at their place of residence.

Article 15

State-run hospitals must have geriatric departments or spare a number of beds for elderly patients under treatment and organize research in therapeutic knowledge and techniques applicable to elderly people.

Article 16

The Ministry of Health shall have to guide medical examination and treatment establishments in health care knowledge and techniques applicable to maintaining elderly people's health: intensify research in the field of care and protection of the health of the elderly; foster and raise the health workers' professional skills in medical examination and treatment for elderly people; apply various forms of education and popularization of general knowledge about physical training so as to help the elderly to increase their capability in preventing and curing diseases, and taking care of their own health.

Article 17

The People's Committees at all levels, political organizations, socio-political organizations, economic organizations, social organizations, socio-professional organizations, units of the people's Armed Forces and all citizens shall, depending on their circumstances, support elderly people in organizing sight-seeing tours of historical sites and scenic places in the country.

Article 18

Investment in building or renovating public utilities shall be made on the basis of taking into account the needs of the elderly in terms of activities and care for them.

Article 19

The State and society shall create favorable conditions for elderly people to enjoy culture and take part in traditional cultural activities of the nation.

Article 20

Mass media agencies shall propagate the Party's lines and undertakings as well as the State's policies and laws on care for elderly people and the promotion of their role and reflections on life, and educate their audiences by developing a sense of respectful care and help for elderly people, praise good people and good deeds reflecting their care of elderly people.

Article 21

The State encourages organizations and individuals, with their own funding sources, to make contributions to and investment in building sanatoriums, health care service establishments, medical therapy and rehabilitation centers, cultural, sport and physical training clubs for elderly people as well as other forms of voluntary assistance to elderly people in the community and social relief establishments.

Article 22

The State encourages elderly people's associations to set up elder-care funds in appropriate forms. The elder-care fund may be formed with voluntary contributions from elderly people, charitable assistance of organizations and individuals inside the country and abroad.

The elder-care fund shall be set up and operated according to the provisions of the law.

CHAPTER IV: STATE MANAGEMENT OVER THE ELDER-RELATED WORK

Article 25

State management over elder-related work includes the following:

♦ Promulgating, amending, supplementing, giving guidance on and organizing the implementation of legal documents, regimes and policies towards elderly people;
♦ compiling statistics on elderly people;
♦ mobilizing, managing and using various resources to boost investment in developing social welfare services for the care of elderly people and the promotion of their role;
♦ supporting activities of elderly people's associations;
♦ supervising, inspecting, settling complaints and denunciations about the implementation of legislation on elderly people;
♦ handling violations in the enforcement of the legislation on elderly people;
♦ establishing international cooperative relations in the care of elderly people and the promotion of their role.

Article 26

The Government shall exercise uniform State management over elder-related work.

The Ministry of Labor, War Invalids and Social Affairs shall be responsible to the Government for providing State management over the elder-related work.

The ministries, ministerial-level agencies, and agencies attached to the Government shall, within the scope of their respective tasks and powers, coordinate with the Ministry of Labor, War Invalids and Social Affairs in providing State management over work related to the elderly.

The People's Committees at all levels shall care for and bring into play the role of elderly people in their respective localities.

Article 27

The Vietnam Fatherland Front Central Committee and the Front's member organizations at all levels shall mobilize families and society to care for, and promote the role of, elderly people.

Article 28

The Vietnam Association of the Elderly is a social organization of elderly people, which has the following responsibilities:

♦ To rally elderly people for participating in the Association's activities, contribute to the implementation of socio-economic programs, the building of a civilized lifestyle and cultured families, the maintenance of political security social safety and order, and the building up and defence of the Fatherland;

♦ to protect the legitimate rights and interests of elderly people, make proposals to the State management bodies on the care for, and the promotion of, the role of elderly people;

♦ to make recommendations to the State bodies on matters relating to the elderly people's legitimate rights and interests;

♦ to represent Vietnamese elderly people in international organizations as well as external relations activities for their interest.

Article 29

The State creates conditions for the Vietnam Association of the Elderly to organize various activities to better care for and promote the role of elderly people.

CHAPTER V: REWARDS AND HANDLING OF VIOLATIONS

Article 30

Organizations and individuals that have recorded outstanding achievements in caring for, assisting and promoting the role of elderly people or in detecting and preventing acting violation of the legislation on elderly people; and elders who set bright examples in social activities, have made good contributions to the cause of national construction and defence, shall be commended and rewarded according to the provisions of the law.

Article 31

Those who infringe upon elderly people's legitimate rights and interests; those who have the obligation to support elderly people but shirk their obligation or maltreat elderly people or commit other acts violating the legal provisions on elderly people, shall, depending on the nature and seriousness of their violations, be disciplined, administratively sanctioned or examined for penal liability; if causing any damage, they shall have to pay compensation according to the provisions of the law.

Abortion Rate

The number of abortions per 1,000 women in the age groups 15–44 or 15–49 in a given year.

Abortion Ratio

The number of abortions per 1,000 live births in a given year.

Age-Dependency Ratio

The ratio of persons in the ages defined as dependent (under 15 years and over 64 years) to persons in the ages defined as economically productive (15–64 years) in a population.

Age-Sex Structure

The composition of a population as determined by the number or proportion of males and females in each age category. The age-sex structure of a population is the cumulative result of past trends in fertility, mortality, and migration. Information on age-sex composition is essential for the description and analysis of many other types of demographic data. See also *population pyramid*.

Age-Specific Rate

Rate obtained for specific age groups (for example, age-specific fertility rate, death rate, marriage rate, illiteracy rate, or school enrolment rate).

Ageing of Population

A process in which the proportions of adults and elderly increase in a population, while the proportions of children and adolescents decrease. This process results in a rise in the median age of the population. Ageing occurs when fertility rates decline while life expectancy remains constant or improves at the older ages.

Anti-natalist Policy	The policy of a government, society, or social group to slow population growth by attempting to limit the number of births.
Baby Boom	A dramatic increase in fertility rates and in the absolute number of births in the United States, Canada, Australia, and New Zealand during the period following World War II (1947–61).
Baby Bust	A rapid decline in US fertility rates to record-low levels during the period immediately after the baby boom.
Balancing Equation	A basic demographic formula used to estimate total population change between two points in time—or to estimate any unknown component of population change, provided that the other components are known. The balancing equation includes all components of population change: births, deaths, immigration, emigration, in-migration and out-migration.
Birth Control	Practices employed by couples that permit sexual intercourse with reduced likelihood of conception and birth. The term birth control is often used synonymously with such terms as contraception, fertility control and family planning. However, birth control includes abortion to prevent a birth, whereas family planning methods explicitly do not include abortion.
Birth Rate (or Crude Birth Rate)	The number of live births per 1,000 population in a given year. Not to be confused with the growth rate.
Birth Rate for Unmarried Women	The number of live births per 1,000 unmarried women (never married, widowed or divorced) in the age group 15–49 in a given year.
Brain Drain	The emigration of a significant proportion of a country's highly skilled, highly educated professional population, usually to other countries offering better economic and social opportunity (for example, physicians leaving a developing country to practice medicine in a developed country).

Carrying Capacity	The maximum sustainable size of a resident population in a given ecosystem.
Case Fatality Rate	The proportion of persons contracting a disease who die from it during a specified time period.
Case Rate	The number of reported cases of a specific disease per 100,000 population in a given year.
Cause-Specific Death Rate	The number of deaths attributable to a specific cause per 100,000 population in a given year.
Census	A canvas of a given area, resulting in an enumeration of the entire population and often the compilation of other demographic, social and economic information pertaining to that population at a specific time. See also *survey*.
Childbearing Years	The reproductive age span of women, assumed for statistical purposes to be 15–44 or 15–49 years of age.
Child-Woman Ratio	The number of children under age 5 per 1,000 women in the age groups 15–44 or 15–49 in a population in a given year. This crude fertility measure, based on basic census data, is sometimes used when more specific fertility information is not available.
Closed Population	A population with no migratory flow either in or out, so that changes in population size occur only through births and deaths.
Cohort Analysis	Observation of a cohort's demographic behaviour through life or through many periods; for example, examining the fertility behaviour of the cohort of people born between 1940 and 1945 through their entire childbearing years. Rates derived from such cohort analyses are cohort measures. Compare with *period analysis*.
Cohort	A group of people sharing a common temporal demographic experience that is observed through time. For example, the birth cohort of 1900 is the people born in that year. There are also marriage cohorts, school class cohorts, and so forth.
Completed Fertility Rate	The number of children born per woman to a cohort of women by the end of their childbearing years.

Consensual Union	Cohabitation by an unmarried couple for an extended period of time. Although such unions may be quite stable, they are not regarded as legal marriages in official statistics.
Contraceptive Prevalence	Percentage of couples currently using a contraceptive method.
Crude Rate	Rate of any demographic event computed for an entire population.
Death Rate (or Crude Death Rate)	The number of deaths per 1,000 population in a given year.
Demographic Transition	The historical shift of birth and death rates from high to low levels in a population. The decline of mortality usually precedes the decline in fertility, thus resulting in rapid population growth during the transition period.
Demography	The scientific study of human populations, including their sizes, compositions, distributions, densities, growth and other characteristics, as well as the causes and consequences of changes in these factors.
Dependency Ratio	The ratio of the economically dependent part of the population to the productive part; arbitrarily defined as the ratio of the elderly (ages 65 and older) plus the young (under age 15) to the population in the working ages (ages 15–64).
Depopulation	The state of population decline.
Divorce Rate (or Crude Divorce Rate)	The number of divorces per 1,000 population in a given year.
Doubling Time	The number of years required for the population of an area to double its present size, given the current rate of population growth.
Economic Activity Rate	The proportion of the specified group supplying labour for the production of economic goods and services during a specified period.
Emigration	The process of leaving one country to take up permanent or semi-permanent residence in another.

Emigration Rate	The number of emigrants departing an area of origin per 1,000 population in that area of origin in a given year.
Ethnicity	The cultural practices, language, cuisine, and traditions—not biological or physical differences—used to distinguish groups of people.
Family	Usually two or more persons living together and related by birth, marriage, or adoption. Families may consist of siblings or other relatives as well as married couples and any children they have.
Family Planning	The conscious effort of couples to regulate the number and spacing of births through artificial and natural methods of contraception. Family planning connotes conception control to avoid pregnancy and abortion, but it also includes efforts of couples to induce pregnancy.
Fecundity	The physiological capacity of a woman to produce a child.
Fertility	The actual reproductive performance of an individual, a couple, a group or a population. See *general fertility rate*.
General Fertility Rate (GFR)	The number of live births per 1,000 women in the age groups 15–44 or 15–49 years in a given year.
Government Consumption	Includes all current expenditures for purchases of goods and services by all levels of government, excluding most government enterprises.
Gross Domestic Investment	Outlays in addition to the fixed assets of the economy plus net changes in the level of inventories.
Gross Domestic Product (GDP)	The total output of goods and services for final use produced by an economy by both residents and non-residents. It does not include depreciation of physical capital and degradation of natural resources.
Gross National Product (GNP)	Comprise GDP plus net factor income abroad, which is the income residents receive from abroad for factor services (labour and capital), less similar payments made to non-residents who contribute to the domestic economy.

Gross Reproduction Rate (GRR)	The average number of daughters that would be born alive to a woman (or group of women) during her lifetime if she passed through her childbearing years conforming to the age-specific fertility rates of a given year. See also *net reproduction rate* and *total fertility rate.*
Growth Rate	The number of persons added to (or subtracted from) a population in a year due to natural increase and net migration expressed as a percentage of the population at the beginning of the time period.
High-risk Pregnancies	Pregnancies occurring under the following conditions: too closely spaced, too frequent, mother too young or too old, or accompanied by such high-risk factors as high blood pressure or diabetes.
Household	One or more persons occupying a housing unit.
Human Development Index (HDI)	A composite index based on three indicators: longevity, as measured by life expectancy at birth; educational attainment, as measured by a combination of adult literacy and the combined gross primary, secondary and tertiary enrolment ratio; and, standard of living, as measured by GDP per capita.
Illegal Alien (sometimes called undocumented alien)	A foreigner who has entered a country without inspection or without proper documents, or who has violated the terms of legal admission to the country, for example, by overstaying the duration of a tourist or student visa.
Illiteracy Rate	Calculated as 100 minus the literacy rate.
Immigration	The process of entering one country from another to take up permanent or semi-permanent residence.
Immigration Rate	The number of immigrants arriving at a destination per 1,000 population at that destination in a given year.
Incidence Rate	The number of persons contracting a disease per 1,000 population at risk, for a given period of time.
Infant Mortality Rate (IMR)	The number of deaths of infants under age 1 per 1,000 live births in a given year.

Inflation	A fall in the purchasing power of money reflected in a persistent increase in the general level of prices as generally measures by the retail price index.
In-migration	The process of entering one administrative subdivision of a country (such as a province or state) from another subdivision to take up residence.
Labour Force Participation Rate	It consists of the economically active population in a particular age group as a percentage of the total population of that same age group. The active population is defined as the sum of persons in employment and unemployed persons seeking employment.
Least Developed Regions (LtDRs)	As of 12th April 2001, there are 49 countries recognised by the United Nations General Assembly as Least Developed Regions. The list includes nine Asian countries: Afghanistan, Bangladesh, Bhutan, Cambodia, Laos, Maldives, Myanmar, Nepal, and Yemen.
Less Developed Regions (LDRs)	It comprises all regions of Africa, Asia (excluding Japan) and Latin America and the Caribbean and the regions of Melanesia, Micronesia and Polynesia.
Life Expectancy	The average number of additional years a person could expect to live if current mortality trends were to continue for the rest of that person's life. Most commonly cited as life expectancy at birth.
Lifespan	The maximum age that human beings could reach under optimum conditions.
Life Table	A tabular display of life expectancy and the probability of dying at each age (or age group) for a given population, according to the age-specific death rates prevailing at that time. The life table gives an organised, complete picture of a population's mortality.
Literacy Rate	The percentage of people aged 15 and above who can, with understanding, both read and write a short, simple statement on their everyday life.
Malthus, Thomas R. (1766–1834)	English clergyman and economist famous for his theory (expounded in the 'Essay on the Principle of Population') that the world's population tends to increase faster than the food supply and that unless fertility is controlled (by late marriage or celibacy), famine, disease, and war must serve as natural population restrictions. See *neo-Malthusian*.

Marital Fertility Rate (MFR)	Number of live births to married women per 1,000 married women in the age groups 15–44 or 15–49 in a given year.
Marriage Rate (or Crude Marriage Rate)	The number of marriages per 1,000 population in a given year.
Maternal Mortality Ratio	The number of women who die as a result of pregnancy and childbirth complications per 100,000 live births in a given year.
Mean Age	The mathematical average age of all the members of a population.
Median Age	The age that divides a population into two numerically equals groups; that is, half the people are younger than this age and half are older.
Medium Variant Projection	The fertility of all countries that had a total fertility above replacement level in 1990–95 is projected to reach replacement level at some point before 2050 and to remain at replacement level from the time it reaches that level until 2050. For countries with total fertility at or below replacement level in 1990–95, fertility levels are projected to remain below replacement level during the whole of the projection period.
Megalopolis	A term denoting an interconnected group of cities and connecting urbanized bands.
Metropolitan Area	A large concentration of population, usually an area with 100,000 or more people. The area typically includes an important city with 50,000 or more inhabitants and the administrative areas bordering the city that are socially and economically integrated with it.
Migration	The movement of people across a specified boundary for the purpose of establishing a new or semi-permanent residence. Divided into international migration (migration between countries) and internal migration (migration within a country).
Mobility	The geographic movement of people.
Morbidity	The frequency of disease, illness, injuries, and disabilities in a population.
More Developed Regions (MDRs)	It comprise all regions of Europe and Northern America, Australia/New Zealand and Japan.

Mortality	Deaths as a component of population change.
Natality	Births as a component of population change.
Natural Increase (or Decrease)	The surplus (or deficit) of births over deaths in a population in a given time period.
Neo-Malthusian	An advocate of restricting population growth through the use of birth control. (Thomas Malthus himself did not advocate birth control as a remedy for rapid population growth.)
Neonatal Mortality Rate	The number of deaths to infants under 28 days of age in a given year per 1,000 live births in that year.
Net Migration	The net effect of immigration and emigration on an area's population in a given time period, expressed as an increase or decrease.
Net Migration Rate	The net effect of immigration and emigration on an area's population, expressed as an increase or decrease per 1,000 population of the area in a given year.
Net Reproduction Rate (NRR)	The average number of daughters that would be born to a woman (or a group of women) if she passed through her lifetime conforming to the age-specific fertility and mortality rates of a given year. This rate is similar to the gross reproduction rate but takes into account that some women will die before completing their childbearing years. An NRR of one means that each generation of mothers is having exactly enough daughters to replace itself in the population. See also *total fertility rate* and *replacement-level fertility*.
Nuptiality	The frequency, characteristics, and dissolution of marriages in a population.
Old Population	A population with a relatively high proportion of middle age and elderly persons, a high median age, and thus a lower growth potential.
Old-age dependency Ratio	Number of persons 65 years and over per persons 15 to 64 years of age.
Out-migration	The process of leaving one sub-division of a country to take up residence in another.
Parent Support Ratio (PaSR)	Number of persons 85 years old and over per 100 persons in the age group of 50 to 64.
Potential Support Ratio (PSR)	Number of persons in the age group of 15 to 64 years per every person aged 65 years or older.

Parity	The number of children previously born alive to a woman; for example, 'two-parity women' are women who have had two children and 'zero-parity women' have had no live births.
Part-time Employment	Refers to people who usually work less than 30 hours a week in their main job.
Perinatal Mortality Rate	The number of fetal deaths after 28 weeks of pregnancy (late fetal deaths) plus the number of deaths to infants under seven days of age per 1,000 live births.
Period Analysis	Observation of a population at a specific period of time. Such an analysis in effect takes a 'snapshot' of a population in a relatively short time period—for example, one year. Most rates are derived from period data and therefore are period rates. Compare to *cohort analysis*.
Population	A group of objects or organisms of the same kind.
Population Control	A broad concept that addresses the relationship between fertility, mortality and migration, but is most commonly used to refer to efforts to slow population growth through action to lower fertility. It should not be confused with family planning. See also *family planning*.
Population Density	Population per unit of land area; for example, persons per square mile or persons per square kilometer of arable land.
Population Distribution	The patterns of settlement and dispersal of a population.
Population Explosion (or 'Population Bomb')	Expressions used to describe the worldwide trend of rapid population growth in the 20th century, resulting from a world birth rate much higher than the world death rate.
Population Increase	The total population increase resulting from the interaction of births, deaths and migration in a population in a given period of time.
Population Momentum	The tendency for population growth to continue beyond the time that replacement-level fertility has been achieved because of the relatively high concentration of people in childbearing years.
Population Policy	Explicit or implicit measures instituted by a government to influence population size, growth, distribution or composition.

Population Projection	Computation of future changes in population numbers, given certain assumptions about future future trends in the rates of fertility, mortality and migration. Demographers often issue low, medium and high projections of the same population, based on different assumptions of how these rates will change in the future.
Population Pyramid	A bar chart arranged vertically, that shows the distribution of a population by age and sex. By convention, the younger ages are at the bottom, with males on the left and females on the right.
Population Register	A government data collection system in which the demographic and socio-economic characteristics of all or part of the population are continuously recorded. Denmark, Sweden and Israel are among the countries that maintain universal registers for demographic purposes— recording the major events (birth, marriage, death) that happen to each individual so that up-to date information on the whole population is readily available. Other countries, like the United States, keep partial registers, such as social security and voter registration, for administrative purposes.
Postneonatal Mortality Rate	The annual number of deaths of infants ages 28 days to 1 year per 1,000 live births in a given year.
Prevalence Rate	The number of persons having a particular disease at a given point in time per 1,000 population at risk.
Pronatalist Policy	The policy of a government, society or social group to increase population growth by attempting to raise the number of births.
Public Expenditure on Health	Recurrent and capital spending from central and local government budgets, external borrowings and grant, including donations from abroad and social insurance funds.
Push-Pull Hypothesis	A migration theory that suggests that circumstances at the place of origin (such as poverty and unemployment) repel or push people out of that place to other places that exert a positive attraction or pull (such as a high standard of living or job opportunities).

Race	Race is defined primarily by society, not by genetics, and there are no universally accepted categories.
Rate of Natural Increase (or Decrease)	The rate at which a population increases (or decreases) in a given year due to a surplus (or deficit) of births over deaths, expressed as a percentage of the base population.
Remarriage Rate	The number of remarriages per 1,000 formerly married (that is, widowed or divorced) men or women in a given year.
Replacement-Level Fertility	The level of fertility at which a couple has only enough children to replace themselves, or about two children per couple.
Reproductive Age	See childbearing years.
Reproductive Health	Reproductive health is a state of complete physical, mental, and social well-being and not merely the absence of disease or infirmity, in all matters relating to the reproductive system and to its functions and processes.
Sex Ratio	The number of males per 100 females in a population.
Social Mobility	A change in status (for example, an occupational change).
Stable Population	A population with an unchanging rate of growth and an unchanging age composition as a result of age-specific birth and death rates that have remained constant over a sufficient period of time.
Survey	A canvas of selected persons or households in a population usually used to infer demographic characteristics or trends for a larger segment or all of the population. See also census.
Survival Rate	The proportion of persons in a specified group (age, sex or health status) alive at the beginning of an interval (such as a five-year period) who survive to the end of the interval.
Tax Revenue	Compulsory, unrequited, non-repayable receipts collected by central governments for public specific purpose.
Total Fertility Rate (TFR)	The average number of children that would be born alive to a woman (or group of women)

during her lifetime if she were to pass through her childbearing years conforming to the age-specific fertility rates of a given year. This rate is sometimes stated as the number of children women are having today. See also *gross reproduction rate* and *net reproduction rate*.

Unemployment All people above a specified age who are not in paid employment or self-employed, but are available and have taken specific steps to seek paid employment or self-employment.

Urban Countries differ in the way they classify population as 'urban' or 'rural.' Typically, a community or settlement with a population of 2,000 or more is considered urban. A listing of country definitions is published annually in the *United Nations Demographic Yearbook*.

Urbanization Growth in the proportion of a population living in urban areas.

Vital statistics Demographic data on births, deaths, fetal deaths, marriages and divorces.

Young Population A population with a relatively high proportion of children, adolescents and young adults, a low median age, and thus a high growth potential.

Youth Dependency Ratio Number of persons aged 0–14 years per 100 persons aged 15–64 years.

Zero Population Growth A population in equilibrium, with a growth rate of zero, achieved when births plus immigration equal deaths plus emigration.

(The glossary incorporates materials from Population Reference Bureau's [PRB] *Population Handbook, 4th International Edition,* with permission from Ellen Carnevale Director of Communications, Population Reference Bureau, 1875 Connecticut Ave., NW, Suite 520,Washington, DC 20009.)

SELECT BIBLIOGRAPHY

Andrews, G.R. and M.M. Hennink, 'The Circumstances and Contributions of Older Persons in Three Asian Countries: Preliminary Results of a Cross-national Study', *Asia-Pacific Population Journal*, 7(3): 127–46, 1992.

Araki, S. and K. Murata, 'Factors Affecting Suicide in Young, Middle-aged and Elderly Men, *Journal of Biosocial Science*, 18(1): 103–8, 1986.

Attig, G.A. and K. Chanawongse, 'The Elderly as Active Community Health Leaders: A Complementary Strategy for the Promotion of Community-based Primary Health Care Information', *Apacph-Clearinghouse Bulletin*, 2(4): 28–39, 1988.

Bali, Arun P. (ed.), *Understanding Greying People of India*, Inter-India Publications, New Delhi, 1999.

Bose, A.B., 'Policies and Programmes for the Ageing in India', in *The Ageing of Asian Populations*, Proceedings of the United Nations Round Table on the Ageing of Asian Populations, Bangkok, 4–6 May 1992. United Nations, Department for Economic and Social Information and Policy Analysis, New York, 1994.

———, 'Ageing in India', *Zeitschrift fur Gerontologie*, 19(2): 96–100, 1986.

———, 'Aspects of Ageing in India', *Social Action*, 32(1): 1–19, 1982.

Bose, Ashish, 'The Condition of the Elderly in India: A Study in Methodology and Highlights of a Pilot Survey in Delhi', UNFPA Project Report, Mimeo, unpublished, 1997.

Bose, Ashish and Shankardass Mala Kapur, *Growing Old in India: Voices Reveal, Statistics Speak*, B.R. Publishing Corporation, New Delhi, 2000.

Bosworth, B. and G. Burtless, *Aging Societies: The Global Dimension*, Brookings Institution Press, Washington, D.C., 1998.

Budak, M-AE, Liaw K-L and H. Kawabe, 'Co-residence of Household Heads with Parents in Japan: A Multivariate Explanation', *International Journal of Population Geography*, 2(2): 133–52, 1996.

Cain, M., 'Consequences of Reproductive Failure: Dependence, Mobility and Mortality among the Elderly in Rural South Asia', Working Paper No. 119, Population Council, Center for Policy Studies, New York, 1985.

———, 'Consequences of Reproductive Failure: Dependence, Mobility and Mortality among the Elderly in Rural South Asia', *Population Studies*, 40(3): 375–88, 1986.

———, 'The Material Consequences of Reproductive Failure in Rural South Asia,' in Daisy Dwyer and Judith Bruce (eds), *A Home Divided: Women and Income in the Third world*, pp. 20–38, Standford University Press, Standford, California, 1988.

Cain, M.T., 'Widows, Sons, and Old-age Security in Rural Maharashtra: A Comment on Vlassoff', *Population Studies*, 45(3): 519–28, 1991.

————, *Ageing of Asia: An Investigation into its Nature and Social Dynamics with Special Reference to Japanese, Thai and Indian Elderly*, MRG Publications, Kolkata, 2002.

————, 'Adjusting to an Aging Labour Force', MRG Policy Development Studies No. 5, Millennium Research Group, Kolkata, 2000.

————, 'Asian Demographic Transition in the eyes of Population Pattern Changes in Kerala', India MRG Policy Development Studies No.7, Millennium Research Group, Kolkata, 2000.

————, 'Fifty Years of Asia's Demographic Change: A Simple Trend or a Miracle?' MRG Policy Development Studies No.8, Millennium Research Group, Kolkata, 2000.

————, 'Population Ageing in Asia: A Demographic Blessing or Curse?' MRG Policy Development Studies No. 6, Millennium Research Group, Kolkata, 2000.

————, 'Population Growth and Economic Development: Lessons from Selected Asian Countries', MRG Policy Development Studies No.1, Millennium Research Group, Kolkata, 2000.

————, 'Social Security Programs and Retirement the World', MRG Policy Development Studies No.4, Millennium Research Group, Kolkata, 2000.

————, 'The Dynamics of an Ageing Population in the Developed Countries: Lessons for the Developing countries of Asia', MRG Policy Development Studies No.2, Millennium Research Group, Kolkata, 2000.

————, 'The Economics of Ageing', MRG Policy Development Studies No.3, Millennium Research Group, Kolkata, 2000.

————, 'Population Ageing and its Impact on the Need for Health Care Facilities: Comments from the Experience of Japan and Thailand', Occasional Paper DSSEAS, Calcutta University, 1998.

————, 'Population Ageing in South Asia and its Socio-Economic Implications', Occasional Paper, DSSEAS, Calcutta University, Kolkata, 1995.

Chanana, H.B. and P.P. Talwar, 'Ageing in India: Its Socio-economic and Health Implications', *Asia-Pacific Population Journal*, 2(3): 23–38, 1987.

————, 'Implication of Demographic Goals in AD 2000 for Ageing Population in India', *Health And Population: Perspectives And Issues*, 9(2): 67–79, 1986.

Chaturvedi, Y.N., 'Statement: India', Presented at the United Nations Commission on Population and Development, Thirty-second session, New York, March 22–31, 1999. Web address: http://www.undp.org/popin/unpopcom/32ndsess/state.htm.

Chayovan, N., J. Knodel and S. Siriboon, 'Thailand's Elderly Population: A Demographic and Social Profile based on Official Statistical Sources', *Comparative Study of the Elderly in Asia*, Research Report No. 90–2, University of Michigan, Population Studies Center, Ann Arbor, Michigan, Sep. 61, p. 32, 1990.

Chayovan, N., M. Wongsith and C. Saengtienchai, 'Socio-economic Consequences of the Ageing of the population in Thailand: Survey Findings', Project Report, ASEAN Population Programme, Chulalongkorn University, Institute of Population Studies, Bangkok, Thailand, p. 183, 1988.

Chen, A.J., G. Jones, L. Domingo, P. Pitaktepsombati, H. Sigit and M.B. Yatim, *'Ageing in ASEAN: Its Socio-economic Consequences'*, Institute of Southeast Asian Studies, Singapore, 1989.

Chesnais, J., 'Demographic Transition Patterns and their Impact on the Age Structure', *Population and Development Review*, 16(2): 327–36, 399, 401, 1990.

Clark, R.L. and N. Ogawa, 'Public Attitudes and Concerns about Population Ageing in Japan', *Ageing and Society*, 16(4): 443–65, 1996.

Cole, Thomas R., W. Achenbaum, Jakobi Andrew, L. Patricia and Robert Kastenbaum (eds), *Voices and Visions of Aging: Toward a Critical Gerontology*, Springer Publishing Company, New York, 1993.

Cornell, L.L., 'Gender, Risk, and Security in Old Age', Working paper No. 28, Population Institute for Research and Training [PIRT], Indiana University, Bloomington, Indiana, p. 49, 1990.

Dandekar, K., *The Elderly in India*, Sage Publications, New Delhi, 1996.

Das Gupta, M., 'The Effects of Discrimination on Health and Mortality', in: *International Population Conference/Congress International de la Population*, New Delhi, September 20–27, 1989, Vol. 3, pp. 349–65, International Union for the Scientific Study of Population, Liege, Belgium, 1989.

Das Gupta, M., T.N. Krishnan and L.C. Chen, 'Overview', in Monica Das Gupta, Lincon C. Chen and T.N. Krishnan (eds), *Women's Health in India: Risk and Vulnerability*, pp.1–16, Oxford India Paperbacks, New Delhi, 1998.

Deaton, A. and C.H. Paxson, 'Patterns of Ageing in Thailand and Côte d'Ivoire', Working Paper No. 81, LSMS, Washington, D.C., World Bank, 1991.

Denton, F.T. and B.G. Spencer, 'Population Ageing and the Maintenance of Social Support Systems', QSEP Research Report No. 320, McMaster University, Faculty of Social Sciences, Program for Quantitative Studies in Economics and Population, Hamilton, Canada, 1996.

Desai, K.G., *Ageing in India*, Tata Institute of Social Sciences, p. 179, TISS Series No. 52, Bombay, 1982.

Dharmalingam, A., 'Old Age Support: Expectations and Experiences in a South Indian Village', *Population Studies*, 48(1): 5–19, 1994.

Dinesh, B.M. and P.H. Rayappa, 'The Aged and their Work Status in Rural Areas', *Demography India*, 12(1): 38–51, 1983.

East-West Center, Population Institute, '*Summary of Proceedings: United States-Japan Conference on Ageing*', December, 5–9, 1983, East-West Population Institute, Honolulu, Hawaii, p. 56, 1984.

Feeney, Grifith and Andrew Mason, 'Population in East Asia', in Andrew Mason (ed.), *Population Change and Economic Development in East Asia: Challenges Met, Opportunities Seized*, Stanford University Press, Stanford, California, 2001.

Fukawa, T., 'Independence of the Elderly and its Consideration from Demographic and Economic Points of View', *Jinkogaku Kenkyu/Journal of Population Studies*, (16): 17–27, 1993.

Furuya, K., 'Employment of Aged People: Comparison between the U.S. and Japan', NUPRI Research Paper Series No. 14, Nihon University, Population Research Institute, Tokyo, Japan, 1983.

Gendell, M., 'Trends in Retirement Age in Germany, Japan, Sweden, and the United States Since the 1960s', Presented at the Annual Meeting of the Population Association of America, Washington, D.C., March 27–29, 1997.

Gokhale, S.D., 'Towards Productive and Participatory Ageing in India', in *The Ageing of Asian Populations*, Proceedings of the United Nations Round Table on the Ageing of Asian Populations, Bangkok, 4–6 May 1992, United Nations, Department for Economic and Social Information and Policy Analysis, New York, pp. 76–87, 1994.

Gokhale, S.D., N. Pandit and R. Raj, *Economic Potential of the Elderly and Local Level Policy Development on Consequences of Ageing in India*, Asian Population Studies Series No. 131-B, United Nations, New York, 1994.

Goldberg, Beverly, *Age Works: What Corporate America Must Do To Survive the Greying of The Workforce*, The Free Press, USA, 2000.

Goldman, N. and S. Takahashi, 'Old-age Mortality in Japan: Demographic and Epidemiological Perspectives', OPR Working Paper No. 94-1, Princeton University, Office of Population Research [OPR], Princeton, New Jersey, 1993.

Gopalan, C., 'The Population Problem: Its Qualitative Dimension', *Demography India*, 11(2): 167–77, 1982.

Goyal, R.S., 'The Problem of Ageing', *Population Education News*, 15(6): 4–8, 1989.

Green, Bryan S., *Gerontology and the Construction of Old Age: A Study in Discourse Analysis*, Aldine de Gruyter, New York, 1993.

Greenspan, A., 'Shifts in Household Demographics Herald Economic Changes for Thailand', *Asia-Pacific Population and Policy*, (25): 1–4, 1993.

Grover, D., 'Population Change and Social Security in India', in S.N. Singh, M.K. Premi, P.S. Bhatia and Ashish Bose (eds), *Population Transition in India*, vol. 2, pp. 55–62, B.R. Publishing, Delhi, 1989.

Guha Roy, S., '*Perspectives on Population Ageing in India*', in S.N. Singh, M.K. Premi, P.S. Bhatia and Ashish Bose (eds), *Population Transition in India*, vol. 1, B.R. Publishing, Delhi, 1989.

———, 'Demography of Ageing: Indian Experience', *Journal of Indian Anthropology and Sociology*, 20: 258–83, 1985.

Gui, S., 'Elderly Populations in the Jingan District of Shanghai and the Special Districts of Tokyo: A Comparative Analysis', *Chinese Journal Of Population Science*, 1(4): 459–69, 1989.

Gulati. L., 'Population Ageing and Women in Kerala State, India', *Asia-Pacific Population Journal*, 8(1): 53–63, 1993.

———, 'Dimensions of Female Ageing and Widowhood: Insights from Kerala Experience', *Economic and Political Weekly*, 27(43–44): WS93–9, 1992.

Gulati, L. and S.I. Rajan, 'Social and Economic Implications of Population Ageing in Kerala, India', *Demography India*, 19(2): 235–50 1990.

Hanada, K., 'Co residence of Family Members and In-home Care of the Aged', *Jinko Mondai Kenkyu/Journal of Population Problems*, 46(4): 32–48, 1991.

———, 'The Mortality of Centenarians in Japan', *Jinko Mondai Kenkyu/Journal of Population Problems*, 190: 50–4, 1989.

Hiebert, Paul G., 'Old Age in a South Indian Village', in Pamela T. Amoss and Steven Harrell (eds), *Other Ways of Growing Old: Anthropological Perspectives*, pp. 211–26, Stanford University Press, Stanford, 1981.

Higuchi, K., 'Women in an Ageing Society', in *Added Years of life in Asia: Current Situation and Future Challenges*, Asian Population Studies Series No. 141, United Nations, Economic and Social Commission for Asia and the Pacific (ESCAP), Bangkok, Thailand, 1996.

Hirosima, K., 'A Decomposition of Household Status Transition of Japanese Elderly', *Journal of Economics*, 24(3): 1–41, 1998.

Hirosima, K., 'Projection of Living Arrangements of the Elderly in Japan: 1990–2010', Working Paper Series No. 22, Institute of Population Problems, Tokyo, Japan, 1995.

————, 'A Basic Demographic Condition for Living Arrangements: Formal Demography of Parent-child Co-residentially', Working Paper Series No. 6, Institute of Population Problems, Tokyo, Japan, 1990.

————, 'Demographic Analysis of Parent-child Co-residentiality in Post-war Japan', Jinko Mondai Kenkyu/Journal of Population Problems, 169: 31–42, 1984.

Hirosima, K., M. Oe, C. Yamamoto, F. Mita and K. Kojima, 'Study on the Model Projecting the Elderly's Living Arrangements. Projection of Living Arrangements of the Elderly in Japan: 1990–2010', Report on Special Study Project No. 12, Institute of Population Problems, Tokyo, Japan, p. 108, 1995.

————, 'Projection of Household Conditions of the Elderly in Japan', Jinko Mondai Kenkyu/Journal of Population Problems, 50(2): 25–51, 1994.

Holmes, Ellen Rhoads and Lowell D. Holmes, Other Cultures, Elder Years, Thousand Oaks, Sage Publications, 1995.

Honda, H., 'Statement: Japan', Presented at the United Nations Commission on Population and Development, Thirty-second session, New York, March 22–31, 1999. Web address: http://www.undp.org/popin/unpopcom/ 32ndsess/state.htm.

Horioka, C.Y., 'The Determinants of Japan's Saving Rate: The Impact of the Age Structure of the Population and Other Factors', Economic Studies Quarterly, 42(3): 237–53, 1991.

————, 'Why is Japan's Private Saving Rate So High?', ISER Reprint Series No. 145, Osaka University, Institute of Social and Economic Research (ISER), Osaka, Japan, 1989.

Horiuchi, S. and J.R. Wilmoth, 'Assessing Effects of Mortality Reduction on Population Ageing: An Analysis of the Elderly Female Population in Japan', Paper presented at the Population Association of America Annual Meeting, Baltimore, Maryland, March 30 to April 1, 1989.

————, 'Deceleration in the Age Pattern of Mortality at Older Ages', in Demography, 35(4): 391–412, 1998.

————, 'The Long-term Impact of War on Mortality: Old-age Mortality of the First World War Survivors in the Federal Republic of Germany', Population Bulletin of the United Nations, 15: 80–92, 1983.

Husain, M.G., Changing Indian Society and Status of Aged, Mainak Publications, 1997.

Imaizumi, Y., 'Mortality in the Elderly Population Aged 65 and over in Japan: Geographical Variations', Jinko Mondai Kenkyu/Journal of Population Problems, 48(1): 16–31, 1992.

Imhof, A.E., 'What has the Longevity in Europe and Japan to Teach India?', Demography India, 15(1): 1–25, 1986.

Ishibashi T., 'Classifying the Economically Productive Population as Persons Aged', Integration, 58(19), 1998.

Ishii, T., Y. Hosoda and K. Maeda, 'Cause of Death in the Extreme Aged: A Pathologic Survey of 5,106 Elderly Person's 80 years Old and Over', Age and Ageing, 9(2): 81–89, 1980.

Ishikawa, A., 'Decomposition of Population Ageing in Japan since 1947', Jinko Mondai Kenkyu/Journal of Population Problems, 45(3): 56–65, 1989.

Izutsu, S. and C.L. Rose, 'The Quality of Life in an Ageing Society', in *Ageing: Quality of Life in Ageing Societies*, Summary of proceedings, Japan-United States Conference on Ageing, September 15–18, 1986, Tokyo, Japan, Nihon University, Population Research Institute, Japan-United States Conference on Ageing Organising Committee, 1987.

Jain, S. and P. Dave, 'A Comparative Study of Conjugal Relationships in Young, Middle-aged and Elderly Couples', *Journal of Family Welfare*, 28(4): 18–24, 1982.

Japan International Social Security Association, *Outline of Social Insurance in Japan, 1999*, Japan International Social Security Association, Tokyo, 1999.

Japan Policy Office for the Aged, *Ageing in Japan*, Policy Office for the Aged, Tokyo, Japan, 1983.

Japan Statistics Bureau, *The Population of Advanced Age*, Population Census, 1980, Statistics Bureau, Tokyo, Japan, p. 152, Monograph Series No. 8, 1984.

Japan-United States Conference on Ageing, *Ageing: Quality of Life in Ageing Societies*, Summary of the proceedings, September 15–18, 1986, Japan-United States Conference on Ageing Organising Committee, Nihon University, Population Research Institute, Tokyo, Japan, 1987.

Jitapunkul, S., S. Bunnag and S. Ebrahim, 'Effectiveness and Cost Analysis of Community-based Rehabilitation Service in Bangkok', *Journal of the Medical Association of Thailand*, 81(8): 572–8, 1998.

JOICFP News, *Ageing conference—Towards a Co-operative Future*, Spec No:1–2, Japanese Organization for International Cooperation in Family Planning, 1999.

———, *Rapidly-aging Society Challenges the 21st century*. (302)2, Japanese Organization for International Cooperation in Family Planning, 1999.

Jones, G.W., 'Consequences of Rapid Fertility Decline For Old Age Security in Asia', Working Papers in Demography No. 20, Australian National University, Research School of Social Sciences, Division of Demography and Sociology, . Canberra, Australia, 1990.

Kamo, Y., 'A Note on Elderly Living Arrangements in Japan and the United States', *Research on Aging*, 10(2): 297–305, 1988.

Kanbargi, R., 'Old Age Security and Fertility Behaviour: Some Research Issues', *Journal of the Indian Anthropological Society*, 20(3): 226–37, 1985.

Kanchanakitsakul, M., 'Factors Affecting Satisfaction of Thai Senior Citizens Living with their Children', *Journal of Population and Social Studies*, 8(1): 143–62, 1999.

Kaneko, T., 'Population Problems Appeared by the Age Group 1. Elderly and Employment', *Jinko Mondai Kenkyu*, 137: 7–12, 1976.

Kargl, I., *Old Age in Japan: Long-term Statistics*, Beitrage zur Japanologie, Vol. 24, Universitat Wien, Institut fur Japanologie, Vienna, Austria,1987.

Kato, R., 'Transition to an Aging Japan: Public Pension, Savings, and Capital Taxation', *Journal of the Japanese and International Economies*, 12(3): 204–31, 1998.

Kertzer, David I. and Schaie K. Warner (eds), *Age Structuring in Comparative Perspective*, Lawrence Erlbaum Associates, Hillsdale, 1989.

Kimble, Melvin A., Susan H. McFadden, James W. Ellor and James J. Seeber (eds), *Aging, Spirituality, and Religion: A Handbook*, Fortress Press, Minneapolis, 1995.

Knodel, J. and S. Siriboon, 'Thai Elderly who do not Co-reside with their Children', Presented at the International Population Conference/Congress

International de la Population, Montreal, Canada, August 24 to September 1, Sponsored by the International Union for the Scientific Study of Population (IUSSP), 1993.

Knodel, J., N. Chayovan and S. Siriboon, 'The Impact of Fertility Decline on Familial Support for the Elderly: An Illustration from Thailand', *Population and Development Review*, 18(1): 79–103, 1992.

———, 'The familial Support System of Thai Elderly: An Overview', *Asia-Pacific Population Journal*, 7(3): 105–26, 1992.

———, 'The Impact of Fertility Decline on the Familial System of Support for the Elderly: An Illustration from Thailand', Working Paper No. 36, Population Council, Research Division, New York, 1992.

Kobayashi, K., 'Attitudes Toward Children and Parents', in Population Problems Research Council, the Mainichi Daily News and the Japanese Organisation for International Co-operation in Family Planning (JOICFP) (eds), *Fertility and Family Planning in Japan*, pp. 203–23, Tokyo, Japan, JOICFP, 1977.

———, 'Ageing Research in ODA, with Particular Reference to the NAS Workshop on Ageing Demography', *Jinko Mondai Kenkyu/Journal of Population Problems*, 45(3): 66–76, 1989.

Kojima, H., 'Ageing in Japan: Population Policy Implications', *Korea Journal of Population and Development*, 24(2): 197–214, 1995.

Kono, S., 'Well-being among Children and the Aged in Japan', *Jinko Mondai Kenkyu/Journal of Population Problems*, 184: 1–18, 1987.

Kono, S., 'Well-being among Children and the Aged in the Ageing Society', *Jinkogaku Kenkyu/Journal of Population Studies*, 13: 5–13, 1990.

———, 'Changes in the Family Life Cycle and the Issues of the Three-generation Household in Japan', in Zeng Yi, Zhang Chunyuan, and Peng Songjian (eds), *Changing family structure and population Ageing in China: A Comparative Approach*, Peking University Press, Beijing, China, 1990.

———, 'Population Ageing in Japan, with Reference to China', *Asia-Pacific Population Journal*, 2(3): 3–22, 1987.

———, 'The Ageing of Populations', *Populi*, 14(3): 32–9, 1987.

———, 'Population Problems and Challenging Studies for Solution', *Acta Obstetrica et Gynaecologica Japonica*, 32(9): 1185–92, 1980.

Kuroda, T., 'The Nature and Policies of Population Ageing in Japan', in *The Ageing of Asian Populations*, Proceedings of the United Nations Round Table on the Ageing of Asian Populations, Bangkok, 4–6 May 1992, United Nations, Department for Economic and Social Information and Policy Analysis, New York, 1994.

———, 'Population Ageing in the Context of Urbanisation and Industrialisation', Population Research Leads No. 33, UN Economic and Social Commission for Asia and the Pacific (ESCAP), Bangkok, Thailand, 1989.

Kurosu, S., 'Suicide in Rural Areas: The Case of Japan 1960–1980', *Rural Sociology*, 56(4): 603–18, 1991.

Lamb, V.L., *'Active Life Expectancy of the Elderly in Selected Asian Countries'*, NUPRI Research Paper Series No. 69, Nihon University, Population Research Institute, Tokyo, Japan, 1999.

Lee, R.D., W.B. Arthur and G. Rodgers, *Economics of Changing Age Distributions in Developed Countries*, Clarendon Press, Oxford, 1988.

Levy, M.L., 'The Population of the Europe of Ten', *Population et Societies*, 181: 1–3, 1984.

Li, Z., Y. Morikawa, H. Nakagawa, K. Yoshita, M. Tabata, M. Nishijo, M. Senma, S. Kawano, T. Kido and Y. Chen, 'Comparison of Mortality Rates of Elderly People in China and Japan', *Japanese Journal of Health And Human Ecology*, 58(6): 336–43, 1992.

Mainichi Shimbun, 'Signs of Still More Reduction in Birth Rate: A Quietly Advancing Ageing Society' May 19, 1977.

Majumdar, B., 'The Problem of Ageing in Rural Bengal', *Economic Affairs*, 29(1): 63–9, 1984.

Manton, K.G. and J.W. Vaupel, 'Survival After the Age of 80 in the United States, Sweden, France, England, and Japan', *New England Journal of Medicine*, 333(18): 1, 232–5, 1995.

Manton, K.G., 'Mortality Patterns in Developed Countries', *Comparative Social Research*, 7: 259–86, 1984.

Martin, L.G. and N.O. Tsuya, 'Japanese Women in the Middle: Work and Family Responsibilities', Presented at the Annual Meeting of the Population Association of America, Denver, Colorado, April 30 to May 2, 1992.

Martin, L.G., 'Population Ageing Policies in East Asia and the United States', *Science*, 251(4993): 527–31, 1991.

————, 'The Greying of Japan', *Population Bulletin*, 44(2): 1–43, 1989.

Maruo, N., 'The Impact of Population Ageing on the Social Security Expenditure and Economic Growth in Japan', *Jinkogaku Kenkyu/Journal of Population Studies*, 10: 7–24, 1987.

Mason, A. and B.O. Campbell, 'Demographic Change and the Thai economy: An Overview', in Burnham O. Campbell, Andrew Mason and Ernesto M. Pernia (eds), *The Economic Impact of Demographic Change in Thailand, 1980–2015: An Application of the Homes Household Forecasting Model,* pp. 1–52, Honolulu, Hawaii, East-West Center, 1993.

Matsubayashi, K., K. Okumiya, T. Nakamura, M. Fujisawa and Y. Osaki, 'Global Burden of Disease [letter]', *Lancet*, 350(9071): 144, 1997.

Minakawa, Y., 'Demographic Consideration of Socio-economic Problems in Remote Depopulated Rural Communities', *Jinkogaku Kenkyu/Journal of Population Studies*, (12): 25–35, 1989.

Morioka, K., 'A Japanese Perspective on the Life Course: Emerging and Diminishing Patterns', *Journal of Family History*, 12(1–3): 243–60, 1987.

Mukhopadhyay, B.K., 'An Age Adjustment of Very Young Children of India, 1981 and Reappraisal of Fertility and Mortality Rates—A Model Approach', *Genus*, 42(3–4): 165–80, 1986.

Mullatti, L., 'Families in India: Beliefs and Realities', *Journal of Comparative Family Studies*, 26(1): 13–25, 1995.

Nair, P.S. and S. Santhosh, 'Population Ageing in India: A Study of Trichur District, Kerala', in Aijazuddin Ahmad, Daniel Noin and H.N. Sharma (eds), *Demographic Transition: the Third World Scenario*, Rawat Publications, Jaipur, 1997.

————, 'The Aged in Rural India: A Study of the Socio-Economic and Health Profile', in *Population transition in India, vol. 2*, S.N. Singh, M.K. Premi, P.S. Bhatia and Ashish Bose (eds), pp. 63–70, B.R. Publishing, Delhi, 1989.

Nair, P.S. and S. Santhosh, 'Effect of Declining Fertility on Population Ageing in India: An Application of Coale's Analytical Model', *Genus*, 43(3–4):175–82, 1987.

Nanjo, Z. and K. Kobayashi, *'Method of Computing the Expectation of Life at Old Age on the Basis of the Principle of Agreement with Data'* NUPRI Research Paper Series No. 36, Nihon University, Population Research Institute, Tokyo, Japan, 1987.

National Statistical Office, Thailand, *Population Ageing in Thailand: 1990 Population and Housing Census*. Subject Report No. 2, National Statistical Office, Bangkok, Thailand, 1994.

Nishimura, H. and A. Klinger, 'The Ageing in Hungary and Japan: Comparative Studies About the Developments in the Two Countries', *Kozponti Statisztikai Hivatal*, Budapest, Hungary, 1995.

Noguchi, Y. and D.A. Wise, *Ageing in the United States and Japan: Economic Trends*, University of Chicago Press, Chicago, Illinois, 1994.

Ogawa, N., 'Population Ageing and its Impact Upon Health Resource Requirements at Government and Familial Levels in Japan', NUPRI Reprint Series No. 35, Nihon University, Population Research Institute, Tokyo, Japan, 1990.

———, 'Population Ageing and Household Structural Change in Japan', NUPRI Reprinted Series No. 31, Nihon University, Population Research Institute, Tokyo, Japan, 1989.

———, 'Economic Implications of Japan's Ageing Population: A Macro-economic Demographic Modelling Approach', *International Labour Review*, 121(1): 17–33, 1982.

Ogawa, N. and R. Matsukura, 'Population Change, Women's Role and Status, and Development in Japan: Executive Summary', in *Population Change, Development and Women's Role and Status in Asia*, Proceedings of the Regional Seminar on Population Change, Development and Women's Role and Status, Bangkok, Thailand, 22–24 May 1995, United Nations, Economic and Social Commission for Asia and the Pacific [ESCAP], New York, 1997.

Ogawa, N., N.O. Tsuya, M. Wongsith and E. Choe, 'Health Status of the Elderly and their Labour Force Participation in the Developing Countries along the Asia-Pacific Rim', in Nahiro Ogawa, Gavin W. Jones and Jeffrey G. Williamson (eds), *Human Resources in Development along the Asia-Pacific Rim*, pp. 349–72, Oxford University Press, South-East Asian Publishing Unit, Singapore, 1993.

Ogawa, N., Y. Saito, S. Yao and Q. Xu, Population Projections for China 1985, Research Report No. 1, Tokyo, Japan, Japanese Organization for International Co-operation in Family Planning (JOICFP), [7], 55 p. (UNFPA Assisted Project: CPR/85/P54, 'Development of Research on the Aged for Policy Making Purposes' Research Report No. 1), [1985].

Ogawa, N. and D.B. Suits, *'Preferences of an Ageing Labour Force Toward Retirement Options'*, NUPRI Research Paper Series No. 13, Nihon University, Population Research Institute, Tokyo, Japan, 1983.

Ohno, Y., 'Implications of the Declining Mortality in Japan', Paper presented at the Meeting on Analysis of Trends and Patterns of Mortality in the ESCAP Region, 13–19 November, Bangkok, 1984.

Okazaki, Y., 'Coping with the Declining Birth Rate, *Economic Eye*, 2: 20–3, 1981.

Oshio, T. and N. Yashiro, 'Social Security and Retirement in Japan', NBER Working Paper No. 6156, National Bureau of Economic Research, Cambridge, Massachusetts, 1997.

Otani, K., 'Birth Trends, Survival Improvements, and Ageing', *Review of Social Policy*, 6: 17–43, 1997.

Otomo, A., 'Mobility of Elderly Population in Japanese Metropolitan Areas', *Jinkogaku Kenkyu/Journal of Population Studies*, (4): 23–8, 1981.

Palmore, Erdman B. (ed.), *Developments and Research on Aging: An International Handbook*, Greenwood Press, Westport, CT, 1993.

Panda, P.K., 'The Elderly in Rural Orissa—Alone in Distress', *Economic and Political Weekly*, 33(25): 1545–50, 1998.

Parant, A., 'Demographic Ageing: A New Challenge for Japan', *Espace, Populations, Societes*, 2(306): 357–64, 1987.

Pardthaisong, T., 'Psychosocial Aspects of Ageing', *Journal of Population and Social Studies*, 2(2): 185–203, 247–8, 1990.

Pati, R.N., *Population, Family, and Culture*, Ashish Publishing House, New Delhi, 1987.

Phalakornkule, S., *Country Policy Development for the Elderly at the Local Level in Thailand*, p. 43, Asian Population Studies Series No. 131-E, United Nations, New York, 1994.

Piriyathamwong, N. and D. Phillips, 'Study of Family Support for Elderly People in Rural Thailand', in *UK/Thai Collaborative Research Development in Reproductive and Sexual Health*, Proceedings of the Symposium on the Mahidol-Exeter British Council Link, edited by Nicholas Ford, Aphichat Chamratrithirong. Nakhon Pathom, Thailand, Mahidol University, Institute for Population and Social Research (IPSR), pp. 65–71, 1993.

Porapakkham, Y. and P. Prasartkul, 'Cause of Death: Trends and Differentials in Thailand', in Harald Hansluwka, Alan D. Lopez, Yawarat Parapakkham and Promote Prasartkul (eds), *New Developments in the Analysis of Mortality and Causes of Death*, pp. 207–37, Mahidol University, Institute for Population and Social Research, Bangkok, Thailand, 1986.

Pramoalratana, A., 'Familial, State and Community Support of the Old in a Rural Community in Thailand', in *The Ageing of Asian Populations*, Proceedings of the United Nations Round Table on the Ageing of Asian Populations, Bangkok, 4–6 May 1992, United Nations, Department for Economic and Social Information and Policy Analysis, New York, 1994.

Puri, N., 'A New Strategy for Family Welfare in the Corporate Sector', *Journal of Family Welfare*, 36(4): 14–9, 1990.

Radha Devi, D.S. Santosh, A. Asharaf and T.K. Roy, *Aged in a Changing Society: A Case study of Kerala,* International Institute for Population Sciences, Deonar, Mumbai, 2000.

Rajan, S.I., 'Ageing in Kerala: One More Population Problem?', *Asia-Pacific Population Journal*, 4(2): 19–48, 1989.

Reddy, P.H., 'Epidemiologic Transition in India', in S.N. Singh, M.K. Premi, P.S. Bhatia and Ashish Bose (eds), *Population Transition in India*, vol. 1, pp. 281–90, B.R. Publishing, Delhi, 1989.

Registrar General, India, *Census of India, 1991, Ageing Population of India, An Analysis of 1991 Census Data*, New Delhi, 1999.

Ridker, R.G., 'A Proposal for Family Planning Bond', Unpublished, p. 40, 1968.

Rogers, A., J.F. Watkins and J.A. Woodward, 'Interregional Elderly Migration and Population Redistribution in Four Industrialised Countries: A Comparative Analysis',

Population Program Working Paper No. WP-89-9, Institute of Behavioural Science, Population Program, University of Colorado, Boulder, Colorado, 1989.

Rogers, A., W.H. Frey, P. Rees, A. Speare and A. Warnes, *Elderly Migration and Population Redistribution: A Comparative Study*, Belhaven Press, London, 1992.

Ross, C.E., J. Microwsky and Goldsteen, 'The Impact of the Family on Health', *Journal of Marriage and the Family*, 52: 1059–78, 1990.

Sakai, H., 'The Elderly Migration: Characteristics and Reasons', *Jinko Mondai Kenkyu/Journal of Population Problems*, 45(3): 1–13, 1989.

———, 'A Study of the Socio-economic Correlates of Japanese Life Expectancy at 60 years and Over', *Jinko Mondai Kenkyu/Journal of Population Problems*, 180: 46–51, 1986.

Salas, R.M., 'Ageing: A Universal Phenomenon', *Populi*, 9(4): 3–7, 1982.

———, 'International Co-operation in Ageing', Statement made at the Nihon University Population Research Institute, November, 1982, *Mainichi Japan Daily News*, p. 2, 1982.

Sarkar, B.N., *Demography of Aged People*, Indian Academy of Social Sciences, Survey Research Centre, Calcutta, 1989.

Schulz, J.H., A. Borowski, W.H. Crown, S. Hoshino, A. Kumashiro, T. Leavitt and K. Takada, 'Economics of Population Ageing: The "Graying" of Australia, Japan, and the United States', Auburn House, New York/London, 1991.

Seike, A., 'The Effect of Employees Pension on the Labour Supply of the Japanese Elderly', Presented at the Annual Meeting of the Population Association of America, Baltimore, Maryland, March 30 to April 1, 1989.

Sen, A. and S. Sengupta, 'Malnutrition of Rural Children and the Sex Bias', *Economic and Political Weekly*, 18(19/21): 855–64, 1983.

Serow, W.J. and M.E. Cowart, 'Demographic Transition and Population Ageing within Caribbean Nation States', Working Paper No. WPS 98–142, Florida State University, College of Social Sciences, Center for the Study of Population, Tallahassee, Florida, 1998.

———, 'Patterns of Rural-Urban Migration among the Elderly', Working Paper No. WPS 89–53, Center for the Study of Population, Florida State University, College of Social Sciences, Tallahassee, Florida, Center for the Study of Population, 1989.

Sharma, M.L. and T.M. Dak, *Ageing in India: Challenge for the Society*, Ajanta Publications, Delhi, 1987.

Sharma, S.P. and P. Xenos, 'Ageing in India: Demographic Background and Analysis', based on census materials, Occasional Paper No. 2, Office of the Registrar General, New Delhi, 1992.

Shimizu, H., 'Regional Differences in Family Patterns in an Ageing Society', *Jinkogaku Kenkyu Journal of Population Studies*, 7: 41–7, 51–2, 1984.

———, 'Living Arrangement of Aged People in Rural Areas: A Comparison of Rural Areas in North-eastern and South-western Districts', *Journal of Population Problems*, 156: 39–53, 1980.

Stoller, Eleanor Palo and Rose Campbell Gibson (eds), *Worlds of Difference: Inequality in the Aging Experience*, Pine Forge Press, Thousand Oaks, 1994.

Takahashi, S., 'Health and Mortality Differentials among the Elderly in Japan: A Regional Analysis with Special Emphasis on Okinawa', Working Paper Series No. 17, Institute of Population Problems, Tokyo, Japan, 1993.

Takahashi, S., 'Effects of Fertility and Mortality Change on Aspects of Ageing in Japan', *Jinko Mondai Kenkyu/Journal of Population Problems*, 46(3): 1–15, 1990.

———, 'The Japanese Mortality Change and its Effect on Population Age Structure', *Jinko Mondai Kenkyu/Journal of Population Problems*, 180: 1–10, 1986.

Thomas, L. Eugene and Susan A. Eisenhandler (eds), *Aging and the Religious Dimension*, Auburn House, Westport, 1994.

Thursz, Daniel, Charlotte Nusberg and Johnnie Prather (eds), *Empowering Older People: An International Approach*, Auburn House, Westport, 1995.

Tilak, Shrinivas, *Religion and Aging in the Indian Tradition*. State University of New York Press, Albany, 1989.

Toshitani, N., 'Coresidence with Parents and Marriage in Recent Japan', *Jinko Mondai Kenkyu*, 47(3): 72, 1991.

Uchino, S., 'Elderly Migration in Japan—A Newly Emerging Trend and its Analysis', *Jinko Mondai Kenkyu/Journal of Population Problems*, 184: 19–38, 1987.

United Nations, Economic and Social Commission for Asia and the Pacific (ESCAP), *Population Ageing: Review of Emerging Issues*, Asian Population Studies Series, No. 80, Report, proposed study design and selected background papers from the Meeting on Emerging Issues of the Ageing Population, 22–26 September 1986, Economic and Social Commission for Asia and the Pacific, Bangkok, Thailand, 1987.

Vatuk, S., 'The Indian Woman in Later Life: Some Social and Cultural Considerations', in Monica Das Gupta, Lincoln C. Chen and T.N. Krishnan (eds), *Women's Health in India: Risk and Vulnerability*, pp. 289–306, Oxford India Paperbacks. New Delhi, 1998.

Vaupel, J.W. and B. Jeune, 'The Emergence and Proliferation of Centenarians', Population Studies of Ageing No. 12, Odense Universitet, Center for Helsetjen-esteforskning og Socialpolitik, Odense, Denmark, 1994.

Vlassoff, C., 'Rejoinder to Cain: Widows, Sons, and Old-age Security in Rural Maharashtra: A Comment on Vlassoff', *Population Studies*, 45(3): 529–3, 1991.

Vlassoff, M. and C. Vlassoff, 'Old Age Security and the Utility of Children in Rural India', *Population Studies*, 34(3): 487–99, 1980.

Wakabayashi, K., 'An Approach to the Problems of Elderly Women', *Jinko Mondai Kenkyu/Journal of Population Problems*, 163: 44–68, 1982.

Way, P.O., 'Issues and Implications of the Ageing Japanese Population', CIR Staff Paper, Bureau of the Census, Center for International Research, Washington, D.C., 1984.

Weinstein, W., T.H. Sun, M.C. Chang and R. Freedman, 'Co-residence and other Ties Linking Couples and their Parents', in Arland Thornton and Hui-Li Sheng Lin (eds), *Social Change and the Family in Taiwan*, University of Chicago Press, Chicago, 1994.

Wilmoth, J.R., 'Are Mortality Falling at Extremely High Ages: An Investigation Based on a Model Propose by Coale & Kisker', Presented at the Annual Meeting of the Population Association of America, Cincinnati, Ohio, April 1–3, 1993.

Wongsith, M. and S. Siriboon, 'Family and the Elderly: Case Study of Bangkok and Phra Nakorn Sri-Ayuddhaya', CPS Publication No. 273, Chulalongkorn University, College of Population Studies, Bangkok, Thailand, 1999.

Wongsith, M., 'Attitudes of the Adult Towards the Elderly', Chulalongkorn University, Institute of Population Studies, Bangkok, Thailand [5], 34 p. [1992].

World Health, 'Ageing: The Surest Demographic Reality of the Next Century', *World Health*, 51(2): 26–7, 1998.

Yadava, K.N., S.S. Yadava and C.L. Sharma, 'Socio-economic Factors and Behavioural Problems of the Elderly Population: A Study of Rural Areas of Eastern Uttar Pradesh', *Ageing and Society*, 16(5): 525–42, 1996.

———, 'A Study of Socio-economic Factors and Behavioural Problems of the Aged Persons in Rural Northern India', *Demography India*, 25(1): 21–34, 1996.

Yadava, K.N., S.S. Yadava and D.K. Vajpeyi, 'A Study of Aged Population and Associated Health Risks in Rural India', *International Journal of Ageing & Human Development*, 44(4): 293–315, 1997.

Yamaguchi, K., 'Age and Sex Composition of the Population', Country Monograph Series No. 11, United Nations and Economic and Social Commission for Asia and the Pacific (ESCAP), Population Division. Population of Japan, United Nations, New York, pp. 74–95, 1984.

Yamamoto, C., 'Note on Family and Household Status of the Japanese Aged Population', *Jinko Mondai Kenkyu/Journal of Population Problems*, 156: 58–62, 1980.

Yanagishita, M. and J.M. Guralnik, 'Changing Mortality Patterns that Led Life Expectancy in Japan to Surpass Sweden's: 1972–1982', *Demography*, 25(4): 611–24, 1988.

Yashiro, N., 'Aging of the Population in Japan and its Implications to the Other Asian Countries, *Journal of Asian Economics*, 8(2): 245–61, 1997.

Aadhar, 360–61, 386
Aaron, H.J., 208–09
Acquired Immunodeficiency Syndrome (AIDS), 151–52, 319–21
Active ageing, process of, 306–07
Adult literacy policies and programmes, 340–41
Age consciousness, concept of, 217
Age distribution, of Indian population, 187
Aged, *see*, Elderly/aged population
Aged 60 or 65 years and above, 164, 166
Aged–child ratio (Ageing Index), 167–68, 187; *see also*, Ageing indices
Aged dependency ratio, 43–52, 167, 169–70, 187
Ageing/population ageing, alternative dependency measures, 173–76; as function of fertility and mortality, 189–90; awareness about, 304–06; by distance from Metropolitan Centre, 135; capital formation and, 207–08; causes of, 81–155; characteristics of, 34–41; consumption and, 200–01; definition of, 159; demographic aspect of, 33–78; demographic transition and, 99, 101–07; dependency measures, 167, 169–73; deprivation and, 227–30; development and, 193–230; economic development and, 193–95; education and literacy, 339–43; family structure changes and, 222–24; feminisation of, 52–53; fertility and mortality elements in, 107–32, 138–53, 155, 189–90; gender dimension of, 249–50; graceful ageing, 303–46; health care costs and, 203–07; in India, 107–15; in Japan, 110–12, 117, 119–29; indices, 174–75, 177–83; intergenerational tensions, 210–14; labour supply and, 199–200; measures of, 160–74; migration and, 132–38, 155; P–index of, 177–83; politics, 214–19; population momentum and, 153–55; process of, 33–34; productivity and, 195–99; progressive demographic of aged, 53–58, 254–56; remuneration relations, 196–97; rural economy and, 250–54; Ryder's alternative measure, 175–77; *see also*, Elderly/aged population; social security system for, 208–10, 212; social setting for, 338–46; society and, 219–24; sociological premises on, 219–21; speeds of, 82–86; spread of, 34–41; traditional measures, 160–68; trends, 35–36; urban and rural population proportion in, 136–37; women and, 224–27; World Assemblies recommendations, 389–418
Ageing indices, 167–68, 174–75, 177–83; evaluation of, 174–75;

P-index, 177–83; population
pyramid slope as, 183–88;
Q-index, 178, 182–83
Agewell, 360
American Association for the Retired
Persons, 212
Americans for Generational Equity
(AGE), 211
Andrews, G.R., 201
Annapurna scheme, 375
Asia, aged population distribution in,
38–40, 83–84; aged proportion
and life expectancy at birth in,
103–05; ageing in, 33–78;
demographic transition in, 99;
demographic transition
index—other economic and
demographic variable relations
for, 93–97; dependency ratio in,
44–45; elderly labour force in, 65;
health care expenditures in, 206;
healthy life expectancy level in,
76–77; illiteracy among elderly
in, 69–71; intergenerational
balance trends in, 42–43; life
expectancy at age of 60 in, 56–57;
marital status of elderly in,
72–73; parent support ratio in,
50–52; potential support ratio in,
46–49; rural–urban sex ratio of
population 60 years and above,
250; sex ratio in, 60–62; speed of
ageing in, 82, 84–85; TFR in,
104–07; trends in ageing, 35–37,
56–57; workforce participation of
elderly in, 67
Automobile Association of Upper
India (AAUI), 381

Barro, R.J., 209
Basu, Alaka, 178
Basu, Kaushik, 178
Becker, G.S., 130
Bengtson, V.L., 216
Bima Nivesh, 378–79
Binney, E., 213
Binney, Estes, 213

Binstock, R., 213
Binstock, R.M., 218
Bongaarts, John, 267
Borsch-Supan, A., 203
Bos, Edward, 206
Brahmacharya, 159
Brennan, Ellen, 153
British Commission on Population
report, 195–96
Brockerhoff, M., 153

CCS (Pension) Rules, 1972, 376
Caldwell, J.C., 129–30, 142–43
Callahan, Daniel, 211–12
Capital formation, ageing and,
207–08; pension and, 208–10
Central Government Health
Scheme, 291
Central Pay Commission,
Fifth, 354, 375
Chellaraj, Gnanaraj, 206
Children under 15 years of age,
164, 166
Citizens' Health Insurance (CHI),
Japan, 293
Cleland, J., 130
Code of Criminal Procedure 1973
India, 276, 355–58
Community participation, by aged,
309–10
Consumption and ageing, 200–01
Contributory Provident Fund (CPF),
376–77
Cox, D., 280
Crime in India, 367
Crude birth rate (CBR), 85–86
Crude death rate (CDR),
125–26, 138
Cumming, Elaine, 216

Daniels, N., 213
Dave, S.A., 371
Dearness Relief (DR), to pensioners/
family pensioners, 376–77
Delhi Transport Corporation
(DTC), 381
Demeny, Paul, 87

Demographic transition index (DTI), economic and demographic indicators relations with, 92–97

Demographic transition stages, ageing and, 99, 101–07; factors affecting death and birth rates and, 88–89; factors influencing supply and demand of children during, 130–31; in Asia, 99–101; TFR and life expectancy in, 89–97; theory of, 86–88

Dependency burdens of aged, 43–52; dependency ratio, 44–46, 167, 169–70; parent support ratio, 49–52, 169; potential support ratio, 44, 46–49, 169

Dependency ratio of aged, rural-urban differences, 247–48; trends in, 44–45, 167, 169–70

Dharmasastra, 159

Dignity Dialogue, 387

Dignity Foundation, 387

Disability, among aged, 288–90

Disability Adjusted Life Expectancy (DALE), 74–78

Easterlin, R.A., 130

Economic development, and ageing, 193–95

Economic support, to aged/elderly, 274–75, 324–27

Elderly/aged population, absolute number and proportion of in Asia, 37, 39–41; ageing of, 53–58, 254–56; alcohol use, 311–12; bills payments, 383–84; changing proportions of, 41–43; chronic conditions affecting, 419; chronic disease/sex among, 286–87; community participation by, 309–10; continent-wise distribution, 36–38, 83–84; co-residence of, 264–65; demographic aspects of, 33–78; dependency burdens of, 43–52; dependency ratio, 167, 169–70; 247–48; deprivation of, 227–30;

disability among, 288–90; economic activities of, 268–72; economic dependence of, 271, 273; economic support to, 274–75, 324–27; emergency situations, 336–37; family support to, 315–17; feminisation of, 52, 58–63, 256–57; financing health care of, 323–24; government support to, 317–18; health care, 384–85; health facilities for, 291–93; health policy support, 318–21; health status of, 74–78, 283, 285–88; healthy eating, 310–11; helpline for, 385; household chores by, 309–10; housing for, 331–34, 396–98; income tax return, 383; international cooperation for, 345–46; labour force, 64–67; literacy status, 66, 68–71, 260–62; living arrangements of, 261, 263–68; marital status of, 68, 72–74, 257–59; medication, 312; mental problems, 321–23; migrant elderly, 336; NSSO survey on, 240–42; by number of surviving children, 263; old age homes, 384; Ordinance in Vietnam on, 421–29; ownership and management of financial assets/property, 280, 282–83; parent support ratio, 49–52, 169; pension policies for, 328–30; physical activity, 308; physical environment for, 330–34; policies and programmes in India on, 355–87; potential support ratio of, 44, 46–49, 169; protection of elderly consumers, 396; railway ticket booking for, 383; region-wise distribution of, 34–41; retirement benefits, 280–81; right to honourable death, 343–45; rural economy and, 250–54; rural elderly, 334–36; rural-urban composition,

242–50, 256; schemes providing
cash benefits to, 282–83; *see
also*, Ageing; self-support by,
308; self-protection measures,
312–15; sex distribution of,
58–59, 243–44, 255, 257;
smoking, 311; social activities of,
293–94; social security to,
275–83, 328–39; Socio-economic
characteristics of, 63–78; special
counters for, 383–85; status in
India, 239–99; telephone for, 385;
transportation for, 334; travel
friendly programmes, 381–83; in
voting age population, 215;
voting behaviour of, 216–19;
women among, 61–62; women
as percentage of, 60; work
participation rate for, 268–69
Elderly Health Index, 295
Elderly Status Index (ESI), 183,
294–98; for India, 295–97
Employees State Insurance
programmes, 291

Family and Medical Leave Act of
1993, US, 214
Family structure, ageing and, 222–24
Family support, to aged, 315–17
Feldstein, M.S., 209
Feminisation, of elderly, 256–57
Fertility, ageing as function of,
189–90; competition at all levels
and, 127; decline theories of,
129–32; determinants of, 124–32;
factors influencing, 130, 132; in
India, 107–15; in Japan, 110–13,
115–20, 124–32; marriage
unpopularity and, 127–28; mass
consumption society and, 128;
role in population ageing,
107–20; urban and rural, 136,
138, 245; women against fertility
and, 129
Finance Act, 1992, 377
Financing health care, for aged,
323–24

Fixed Period, 343
Forbes, 210
Free Health care to the Poor,
Elderly and School Children
Scheme, 292

General Insurance Corporation, 291
Gerdtham, Ulf-G., 203
Getzen, Thomas E., 203
Goode, William J., 220
Government Managed Health
Insurance (GMHI), Japan, 293
Government–sponsored schemes, for
old age income security, 277–78
Government support, to aged,
317–18
Graceful ageing, community
participation for, 309–10;
economic support for, 324–27;
emergency situations, 336–37;
family support in, 315–17;
financing health care, 323–24;
government support in, 317–18;
health policy support for,
318–21; healthy eating for, 310–11;
household chores for, 309–10;
housing for, 331–34; medication,
312; mental problems, 321–23;
pension policies, 328–30;
physical activity for, 308–09;
physical environment for, 330–34;
policies content for, 326–27;
process, 306–07; reducing
smoking for, 311–12; self-
protection measures, 312–15; self-
support for, 308; social security,
328–30; social setting for, 338–46;
transportation for, 334
Gratuity, 377
Great Depression of 1930, 195
Grihasthashrama, 159
Group Medical Insurance
Scheme, 380
Guha, Roy S., 176

HIV, 151–52, 319–21
Habakkuk, H.J., 198

Hauser, P.M., 182
Health Card Programmes, Thailand, 292
Health care costs and ageing, 203–07
Health facilities, for aged, 291–93
Health policy support, to aged, 318–21
Health status, of aged, 74–78; of elderly, 283, 285–88
Healthy eating, for aged, 310–11
Healthy life expectancy level, in Asia, 76–77
Heller, P.S., 212
Helpline, for aged, 385–86
Henry, William E., 216
Heritage Medical Centre, 387
Hindu Adoption and Maintenance Act, 1956, 276, 355
Hon, Vivian, 206
Household chores, by aged, 309–10
Housing for aged, 201–03, 331–34
Hudson, R., 210
Hudson, Robert, 217
Human development index (HDI), 144–49, 183

I-gap of ageing, 178, 182–83
Illiteracy rate, among elderly, 68–73
Income Tax Rebate, 377
India, policies/programmes on aged in, banking sector, 387; Code of Criminal Procedure 1973, 356–58; constitutional provisions, 355; disposal of court cases, 386; health care, 384–85; helpline, 385–86; insurance schemes, 378–80; Integrated Programme for Older Persons, 371–72; legal arrangements in States, 358–59; magazines for elderly, 387; mobile medicare unit programme, 387; national level programmes, 371–80; NCOP, 360–61; NOAP, 373, 375; NPOP, 359, 361–70; OASIS, 371; Old Age and Widow Pension schemes,

373–75; old age homes, 372–73, 384; pension/family pension schemes, 375–76; Scheme of Assistance for Constructions of Old Age Homes, 372–73; special counters for aged, 383–84; taxation, 377–78; telephone connection, 385; for travel, 381–83
Indian Airlines, 383
Indian Majority Act 1875, 356
Indira Gandhi Bhumihin Vrudh Sheth-Majdoor Sahayog Yojana, 373
Infant mortality rate (IMR), 139–41, 144, 150–51
Insurance Schemes, 378–80
Integrated Programme for Older Persons, 371–72
International balance in proportion of elderly, changes in, 41–43
International Labour Organization (ILO), 306
International Network for the Prevention of Elder Abuse, 341
International Plan of Action on Ageing 2002, 306, 414–15, 418

Jain, S., 280
Jan Arogya, 380
Japan, age-child ratio in, 119; age-specific mortality rates in, 121; aged proportion in, 110–12, 117, 119; causes of death in, 122–23; crude birth rate, 125–26; fertility and mortality factors in population ageing in, 115–20; fertility decline and its determinants in, 124–29; health facility for aged in, 292–93; indices of ageing in, 178, 180–83; life expectancy in, 110–13, 116, 121–23; marriage unpopularity in, 127–28; mass consumption society, 128; mortality determinants of, 120–24; net reproduction rate, 125–26; TFR

in, 110–12, 125–26; women against fertility in, 129
Jeevan Akshay, 378
Jeevan Dhara, 378
Jet Airways, 383
Jimenez, E., 280
Jones, G.W., 142

Keyfitz, N., 212
Kim, Young J., 154
Knodel, J., 142
Kotlikoff, Laurence, 211
Kuroda, T., 182

Labour force, elderly participation in, 164–66
Labour supply, and ageing, 199–200
Laslett, P., 211, 220
Laundry, Adolph, 87
Lee, Sang–Hyop, 265
Leibenstein, H.M., 130
Lesthaeghe, R., 129
Liao, Tim Futing, 190
Life expectancy, aged proportion and, 102–04, 108, 110–12; at age of 60, 55–56, 113–14, 176; at age of 65, 176; at age of 70, 176; at birth, 55, 93–97, 102–04, 108, 110–12, 116, 139–41, 144–48, 150, 247; causes of death and, 122–23; demographic transition stages in terms of, 89–97; increase in, 55; of males/females, 113–14, 122–23; TFR and, 89–97
Life Insurance Corporation, 291
Literacy, among elderly, 66, 68–71, 260–62
Living arrangements, 261, 263–68
Longman, P., 211

Maed, Akiko, 206
Magazines, for elderly, 387
Maharashtra State Road Transport Corporation (MSRTC), 381
Malaker, C.R., 176
Mankiw, N.G., 202

Manning, Willard G., 207
Manton, K., 298
Manu, 159
Marital status of elderly, in Asia, 72–73; in world regions, 72
Married Women's Property Act (MWPA), 1874, 378
Mason, A., 265
Mean age, 163
Measures of ageing, aged–child ratio, 167–68; alternative dependency measures, 173–74; dependency measures of, 167, 169–70; mean age, 163; median age, 163–65; old age dependency ratio, 167, 169–70; parent support ratio, 169; potential support ratio, 169; problems of, 173; proportion of children under 15 years of age, 164, 166; proportions of aged 60 or 65 years and above, 160–63; total dependency ratio, 171–73; traditional measures, 160–68; youth dependency ratio, 171–72
Median age, 163–65
Medical Insurance Scheme, 379–80
Medication, 312
Mediclaim, 379–80
Meiji Restoration (1868), 127
Mental problems, 321–23
Miai Kekkon (matchmaking system), Japan, 128
Migrant elderly, 336
Minkler, M., 213
Mishra, U.S., 248
Mobile medicare unit (MMU) programme, 386
Moody, H., 214, 222, 338
Mortality, age specific rates, 121; ageing as function of, 189–90; decline in, 151–53; determinants of, 138–53; female education and, 144–49; female excess over male life expectancy and, 144–48, 150; HIV and AIDs and, 151–52; human development index and, 144–49; in Japan, 120–24; over

urbanization and, 152–53; proportion of GDP spent on health and, 144–48; purchasing power parity and, 143–48; role in population ageing, 107–20

Murthy, N.R. Vasudeva, 203

Mutual Aid Associations (MAAs), Japan, 292

National Commission on Labour, 366

National Council for Older Persons (NCOP), 360–61

National Health Insurance (NHI), 203

National Labour Institute, 366

National Old Age Pension Scheme (NOAPS), 279, 373, 375

National Policy on Older Persons (NPOP), plan of action 2000–2005 adopted by Ministry of; Agriculture, 369; Civil Aviation, 369; Communications, 368; Finance, 364; Food and Consumer Affairs, 369–70; Health and Family Welfare, 362–64; Home Affairs, 367; Human Resource Development, 365–66; Industry, 370; Information and Broadcasting, 368; Labour, 366; Law, Justice and Company Affairs, 367; Parliamentary Affairs, 370; Personnel, Public Grievances and Pensions, 366–67; Petroleum and Natural Gas, 369; Planning, 370; Railways, 368–69; Rural Development and Employment, 364; Science and Technology, 370; Social Justice and Empowerment, 361–62; Surface Transport, 369; Urban Affairs and Employment, 365

National Policy on Older Persons (NPOP) 1999, 359

National Sample Survey Organisation (NSSO), 239; survey on aged, 240–41

National Social Assistance Programme (NSAP), 371

Nayar, Usha S., 159

New India Assurance Co. Ltd. (NIAC), 379

Notestein, Frank W., 81, 87, 129, 193

O'Connel, Joan M., 203

Ogawa, N., 117

Old Age and Survivors Insurance, 208

Old Age and Widow Pension in Maharashtra, 373

Old Age homes, 384

Old age income security in India, government-sponsored schemes for, 277–78

Old Age Social and Income Security (OASIS) Project, India, 329, 371

Older population, ageing of, 53–58; demographic profile of, 52–63; feminisation of elderly, 58–63; see also, Elderly/aged population; women among, 60–63

Oldest among old, age distribution of, 54–57; concerns of, 53; life expectancy at age of 60 and 56–57

Order for Maintenance of Wives, Children and Parents, 356–58

Ordinance on Elderly People in Vietnam, general provisions, 421–23; rewards and handling of violations, 429; state management over elder-related work, 427–28; supporting and caring for elderly people in, 423–27

Palmore, E., 298

Parent support ratio (PaSR), 49–52, 169

Penal Code of 1980, China, 275

Pension, 198, 200; capital formation and, 208–10; family pension and, 375–76; policies for aged, 328–30

Physical activity by aged, 308–09
Physical environment, for aged, 330–34
P-index, of ageing, 177–83; of poverty, 177–78;
Planning Commission, 370
Population ageing, *see*, Ageing/Population ageing
Population Association of America, 211
Population momentum, 153–55
Population pyramid slope, as ageing index, 183–88
Post-retirement employment, 198
Potential support ratio (PSR) of aged, trends in, 44, 46–49, 169
Preker, Alexander, 206
Preston, Samuel, 211
Private pensions plans, 380
Productivity and ageing, 195–99
Public Health System, Thailand, 291–92
Public Insurance for Public Sector Employees, 292
Pythogoras, 159

Q-index of ageing, 178, 182–83
Quadagno, J., 220

Rajan, S.I., 248
Rajasthan State Road Transport Corporation (RSRTC), 381
Rapid population growth (RPG), problem of, 81
Richman, R., 211
Riemer, Yosef, 218
Robertson, A., 213
Rosenstone, Steven J., 217
Rowland, D.T., 154–55
Rural ageing, gender dimension of, 249–50
Rural economy and ageing, 250–56
Rural elderly, 334–36
Rural poverty decline in India, 252
Russo, Gerard, 265
Ryder, N., 175–77

Sahara India Airlines, 383
Sanyasa, 159
Sarma, P. Sankara, 248
Scheme of Assistance for Construction of Old Age Homes, 372–73
Schmahl, W., 212
Schoen, Robert, 154
Schultz, T.W., 130
Second career, 198
Self-protection measures, by aged, 312–15
Sen, A.K., 177
Senior Citizens Unit Plan (SCUP), 291, 379
Senior Heritage Selections, 387
Simon, J.L., 198
Single elderly, 257–59
Smoking, 311–12
Social activities, of aged, 293–94
Social ageing, definition of, 227
Social Defence Bureau, 371
Social security, to aged, 328–30; for elderly, 275–80
Social Security Scheme for Private Sector Employees, 292
Social setting for graceful ageing, education and literacy, 339–41; international cooperation, 345–46; neglect, abuse and violence, 341–43; peaceful resolution to intergenerational tensions, 338–39; right to honourable death, 343–45
Society, ageing and, 219–24; family structure, 222–24; sociological premises on, 219
Society Managed Health Insurance (SMHI), Japan, 292
Socio-economic characteristics of elderly, 63–78; health status, 74–78; labour force participation, 64–67; literacy status, 66–71; marital status, 68, 72–74
Stagner, M., 211
Statutory Retirement Ages (SRAs), 175, 349–54

Strate, John, 217
Suicides and Accidental Deaths in India, 367

Tamil Nadu Transport Corporation, 381
Taxation, 377–78
Telephone connection, for aged, 385
Thompson, D., 212
Thompson, Warren S., 129
Total dependency ratio, 171–73
Total fertility rates (TFR), aged proportion and, 104–12; demographic transition stages in terms of, 89–97; life expectancy and, 89–97
Transportation, for aged, 334
Travel friendly programmes for aged, by air, 382–83; by road, 381; by train, 381–82
Trollope, Anthony, 343

Ukpolo, victor, 203
Unit Trust of India, 291

Vanaprastha, 159
Varistha Pension Bima Yojana, 380
Vietnam Association of the Elderly, 428
Visaria, L., 255
Visaria, P., 255
Voting behaviour, of aged, 216–19

Wage and age relations, 196–97
Weber, Max, 127
Weil, D., 202
Widow pension in, Karnataka, 373; Kerala, 375; West Bengal, 374
Wilson, C., 130
Wolfinger, Raymond E., 217
Women and ageing, 224–27
Work participation rate of elderly, 269–72; by class of worker status, 271–72; by industrial category, 270
World Assembly on Ageing recommendations on, data collection and analysis, 409–10; education, 406–09; family, 398–400; health care and nutrition, 389–96; housing, 396–98; income security and employment, 402–06; political declaration of, 414–18; protection of elderly consumers, 396; research, 412–13; social welfare, 400–02; training and education, 410–12
World Fertility Survey (WFS), 239, 245
World Health Organization (WHO), 306, 318–19

Youth dependency ratio, 171–72, 248

Zimmer, Zachary, 267
Zweifel, Peter, 203

ABOUT THE AUTHOR

Rajagopal Dhar Chakraborti is a senior Reader in the Department of South and Southeast Asian Studies, Calcutta University, Kolkata, of which he was a former Director. He is also Visiting Faculty at the United Nations International Institute on Ageing, Malta. Till recently, Dr Chakraborti was Visiting Professor at China Renmin University, Beijing, and Nankai University, Institute of Population and Development, People's Republic of China. He has previously taught at the Centre for Development Studies, Trivandrum; St. Xavier's College, Kolkata; and the Indian Institute for Social Welfare and Business Management, Kolkata. He has also served as the Deputy Registrar of Calcutta University and been a Visiting Fellow at the London School of Economics and Political Science. A recipient of the prestigious Asia Fellowship and The Wellcome Trust Post Doctoral Fellowship, Dr Chakraborti is widely travelled and has several publications to his credit including *Quantitative Methods* (2001) and *Ageing of Asia* (2002).